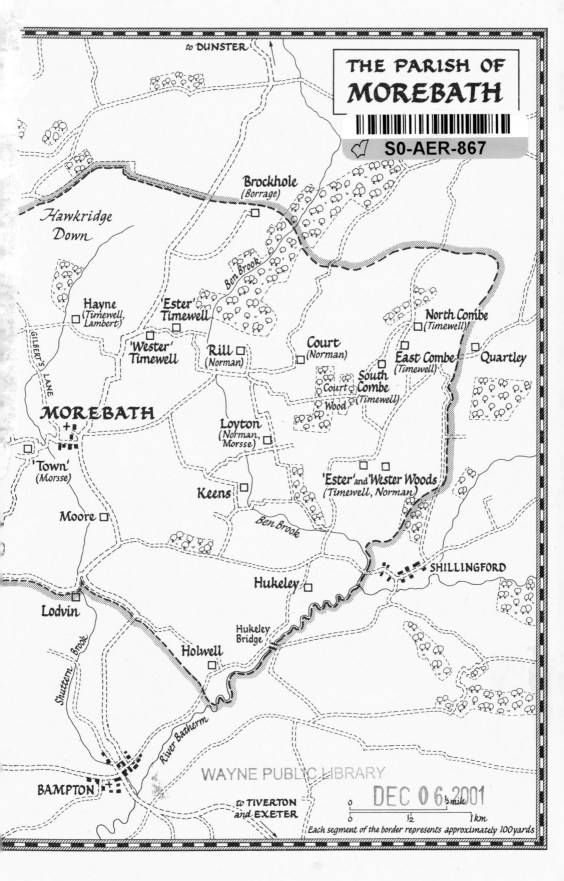

THE PARISH OF
MOREBATH

to DUNSTER

Brockhole
(Borrage)

*Hawkridge
Down*

Ben Brook

Hayne
(Timewell,
Lambert)

'Ester'
Timewell

North Combe
(Timewell)

'Wester'
Timewell

Rill
(Norman)

Court
(Norman)

East Combe
(Timewell)

Quartley

GILBERT'S LANE

Court
Wood

South
Combe
(Timewell)

MOREBATH

Loyton
(Norman,
Morsse)

'Town'
(Morsse)

Keens

'Ester' and 'Wester Woods
(Timewell, Norman)

Moore

Ben Brook

SHILLINGFORD

Hukeley

Lodvin

Shutterm Brook

Hukeley
Bridge

Holwell

River Baxherm

to TIVERTON
and EXETER

0   ½ mile
0   ½   1 km

Each segment of the border represents approximately 100 yards

THE VOICES OF MOREBATH

Eamon Duffy

The Voices of Morebath

Reformation and Rebellion
in an English Village

Yale University Press
New Haven and London

Typeset by Northern Phototypesetting Co. Ltd, Bolton
Printed in Italy

LIBRARY OF CONGRESS CATALOGING-IN-PUBLICATION DATA

Duffy, Eamon.
   The voices of Morebath : reformation and rebellion in an English village / Eamon Duffy.
      p.   cm.
Includes index.
   1. Reformation—England—Morebath. 2. Morebath (England)—Church history—16th century. 3. Trychay, Christopher, ca. 1490-1574. I.
Title.
   BR377.5.M67 D84 2001
   274.23'52‒DC21

2001001477

FRONTISPIECE: *The Alchemist*, by Pieter Bruegel the Elder, 1558? detail. Staatliche Museen, Berlin
TITLEPAGE: Sir Christopher Trychay's signature, from a list of regulations for the maintenance of the church hedge [Binney 38 / Ms 181], see pp. 50‒1.

for
Jonathan, Hester, Pippa
at their goyng forthe

Contents

Acknowledgements

While writing this book I have accumulated obligations to a host of friends and colleagues who have offered insight, advice, information, expertise, hospitality or merely an indulgent ear – Dr Ian Arthurson, Mr T. Cooper, Dr David Crankshaw, Professor Pat Collinson, Dr Beat Kumin, Dr Joanna Mattingly, Professor John Morrill and and Ms Helen Weinstein. I owe special debts of gratitude to Sir David and Lady Calcutt for hospitality on Exmoor and for the sight of an archdeacon chasing someone else's hat, to Jim and Mabel Vellacott of Bampton and Morebath – Jim and Mabel 'at Wode' – who walked and talked me round the farms of Morebath, to Richard and Caryl Rothwell of Little Timewell for access to the estate map of Morebath Manor, to Professor Diarmaid MacCulloch for making me think twice, to Dr Neil Jones for unrivalled expertise in Tudor law, to Professor Nicholas Boyle, who read every word and commented constructively on almost all of them, and to Dr C. S. Knighton who also read the typescript. I thank them all. Professor Nicholas Orme has been from the beginning of this project a generous and supportive friend. A glance at the footnotes will reveal how often I have borrowed from his deep knowledge of the religious history of Devon. In addition he has been a tireless source of hospitality, information and guidance, and a healthily sceptical reader: this would have been a far poorer book without him.

The Bethune-Baker fund of the Cambridge Faculty of Divinity and the Morshead-Salter fund of Magdalene College made research grants. John Nicoll and Sally Salvesen at Yale have again proved themselves peerless publishers and warm friends, and Margot Levy was a thorough and intelligent copy editor. I am grateful to the Rector of Bampton and the Devon County Archivist for permission to reproduce pages from the Morebath accountbook, and I am grateful for the efficiency and cooperation of the staffs of the Devon Record Office, the Somerset Record Office, and the West Country Studies library. The final stages of the book were completed as McCarthy Professor at the Gregorian University, Rome, in the gracious setting of the Collegio Irlandese, where I was welcomed with truly Hibernian kindness by Monsignor John Fleming, Rector, and his staff and students.

Finally, I thank my wife Jenny, best support of all, who has borne heroically with marriage to Sir Christopher Trychay.

A note on names and spelling

This is a book about the voice of a sixteenth-century man; I have therefore
felt it essential to present to the reader what Sir Christopher Trychay wrote,
in the way that he wrote it. I have retained the Tudor spelling in all quotations (this is less difficult to understand than may appear at first glance –
readers who are daunted should try reading the passages aloud, and will be
surprised how often the sense clarifies itself. I offer such brave readers three
clues – Sir Christopher uses 'y' to speak about himself, 'I'; he uses a separate
word, 'ys', to indicate a genitive, where we now use an apostrophe s –
'John Wode ys brother' for 'John Wode's brother'; and he frequently uses
double s or double t where we use sh or tch – '*parysse*' for parish, 'fett' for
'fetched'). But for comfort's sake, and since it is my hope that readers other
than professional historians may find the story of sixteenth-century
Morebath of interest, all extended quotations are followed by a modernised
version, printed in italics. In shorter quotations, I have translated all hard
words in square brackets, and I have translated all the Latin.

The 1904 edition of the Morebath accounts by J. Erskine Binney, while
not quite complete and sometimes inconsistent in capitalisation and division
of the text, is basically reliable. I have worked from the manuscript in the
Devon Record Office in Exeter, but since the printed edition is the version
of the accounts available to most readers of this book, I have chosen to
quote from Binney's text, except in the few places (clearly indicated) where
his transcription positively misleads. For those who wish to pursue them,
page references to the current (but chaotic) binding of the manuscript are
given immediately after the page numbers in Binney's edition.

For clarity's sake, I have provided arabic equivalents for all roman numbers, even in the Tudor text, and in translating money sums have used the
modern symbols for pounds, shillings and pence. I have silently expanded
all conventional abbreviations, and have very occasionally and very conser-
vatively added punctuation to clarify specially complex passages. Following
a misleading Victorian convention, Binney transcribed the obsolete letter
'thorn' as 'y': I have substituted the more accurate 'th'. The obsolete letter

'yog', which he transcribed as 'z', presented greater problems. There is no stable modern equivalent for Sir Christopher's somewhat erratic use of this symbol, and it never assists the sense. I have thought it simplest to omit it.

Spelling of family and place names vary greatly in the manuscript: outside direct quotation, I have opted for the spelling in the modern ordnance survey maps of Morebath, and have also used the generally current versions of family names such as 'Hurley' (instead of 'Hurly'): the only exception is Sir Christopher's own surname, which I have spelt throughout as he did.

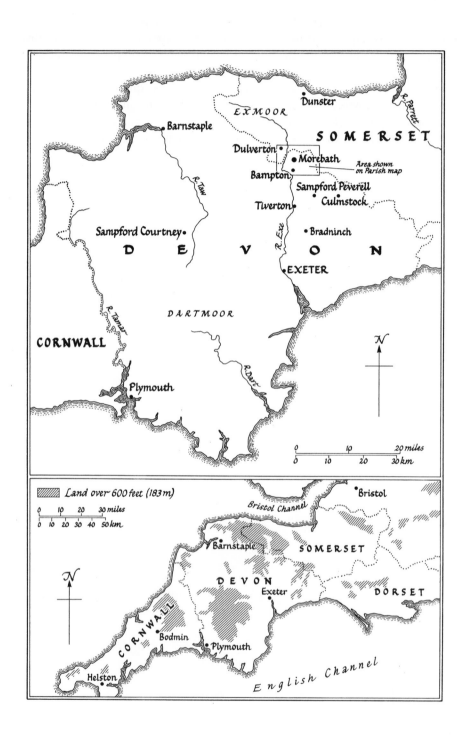

Land over 600 feet (183 m)

Preface

This is a book about a sixteenth-century country priest, and the extraordinary records he kept. It deals with ordinary people in an unimportant place, whose claim to fame is that they lived through the most decisive revolution in English history, and had a priest who wrote everything down. Morebath was and is a tiny Devonshire sheep-farming village, which in the sixteenth century was made up of just thirty-three families, working the difficult land on the southern edge of Exmoor. The bulk of its conventional Tudor archives have long since vanished: there are no manorial records, and most of the ancient wills of the region went up in smoke during the bombing of Exeter in the Second World War. But for more than fifty years through all the drama of the English Reformation, Morebath had a single priest, Sir Christopher Trychay (his surname is pronounced 'Trickey', to rhyme with Dicky, and Catholic priests then were called 'Sir' as now they are called 'Father'). Sir Christopher was vicar of Morebath from 1520 until his death in 1574. Opinionated, eccentric and talkative, he kept the parish accounts on behalf of the churchwardens. There are more than two hundred surviving sets of churchwardens' accounts from Tudor England, but none of them like Morebath's. Almost everywhere else these accounts are what they sound like – bare bones, dry records of income and expenditure. The Morebath accounts contain all that, but they are packed as well with the personality, opinions and prejudices of the most vivid country clergyman of the English sixteenth century, and with the names and doings of his parishioners. Through his eyes, or rather, through his voice, talking, talking, talking – for he wrote these accounts to be read aloud to his parishioners – we catch a rare and precious glimpse of life and death in an English village. His accounts reveal its complex social life, its strains, tensions and conflicting personalities, its search for internal harmony, its busy pre-Reformation piety, its struggles to meet the growing demands of the Tudor war-effort against Scotland and France.

They also offer a unique window into a rural world in crisis, as the progress of the Reformation inexorably dismantled the structures of Morebath's corporate life, and pillaged its assets. W.G. Hoskins, in the best book ever written about Devon, chose Morebath as the perfect example of a sleepily conformist country community, haplessly accepting all that happened to it, and almost everyone who has used the accounts since Hoskins wrote in the 1950s has taken much the same view. In fact, Sir Christopher Trychay's accounts provide us with our only direct evidence of the motives which drove hitherto law-abiding West Country men into a disastrous rebellion against the Crown which left at least three thousand men dead and the West Country traumatised. Far from being mutely conformist, Morebath was one of the Devon villages which joined the doomed Prayer Book rebellion of 1549. In that year the avalanche of change loosed by the Reformation swept Morebath into armed protest. Amazingly, the priest carefully documented the equipping and financing of the young men of Morebath to join the peasant army besieging Exeter, in revolt against the religious Reformation, and the financial and social crisis presided over by the boy-king Edward VI's divided government.

The siege ended in bloody defeat and a wave of executions. Morebath, its church bells confiscated and silenced, shared in the punishment imposed on all the towns and villages of Devon and Cornwall. And, despite an eagerly welcomed period of rebuilding of the old order under Mary Tudor, the Reformation stabilised under Elizabeth, and permanently transformed Morebath. For the last twenty years of his life the priest, garrulous as ever, documents a changed community, reluctantly Protestant, no longer focussed on the religious life of their parish church but increasingly preoccupied with the secular demands of the Elizabethan state, the equipping of armies and the payment of taxes.

I have wanted to write Morebath's story since I first encountered its priest and his remarkable accounts while working on another book, *The Stripping of the Altars*. That book set out to explore the Catholic world-view which was the religion of most English people on the eve of the Reformation, and the impact of radical religious change on the majority who would have liked things to stay more or less as they were. The present work is in one sense a pendant to that larger study. But I hope that it is more, above all that it offers a convincing portrait of a remarkable man, and a sense of what the world looked like through his eyes.

The Morebath accounts are well known. A learned Victorian vicar of Morebath, J. Erskine Binney, printed an excellent transcription almost a century ago, and most recent historians of the English Reformation, myself included, have drawn on his edition. But all of us have used the accounts essentially as a quarry for facts, or have picked for quotation the same two or three colourful passages in which Sir Christopher denounces the Reformation or gives thanks for Queen Mary's rebuilding of Catholicism. In this book I have tried to stand back and allow Sir Christopher's unique fifty-year conversation with his people to speak for itself. I have been astonished as I have attended to that conversation how much of the texture of the life of country people a world away from us has emerged.

Tudor England had no such thing as a typical village, and I do not offer Morebath in proof of any thesis. A study of the Reformation in an Essex or Suffolk village, in the Stour Valley, say, where many ordinary men and women welcomed the Protestant gospel and eagerly embraced it, would look very different. Morebath and its priest, however, do offer us a unique and vivid insight into a rural world which has otherwise left little trace: ruffling the pages of Sir Christopher's book we hear once again a chorus of forgotten but fascinating voices. I hope the reader finds them as rewarding to listen to as I have done.

Illustrations

The maps on the endpapers and p. xii were drawn by Reginald Piggott.
The detail of the Culmstock cope is reproduced by kind permission of the
Rector and Parish Council of Culmstock. The chapter decorations on pp.
32, 46, 47, 65, 83, 84 and 110 depicting Catholic sacraments and celebrations are from the Cambridge University Library copy of an unpaginated
Sarum Book of Hours printed in 1507 by Simon Vostre (STC 15905); those on
pp. 142, 151, 168, 169, 181 and 190 depicting Reformed sacraments and
works of charity are from the 1578 *Book of Christian Prayers* (STC 6429); that
on p. 152 is from *The Shepardes Kalendar* (STC 22412). They are reproduced
by kind permission of the Syndics of Cambridge University Library. Other
illustrations are from the following sources: p. 1 John Fitzherbert, *New tracte
for husbade men* [1525?]; p. 24 Baptista Spagnuoli, *Lyfe of saynt George*
[1515?]; p. 111 Sir Thomas Mallory, *Le morte dathur* [*sic*] [1498].

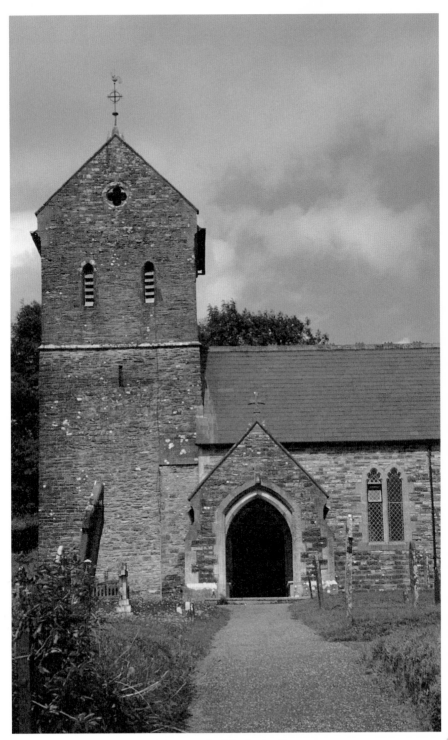

Morebath church, with its distinctive 'saddle-backed' tower.

The north aisle or 'almatory', a favourite place for burial with the parish elite, and the site of St Sidwell's altar: this is the one part of the modern church interior Sir Christopher would recognise.

Gilbert's Lane, the medieval main road from Morebath Town to Hayne Cross: the section northwards to Bury and Dulverton retains its unmetalled surface and is now a bridle-path: the tarmac surface in the picture is of course modern.

The surviving (probably) Tudor part of Timewell, one of the principal farms of the parish, and scene of the disastrous betrothal of Margaret Timewell on St George's day 1537 (below p. 61)

Brockhole, one of the remotest farms in Morebath: under the modern porch and pebbledash the layout of a medieval Devon longhouse is visible. People and animals shared a single roof on either side of a central entrance.

These cottages at Rill stand near the probable site of Morebath's Tudor Mill, home of the Scely family.

The view north across the parish towards the Easter and Wester Timewells and the Somerset border.

Morebath parish looking south from the Somerset border.

Sheep grazing in a Morebath field.

John Greneway's ships carried Exe-valley wool to Northern Europe: a carving from the Greneway chantry-chapel , Tiverton parish church.

Embroidery from a late medieval cope, preserved at Culmstock parish church, Sir Christopher's home parish. From left to right the saints are St James, St Apollonia and an unidentified Apostle

Prosperous Devon lay piety: the Greneway chantry and porch at Tiverton, built with the proceeds of an Exe-valley wool fortune: Joan Greneway was a benefactor of Morebath church.

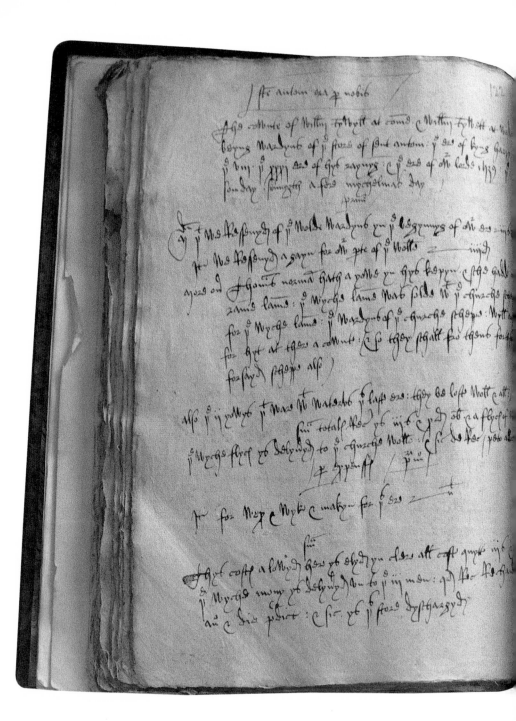

Morebath Churchwardens' Accounts, Devon Record Office, Exeter, 2983/PW1.

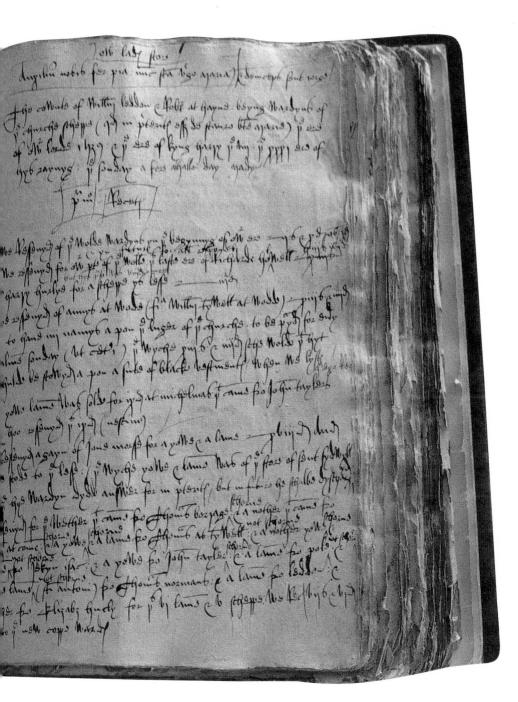

The reformation begins: the count of Our Lady's store, 1539 (right hand page) was the last year in which any Morebath 'store' operated under the patronage of the saints: in the heading here Sir Christopher invokes the Virgin's aid in latin, but adds 'and from now on, St George' (the parish patron). From the following year the account is headed simply 'the church sheep'.

Recording the final surrender of the parish's vestments and plate to the Crown in 1552, Sir Christopher for the first time copies out Edward VI's title as 'supreme head' of the Church. In the margin he writes enigmatically, 'not[e] the style of the kyng'.

A Place Apart

Morebath is a remote Devonshire community on the rain-swept southern edge of Exmoor, ten miles north of Tiverton, twenty-five miles north of Exeter. Now as in the sixteenth century there is not much that can convincingly be described as a village, just a huddle of houses round a small gaunt church, gutted and rebuilt by the Victorians, and a wider scatter of farms across the foothills and valleys that run down to the river Exe from the moor. The parish forms a compact rectangle, three and a half miles by two and a half, on the southern skirts of Exmoor. To the west it is flanked by the valley of the Exe, from which it rises steeply between six hundred and a thousand feet above sea level, and runs east along the country boundary with Somerset, which forms its northern edge. To the south it stops just short of the market town of Bampton, from which it is separated by the river Bathern, while on the north-west its nearest neighbours are the Somerset village of Brushford and the market town of Dulverton, in the valley of the river Barle.

Nowadays a visitor is likely to approach Morebath via the A396, the scenic road which runs from Tiverton along the Exe to Bampton, and from Bampton on to Exebridge, on the south-western side of the parish. But the road from Bampton to Tiverton in the sixteenth century was more tortuous: it ran southwards along the ridge tops well to the east of the Exe, avoiding the valley bottom to follow the higher ground. The geography of the parish was changed decisively in November 1873, when the Devon and Somerset Railway opened a line to Barnstaple via Dulverton,[1] and Morebath became the main station for Bampton and the surrounding villages. New carriage routes from Bampton and Shillingford were cut across the valleys to Morebath station, easing access to what had once been, even by Devon standards, one of the county's remotest communities.

The roads of Tudor Morebath were narrow, deeply banked and hedged in the Devon manner, poorly surfaced with soft slate, river gravel, and stones gathered from the fields, broken by fords and often awash with mud and water during the incessant winter rains drawn down by the moor, impassable in hard weather.[2] Even in modern times, during the winter of 1963 every road in Morebath filled to the height of the hedges with layer upon layer of frozen snow. For weeks the only way in or out of the village was across the higher fields, where driving wind had kept the snow from settling. In Tudor England's savage 'little Ice Age' the parish must often have been totally isolated. Even the hardy long-woolled sheep which were the mainstay of Tudor Morebath's economy were vulnerable to the inhospitable moorland winters of the sixteenth century. The annual sheep counts of the church flocks are punctuated by reports of animals 'lost and gone', 'drowned', 'dede and gone wolle and all', or 'lost at crystmas'.[3]

North Devon was sheep country, above all here on the skirts of the moor, for, as an early Stuart survey of the county observed, 'moors and hills are untractable to tillage'. In much of the parish the land was 'lean and barren ... churlish and unthankful to the husbandman's labour'.[4] Some corn was grown – at best wheat and barley, but mostly rye and oats, the staples which until the nineteenth century provided the whole region with its black bread and small beer.[5] A narrow ridge of good red loam reached westward into Morebath from the direction of Shillingford, and the farms to the east of the church – Loyton, Keens, the two farms or 'bargains' at Wood – all benefited from this fertile soil. But the valley floor was solid clay, cold and sodden in winter, and the thin sour soils of the hill farms in the northern half of the parish were good only for grazing. The northern half of the parish was still comparatively heavily wooded in Tudor times, with beech and especially oak available in abundance for even the most extensive building work: the woodland was coppiced for fuel and fencing.[6]

There are many small and isolated places in this border country on the fringe of the moor, but Tudor Morebath was one of the smallest communities in the Hundred of Bampton and the region generally. A set of regulations preserved in the parish records for the collection of the ecclesiastical tax known as 'Peter's Pence', dating from 1531, reveals that there were just thirty-three households in the parish, five of them cottagers, the rest tenant-farmers or 'placeholders'.[7] Most were tenants of the Manor of Morebath, whose lord was the local priory of Barlinch, 'one of the poorest, remotest monasteries of medieval Somerset', by the 1530s a somewhat run-down house of six Augustinian canons and a prior, with an income of under £100 a year, much of it derived from Morebath. After the dissolution in 1536 the manor was acquired by Sir John Wallop, gentleman of the Privy Chamber, and in due course passed to his son Henry. A couple of the cottagers at Exebridge were tenants of the Sydenhams of the neighbouring Somerset parish of Dulverton. The Sydenhams also grazed sheep on sixty acres of moorland in the north of the parish at Hawkridge Down.[8]

The sixteenth-century parish consisted of a series of farms, distributed more or less evenly over the surrounding hills. Some of the smaller holdings are now difficult to place, but most remain. To the east was Combe, a cluster of households belonging to the Timewell clan, one of the dominant families in the parish. Slightly to the west, on the next hillside, was Court, the base for another of the richest households in Morebath, the Norman family. Directly east of Court was Rill (now Morebath Manor), also farmed by a branch of the Normans. North and slightly west of Court was the small hill farm of Brockhole, eventually held by the Borrage family whose main base was at Warmore, but evidently a difficult let. Even today it is hard to find, the farmhouse tucked two fields away from the nearest road, an 'outlandish place' as one Morebath resident described it to me. In the mid-Tudor period it was often without a tenant. Moving west and south again, closer to the parish centre, was Timewell, like Combe divided into an 'ester' and 'wester Tymewyll', and housing several branches of the ubiquitous Timewell clan. In the valley at the western side of the same hill was Hayne, until the beginning of Elizabeth's reign also held by Timewells, then passing to the Lambert family. To the west of Hayne was Warmore, farmed by the Borrage family. On a steep rise above the river, but facing north towards Warmore, was Burston, where there were more Timewells; west of that towards Brushford was Perry, and at the western foot of the rise, in the valley, was Poole, held by yet more Normans.

At the southernmost point of the western border of the parish was Exebridge, where there was a huddle of cottages but no major farmstead though Grants, on the Bampton side of the parish boundary, was farmed by more Timewells and features regularly in Morebath parish affairs. Immediately south of the village centre was Moore. In a farm slightly west of the village centre, and therefore called 'Town', lived the richest family of all, the Morsses. Just under a mile to the east of the church was Loyton, with one household occupied by another branch of the Norman family, though there were Morsses here too. To the east of Loyton were the 'ester' and 'wester' Woods, farmed by yet more Timewells and Normans. At the southern end of the eastern boundary was Hukeley, and the Hukeley bridge over the river Bathern which flows south to join the Exe below Bampton.[9] On the fringes to the east was Quartley, technically part of Bampton parish but closer to Morebath church and once again farmed by the Timewells and so, like Grants, its western counterpart, often drawn into Morebath affairs. The location of the mill is uncertain: it may have been near the cluster of cottages at Exebridge, but by the eighteenth century there were two mills on the Ben Brook, which runs through the Easter and Wester Timewells, past Rill, Loyton and Keens to join the Bathern at Hukeley, one to the south of Loyton (Keens Mill), the other marked now only by an old mill leet near Rill cottages: either of these is a likely enough site for the Tudor mill.[10] There were also a number of smaller holdings, farmed by established families along with 'the home place' – 'priers hay' and 'Galberdis yatte', which I have not been able to locate, and 'Bollyn', a stretch of land with a house, long since disappeared, between Loyton and Keens. Field sizes on these farms were small, ranging from one to fifteen acres, most at the lower end of the scale.[11]

Surnames in Morebath were often simply the farm name – Alsyn at Perry, John at Moore, William at Timewell, Robert at Wood – and the priest often identifies householders by a single-word reference to their farm – Burston, Court, Wood – as even minor Scottish lairds are still addressed. However, occupational and family surnames were also freely used: George the Smith is interchangeable with George Smith; John Hukeley is called John Smith in 1537,[12] presumably because of his occupation; Lucy Scely, widow of the miller William, is Luce at Mill, and Thomas Borrage, who seems to have taken over the mill in the late 1540s, calls himself Borrage but is referred to by the Commissioners appointed by the crown to handle the confiscation of Devon bells in 1549 as Thomas Mill. Occasionally, patronyms are used as surnames – Lewis Trychay's daughter Joan occurs as 'Jone Lewys', as indeed does his wife.[13] It is all very confusing.

As it happens, despite the loss of the manorial records, the pre-1558 parish registers and almost all the wills of the region, we are specially well placed to calculate the population of Tudor Morebath. A combination of the parish priest's obsessive penchant for list-making and the fiscal and military efficiency of the Tudor state has provided us with lists of the Morebath tax-payers in 1524 and 1545 (55 and 48 names respectively),[14] the tenants of the manor of Morebath in 1532 (33 names), again in 1546 (31 names or farms), 1557 (24 names), and again in 1558 (31 names),[15] the names of all the unmarried men and maidens in April 1534 (105 names, 68 of them men, but including an uncertain number of men and women with connections to the parish while living outside it, like the two chaplains from Bampton named there),[16] a list of the wives in 1554 (27 names),[17] a list of householders in 1554 (32 names),[18] and a muster roll of 1569 listing 41 able-bodied men between the ages of 16 and 60.[19] Despite the large number of 'young men and maidens', inflated by the inclusion of outsiders, these sources combine to suggest a population of not many more than 150 men women and children through the mid-Tudor period.[20]

In so small a community, everyone was known and communal life intense, even perhaps at times claustrophobic. The parish church was by no means its only focus. Since almost everyone was a tenant of Morebath Manor, the Manor Court and the obligations and relationships which flowed from it feature large in Morebath's records,[21] even though the court records themselves have long since disappeared. The court and its officials were used to settle parish disputes and regulate common obligations – to the Crown, to the church, to one another – which strictly speaking had nothing to do with the Manor and its farms, and the priest recorded it all in the church book.[22] At Morebath, no rigid distinction was drawn between the community at prayer, and the community as it went about its business.[23]

The restoration of Morebath church by Butterfield in the late 1870s scraped away most of its history along with its seventeenth-century plaster and eighteenth-century woodwork. It now has an unglamorous railway-age gothic interior which retains few traces of its late medieval and Tudor evolution. It is not clear how much the curious saddle-backed top to the tower owes to this restoration, though Butterfield clearly did not altogether invent it: Richard Polwhele, the eighteenth-century historian of Devon, noted that the tower was in shape 'a rectangular parallelopepidon', that is, a box topped by a prism. But the windows were certainly altered and made smaller: a burglar could not now enter the church this way, as one did in 1534, and the modern tower roof cannot in fact be reached from within, so that all major repairs require elaborate scaffolding.[24] In the sixteenth century the tower was forty-two feet high, almost twice the height of the church itself, its bells in constant need of minor outlay on ropes and stays and greasing. Even with the north aisle, the church interior was never large – sixty-five feet long by twenty-nine at its widest, a tight fit even for 150 people, which was no doubt why the aisle, with its handsome barrel vault, was added sometime in the fifteenth century, the one interior feature of the present building we can be sure its Tudor parishioners would recognise.[25] This aisle, or 'almatory' as their priest preferred to call it,[26] was a favourite place for burials, especially after the cult of St Sidwell took hold at the side altar which was located there. The wealthier men and women of Morebath regularly left the sum of 6/8d for a grave in the church, and the priest notes when someone was buried there, 'for he/she lyeth in the almatory', which happened often enough for him to keep a nervous tally of the numbers of 'corps beryd ... yn the church *actenus* [so far]'.[27] The tower and nave of the church were roofed with lead laid over timber, the aisle with tiles, and the roof, like the bells, was a constant demand on parish resources, its gutters in perpetual need of attention, its lead lifting clean away, 'ryppyd with the wynd' in 1545, so that a plumber spent the best part of a week lodging in the parish to fix it down again. In the 1520s and 1530s the parish had an annual maintenance contract with a travelling plumber 'when he cummyth thys ways ... to mendd all fawtis a pon our churche and gutters and towre', 'to keppe us dry', on one occasion the plumber was given old pewter plates from the church house in part payment for this work.[28] From the 1520s to the early 1540s, in any case, a stream of devotional investment by parishioners and priest must have made the interior seem a constant building site, stacked with boards and building materials as new high and side altars were installed, along with new screens, new standings or tabernacles for the images, a new High Cross, a new floor and a complete re-pewing.[29] Morebath church had only two altars but many images, most of them standing in niched tabernacles, curtained and gilded, and with candles or lamps in bowls or basins or branched candlesticks of timber or latten (a type of brass) burning before them during service time. Parish business was conducted there, bargains concluded, contracts signed and debts paid, 'here before the quyre dore',[30] and parishioners were prone to linger there long after service was done, so that the exasperated clerk who kept the keys was forced to knock loudly on the door to hurry them home.[31]

After the church, the most important building in the parish was the church house, also called the church ale-house.[32] Located on the south-east side of the churchyard, in the cluster of ten or eleven dwellings that made up the village centre or 'Morebath town', it was the parish's place of public entertainment, a two-storey building furnished with a fireplace and spit, with cups and platters and trenchers of treen [turned wood] and tin and pewter: its tressle tables and tablecloths were sometimes loaned to parishioners for events like weddings.[33] Visiting merchants could hire a 'sete' or stall there to sell their wares, like William the merchant who had a 'standing' in the house in 1535, or the Tiverton ciderman John Walshman, who sold cider there for four weeks in 1538.[34] The 'pleers' [players] who paid 12d to the wardens to perform in Morebath at Easter 1533 may well have been hiring the church house.[35] Above all, the fund-raising banquets known as church ales, organised by the churchwardens and by the Young Men of the parish (the 'grooming ale'), and which between them provided the bulk of the parish's income, were held here. Beer brewed or bought by the wardens and food cooked in the church house itself were sold and served at these ales: in 1527 the menu at the high wardens' ale included a roast lamb from the church flock, which had accidentally bled to death after being castrated.[36] By Elizabeth's reign, and perhaps before, minstrels and a local man, John Timewell the harper, were being paid to entertain the drinkers.[37] Parishioners were expected to attend and spend their money, and official representatives came and supported from surrounding parishes, a favour which had to be returned when the parishes concerned held their own ales.[38]

This was not merry England, however. Friction was as notable a feature of this intensely communal life as harmony. On St George's day 1537 the whole parish attended a party at Timewells for the betrothal of Margaret Timewell and William Taylor. But we catch a glimpse of the event only because it was a disaster, with tempers flaring and two of the guests 'a most by the eris', so that the whole parish 'resonyd shamfully' all that day: poor Margaret Timewell. The language in which the priest reports the incident is value laden, a rhetoric designed to shame 'froward fellows' and to persuade the 'parish universall' to cease 'trobyll or vexacion: and 'be contendyd to be ordred', so as to have 'unite and pece a mongg us'. The quest for unity and peace, at Morebath as everywhere else in Tudor England, was an ideal eagerly pursued because often lacking.[39]

Small and remote as it was, we would be quite mistaken in dismissing Morebath as one of what seventeenth-century puritans liked to call the 'dark corners of the land'. A serviceable road ran from Exeter to Bampton, and Bampton itself was a bustling place, claiming 600 houselling folk (communicant adults) in the 1540s, and supporting a community of gentry, merchants, tradesmen, artisans, lawyers and parish and chantry clergy, representatives of all of whom feature in the Morebath accounts.[40] Morebath parishioners and their priest attended ales, employed workmen and transacted business in the surrounding towns and villages like Dulverton, Brushford and Bampton itself, attended the court at Bradninch as part of the sheriff's twice-yearly progress through the county (the 'sherows towrne'), and regularly travelled on ecclesiastical or civil business to Exeter or, nearer at hand, to Oakford, Uffculme, Sampford Peverell and Tiverton. Morebath was one of the churches 'next ionyng [joining] unto Tyverton' which in the 1530s attracted the minor benefaction of a corporas case[41] from Joan Greneway, widow of the richest man in Tiverton, who had so magnificently extended his parish church of St Peter there with a chantry aisle and its splendid south porch.[42] When they needed a lawyer in 1532 they employed one of the most distinguished in the country, who had a house at Wellington in Somerset, and the unbeneficed priest who made and repaired their church's vestments lived at Dunster, near the Somerset coast and the Bristol Channel.[43] At least one parishioner travelled sufficiently regularly to London on business to be given errands to perform for the parish. Books and church furnishings beyond the resources of Bampton, Tiverton or Exeter thereby found their way to Morebath, and along with them, no doubt, budgets of news of the outside world.[44]

Nor was the parish without educational resources. The chance survival of some pages from a notebook used in the binding of one of the Luttrell Manuscripts now in the Somerset Record Office establishes the existence of a school at Barlinch in the early years of Henry VIII's reign, offering the standard grammar-school curriculum and taught by 'Master David Juyne'. A visitation of the priory in 1510 had required the canons to make good the lack of such an educational provision, stipulated in their rule,⁴⁵ and Juyne's appointment was almost certainly the result. The first objective of such teaching would have been the preparation of novices for ordination and the education of any choir and serving boys attached to the house, but Barlinch was too small and poor to have had many such pupils, and the presence of a competent schoolmaster there must certainly have attracted a wider clientele. The syllabus Juyne followed was identical to that available in the established schools in larger centres of population. The scrappy notes which survive from some early sixteenth-century Barlinch schoolboy's copy-book include quotations from standard grammar-school texts like Alain de Lille's *Liber Parabolorum* and Robert Grosseteste's *Stans Puer ad Mensam*; a Latin sentence declaring that 'we are all off to the swimming-pool' suggests that the proximity of the Exe was appreciated by the boys, and an English sentence prescribed for translation declaring that 'I ha[v]e ete my belyfull of coloppes and egges today' [bacon and eggs] suggests a down-to-earth approach by the schoolmaster in his choice of illustrative material. We have no way of knowing whether the sons of the farmers of Morebath made the two-mile walk across the moor or up the valley of the Exe to Barlinch, but the opportunity was certainly there, and there is evidence in the accounts of literacy in the parish, even among the cottagers and wage-earners.⁴⁶

There were no very rich men in Morebath, and the gap between the well-to-do and the poor was narrower than in many more prosperous communities. The lay subsidy for 1524 lists fifty-five tax-payers, assessed at sums ranging from £1 in wages – the normal valuation for farm labourers – to £14 in goods, held by William Morsse, with John Norman senior a close second at £13/6s/8d; other indications in the accounts suggest that Norman was under-assessed in 1524, and may in fact have been the wealthiest man in the parish. Only five parishioners in all – two Normans, two Morsses and a Timewell – were rated at more than £10, and these families, together with the Raws and the Borrages, consistently show up in subsidy and muster rolls and in manorial and parish setts [local taxes] and rates as the wealthiest in the parish. As these modest figures suggest, Morebath was a parish without resident gentry, though the nearest gentry household, that of the Sydenhams of Dulverton, was not far away, just over the parish boundary in Somerset. Members of the Sydenham family were called in on several occasions to help sort out parish rows, and Morebath's priest, Sir Christopher Trychay, was clearly on excellent terms with them. Edward Sydenham, the family patriarch, had married into the Combe family of Dulverton at the beginning of Henry VIII's reign. He came originally from

Culmstock in Devon, the priest's home village, and he must have known Sir Christopher's parents since he occurs along with Thomas Trychay senior, almost certainly the priest's father, in a list of jurors in a Culmstock manorial court roll in 1509.[47] Though he was not a beneficiary of Sydenham's will, Sir Christopher paid the parish the large sum of 3/= in 1543 for a knell 'for Mr Edward Sydenham ys sowle', too much for ringing simply on the burial day and month's mind. It probably represents payment for the elaborate tolling of the great bell every night for a month, a practice which continued to mark the obsequies of the more prosperous inhabitants of the Morebath even in Elizabeth's reign.[48] It is too costly a gesture for casual acquaintance, and suggests a relationship of real friendship or perhaps of patronage and clientage.

Seventeen Morebath parishioners were assessed at £1 in wages or goods in 1524, the standard figure for farm labourers or poor cottagers. They formed a third of the parish, therefore just about the county average. These poor men included Lewis Trychay, the priest's brother. Thirteen parishioners were assessed at £2, while the remaining nineteen were assessed between £3 and £8, the majority in the £3–£4 range.[49] It was a mixed farming area, with a range of livestock, from beef and dairy cattle to geese and chickens. But Devon's largest industry was the production of the ribbed woollen cloth known as kersey or 'Devon Dozen', by the beginning of Henry VIII's reign already transforming the fortunes of north and mid-Devon wool-towns like Tiverton.[50] John Greneway's alms houses and his chantry chapel, blazoned with his merchant's mark and carved with a fleet of his wool ships, proclaimed this new prosperity.[51] The Exeter chronicler John Hooker wrote that in the region 'there is no market nor village nor scarse any privat mannes house where in theise clothes be not made, or that there is not spynninge and cardinge for the same ... wheresoever any man doth travell you shall fynde at the ... foredore of the house ... the wyffe their children and their servantes at the turne spynninge or at their cardes cardenge and by which comoditie the comon people do lyve'.[52] Morebath certainly shared in this activity: there was a weekly sheep and wool market at Bampton, and in Morebath sheep-grazing dominated the high ground in the parish, as wool dominated the parish economy; every householder in Morebath had one or more (mostly small) flocks of sheep. Many parishioners, including the vicar, also kept pigs. The parish had a smithy, a mill, and a pound to keep sheep which had strayed or were awaiting sale. Everyone with land grew corn, at best wheat and barley, but on the higher, rougher ground, oats and rye. The heather and gorse of the moor itself provided pollen for hives of bees, though bee-keeping seems to have been a specialism of the Morsse family, who regularly made up the wax for the lights in the church and who were paid to look after the butts of bees left by members of the vicar's family and by parishioners to maintain a light before the statue of St Sidwell. Their proximity to the parish church also meant that the Morsses were regularly paid to lodge artisans working on the church and that equipment and building materials used in the repair of the church, from the loan of a ladder to the carrying of water for mixing cement and thatching reed for the church house, were fetched – and paid for – from the Morsse homestead.[53]

A few of the better houses in the parish may have been of stone – there are remnants of what may be Tudor stone building in the farms at Wood and elsewhere.[54] But the majority were of thatch and cob, that extraordinary mixture of clay, straw and gravel which, kept properly roofed and limewashed, sets hard as brass and endures for centuries, but which melts away to mud if the weather is let in. The layout of the houses of Tudor Morebath is less certain: most were probably the two- or three-roomed type divided by a cross-passage which is the commonest medieval house form in Devon. But if appearances are anything to judge by, Brockhole, the remote hill farmhouse in the north of the parish, preserves under its pebbledash and flimsy modern porch the powerful lineaments of a Devon longhouse, in which the family living quarters were on the higher ground to one side of the cross passage, the shippon for the animals sloping away (for the sake of drainage) on the other, but all under one roof. In this arrangement, the bodies of the oxen provided an additional source of heating for their human companions in winter. Longhouses are essentially a Dartmoor phenomenon but they were also found on Exmoor, and Brockhole may suggest that the upland farms in Tudor Morebath followed this ancient pattern.[55]

We get a snapshot of the contents of a typical Morebath farmhouse and yard from the 1531 inventory of the goods of the widow Katherine Robbyns, whose husband William had been assessed at £3 in goods in 1524. She had been well clothed, with two kirtles to wear over her linen petticoat, black for everyday wear, crimson with matching mantle for best. To protect her against the bleak moorland winters she had a woollen 'knytter' or jumper, and at her girdle she wore a splendid and expensive rosary of coral, 'dubbyll gawdyd with amber' and with Pater Noster beads of silver, hung from 'a ryng lyke a hope'.[56] Even her best clothes, however, were probably old-fashioned. Morebath women, like country women everywhere in early Tudor England, passed their garments of state on from generation to generation. Such gowns were sometimes left to the church, but they were usually redeemed for cash by the family and passed to the women-folk in the next generation. Katherine Robbyns in her finery would probably have elicited a curled lip or a condescending smile from the wives of the citizens of Exeter, though they might well have coveted her rosary, as the wife of John Tutlake her executor evidently did, since she eventually bought the beads from the church.[57]

Katherine's bed had three blankets, a 'hyllyng' or coverlet and a bolster, her table was covered with a linen board-cloth; she had eight pewter dishes and a salt-cellar; she had two silver spoons, one of which however was at pledge with a neighbour who had loaned her 10d, almost certainly because of Morebath's recurrent shortage of ready coin rather than through poverty. She had three wooden coffers, one of them 'great', and her kitchen was equipped with a range, pans, pots, basins and 'greater and lesser' bowls of brass and of earthenware, a mortar, a gridiron, the hanging for a crock, and a goose pan. She had two gallons of butter, ten and a half bushels of rye, seven pecks of malt, and a bowl with a 'lytell wotmelle [oatmeal] in store'; still standing on her land was the 'rye and the whett of this ere'. Three flitches of bacon hung from the rafters. She had the inevitable 'torne' or distaff, two carding combs, three pounds of yarn and and eleven pounds of wool, 'the blake and the blew'. She had casks and crocks and sieves for brewing beer, and 'a pype and 3 lytell caskes' to put it in. In the dairy she had milking buckets, pans and cheese vats. A plough, a harrow, a sown saddle, a 'teng' [a harness for a pack-saddle or pannier] and a bag stood or hung in the outhouses. Her livestock comprised the plough ox, a bullock, three cows, two calves, a mare and a colt, thirteen sheep, a sow, a goose and its gander, two hens and their cock, and there was a dray-full-and-a-half of hay to feed or bed them all. She died, as she had lived, in modest comfort, nursed with spice and ale and candles. At her burial and month's mind there were doles of bread and ale, and funeral baked meats of beef and mutton garnished with raisins and mustard.[58]

Between the living standards of middling farmers like William and Katherine Robbyns and the cottagers and smallholders assessed at just £1 in goods or wages there may not in fact have been all that much difference in practice. Lewis Trychay, the priest's brother, started life in Morebath town as a cottager assessed at £1, and regularly features in parish lists and levies as one of the poorest men. By the 1540s, however, while still among the poorer parishioners, he had progressed to tenancy of one of the farms of Morebath manor, and was very active in parish business, helped on no doubt by the fact that his brother was the priest. Harry Hurley was also a cottager assessed at £1, but Harry was one of a handful of men who gave an oak to the making of the church's new benches in 1534, he was able to donate a pair of candlesticks worth 20d to St Sidwell's altar in the same year, and his bequest of 6/8d at his death in 1543 suggests burial in church, the mark of a man of substance in Morebath. His son William was also nominally among the poorer men of the parish, but he too was one of the leaders of parish affairs in the 1540s and 1550s, and he certainly had sources of income other than his smallholding, perhaps trading in wool, for his business took him frequently to London.[59]

Men assessed at only £1 therefore played a full part in parish life, serving alongside the well-to-do as wardens of the stores and as churchwardens, appearing with other leading parishioners to support the wardens at visitations, riding to the hundred and manor courts to answer for the parish.[60] But the community made allowance for their sometimes straitened circumstances, since some of those elected to serve as wardens lived very near the poverty line. John Isak was assessed at £2 in 1524. His son Robyn shows up in parish and manorial setts as one of the poorest men in the parish, yet he was High Warden in 1555 and again in 1562. By 1568 he had fallen ill, and both the Young Men's store and the High Wardens were making payments to a 'leche' [a 'leech' or doctor] on his behalf; by 1572 he was a pauper, receiving parish hand-outs.[61] When another poor parishioner, John Wood, mislaid 18d of parish money entrusted to him by one of the wardens, the parish eventually wrote it off as a bad debt because 'hyt ys more cherite to geve hyt hem then to take hyt frome hem' – though not before they had nagged away about it for fourteen years![62] It was recognised that service as churchwarden might be time-consuming, a serious matter for a wage-earner paid by the day, and also that outlay for parish expenses might involve the warden in personal expense or at any rate short-term cash-flow problems. When poor men were elected, therefore, they were sometimes allowed to decline the office, paying only a nominal fine for refusal of service, or being let off with no fine at all. When the cottager Richard Don was elected High Warden in 1544 he paid only £2 of wax 'for hys dyscharge', and when the even poorer Exebridge cottager Marke was due to serve, 'the parysse forgave hyt hem'.[63]

Until the reign of Edward VI, however, the poorest of all are concealed from us in the Morebath sources. Poor there certainly were, though we have virtually no hard information about beggars and the destitute in Morebath and its region for most of the Tudor period, and even servants and labourers like 'Harry Tanner's wife' often surface first and last only when someone buys a funeral knell for them, or pays for their burial.[64] The poor do occasionally appear in the accounts in their own right, like John Huintte or Alice Oblye the servant of Thomas Zaer, paying 1d or 2d for the 'occupying of the alms light', a contribution to the maintenance of the communal light burned in memory of the parish dead and the nearest the poor could approximate to the ceremonies with pall and candles and ringing of knells which marked the obsequies of the well-to-do.[65] With the Edwardine regime's emphasis on the substitution of alms to the poor for all other forms of 'good works', and in particular the order that ecclesiastical linen rendered redundant by religious reform be given to the poor, the paupers or at any rate the marginal men of Morebath become visible – Marke at Exebridge, William Bicner, from a family whose members appear elsewhere in the accounts delving stone at Lodvin quarry, Thomas Sexton (the grave-digger), Richard Cruce, John Wood, all recipients of old surplices or altar cloths on St George's eve 1549, some openly in the face of the parish and some secretly, perhaps to spare their feelings.[66] Periodic donations to paupers like '[W]hyte the begger' or the occasional demobbed sailor feature in the Elizabethan accounts,[67] and with the commencement of the register of baptisms, weddings and burials in 1558, the homeless poor who increasingly haunted the Elizabethan social imagination if not always their conscience, stalk or stagger into Morebath – 'Alice a poore walking woman which died at Robert Isac's' in March 1560, or Joan, another poor walking woman who died in the parish in October 1563, or the succession of 'poor walking women' brought to bed of base-born children in Morebath barns and outhouses – in November 1562, August 1563, October 1572.[68]

The register also gives us a firmer grip on the experience of birth and death in Tudor Morebath. From 1558 we can trace the arrival of every new child in the village, including those who may not have been entirely welcome, like the bastard sons born to the unmarried daughters of some of Morebath's most prominent families – John, born to Margaret Morsse in March 1566, James to Mary Timewell of Burston in November 1568. But it is death rather than birth which the registers bring into sobering focus. Morebath seems to have avoided major outbreaks of epidemic disease, like the sweating sickness that ravaged other parts of north and north-west Devon in the 1550s, but it had constant acquaintance with untimely death.[69] Even before the burial registers begin this is visible in the mortuary bene-factions that commemorate the young – Walter More 'a yong man' and John Tayler alias Iosse 'a yong man' in 1529, Joan Hukeley and the priest's niece Joan Trychay in 1531, William Robbyns 'a yong man' the same year, Alsyn the daughter of Thomas Timewell at Combe in 1532, John Don of Exebridge 'a yonge man'and Christopher Morsse 'filius William Morse' in 1534, John Webber and Christina Goodman in 1537, Thomas Zaer 'a yong man' in 1538. The litany is relentless, the brief entries in the accounts of gifts for knells or candles the trace of the most terrible of afflictions, a parent's mourning for their child. Most will have succumbed to disease, some to mischance, like the unnamed 'ladd that was killed with the knyffe', a stranger from Stoodleigh who leapt to his horse at Exebridge in 1558 and impaled himself on his own dagger, leaving the parish with elaborate and expensive arrangements to make for the inquest.[70]

With the commencement of the register the pathos of this everyday experience of mortality in Tudor Devon comes into sharper focus. James Goodman's son Christopher was baptised in church by Sir Christopher Trychay on 13 October 1564: he had been born with a twin brother, bap-tised in the birthing room at home, but certain not to survive and so not given a human name – the midwife bizarrely christened the little scrap of mortality 'Creature'. Perhaps the doomed baby had been christened after only its head had appeared and its sex was not yet known. This was evidently the custom of the parish – the register for 31 May 1560 records the burial of Alice the wife of William Morsse, along with 'her child Creature', presumably another hopeless birth baptised to ensure the salvation of the child's soul and its material equivalent, the dignity of Christian burial. Christopher Goodman's mother did not long survive the death of her 'Creature': she lingered a week, but she herself was buried on 22 October. Goodman already had a three-year-old son, and with two young children to care for he could not afford the luxury of long mourning. Within six months he had remarried: the first child by his new wife, Joan Morsse, was another October birth, baptised Mary on 4 October 1567; it was to be another October death also, for this child too was buried a fortnight later, though this time the mother would survive to bear two more sons.[71] The Goodman family's experience could be replicated several times over from the Tudor registers of Morebath, as of most other English parishes. This brutally high level of mortality among their children may explain the custom, maddening to the historian trying to pick his way through meagre documentation, of naming several children of the same generation of the same family with the same name. In 1534 the branch of the Timewell family farming at Wood in Morebath had three unmarried sons, all called John, identified by the priest in a note of that year as John maior, John minor and John minimus.[72] Lawrence Stone has famously suggested that the men and women of early modern England were hardened to the loss of their children in infancy, held themselves back from bonding until the dangerous early years were passed, and did not grieve as we would grieve.[73] Believe it who can: Tudor hearts were as breakable as ours, and one can only speculate about the impact of such relentless misfortune on the sensibilities of the men and women of early modern Morebath.

Most of our knowledge of Tudor Morebath derives from a single source, the parish accounts kept by one man, vicar through all the changes of Reformation and Counter-Reformation from 1520 to 1574. Sir Christopher Trychay arrived in Morebath on 30 August 1520.[74] Despite the title, he was not of course a knight. Non-graduate priests were conventionally given the honorific 'Sir' or, in Latin, 'Dominus', though this was a form of respect which by the sixteenth century could sometimes carry undertones of irony, as a street-vendor nowadays might call his customers 'squire': 'Sir John Lacklatin', the ignorant country priest, was a conventional figure of fun. Morebath's priest was a countryman, but by no means a lack-latin. He was not exactly a local man, having been born twelve miles away at Culmstock, where his father Thomas still lived. There are two Thomas Trychay's listed in the 1524 subsidy rolls for Culmstock, assessed at £2 and at £5. His father was probably Thomas Trychay senior, a man of substance and reeve of the Manor of Culmstock in 1510–11, but most of the eight Trychays listed in the subsidy returns for Culmstock were assessed at £1 in wages, so the vicar's origins were humble. They were evidently comfortable enough to ensure him a decent education, however: he could express himself fluently if often rather wildly in Latin as well as English, at his death he left a collection of books to a favourite nephew, and his handwriting, at least to begin with, is handsome and disciplined.[75]

Sir Christopher must have been born in the early 1490s: he was ordained acolyte in September 1514, subdeacon and deacon in March 1515, and priest on 2 June 1515, 'ad titulum prioratus de Frithelstock' [to the title of the priory of Frithelstock].[76] In order to avoid huge numbers of unemployed clerical scroungers, the medieval Church required every ordinand to have a 'title', nominally a guarantee of employment, but if this had ever worked, by the end of the Middle Ages it was essentially a legal fiction. The granting of titles to candidates for ordination to the secular clergy was standard procedure for the religious houses of Devon, as indeed everywhere else in early Tudor England. In most cases this must have been no more than a formality, a convenience for which candidates may have paid a fee.[77] The monasteries could not possibly have provided employment for all the clergy to whom they gave titles, even though a good many chaplaincies, chantries and curacies were in the hands of religious houses, and some of these did find their way to the men granted such titles.[78]

It is often assumed that men seeking a title for ordination went to their nearest religious house, so there is a puzzle about Trychay's use of a title from Frithelstock, an Augustinian priory near Torrington, miles away on the other side of the county. Many religious houses had schools or choirs attached, and it is just possible that Trychay may have been a pupil at Frithelstock, though the strong devotion to the Exeter saint Sidwell which he brought to Morebath and set about fostering there suggests an education in Exeter itself. At any rate, in his case the Augustinian connection was possibly more than a titular formality, for the vicarage of Morebath was in the gift of another Augustinian house, at Barlinch, and it was the prior of Barlinch, 'my patrone', who presented Trychay to Morebath in 1520. But it may be that family connections rather than any special affiliation with the Augustinian order explain Trychay's preferment. It seems likely that his claims were pressed on the prior of Barlinch by Edward Sydenham, a friend of Trychay's family and, as one of the largest landowners in Dulverton, a close and influential neighbour of the priory. If Sydenham did use his influence to help Trychay to the security of Morebath vicarage, this would account for the priest's gift of 3/= for a knell for the repose of Sydenham's soul in 1543. [79]

We do not know what Sir Christopher was doing between his ordination and his arrival in the parish where he was to spend the next fifty-four years. The likelihood is that he eked out a precarious living as a chantry or stipendiary priest of some sort, without security or prospects, as most newly ordained clergy were obliged to do. The vicarage of Morebath , indeed, was itself only a modest security. Recorded in Henry VIII's *Valor Ecclesiasticus* as worth a mere £8, it was not the poorest living in the region, and was certainly enough for a single man to live on, but it was by no means a plum. Two miles away, the living of Bampton was worth £20, and Trychay's own home parish of Culmstock was worth £16.[80] Nevertheless, Trychay's £8 put him at least on a par with most of his parishioners, and by contrast with what may well have been lean years before, he clearly viewed his arrival in Morebath as a homecoming to permanence and security. Twenty years on, recalling his arrival on 30 August 1520, he wrote, in a jubilant quotation from psalm 117, 'et in eo anno dextera domini exaltavit me' [and in that year the right hand of the Lord raised me up].[81] But in retrospect, it is clear that the arrival of Sir Christopher in Morebath was to be at least as momentous for the parish as for the priest.

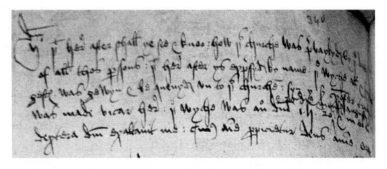

Sir Christopher heads a list of parish benefactors with a jubilant note recording his own arrival in Morebath on 30 August 1520
[Binney 19–20 / Ms 340]

CHAPTER TWO

The Voices of Morebath

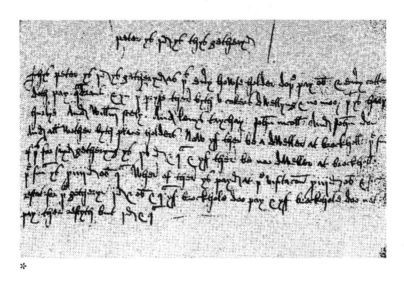

*

I A BOOK OF ACCOUNTS

All the voices of Tudor Morebath are one voice, caught between the pages of a single book. More than two hundred sets of Churchwardens' accounts survive from Tudor England, and the accounts of the parish of Morebath, available in print since 1904, are among the best known and most widely used of them.[1] The large quarto manuscript, written on rough but still white rag paper, was bound in brown calf covers measuring 23 by 33cm sometime in the first half of the twentieth century, at the Exeter City Library, where it had been deposited by T.W. Glare, vicar of Morebath 1930–56.[2] Now in the Devon County Record Office, it consists of 205 manuscript folios containing, with a few gaps, the accounts from 1527[3] through to 1596. The manuscript in its present state is incomplete. It probably once included all the accounts from the arrival in the parish of Sir Christopher Trychay in August 1520 and it certainly began, as Sir Christopher himself informs us, with an inventory of the 'iuellis [jewels] …

---

* Among the documents inserted into the accounts is this 1531 regulation for the collection of 'Peter's pence', a tax paid to the Pope. The entry incidentally informs us of the total number of farms and cottages in the parish [Binney 34–5 / Ms 357]

with all wother ornamentis of ye churche and of the churche howsse cuppis and all', publicly delivered to successive High Wardens as they took office at the beginning of their year.[4] This inventory, and the first six years of the accounts, are now missing, and the earliest surviving portion begins in the middle of the accounts for the year 1527.

The manuscript itself is a bewildering jumble. Though referred to more than once by its scribe as 'the boke of a cowntis' or 'the churche bok',[5] it was not in fact a single book at all until the early twentieth century, but a bundle of unbound quires, varying slightly in size because bought as they were needed, and added, presumably in some form of loose-leaf cover, to the accumulated accounts of previous years.[6] Unsurprisingly, over the years these quires became jumbled in the parish chest. They were (mostly) correctly ordered, transcribed and eventually published by an able late-Victorian antiquary and former Vicar of Morebath (1889–95), J. Erskine Binney. The very serviceable edition which resulted is an impressive monument to meticulous editorial detective work, but Binney was occasionally defeated by his material. He misread some letters and numbers, being prone in particular to substitute for the figure 2 in the ale account receipts the roman numeral 'x', with a consequent five-fold exaggeration of the drinking capacity of the parishioners of Morebath.[7] A more momentous misreading led him to print 'sent Denys downe ys campe' instead of the manuscript's 'sent davys downe ys campe', and thereby helped disguise from generations of users of the accounts the astonishing fact that in July 1549 the parish of Morebath not only sent a group of young men to join the siege of Exeter and the rebellion against the Prayer Book, but carefully documented the expenses incurred in the process, including the names of the leading parishioners involved in funding this act of high treason.[8] Less seriously, Binney was occasionally misled into running together parts of different accounts,[9] while two pages of the High Wardens' accounts for 1528,[10] and two more from 1571,[11] evaded his scrutiny altogether, were omitted from his edition, and remain unprinted.

In any case, when the manuscript was passed to the Exeter Library in its unbound state, Binney's careful collation of the pages was undone.[12] The library's binder could not read Tudor handwriting, and he or someone else evidently dropped the pages. They were therefore sewn into their new binding in total disorder, ignoring the sequence which Binney had laboriously established. So the bound manuscript begins with twenty-six pages containing the accounts for 1570 to 1575, then leaps abruptly to the middle of the accounts of 1556, running for forty-six pages through to 1562. It then leaps backwards to the 1520s and 1530s, and so on, with frequent jumps back or forward, through the entire volume. Single years or runs of years are interrupted and distributed randomly through widely separated parts of the book, breaking off in mid-stream to resume anything up to fifty or sixty pages later. The result, even with Binney's edition to hand as a crib, can drive the reader of the manuscript to distraction.

All the accounts up to and including those for 1573 are written in a single bold and clear hand, elegant to start with, coarsening with age into spikiness, occasionally made erratic by illness or stress, marked throughout by easily recognisable features (such as a distinctive letter 'G', always formed by placing point-to-point a diamond and a jagged triangle), and retaining to the end its distinctive energy and dash. The writing is that of the Vicar of Morebath from 1520 until his death in May 1574, Sir Christopher Trychay. Like many Tudor priests, Sir Christopher was the most literate man in his parish. For the fee of 1d a year, even in the early sixteenth century a purely nominal return for the very substantial labour involved, he acted as scribe for the churchwardens and storewardens of his parish. Year by year he copied into the church book the dangerously ephemeral loose-leaf accounts which a mixture of canon law, parochial expectation and ecclesiastical custom required churchwardens to keep. In the process, Sir Christopher audited the accounts, frequently and publicly correcting the wardens' often shaky arithmetic, adding gloss and comment on intentions and outcomes, exhorting the parish to further acts of piety, praising the public-spirited, rebuking the recalcitrant, truculent or grudging. Though the wardens themselves retained the individual 'bill' or 'cownter pane of [their] account',[13] the book, with its file-copies, seems to have remained in the keeping of the priest. Into it he also copied many non-ecclesiastical documents, the common factor of which was that all of them had some bearing on the shared life of the parish community – records of setts (compulsory rates set by parish or manorial officials) and collections for secular obligations like the repair of bridges or the payment of fifteenth and tenths to the Crown, levies for the maintenance of Devon's sea defences or the equipping and financing of the Tudor militia and, in Elizabeth's reign, of colonial armies for Ireland. The result is the fullest and most remarkable of all sets of Tudor churchwardens' accounts, fifty years of uniquely expansive and garrulous commentary on the affairs of a tiny and otherwise obscure rural community in one of the remotest regions of early modern England, during the revolutionary religious and social upheavals of the English Reformation.

History has its fashions, and new generations of historians discover or revalue new types of evidence. Churchwardens' accounts, which survive in greater numbers for early modern England than for any other country in Europe,[14] are, in form at any rate, single-entry balance sheets of the income and expenditure of parishes and their elected officials. With their apparently microscopic focus on small-time getting and spending, their endless catalogues of pious donations and piffling outlay on tiles and timber, the greasing of bells, the repair of roofs and windows, the payment of carpenters, tilers and plumbers, the carriage of shingles and sand and thatching reed, the upkeep of candles and lamps, these accounts were once considered the dreary preserve of county archaeological societies and parochial antiquarians. No longer. Over the last generation, growing interest in the implementation and pace of official religious policy during the Reformation, and a heightened sense of the centrality of the localities for an understanding of early modern society in general, has led historians of religion, politics and of popular culture to place enormous emphasis – and correspondingly high hopes – on churchwardens' accounts.[15] They are increasingly quarried for the information they contain about the nature, priorities and practices of late medieval religion, for detailed assessment of fluctuations in corporate lay religious investment, for information about the local progress of reform and counter-reformation in the mid-Tudor years, and even for clues to the precise dating of the rise of religious and folk customs once considered, simply, 'immemorial'.[16]

There are in fact a range of serious problems in using Tudor parish accounts in any or all of these ways. For a start, the arithmetic of most such accounts, those of Morebath included, is often extremely unreliable. Totals of expenditure or income are frequently miscalculated by amounts ranging from a few pence to several pounds, a phenomenon so widespread as to lead some historians to question the viability of systematic statistical analysis based on them.[17] Clive Burgess in particular has argued that this chronic inaccuracy is not a matter of poor Tudor accounting techniques, nor of low levels of numeracy among the artisans, merchants and yeomen from whom the wardens were mostly recruited, nor of the difficulties for accurate calculation posed by the almost universal use of the cumbersome roman (rather than arabic) system of numerals. Burgess does recognise that practical need for long-term records of parish resources and commitments was a factor in the emergence and preservation of late medieval and Tudor churchwardens accounts. He suggests, however, that many surviving accounts are best viewed not as working financial records but as specially compiled commemorative and propagandist works, designed to celebrate the good works of earlier wardens and parishioners, and to urge living parishioners to imitation. Many such books of accounts, he argues, were indeed constructed by copying, excerpting and summarising real working accounts. They can nevertheless be misleadingly selective, and they systematically disregard numerical accuracy because they were employed by their compilers and understood by their first audiences as essentially symbolic and devotional rather than functional documents. Burgess has also rightly emphasised the incomplete picture of parish activity which emerges from even the fullest churchwardens' accounts. Many crucial parish functions, from the celebration of the liturgy to the control and planning of long-term investment and spending, were managed by parishioners, clerical and lay, other than the wardens, and often in fact superior to them in the parish hierarchy. The activities of these people – the clergy and the parish elite or 'masters' – are therefore often invisible to us, because they were not part of the wardens' remit, and so were not reported in the wardens' accounts.

These warnings about the limitation of churchwardens' accounts as historical sources deserve to be attended to, but they in turn are derived from the study of sets of urban parish accounts from Bristol and London which are themselves far from typical. The splendidly copious accounts of All Saints Bristol, for example, which Burgess has edited, with their elaborate lists of benefactors and commemorative inventories, are manifestly designed both to memorialise and to provoke parochial piety. It is difficult, however, to view the often very bald and sketchy balance sheets which make up the bulk of surviving rural accounts as having much in the way of symbolic or hortatory mileage in them. The more workaday reasons for compiling a book of accounts given in 1498 by the wardens of the Somerset parish of Pilton 'for a remembrance of all such goodes as long therto and to make and tytyll atrew acownttys off all wardens wher withyn and all other things that encresse to the same', were probably just as important.[18] In 1557 much the same reason was given by the wardens of the Devon country parish of Kilmington at the beginning of their book. This was, they wrote, the 'boke of the Rekenyngs and Acount of the Chyrch Wardyns of the Parysche of Kylmyngton and for other Reckenyngs for the sayd Chyrche Always to be hadd yn a redyness for Anye besynes belongyng to or for the same Chyrche'.[19]

'Always to be hadd yn redyness for Anye besynes'. In the West Country as elsewhere, churchwardens were required not only to present an annual account of their stewardship to the parish, but to keep a written copy, which might be examined by the archdeacon at his visitation.[20] Since late medieval visitations were rarely more than triennial events, this meant keeping accounts well beyond the average warden's term of office, and must certainly have provided a motive for the shift from fragile single-sheet accounts to *books* of accounts, easier to store and to use, and less vulnerable to loss or damage. By no means all parishes, however, made this transition. Most accounts will have been compiled first by individual wardens on loose sheets, often written on whatever scraps of paper came to hand – for paper, though cheap enough, could be in the countryside a scarce commodity. But throughout the Tudor century many parishes also retained their fair-copied file versions of these accounts as single paper or parchment membranes, where necessary made up of several sheets glued or stitched end-to-end into a roll, and preserved as sheets or rolls in the parish chest.

This was by no means necessarily a matter of poverty or poor organisation. The best-preserved accounts from Tudor Devon are those from the stannary town of Ashburton – copious, elaborate, well organised and, as it happens, preserved in a paper book, similar in many respects to the Morebath book, but already bound between parchment covers in the sixteenth century.[21] The order and coherence of the Ashburton book, however, depended on the availability within the parish of a succession of sophisticated urban scribes. Bound books of accounts might also be scrappy and disorganised affairs, giving not much more than the names of the wardens and the bare totals of income and expenditure, or might be clogged with rough calculations and illegible crossings out.[22] By contrast, loose-leaf accounts might be well written and carefully preserved. The accounts of many wealthy Exeter city parishes, and of the prosperous towns of Tavistock, Okehampton and Crediton, were kept in loose format on parchment rolls, one for each year.[23] These rolls are very splendid objects, handsomely copied and elaborately ornamented by professional scribes, as the surviving accounts of Exeter parishes like St Petroc and St Mary Steps, preserved in this format, demonstrate.[24]

The impressively formal appearance of these rolls prompts the wider question of the use of all such accounts, whether in rolls, sheets or books – what were they *for*? Most Tudor parishes had some form of public audit, at which the wardens gave an account of income and expenditure, and West Country parishes in general put a high value on consensus and accountability. Officials were expected to act 'with the assent and by the comanndement of the hole parishe ... according to ther olde accustomed usage', and wardens who exceeded or abused their authority were liable to find themselves dragged into the ecclesiastical or civil courts.[25] When in 1519 a bitter financial dispute broke out between the London goldsmith John Amadas and the Devon parish of Tavistock over payment for a silver processional cross, the case in the Court of Requests turned on whether the cross had been ordered not only by the wardens and 'most substancyall men of the same parische', but also with the assent and consent of the parishioners at large. Evidence was produced of a series of meetings at which the cross had been displayed to the parish at large, and of a formal meeting to elicit their consent, announced beforehand by the priest from the pulpit and held when 'the hole parisshens wer assembled to gither upon a holyday'.[26]

Churchwardens' accounts and the annual audit were certainly central to this process of parochial scrutiny and literal *accountability*, and the unrolling and reading of elaborately calligraphed rolls, or the production and opening of large and impressive books, was often no doubt a formal enactment of the relationship between wardens and parish. Precisely how they contributed to it, however, is less easy to say. The substance of the accounts must have been communicated to the parish at the audit in some form or another. In many cases, however, it is hard to believe that the accounts were actually read aloud in their entirety or, if read, that they were closely followed by the parishioners.

One reason for doubting this is the fact that in many parishes the accounts were written down in Latin or, as at Ashburton, in a bizarre maca-ronic mixture of English and Latin, a practice which in many places per-sisted well into the 1540s and beyond. The extent of lay literacy in elementary Latin in early modern society has almost certainly been seriously underestimated: nevertheless, these long lists of transactions in what amounts in some cases to pidgin Latin must have been extremely opaque to many, perhaps to most, hearers. The fact that in many parishes receipts con-tinued to be accounted for in Latin but that the expenditure begins, at varying dates, to be reported in English, may reflect a greater degree of lay engagement and interest in the way the parish's resources were spent, and an attempt by wardens to meet that expectation.[27] But many parishes must have presented no more than summary accounts, and some West Country parishes had a small group of auditors, often the wealthy men of the parish, who had the major say in parish business and who scrutinised the detailed accounts privately before the presentation of brief summaries at the general parish audit.[28] Such summaries might contain explicit references to the fuller accounts contained in separate bills or in the church book – as at Stogursey in Somerset in 1507, where the wardens referred to receipts 'in our seid year of accounte as by a byll byfore the auditors showed and restyth and also yn the boke of receyts more playnly doth appere'.[29]

All of which raises the question as to whether churchwardens' accounts in general should be thought of as literary or oral documents, whether they were conceived as part of the parish archive, or as texts for performance at a public meeting. The likeliest answer is that most accounts were conceived as serving both purposes, but that some were better adapted to public per-formance than others. No doubt wardens often talked the parish through the accounts, using the written account merely as a prompt, as frequently happens nowadays at annual general meetings of societies and clubs. But late medieval and Tudor accounts survive which do look as if they were intended to be read aloud, or which look like very close *post facto* reporting of the parish audit, incorporating the conclusions and outcome of the whole process. From at least the mid-1470s the wardens of the Somerset parish of Croscombe wrote their accounts into a paper book. These accounts were not only composed in English, but their language directly mimicked the action of the meeting at which they were presented. They are written in the present tense, and enact the appearance and report of a succession of parish officials and collectors, some of whom hand over money in the presence of the parishioners, and some of whom do not:

First the Wardence present in the gyfte of Annes Down, modor … xij^d [12^d]
…
Comes the maidens and present in clere of this yer past noght yet …

Comes Harry Mew and Thomas Symons (weavers) and present in nought
...
Comes John Halse and Roger Morris for Roben Hod's revels, presents in xls iv^d [40/4d] ...
Comes William Branch and presents that he hath in his kepyng of the yere last past. Richard Costrell ryng the same yere and Jone Mede ... xxvi^s viii^d [26/8^d] ...[30]

First the Wardens present in the gift of Agnes Down's mother, 12d ...
Comes the maidens and present in clear of this year past naught yet ...
Comes Harry Mew and Thomas Symons (weavers) and present in naught ...
Comes John Halse and Roger Morris for Robin Hood's revels, presents in 40/4d ...
Comes William Branch and presents that he hath in his keeping of the year last past, Richard Costrell's ring the same year and Joan Mede ... 26/8d ...

And so on. As we shall see, the Morebath book fits firmly into this category of accounts: though it was certainly intended by its clerical compiler as a written repository of the parish memory, occasionally cross-referenced for ease of consultation, though it contains some pious and a great deal of exhortatory material, and though some items were quite explicitly notes and memoranda intended for reference rather than public recitation, the bulk of its contents are transcripts not so much of documents as of scripts, the traces in black and white of a man talking.

II THE STORES AND WARDENS OF MOREBATH

For so small a place, Morebath had an astonishingly elaborate internal structure, whose practical arrangements were reflected in the accounts, which were themselves a reflection of the devotional life of the community. The parish church, dedicated to St George, housed a large number of images – notably of the patron St George, depicted in an elaborate three-dimensional scene which included the dragon, together with the princess whom George rescued from the dragon, and her parents, the king and queen.[31] There were two images of the Virgin Mary, one each of St Anthony, St Sunday, St Loy, St Anne, and one of Jesus, whose figure stood in a tabernacle over the one side altar, at the east end of the north isle or 'almatory'. In the year of his arrival, Trychay presented the parish with a new carved and gilded image of the Exeter saint, Sidwell, and she too was placed above this side altar where, with the vicar's encouragement, she rapidly became the dominant devotional focus.[32] Most of the images had lights burning before them, and these lights were maintained by a series of 'stores' or devotional funds provided by the return on wool from small flocks of sheep, by ales, by gatherings 'of devotion', and by individual gifts and bequests. An annual account of income and expenditure for each store was read aloud to the assembled parish, always on a Sunday: to make this possible, the stores accounted at different times of the year. Except in the case of the High Wardens, who generally accounted on the Sunday nearest All Saints, and at any rate always in the winter, and the Maidens, whose account was usually on the 'second sunday in clene lent', accounting days were not rigidly fixed. The Young Men and the Alms Light warden generally accounted together, but on dates which might vary from May to October, and Our Lady's wardens usually in late summer or early autumn. The stores of Morebath were Our Lady's store, St Anthony's store, St Sidwell's store, the store of Jesus, St Sunday's store, the Alms Light store, the Maidens' store, and the Young Men's store. They differed widely in character.

The stores of Sidwell, Jesus and the Alms Light were simply lamp funds, whose income was derived from the sale of wool given to maintain the light as an act of piety, or purchased by the wardens: the income from the wool was supplemented by occasional gifts and bequests of money, clothing or jewellery. The churchwardens, in Morebath always called the High Wardens, routinely accounted for the stores of Sidwell and Jesus as part of their annual accounts, and there were no other officers involved. The Alms Light had its own warden, elected newly each year: until 1538 most of those who were elected High Wardens had already served as Alms Light warden. The Alms Light itself was a taper in a basin burning before the High Cross – evidently only in service time, for the annual sums spent on wax for it were seldom more than a few pence. A light of this sort was a feature of all the churches of the region: it was essentially a light to commemorate the dead, and on this Devon/Somerset border was variously called the Alms Light, the Dead Light or All Soul's Light.[33] St Sunday store had its own warden but, unlike the other stores with wardens, this job was done year after year by the same man, John Norman at Court, described as 'yerly wardyng' of the store. 'St Sunday' was probably an image of the 'Sunday Christ', the wounded body of Jesus surrounded and attacked by implements of work – ploughs, spades, flails and the like. It was an image whose cult had been growing in southern England in the late fifteenth century, and it was designed to promote a form of sabbatarianism – the strict observance of the church's rules about abstention from servile work on Sundays and Holy Days. It is a devotion which may well have appealed especially to the well-to-do and respectable, and, to judge from John Norman's appearances in contemporary tax assessments and parish levies, he was possibly the wealthiest man in Morebath. He may have donated the image and founded the store.[34] St Anthony's store had two annually elected wardens. The income from the store's sheep, varying from 6/= to 10/= a year, maintained a light which rarely cost more than 9d, and usually not so much. As with other stores, the surplus went to the High Wardens' stock. St Anthony's store differed from all the other church stores in benefiting from regular gifts of pigs as well as sheep. St Anthony was patron saint of farm animals, and was normally portrayed accompanied by a 'tantony pig', so these gifts should probably be understood as a distinctive and practical devotional gesture.[35]

None of these stores should be thought of as 'guilds': they were purely and simply funds, with the single complication required by the management of livestock. The Maiden store was another matter. The Maidens probably included all unmarried girls of twelve or so, the age at which girls began to take communion.[36] They maintained a light before the statue of the Virgin, before the High Cross and, once her cult had established itself, before St Sidwell. They had no sheep; the income from the store came from an annual 'gathering' that grew steadily throughout the 1530s, though the sums involved were never large: 3/5½d was gathered in 1529, 7/4d in 1538. These gatherings are described as 'of devotion', and the sums involved tapered off after the royal suppression of the cult of images, so, although it is impossible to be sure, they probably involved simple goodwill collections rather than organised gender games like the 'hock-tide' bindings common elsewhere, in which women bound the men of the parish, releasing them only on payment of a forfeit which went to the church.[37] Two wardens were elected each year, always young women, though their fathers occasionally seem to have served in their place, perhaps because the girls elected were just too young or inexperienced to manage the finances.[38]

The Young Men's store, which included all bachelors of communicant age, which for men usually meant about fourteen years and above, played a central role in parish finances and, by implication, its social life. Its main source of income came from an ale, referred to sometimes as the 'grooming ale' and once at least held in Lent.[39] The sums raised at these ales varied wildly, but were normally between £1 and £2, and sometimes more, a significant element in parochial income, which rarely exceeded £7 or £8 a year. There is no way of knowing who attended these ales, but the 'grooming ale' raised on average about half the sum raised by the High Wardens' ales, so it may be that it was essentially a youth event, attended by the younger and unestablished people of the parish. There are no other payments from the Young Men in the parish accounts, which means that at Morebath they probably did not engage in the 'hoggling' and 'plough' frolics by which Young Men elsewhere raised parish funds, though the 'harrow tyne' disposed of by the churchwardens at the Reformation suggests that a plough ceremony of some sort might have been a feature of Morebath's ritual year.[40] The Young Men maintained the taper before the church's patronal image of St George, and two lights before the 'high cross' or rood: in the early 1530s they several times accounted to the parish on Holy Rood day. Again, they had two wardens elected afresh each year, and as with the Maidens, when boys too young or gormless to serve were elected, their fathers (or mothers) were expected to take on the responsibility.[41]

The store of Our Lady was the most important store in the parish. Like the others it existed to maintain a light, in this case before the principal image of the Virgin. The two wardens of this store derived the bulk of their income from the church's largest flock of sheep, called 'Our Lady's sheep', normally from about twenty to two dozen and producing about forty pounds weight of wool each year. Like all the church sheep, this flock was distributed piecemeal to individual parishioners, who were responsible for accounting to the wardens for the animals in their care at the end of the year, and for handing in the fleeces after shearing. The sheep of each store had a distinctive mark cut in their ears, and were put to graze with the parishioner's own flock. All the profits went to the church, though the custodians sometimes seem to have been allowed to buy the sheep and lambs in their care, perhaps below market prices, and sheep were also bought and sold between stores, the wardens carefully accounting to the wardens of Our Lady's store for all such transactions.[42] Each year at the account the whereabouts of every sheep was minutely reported to the assembled parish. No penalties were exacted for the accidental loss or death of sheep, inevitable in a moorland parish, [43] though if the corpse was found in time the fleece was handed over to the wardens.[44] The wool from these sheep generated an annual income of about 30/= or 40/=.

The system of parochial obligation involved in the maintenance of these church flocks was quite remarkable. Many West Country parishes drew income from sheep and cattle, but most seem to have operated some sort of profit-sharing system, whereby parishioners were paid to keep the sheep and cows, or themselves paid a fee for the hire of the animals, keeping the wool or milk in return, or where parish and custodian split the profits – the system of 'half money', which at Morebath was in fact operated for the maintenance of the church beehives.[45] But keeping one of the Morebath church sheep was considered a parochial obligation, only occasionally refused. As we shall see, each year the priest reported in minute detail on the disposal of the church sheep round the parish, noting explicitly who had or had not animals from the church flocks, and commenting, usually with an edge, on those who refused. Those declining the obligation were expected to pay the church a fine of 3d or 4d called a 'sheep's lease', which was passed on by the wardens to whoever accepted the sheep in place of the recusant parishioner. Occasionally one parishioner paid another directly for this favour, 'for grasse'. These payments of 'a sheep's lease' seem to have come most often from the parish's cottagers, who, with very little grazing land of their own, preferred to pay a money fine rather than having to mortgage precious grass to one of the church sheep. In a community where grazing was at a premium and most flocks were small, the responsibility and labour involved in keeping one or more of the church sheep was a demanding commitment.[46] At any one time, nevertheless, a very large number of parishioners were involved in this particular aspect of parish fund-raising – in 1529, twenty-one householders had church sheep in their keeping, in 1531 twenty-four, just over two thirds of the parish.[47]

With a wider remit than any of these stores were the two 'hye Wardyns of the gooddis and the cattyll of the store of sent iorge',[48] that is, the churchwardens responsible for the central funds of the parish, elected afresh each year from among the heads of households. Both wardens served for just one year and there was no staggering of office, each pair beginning and ending their term of service together. It is clear nonetheless that the two wardens did not carry equal authority. Each year the church 'iulis' or plate, the stock, and the contents of the church house were entrusted to one of the wardens in particular, named first in the account, and that warden was responsible for preparing the account at the end of the year: it is often delivered in the singular – 'I received' or (after 1540) 'he received' – and retrospective references to a previous year's accounts were normally identified by the name of the accounting warden – 'Harry Hurly's account'. When Robin Isac, the senior warden, was absent from the parish during the 1562 account, his fellow warden was able to account only for the proceeds of the church ale: this is almost certainly because the ale was the special responsibility of the junior warden.[49] It was a major responsibility, since the High Wardens' ale was the most important fundraising event of the year, often providing more than half their total receipts. The tendency for one warden to take primary responsibility, evident throughout the accounts, was a special feature of the emergency years of Edward's reign, and became more marked in Elizabeth's reign than earlier; it reached its logical conclusion in the mid-1580s, after Sir Christopher's death, when for about ten years the parish elected only one warden each year.[50]

Election travelled round the parish by farms and cottages, and the head of each household was expected to serve when their turn came round, even where that head was a widow. There were women High Wardens in 1528, 1542, 1543, 1548, 1557, 1561 (when both wardens were women), 1563 and 1572 (when once again both wardens were women). Without knowing the exact location of every household, including the cottagers, it has not been possible to reconstruct the geographical basis for the rota which seems to have operated in such nominations, but rota of some sort there certainly was. John Lambert, who was farming Hayne in the 1560s, served as High Warden in 1564; he was elected to serve again in the following year, this time 'for Webber's bargyn', that is, because he was farming another property or 'bargain', whose turn it evidently was to provide the warden that year.[51]

With so many offices to fill each year, the refusal of parishioners who 'wolde not doo ther diligens'[52] was a serious matter, and finding substitutes could be difficult. Elsewhere in the diocese, parishes sometimes coerced the reluctant by prosecuting them in the ecclesiastical courts for refusal of office in the store or parish wardenships,[53] but Morebath seems always to have managed without such draconian measures. In 1540 William Leddon 'spelyd [spelled or took the place of] the ii [2] wydows at Combe', whose turn it was to serve,[54] and in fact such substitutionary arrangements were common, both for the high wardenship and for the wardenships of the stores. Occasionally they required diplomacy and persuasion, as when in 1537 the Young Men elected Edward Lawton 'but he wolde not have hyt' and so John Borrage was elected 'with the vicars helppe', presumably in the form of clerical arm-twisting.[55] One member of a family might stand in for another – Richard Timewell substituted as High Warden in 1558–9 for his kinsman William at Timewell, and in 1574 'toke the offyce yn hand' for his son William when the latter was elected Young Men's Warden that year.[56] Nicholas Timewell, Richard's father, who died in office in 1558, had himself 'spelyd' the recently widowed Joan Rumbelow in 1556, and she had reciprocated by serving in his turn the following year. Very unusually, he was then re-elected to serve in 1558. Thomas Timewell served as High Warden in 1572 in place of the widow Susan Leddons, because he was now farming at least part of her land.[57] Sometimes the deputy was paid: when William Tayler acted as High Warden 'in vice' George Smyth in 1557, Smyth paid him 3/10d 'pro ejus labore'.[58] Sometimes payments were made directly to the parish, in the form of fines, as when the widow Eylon Norman paid the parish four pounds weight of wax 'for her discharge of the hye Wardynscheppe' in 1546.[59] The wardenships were not the only offices occasionally refused. William Timewell at Wood was one of the Three Men who had played a crucial and very demanding role in 1542 in organising the complete rebuilding of the church house,[60] and then served as senior High Warden the following year. In reporting his work on the church house, the priest had singled William Timewell out as an example of unselfish service to the parish. But these were years of falling income and mounting obligations for the church, and by 1545 Timewell had evidently had enough. The priest reported to the parish that 'now William Tymwell at Wode wyll melle [meddle] no more with these offycis dicit [he says] and sic est dyschergyd nunc et quietus' [and so he is dismissed and the matter rests].[61]

As might be expected in a small community with a small population, service as High Warden was not and could not be restricted to the well-to-do: the essential qualification was headship of a household, and the poor served as well as the prosperous. Of the fifty-five tax-payers listed in the 1524 Subsidy for Morebath, thirty-five can be shown to have held parochial office in the stores or the High Wardenship subsequently. Of the remaining twenty, eleven were assessed at the lowest rate of £1 in wages or goods. They were mostly farm labourers, probably living in other households and so ineligible. Two were widows, whose husbands may have served before the accounts begin. Five of the twenty came within the sort of economic range normally associated with headship of a household and could have been expected to serve, but all these five appear to have died within a few years of the Subsidy return, and so all may have served before Sir Christopher's record begins.[62]

Of the thirty-five in the return who did serve, several fell within the £1 assessment band which in theory at any rate marked them out as poor men. So William Norman of Loyton served as Alms Light Warden in 1529, High Warden in 1533, and Our Lady's Warden in 1537. William Scely, a cottager (but also the parish miller), was Warden of the Alms Light in 1532, High Warden in 1536, and Warden of the Church Sheep in 1540. Richard Robbyns was Alms Light Warden in 1535 and High Warden in 1539. Lewys Trychay, the priest's brother and another cottager, served as Alms Light Warden in 1537, High Warden in 1541 and 1553, and as Sheep Warden in 1546.[63]

At the other end of the scale, the parish plutocracy also served. William at Morsse[64] was High Warden in 1532, Our Lady Warden in 1536, and High Warden again in 1545.[65] John Norman at Court was perpetual warden of the store of St Sunday, High Warden in 1526 and again in 1539, and Warden of St Anthony's store in 1537.[66] Men of their standing were also likely to be elected to the small group of senior parishioners who comprised the 'Four Men' or 'Five Men' – the number varied – 'that have the churche stock yn governansse'. This was an arrangement common in the West Country, whereby a small group of prominent men (in Morebath at any rate, in contrast to the Wardenship, they were always *men*) acted as bankers for the surpluses from all the church stores, and for the High Wardens. At Chagford there were four of them, called 'receptores generales',[67] the 'General receivers', at Dartington they were called 'receivers of the goods of the parish'.[68] Whereas the wardens served for a single year, the Five, Four or Three Men at Morebath held office as long as they were willing: indeed, one crucial aspect of their role was to provide financial continuity, enabling long-term planning and management of resources. They also appeared at Visitations with the Wardens, met extraordinary demands for money imposed in the manorial or Hundred courts, making 'setts' or parish levies afterwards to recoup the outlay, and from time to time were called upon to resolve parish disputes, sometimes with the assistance of the vicar, or under the chairmanship of an outsider, such as the Sydenhams of Dulverton (local Somerset gentry who held land in the parish) or the Steward or Lord of the Manor. To qualify as one of the 'Five Men' financial security was essential, because from time to time they were expected to solve cash-flow problems from their own resources.[69] As we shall see, this aspect of their office was to be crucial in Edward's reign, when they assumed a dominant role in managing the series of crises the Reformation brought to the parish. In Henry VIII's reign a number of parishioners served more than once as High Warden, but seldom with fewer than a dozen years between terms of office, and usually first as junior then as senior warden. In Elizabeth's reign, by contrast, the pool of householders willing or considered eligible to serve evidently shrank: there were more repeat elections, and the gap between first and second terms of office shrunk significantly, in some cases to a mere four or five years.

Throughout the 1520s and 1530s, therefore, in any one year twelve parishioners, eight of them heads of households, held parish office, in addition to the 'Five Men'. The degree of active parochial involvement this demanded from a community as small and relatively poor as Morebath is staggering. It reflects a highly self-conscious community life, in which shared decision-making and accountability were dominant characteristics. Its demands were matched by the degree of responsibility it allowed individuals. A note made by the priest in 1565 about payments to a plumber working on the church roof allows us a glimpse of the young men and the wives of the parish exercising their initiative in the handling of church business. The Young Men's store in 1565 had agreed to contribute towards the costs of repairs to the church. The Young Men's wardens were Thomas Perry and William Scely, but both were evidently too young to transact business on their own, for Scely's father John and Perry's mother Alison were acting on their behalf. It so happened that the plumber's son was 'then at tabyll' in the house of the senior High Warden, John Lambert of Hayne, that is, he was a lodger there that year, perhaps as a servant or farm labourer. To speed the payment of his father's wages, the plumber's son decided to make use of his association with the High Warden. Together with Nicholas Norman, son of the Bailey of Morebath Manor, also a tabler at Hayne, he went to John Scely and, with the agreement of Thomas Perry and his mother, fetched 9/6d from the Young Men's store. 'Thos[e] 2 lad-dis' then took the money to Hayne, so that John Lambert could pay the plumber's bill. The warden was away from home, however, so they gave the money instead to his wife, Alison at Hayne, and there and then 'a pon here tabyll borde sche told [counted] hyt and deliveryd hyt unto the plumer (as the plumer sayth) and thus was the plumer payd'.[70] The incident, trivial in itself, reveals the freedom with which parishioners other than the war-dens, including teenagers and women, might involve themselves in the handling of the parish's resources and the fulfilment of parish obligations. This broad-based accountability in Morebath is built into the very nature of our principal source, the accounts kept by Sir Christopher Trychay.

III SIR CHRISTOPHER TALKING

Morebath was far from unique in having a large number of stores, each with its own finances and wardens, each contributing to parish funds and parish projects, and each reporting to the parishioners at an annual audit. In the early reign of Henry VIII, the twenty or so 'stocks' or stores of the bustling mid-Devon stannary town of Ashburton generated an average income of more than £40 a year, three times the sum directly raised by the churchwardens, though we know of the stores' activities only from the summaries of receipts included in the churchwardens' annual accounts: if the stores presented separate financial reports to the parish, they have not survived.[71] At Chagford, by contrast, annual accounts do survive, not only from the churchwardens and the Four Men, but from the parish's many sub-parochial stores – St Katherine, St Mary, St Anthony, St Eligius, the High Cross, the Hoggeners.[72]

Morebath is unique, however, in the extraordinary verbal immediacy of its accounts, which bear all the marks of being transcripts of a spoken text. Where the vast majority of Tudor parish and guild accounts are desiccated lists of income and expenditure, often compiled wholly or largely in Latin, those of Morebath are vividly personalised and precisely located in a specific time. Each account, whether of one of the stores or of the High Wardens, has the same basic format. Each begins with a title, naming the store, the wardens, the regnal and calendar years and the day (almost always a Sunday) on which the account was presented to the parish. Receipts for the year are then itemised, beginning with the balance received from the previous wardens, any benefactors are named, and the grand total stated. The wardens then 'ask allowance for necessary expenses', once again itemising and totalling expenditure. The account concludes with that year's balance and, if there is a surplus to be passed to the Four Men, names which of them is to act as stockholder. The wardens for the following year are announced, together with that year's working balance; any property held by the store is passed to the new senior warden.

Something like this framework is of course common to most Tudor churchwardens' accounts. At Morebath, however, the skeleton has living flesh. In the first place, until 1540 all the accounts except those of the Maiden Wardens are written in the first person, as if the accounting warden or wardens were speaking directly. So the account of St Anthony's store in 1527 begins: 'Item we ressevyd of the wolde wardyns the laste ere at the begynnyng of our a cownte ... ii^s ii^d [2/2d]', and ends: 'and apon this we a mytte wardens for the ere follyng Robert at More and Geffery More and to Robert this for sayd mony and the wolle was delyveryd the ere and the day before reherssyd'. Wardens often name themselves again at the outset of their itemised account, and not just in the heading. The High Wardens' account for the same year was presented by the senior warden, William at Poole, and begins:

> Memorandum that y William at Pole ressevyd at the begynning of my wardynscheppe of the wolde wardyns xxij^s j^d ob [22/1½d].[73]

And even where names are not invoked, the wardens' ownership of their accounts is underlined by the pervasive use of this first person form. So when in 1529 'wolde dame Rumbelow' left her entire estate to Our Lady's store to help to buy a new image of the Virgin, the wardens prefaced a list of her benefactions with:

> ... we ressevyd by the dethe of Joan Rumbelow wydow to a new image of our Lady the wyche image was her exsector with us Wardyns as ys expressyd be fore a pon her testament.[74]

> *We received by the death of Joan Rumbelow, widow, to a new image of Our Lady, the which image was her executor with us Wardens, as is expressed before upon her testament.*

'Us wardens': the only exceptions to this ubiquitous first person convention are the Maiden Wardens' accounts. These are invariably presented in the third person, as in the account for 1529: 'Memorandum that these for sayd maydyns ressevyd of ye wolde Wardyns ...'.[75] It is not clear whether this difference of address was an example of gender discrimination because the Maiden store was the only one always administered by women, or whether it stemmed from the fact that the Maiden Wardens were often and perhaps always very young girls, whose finances were managed for them by older male relatives, by the High Wardens or by the priest.

If the accounts are precisely located as the utterance of particular named persons, they are also pervaded by a vivid sense of belonging to a quite specific moment, the day on which the accounts were presented. This, of course, is implicit in the dating of each account, but it is constantly underscored by insistent temporal references in the accounts themselves. So the High Wardens in 1530 remind the parish that Robert at Hayne owes the church 13/4d, 'the wyche mony he ys contendyd to delyver un to Thomas Rumbelow *this after nown*'.[76] In 1537 the High Wardens declare that they have money in hand 'to helppe to tyle the churche *as sone as we can gett a man and sande for to doo hyt*', or report in 1539 that 'there ys *delyveryd this present day* to William Leddon xiij^s & iiij^d [13/4d]', or in 1541 inform the parish that 'ys for the v^s [5/=] that Eylon Norman promysyd to bring yn here at Ester ... *sche wyll delyver* hyt to Richard Hucly and ... *ye schall have* a new stremer of sylke agayn sent iorge day gracia divina'.[77] In 1538 the wardens of Our Lady's store report that one of the sheep ' ys not yett schorne (nor lyke to be this ere)'.[78] In an entry in the account of Thomas Rumbelow, High Warden with John Norman at Wood in 1531, we are even more precisely located in the 'now' of the account, the Sunday before All Saints day (in that year, Sunday 27 October), looking both backwards and forwards as we are moved systematically through past, present and future tenses:

> Item y ressevyd of Thomas Borrage to the store of Sent Sydwyll a yowe hogg [i.e. an unshorn yearling ewe] the wyche John Morsse *hath now* yn kepyng and *her flyes of this ere ys putte* a mong the wolle of the store of Jhesu: unde Sent Sydwyll ys store *must have* for the flyes *a nother ere* ... iiij^d [4d].[79]

> Item I received of Thomas Borrage to the store of St Sidwell a ewe hogg (i.e. an unshorn yearling ewe), the which John Morsse hath now in keeping and her fleece of this year is put among the wool of the store of Jesus: whence St Sidwell's store must have for the fleece next year 4d.

All of which, on the face of it, might seem to suggest that Tudor Morebath was a parish of extraordinarily articulate and literate men and women, who year after year wrote down and presented to the parish a series of accounts quite unlike those of any other Devon parish of the period in the precision and vividness with which they evoke the dynamics of the parish audit. In place of a series of balance sheets, it seems, we have a sophisticated succession of living voices.

Inevitably, of course, matters are not so simple. To begin with, all of the accounts are quite explicitly compiled, or at any rate written down, by one man, not many. The High Wardens' accounts each year pay 1d 'for wretyng this a cownte and all wother this ere paste', to the vicar.[80] There was far more to this than merely copying other people's work into a book. In some cases at least, and perhaps usually, Sir Christopher did work from an existing written account provided by the wardens. Not only does he several times refer to the warden retaining 'the cownter pane of this a cownte' or 'the copy istius competus',[81] but from time to time he criticises the details of the accounting, above all the warden's arithmetic. In the account of Our Lady's store in 1538, prepared by the senior warden John Taylor, for example, the total receipts were announced as 38/11½d, but the priest adds at once 'but y wyne [I ween] hyt ys wrong caste for taylor by a 1d to moche'. Similarly, in the High Wardens' accounts for 1565, in announcing the total receipts the priest comments, 'y got the wardyn here by my cast 12d inn hys ressetis for he cast his ressettis furst ivli v^s & vj^d [£4/5/6d] where as he ressvyd not so moche by xij^d [12d] by my cast'.[82]

This correction of the wardens' arithmetic simultaneously reveals to us the presence of the priest, not only writing down the account but reading it to the parish, and establishes a distance between scribe and warden, since it makes it clear that the financial substance of the account remained the wardens' own. Morebath wardens certainly felt themselves responsible for the accounts presented in their names, if only because they were liable to be out of pocket if there was a deficit, or pursued for outstanding debts if they had not managed to balance the books. In 1540 the senior sheep warden, William Scely, spent 4/= of the wool money from the church sheep to meet a parish obligation for the repair of a local bridge. This was a perfectly legitimate transaction, for church funds were often drawn on to meet parish debts in this way. Scely, however, was a poor man, one of the parish's five cottagers, and he worried that he might be expected to handle the cashflow problem which would arise from the gap between reporting the 4/= deficit and his eventual recovery of the money from the parish. He therefore refused to present an account at all until the money was repaid to the sheep stock. The account was presented six months late to the parish, on Sunday 27 March 1541, as the priest grumbled in copying the account, 'that schulde y be made a fore Allhallow day but he keppt a way 4s so 1d [four shillings less a penny] of the churche money the wyche he be stoyd hyt a bout Exbryge and so keppt our mony tyll he was payd'.[83] When in 1558 the senior warden Nicholas Timewell at Hayne died in office, his partner John Wood, a poor man, was uneasy about the account presented in their joint names, which he had not compiled. So the priest, having read out the joint account, reported to the parish that 'yet for pleasure and partly to qualifye there mynd hereafter follyth John Woddis singular cownt for hys owne discharge what he resseuyd and payd'.[84]

The wardens, therefore, owned their own accounts. Yet equally clearly, the priest was far more than the scribe of the wardens of Morebath. He certainly sometimes compiled the first version of the formal account himself from information supplied by the accounting warden: in 1559 that process becomes visible to us because the accounting warden, John Norman at Poole, amazingly forgot to report 9d spent on oiling the bells, taken from money meant to be devoted to equipping the church once more for reformed worship, with the Bible, Homilies and Erasmus' *Paraphrases*. At the end of the annual account, therefore, having reported the closing balances, the priest added a second, shorter account on John at Poole's behalf, 'as here aftyr follyth the wyche was out of hys memory tyll this cownt was made'.[85]

Even without such clues, however, the purely formal aspects of the accounts constantly alert us to the role of the priest in their composition. All the accounts follow a common and tightly ordered set of conventions of organisation, presentation and language, and they are marked throughout by a distinctive English timbre and an equally distinctive repertoire of Latin words and phrases. Together, these stylistic traits reveal an idiosyncratic and garrulous personality, a single voice, the same no matter whose name heads the bill. This is not primarily a matter of accent or dialect, though the spelling of the accounts often preserves for us the unmistakable burr of a deep Devon accent – the font is always the 'vawnte', the altar the 'awter', the workmen who cut up trees in the wood are 'zaers' and what they are doing is 'zayng', large trees are 'grette', the elderly are 'wolde' and the woods are full of 'wokes', oatmeal is 'wotmeal', wardens travel not to Oakford but to 'wocford', money spent by the vicar is 'ledde out' or 'ledde forth' on the church's behalf, workmen renew the 'pwontyng' on the church, a poker is a 'vyre pyke', the priest's brother rides to Exeter to make payments for the 'vyre bykyn' [fire beacon] and we hear of a 'noke', a 'nox' and a 'nonest' woman.[86] But the pervasive tone of voice in the accounts is rooted in more than dialect, it reflects a distinctive mind-set, which is established in the earliest surviving accounts and which persists when, in 1540, the conventional use of the first person is dropped and all the accounts are explicitly delivered in the third person – no longer the 'I' or 'we' of the named wardens, but 'yn the begynnyng of *there* ere *they* resseuyd of the wolde Wardyns'.[87] Even before that change of person, the presence of the priest is manifest in the accounts, commenting on their content, shaping their rhetoric.

His Latin alone would alert us to this. It contains a good deal of the scribal pidgin we find in the Ashburton and many other Devon accounts – conventional shorthand snippets of clerkly jargon – 'summus totalis receptionis ys ... xxxv^s ij^d, unde petunt allocari for expenssis ...'.[88] But many of the Latin tags and phrases are decidedly devotional, with a liturgical resonance that betrays the priest. The accounts of the individual stores are usually prefaced with a brief invocation to their patron saint – 'Sancte Antoni ora pro nobis' [St Anthony pray for us], 'Auxilium fer nobis pia nunc sancta virgo Maria' [Now bring us help, o loving Virgin Mary].[89] From 1540, when the Henrician attack on the cult of the saints led to the merging or abolition of the lesser stores, the priest opened that sheep count not with an invocation to the Virgin, but with the psalm verse used at the opening of the hours of the breviary, 'Deus in adiutorium meum intende' [O God, come to my help], though he continued to invoke the parish patron, St George, before the High Wardens' accounts – all of which demonstrates a degree of sophisticated theological nuance (and a sense of ecclesiastical politics and prudence) not very common among the rural laity.[90] Reporting the pious intention of benefactors or wardens, the parishioners are told 'ye schall have a new stremer of sylke agayn sent iorge day *gracia divina*'.[91] Even a note (in the High Wardens' accounts for 1530) describing the mark in the ear which distinguished the sheep of the store of Jhesu from the sheep 'of our Laydy merke' can conclude with a liturgical flourish – 'they have a gayn a ob a pon the new ere *in seculum seculi amen*' [for ever and ever Amen].[92]

The priest was also prone to drop into Latin when matters directly affecting his own concerns were being reported, or when he wished in some way to distance himself from what was being said. For almost twenty years, as we shall see, Sir Christopher encouraged the parish to save for a fine new set of black vestments for requiem masses. He launched this project by donating the small tithes paid to him each year by the parish for the church sheep (in return for which the tithing honey and wax were to be given to him already processed or 'made', rather than unseparated in the butt or the comb). A parishioner named Harry Hurley, one of Our Lady's wardens that year, was elected by the parish to act as trustee for the slowly mounting fund thus created, and from 1529 its progress was reported annually to the parish in the account of the Wardens of Our Lady's store. At that point in the accounts, the priest almost invariably speaks directly to the parish, in a characteristic macaronic mixture of English and Latin phrases referring to 'my tithes': 'Et sic restat nunc [so there remains now] yn Harry Hurlye ys hands de meis decima [of my tithes] xiij^s [13/=] ...'; the vestments will be bought, he tells the parish, 'quando placeth Vicarius parochiaeque' [when the Vicar pleases – and the parishioners]. 'And to this agayn Harry Hurlye hath ressevyd thys present day ... xiiij^d (and mi xij^d) [14d and my 12d] and sic [so] Harry Hurlye hath in his hande now xl^s (and 5 nobyllis and xij^d nunc in meis) [40/= (and 5 × 6/8d and 12d now in my hands)] and sic in toto [and so in all] (by sydis Courte hys vs and the xiv^d puellarum [5/= and the 14d from the maidens] ys iij^{li} & xiv^s & iiij^d [£3/14/4d]'.[93]

Some of this may have been simply a matter of routine accountancy shorthand, but the priest often seems to use a Latin word or phrase also to establish distance between himself and what he is reporting. Sometimes the effect is faintly sardonic, as when he reports a claim he does not necessarily believe, for example the loss of one the church ewes: 'the yewe that [John Waters] hadde that came from William Tymwell ys gon (*ut dicit*) [so he says]'.[94] More often, it simply signals reported speech, as when he records the progress of a benefaction promised by a parishioner:

> Ys for the gefth of Thomas at Tymwell the wyche was vj^s & viij^d [6/8d] hyt was be stowyd yn payntyng of the sylyng a bowt the hye crosse parte of hyt and the rest of hyt schall come yn a banner *dicit* very shortly *sperat*.[95]

> *As for the gift of Thomas at Timewell, the which was 6/8d, it was bestowed in painting the ceiling above the high cross, part of it, and the rest of it shall come in a banner, he says, very shortly, he hopes.*

But we do not need to look to such oblique evidence to catch the sound of Sir Christopher's voice. Dozens of entries make it plain that he not only wrote out all the accounts, but that it was he who read them aloud to the parish on behalf of the wardens on their accounting Sunday. We can be sure of this because in the process he often takes the opportunity to drop the *persona* of the reporting warden, and to address his parishioners directly. This becomes especially clear after 1540, when all the accounts go into the third person, but it is liable to happen anywhere, as in the High Wardens' accounts for 1535, when he breaks off in the middle of reporting a series of expenses for the roofing of the north aisle, to note that 'this churche hadd a sak of lyme of me Sir Christopher vicar for the performing of this for sayd work (and more a lytyll) for the wyche y wyll have a nother good sak this somer follyng.'[96] Again, in the account of Our Lady's store in 1529, the year in which he launched the black vestment fund, he interupts the flow of reported expenses to note that:

> ... sic restat in Harry ys hande now de decimis ij^s viij^d [2/8d] and at the next a cownte y schall be answeryd where this mony schall go to a blacke pere of vestments or noo.[97]

> *Thus resteth in Harry's hande now from my tithes 2/8d and at the next account I shall be answered whether this money shall go to buy a pair of black vestments or not.*

He returned to the issue the following year at the same point in the accounts, reporting that he was now ready to pass the receipts from that year's wool-tithe to Harry Hurley 'whiche ... shall reste yn my hande tyll my hony be made', and declaring that:

Ys for the vestmentis of blacke we be full a greyd that these decimas schall pay for hyt all to gethers thoffe hyt be never so moche above xx^s [20/=] and yff y dey a for this be to xx^s y wyll make hyt xx^s.[98]

As for the vestments of black we be full agreed that these tithes shall pay for it altogether though it be never so much above 20/=, and if I die before this be to 20/=, I will make it 20/=.

In each case, having dealt with this matter, he immediately resumed the account, in the assumed voice of the wardens 'item we payd to the payntyng of Jhesu ... xv^s & iiij^d [15/4d]'.[99]

'We be full a greyd.' The accounts and account days, therefore, were more than an opportunity for the priest to press his own agenda on the parish: they also provided him with an opportunity to present a particular model of the parish community to itself. The accounts are saturated with a rhetoric of collective identity and shared responsibility. The parish meeting itself is constantly alluded to — contracts for work are made and debts paid '*coram parochianos*' or '*thys day ante parochianos*' [in the presence of the parishioners, before the parishioners],[100] and financial undertakings entered into 'of hys fidelite before the parysche promissyd'.[101] The sheep wardens are '*our* Wardyn of the churche scheppe',[102] expenditure undertaken by the wardens is the responsibility of the whole parish. When in 1539 a parishioner on a trip to London was authorised to spend a bequest of 5/= on a banner for the church, the High Wardens' account declared that 'yff hyt coste more money ye must be content to ley more to hyt and yff hyt costte lesse ye schall have that ys lefth ...'.[103] In the 1520s and 1530s, as we shall see, this sense of the parish collectivity was articulated in predominantly religious and sacral terms; the Edwardine Reformation was a watershed, drastically reducing the repertoire of cultic forms of social organisation and representation available to the parish. Nevertheless, even in the late 1560s the priest was insisting on this collective dimension of the parish as strongly as ever, for example when he urged the listeners to the High Wardens' account in 1567,

and of this forsayd mony se you a fore ye depart what the wardyn shall have and to whome the rest shalbe dedit [given] where by the parysshe may be answeryd of hyt when so ever they have nede.[104]

and of this aforesaid money, see before you depart what the warden shall have and to whom the rest shall be given, whereby the parish may be answered for it whensoever they have need.

The accounts are also full of the sound of reported speech, as in the High Warden's account for 1554:

Item ys for the v^s [5/=] that Thomas Rumbelow gave to the churche ... the wydow hath made answer and sayth that yow schall have hyt when ye wyll. Item ys for the vl^s & viij^d [6/8d] for Roiger Bodd ys grave with wother bequesth...hyt ys answeryd that Annys [Agnes] Bodd wylbe here schortly and pay hyt.[105]

Item as for the 5/= that Thomas Rumbelow gave to the church … the widow hath made answer and saith that you shall have it when you will.
Item as for the 6/8d for Roger Budd's grave with other bequests … it is answered that Agnes Budd will be here shortly and pay it.

Reported transactions of this sort are usually represented not as units of bookkeeping but as the outcome of processes of negotiation, often signalled by the priest's declaration that a parishioner 'is contented' to see something done. So, in the High Wardens' accounts for 1537:

Item we resseyved by the deth of Anys at Hayne a gowne and a ryng yn prisse of xij^s [12/=] in the wyche mony Nicolas at Hayne ys contendyd to sende to London by William Hurly when he goyth thether nexte and to by us a baner of sylke and so to bryng hyt yn to this churche: and yff the banner doo not coste the full xij^s he sayth ye schall have that ys left when the banner cummyth yn to this churche'.[106]

Item we received by the death of Agnes at Hayne a gown and a ring in price of 12/=, in the which money Nicholas at Hayne is contented to send to London by William Hurley when he goeth thither next, and to buy us a banner of silk and so to bring it in to this church: and if the banner do not cost the full 12/= he saith ye shall have that is left when the banner cometh in to this church.

This 'contentment' here is not a settled state of mind, but the outcome of a negotiation, something manifestly elicited from the parishioner by the priest himself. In this same year, 1537, the priest was coaxing the parish on to a number of pet projects – notably the adornment of the altar of his favourite St Sidwell. As ordinary mortuary benefactions came into the church, therefore, he suggested to the executors that they should be directed specifically to these projects. So when Christina Waters died and left a cup worth 16d to the church, the money, plus a further 3/= donated by her husband, was spent on St Sidwell, 'the wyche mony Waterus ys contendyd to pay to the same worke for this intent to have hys wyfe ys name a pon the churche boke to be prayd for every Palme Sonday *ut ceter.*[107] But reported speech, direct or indirect, could also be used to record less satisfactory outcomes to negotiations. In the Alms Light account for 1538 a more difficult parishioner is reported:

William at Tymwell hathe a wether hogg of this store yn hys kepyn. Item for syngyn and wex pro anima Joahannis at Lawton he wyll pay noth, he sayth.[108]

William at Timewell hath a wether hogg [an unshorn yearling castrated sheep] of this store in his keeping.
Item for singing [the requiem mass] and wax for the soul of John at Lawton he will pay not, he saith.

Rather implausibly, however, the occasions which provided Sir Christopher with his best opportunity to set before the parish this repertoire of rhetorical devices, designed to maintain and promote an idealised image of their unity and mutual obligations, were the annual sheep counts. The fullest of these each year was the account of the store of Our Lady, to which after 1539 all the church flocks were assimilated. Every parish which drew income from livestock must have kept records of where the animals were lodged, and lists of parishioners with the number of animals in their keeping are a feature of other parish accounts of the period.[109] But these are simply lists of names and numbers, whereas the Morebath sheep counts are astonishingly circumstantial. The Morebath church sheep were distributed, in principle, one to a household. If a ewe had a lamb in the course of the year, that lamb was passed as soon as it was weaned to another parishioner, so that no one should be burdened with more than the statutory single animal from a given store, though some parishioners might have sheep from more than one store. Surplus sheep for which a custodian could not be found were taken to the village pound and sold. This meant that in a given year, two thirds or more of the households in the parish had at least one of the church sheep, and young animals were being passed from one farm to another in the course of the year, as parishioners and wardens tried to spread the burden of responsibility fairly. The sheep counts were therefore the most concrete expression of the demands which the parish made on the parishioners of Morebath, and of their mutual obligations, and in reporting them the priest made the most of it. Short extracts from these counts fail to convey the full effect, which is best grasped by considering a more or less complete count. Each count was introduced by a ritual formula which varied only a little year after year: 'Now how many of our Lady scheppe be dede and gon this ere: and how many there be as yett a lyfe and yn hoo ys kepyng they be now schall ye have knolyge of' ['*Now how many of Our Lady's sheep be dead and gone this year: and how many there be as yet alive and in whose keeping they be now shall ye have knowlydge of*'], or 'a gayn ye schall hyre' or 'yn hoys kepyn they be now y wyll schow you'.[110]

Here is the slightly abbreviated count for 1536:

John Morsse hath yn hys kepyn a wether [castrated sheep] solde. John Goodman ys wether ys solde and he hath yn hys kepyn a nother lambe that came from John at Courte. John Waterus hath none of this store but he hath 2 yowys of sent Anthonys store. Joan at Pole ys wether ys solde and so now sche hath non of no store as yett. John at Burston a wether. Jekyn isac a yow and no lambe this ere. Thomas Borrage ys wether ys dede and he brosth home ye fell wolle and he hath yn hys kepyn a wether lambe that came fro Richard Webber. Thomass Rumbelow a wether, William Tymwell a wether. Robert at Hayne a yowe and no lambe this ere. And ys for the wether hogg [castrated unshorn yearling sheep] that was brosth with him of the store of sent Sydwyll that came fro Richard Robyns that wether ys now with Richard at Wode yn our Lady merke. ... John at Courte a yowe and her wether lambe ys delyvered un to John Goodman ... Richard Raw ys yowe ys dede and lost wolle and all and so he hath a wether lambe that came from John Smyth. William at Combe a wether. William Leddon a yowe hogg [unshorn yearling ewe]. William Tymwell at Wode ys yowe ys dede and he hath yn hys kepyn a yowe hogg that came the laste ere fro Waterus of the store of sent Antoni and was put yn our Lady merke ... William Norman hath non but he will find on dicit [he says] ... Richard Robyns hath non of this store but he hath a yowe and a lambe of sent Sydwyll ys store. Robert at More a yowe hogg. Levys Trychay a wether hogg.[111]

John Morsse hath in his keeping a wether, which has been sold. John Goodman's wether is sold and he hath in his keeping another lamb that came from John at Court. John Waters has none of this store, but he hath two ewes of St Anthony's store. Joan at Poole's wether is sold and so now she hath none of no store, as yet. John at Burston a wether. Jekyn Isac a ewe and no lamb this year. Thomas Borrage's wether is dead and he brought home the fell wool and he hath in his keeping a wether lamb that came from Richard Webber. Thomas Rumbelow a wether, William Timewell a wether. Robert at Hayne a ewe and no lamb this year. And as for the wether hogg that was brought with him of the store of St Sidwell, that came from Richard Robyns, that wether is now with Richard at Wood in Our Lady's mark ... John at Court a ewe and her wether lamb is delivered unto John Goodman ... Richard Raw's ewe is dead and lost, wool and all, and so he hath a wether lamb that came from John Smith. William at Combe, a wether. William Leddon a ewe hogg. William Timewell at Wood's ewe is dead, and he hath in his keeping a ewe hogg that came the last year from Waters, of the store of St Anthony, and (which) was put in Our Lady's mark ... William Norman hath none, but he will find one, he says ... Richard Robyns hath none of this store but he hath a ewe and a lamb of St Sidwell's store. Robert at More a ewe hogg. Lewis Trychay a wether hogg.

These lengthy counts were embedded in the longest accounting session of the year, which throughout the 1530s and 1540s included the same day a progress report on the fund for the black vestments. They involved an element of display as well as report, for the wool from the sheep was evidently not just mentioned but often physically displayed at the count – when listing sheep that had died or been sold, but whose wool had been saved or retained for the store, the priest often displayed the wool itself: 'but yett here ys her wolle' or 'here ys the flecis'.[112]

The sheep counts themselves sound uncannily like the recitation of a litany and that was certainly intentional, for there is a very obvious sense in which they were indeed ritual texts. Over the twenty years for which they exist the names of the individuals mentioned in these counts change, of course, but the order in which the farms and households occur does not, the priest always following the same sequence with only insignificant variations from year to year. Most of the personal names can be related to particular farms, and plotted on a map. When we do so, it becomes clear that the sequence in fact constitutes a carefully structured circuit of the parish, a sort of verbal beating of the bounds, starting near the church with the Morsse household at Morebath Town, and moving clockwise to the households in the west of the parish, through Exebridge and Poole, then north to Burston, Warmore and Hayne, eastwards to the two Timewells, on to Court and Combe, then southwards again to Loyton and the cluster of farms at Wood, on to Hukeley bridge, and so back to Morebath town via Moore: the last name is always the priest's brother Lewis, whose cottage was near the church at Morebath town. The sheep count was thus no mere exercise in accountancy but a carefully crafted parochial ritual, the recitation of which served to display the community and its relationships to itself in a peculiarly concrete way. The detailed account of the movement of lambs from one farm to another enacted the sharing of communal burden, the bond of neighbourhood. Those without sheep in their care were mentioned but excused, provided they expressed a willingness to keep one of the sheep when required. The merely uncooperative were liable to be singled out for criticism. So in 1539 Sir Christopher reported that 'John Burston hath no scheppe of no store', and went on to emphasise in two different places in the count that William Leddon had been obliged to keep *two* sheep that year because he had

a nother wether hogg ... yn hys kepyn that came from Richard Hucly that schuld y be brofth with John at Borston but he wold have non.

another wether hogg...in his keeping that came from Richard Hukeley, that should have been brought to John at Burston but he would have none.

In 1536 he reported that

ys for the yowe hogg that was brosth yn the pownde the last ere for William Norman to keppe (but he wolde not have hyt) sche hathe byn the moste parte all this ere with Thomas Tymwell and now sche ys with Richard Hucly to kepe yn sent Antonys merke.[113]

as for the ewe hogg that was brought into the pound the last year for William Norman. to keep (but he would not have it) she hath been the most part all this year with Thomas Timewell and now she is with Richard Hukeley to keep in St Anthony's mark.

The Morebath accounting days and audits, therefore, were far more than simple business meetings at which duly elected parish officials reported to their constituency. They were formal exercises in the construction of community, opportunities for the parish to confront its values and measure the performance of its members, and for the priest to weave round his parishioners a loose rhetorical web designed to school them in the virtues of community.

The special importance for the priest of the sheep counts in particular emerges graphically – and hilariously – from one of the oddest entries in the Morebath book. For much of 1537 the parish was locked in acrimonious debate over the financing of the parish clerk's wages: that year, and maybe because of those disputes, the sheep wardens prepared their account as usual around Michaelmas, but did not present it to the parish. For reasons which are not clear, it was delayed until mid-May 1538. Sir Christopher did eventually read out the account as compiled six months earlier, but carefully and comically updated it, in order to report accurately the present state of the church's flocks. Many of the corrections are patently just that, squeezed in above the line: the effect when read out must have been to enact the passage of time as well as the usual physical circuit of the parish, as he describes the shearing, sale, ageing or death of last year's sheep:

Joan Goodman a wether hogg yn her kepyn last ere *and now hyt ys a wether* [i.e. it had been shorn in the meantime]
Jekyn Isac a yowe and sche hath a yowe lame and her yowe black lame ys delyvered un to John Hucly, *a hogg now hyt ys* [i.e. it is now a yearling, not a lamb]
Thomas Norman a yowe hogg *and now hyt ys a yowe and her lame ys dede*
John Smyth hath both hys yowe y schore ... *and her wether lame remayneth not, beyng now a wether hogg*
Richard Raw a wether *and now hyt ys a hogg*
Richard Hucly ys yowe of sent Antonys merk ys nowe yn our Lady merke for the wyche our Lady Wardyns hath payd Sent Antonys Wardyn *ut praedict est* thys yowe now hath John Taylor bofth y schore and hath fett hyt with William Leddon and so hath Richard Hucly the yowe lame that came fro Willm Morsse yn hys kepyn *and now hyt ys a hogg.*[114]

Joan Goodman a wether hogg in her keeping last year and now it is a wether [i.e. it had been shorn in the meantime]
Jekyn Isac a ewe which has a ewe lamb and her black ewe lamb is delivered unto John Hukeley, a hogg now it is [i.e. it is now a yearling, not a lamb]
Thomas Norman a ewe hogg and now it is a ewe, and her lamb is dead ...
John Smith hath both his ewes shorn ... and her wether lamb remaineth not, being now a wether hogg [i.e. has grown into a yearling]
Richard Raw a wether and now it is a hogg
Richard Hukeley's ewe of St Anthony's mark is now in Our Lady's mark for which

Our Lady's Wardens hath paid St Anthony's warden as aforesaid. This ewe now hath John Tailor bought already shorn, and hath fetched it with William Leddon, and so hath Richard Hukeley the ewe lamb in his keeping that came from William Morsse and now it is a hogg.

These bizarre entries demonstrate just how completely the written text of the accounts at Morebath was conceived as a script for performance, geared to a specific moment and felt to be in need of drastic revision if that moment passed. There is no mistaking the distinctive, even eccentric, voice of the priest in all this, but there is no doubt either that even at his most idiosyncratic, he felt himself to be articulating shared values and perceptions. In 1544 the sheep count was similarly delayed, and once again, seven months late, the priest presented an updated count. He did so, however, not in his own right, but expressly as the mouthpiece of the wardens – as he declared in his preamble to the new count, 'the same forsayd perssons as yett beyng wardyns dothe you to knolyge furder more of the scheppe and of the woll of this ere now to put hyt in order agayn and yff hyt wylbe … what scheppe there be as yett a lyve a gayn ye schall hyre'.[115]

But *all* the accounting days distributed through Morebath's year from the springtime 'second Sunday in clene Lent' when the Maidens normally reported, to the dark months before Christmas when the High Wardens' accounts summed up the year, were opportunities for the priest to articulate and reinforce the values and expectations which underlay the communal life of his parish. Sir Christopher was at the height of his form in the High Wardens' accounts for 1538, in which we hear him deploying all the weapons in his rhetorical armoury – naming the officials, reminding the parish of their collective identity, urging them to participation in community projects, breaking off from the itemising of income and outlay to remind and rebuke individuals who have reneged on promises or obligations. The parish sit on their new benches, and listen to their priest:

Memorandum as for Nicholas at Hayne ys xij[s] [12/=] hys fader and he ys contendyd that hytt schall goo now to a new cope when ye will.

Item of Richarde Webber we resseuyd of the be questh of hys wyfe Jone a gowne and kurtyll: the wyche was sold to John at Pole for xiij[s] & iiij[d] [13/4d] for the wyche mony the iiij men wyll make you a cownt as here after ye schall hyre: and Richard Webber wyll desyre you that ye wyll ley forth this mony a gayn of the churche stoke in remembrans of hys wyfe Jone: when ye bye a new cope to this churche.

Item John Waterus remember yor promysse to the syde auter as ys expressyd the ere be fore a pon Harry Hurlys cownte.

Item Willam at Wode remember your paynter for the hye auter in yor v[s] [5/=] a cordyng to you promysse of the laste ere a pon Harry Hurlye's a cownte.[116]

Memorandum as for Nicholas at Hayne's 12/=, his father and he is contented that it shall go now to a new cope whenever you will.

Item of Richard Webber we received of the bequest of his wife Joan a gown and kirtle: the which was sold to John at Poole for 13/4d for the which money the Four Men will make you account, as hereafter ye shall hear: and Richard Webber will desire you that you will lay forth this money again of the church stock, in remembrance of his wife Joan, when you buy a new cope for this church.
Item, John Waters, remember your promise to the side altar as is expressed the year before upon Harry Hurley's account.
Item, William at Wood remember your painter for the high altar, in your 5/= according to your promise of last year upon Harry Hurley's account.

All the voices of Morebath are one voice.

CHAPTER THREE

The Pursuit of Peace

In copying the accounts of his parish into a book, Sir Christopher knew that he was writing for posterity. The account book was more than a ledger to keep trace of income and spending. It was an archive, designed to record the benefactors of the parish and ensure that they were prayed for, to inform the wardens of their responsibilities, to record collective decisions binding 'ever here after by this boke', an oracle to be consulted in time of dispute.[1] Its margins are littered with cross-references and notes sign-posting particular entries for the benefit of the reader thumbing through it: 'not[e] the store of Sent Sydwyll', 'not[e] my fader ys gefte', 'not[e] the bordis that restyth', 'not[e] the plumer', 'not[e] debz to the black vestments', 'The cownte of the yong men Wardyns in anno domini 1543, loke the 24th leve be fore and *invenies* [you shall find it]'.[2] These are essentially index marks to the file copies of the annual accounts, handy pointers to facilitate reference to an originally oral text. But some items included in the book were quite clearly composed in the first place not to be heard, but to be read. Almost all of these are designed in some way to consolidate the parish's identity and unity, or to heal or forestall division. The keeping of records was thus an aspect of the priest's role in the 'social miracle', the religious healing and sustaining of the bonds of community.

Perhaps the most notable and most obviously religious of these insertions into the Morebath account book is the long and detailed list of benefactions which Sir Christopher compiled in 1540, recording every gift, great and small, made to the church since his arrival twenty years before. The document opens like a public, oral text, with an injunction to prayer: 'Orate pro animabus sequentibus [pray for the following souls]'. This makes it sound as if it were the parish bede-roll, the list of benefactors read out at the annual Palm Sunday commemoration.[3] But the Morebath bede-roll was almost certainly less detailed, consisting probably of just the names of the dead, and it was definitely a different document, which has not survived. In 1539 Agnes Adams, the daughter of William Timewell at Wood, paid 13/4d to have four members of her family commemorated 'a pon the luger [ledger] of the churche to be prayed for every Palme Sunday', but their names do not occur in this list of Sir Christopher's.[4] In any case, that long list, carefully copied with its roll-call of wardens and benefactions, was quite clearly intended in the first place for the eye, rather than the ear:

Nota bene: Memorandum that here after *schall ye see and knoo* how this church was prevaylyd by the dethe of all these persons that here after ys expressyd by name: the wyche all and syngeler geftis was gevyn and be quevyd unto the churche syn y Sir Christopher Trychay was made vicar here ... *cuius anime propicietur Deus anime orate.[5]*

Nota bene: Memorandum *that hereafter shall ye see and know how this church was prevailed by the death of all these persons that hereafter is expressed by name: the which all and singular gifts was given and bequeathed unto the church since I Sir Chrstopher Trychay was made vicar here, ... on whose souls pray God to be merciful.*

The gifts and bequests for each of the twenty years covered by the list are introduced formulaically, each year identified both by its date and by the names of the High Wardens in office at the time, the gifts therefore located both in public time and Morebath time:

Anno Domini 1520 John Hucly and Richard Webber was hye Wardyns of this church: and how the church was prevaylyd by there Wardyng scheppe and by there tyme now schall ye see.

Anno Domini 1520 John Hukeley and Richard Webber was High Wardens of this church, and how the church was prevailed by their Wardenship and by their time now shall ye see

This was a record explicitly intended to last forever, for in it Sir Christopher refers to himself as dead and gone – 'Dominus Christoferus Trychay condam [quondam] istius ecclesie vicarius [Sir Christopher Trychay, one-time vicar of this church]'.[6] Yet it was also emphatically *his* list, compiled with the benefit of access to all the wardens' accounts, and priding itself on making good their omissions. So he details in the third person a series of his own gifts, adding that 'all this for sayd he gave to this churche *thof* [though] *hyt a pere not a pon the cownte of this ere*'.[7] Again, detailing a bequest from his friend, the Brushford chantry priest Sir Edward Nicoll, Sir Christopher informs the reader that the wardens have missed this one, perhaps because Sir Edward gave the money directly to Sir Christopher, 'the whyche ys no thyng spokyn a pon these men a cownt'.[8] All the same, the list was clearly intended as part of the church book, an epitome and guide to the fuller records, designed to be read alongside them: as Sir Christopher comments,

> and yf ye be yn any doute of any man ys gefth loke what ere that ye wyll have and loke a pon that a cownte and there schall ye a see playnly what proffyth this churche toke by the dethe of any man.[9]

All this suggests an acute awareness of the value of the written record, kept not merely to satisfy the requirements of external church authority, but as a crucial resource within the life of the parish, and one that gave its possessor a very concrete advantage in any dispute. Sir Christopher, as the scribe and custodian of the parish accounts, deployed this advantage in his own interest in 1547, when, among many other changes, the church floor was being re-tiled. As in every other Morebath project, Sir Christopher took a keen and active interest in this work, and he himself supplied and paid for half a hundred-weight of tiling stones from his own pocket. He proposed to repay himself for this outlay, he told the parish, by taking possession of four large slabs or steps ('grystis') 'that lay here be fore the quyre dore' (that revealing word 'here', incidentally, places Sir Christopher exactly for us, standing in front of the chancel screen as he talks). If the parish objected, then they must repay him his money 'and ye schall have your grystis stonys a gayn'. Conscious that some of his parishioners might resent this transaction as a trifle high-handed, he reminded them defensively that he himself had donated the slabs in the first place, and that he could give chapter and verse to prove it:

> and yett y gave them to the churche furste and can tell who was Wardyn when ye fett them.[10]

Here the record is being drawn upon by the priest, simply as a matter of fact, to forestall friction in the parish. He 'can tell' who was warden, and when he gave the stones, because it is all written down in his book. Many of the items in the book were plainly compiled with that purpose explicitly in mind. Tudor parishes were contentious places, for the parish, like the manor, was a forum in which the sometimes troublesome obligations of neighbourhood were prescribed and exacted. The communal life of Morebath, as we have seen, made heavy demands on its people. Parish officials had to enforce those obligations and, if they were flouted and persuasion failed, might refer the recalcitrant to external authority, the ecclesiastical or even the manor courts. Until the early Tudor period, most of those parochial obligations were religious, though the Tudor state increasingly harnessed the parish to its own purposes: the Lay Subsidy of 1523–4 was parish based and, as we shall see, secular demands were to be increasingly mediated through the parish structure.

But even before that process of secularisation manifests itself, the Morebath accounts have plenty of examples of the extreme care so small a community needed to take to ensure a fair distribution of responsibility, and of the wary compilation of records to prevent conflict, whether the issue was religious or secular. So in 1531 the priest compiled a guide to the collection of the ecclesiastical tax known as Peter's Pence, paid at the annual visitation and passed on eventually to the Pope. The document is brief, but, incidentally, provides us with our clearest and fullest guide to the number of placeholders and cottagers in Morebath. In it Sir Christopher notes that every 'placeholder' in Morebath pays a halfpenny, every cottager a farthing, and that there would or would not be a surplus depending on whether Brockhole had a tenant, as it often did not.[11] A longer list compiled the following year, not all of which has survived, shows the same concern with the fair distribution of parish burdens. In this list, however, the marking of internal boundaries, literal and metaphorical, is an explicit concern. The churchyard hedge (made, in the Devon manner, of stone walling as well as trees) was maintained by the parish, each of the farms and grazing grounds of the parish being responsible for maintaining a length of hedge proportionate to the size of the holding. By 1532 there had evidently been dispute about the matter, and it was decided to seek a formal order 'by the a vissement of the vicar and of hys paryssyng' [by the advice of the vicar and his parish], which was duly entered in the church book and formally signed by the priest – his only surviving signature –

> Robert Rumbelow for priers hay he makyth a xi fote
> John Don he makyth a xj fotte
> John Norman at Court he makyth a xj fotte now bytt he never made none be fore …
> Thomas Rumbelow for hys home place he makyth a xj fotte and a xj fotte more for Bollyn
> All Hawcrige downe makyth a xj fotte

> *Robert Rumbelow for Priors Hay maketh eleven foot.*
> *John Don he maketh eleven foot*
> *John Norman at Court he maketh eleven foot now, but he never made none before.*
> *Thomas Rumbelow for his home place he maketh eleven foot and eleven foot more for Bollyn*
> *All Hawkridge Down maketh eleven foot*

Sir Christopher concluded this detailed entry with a liturgical flourish, carefully emphasising the informal and peaceable harmony that underlay this formal exercise in the demarcation of boundaries:

> And thus ys the churche hage made from the yeste churche stylle to the west churche style: how bytt there ys more ground yn this for sayd space a lytyll more than the mesure *and that ys made amonggis them pesabylly* and under this manner this churche yerde ys closyd and schalbe fro thense: in seculum.[12]

> *And thus is the church hedge made from the east church style to the west church style. Howbeit there is more ground in this aforesaid space a little more than the measure and that is made amongst them peacably and under this manner this churchyard is closed and shall be from thence, for ever.*

As Sir Christopher's choice of language suggests, the maintenance of the churchyard hedge was plainly a religious obligation, and in itself a powerful expression of the symbolic role of the parish church, the point of convergence in a community where fences and boundaries were important to the preservation of peace: good fences made good neighbours.

These religious dispositions found a close secular parallel in the course of the following year, in the record of two 'setts' or formal levies, imposed on all the tenants of the manor of Morebath to recover 'wold dettis', in one of which the parish sought to defend itself from external attack.[13] The debts concerned were complicated, but both involved the parish's liability for the repair of the two bridges that linked them with the outside world, at Exebridge, where the maintenance costs were shared with the Somerset parish of Brushford, and at Hukeley bridge, where the costs were shared with the Devon parish of Bampton.[14] As these and many subsequent references to the upkeep of the bridges make clear, the responsibility for maintaining them fell squarely on the Manor of Morebath, but was passed on to the tenants of the manor: for this reason, the few cottagers who were not tenants are invariably explicitly exempted from the setts made for this purpose. The money was collected by the tithing man, with payments calculated, as in the case of the churchyard hedge, on the size of land holdings. The money was handed over to the Four Men, who then dispensed it 'to help to pay the demaundis'.

The Exebridge sett was comparatively straightforward, though some of the 'wold dettis' concerned are said, rather improbably, to have been incurred '16 ere a gon' [16 years ago].[15] The collection was designed to recompense parishioners who had 'ledde out' money on behalf of the parish, and for that purpose to extract contributions from others who had been 'be hynd at Exebridge'. Back payments were demanded from everyone so identified – 'for lak of hys plow at Exbrige'.

The other sett 'made this laste ere' (Sir Christopher's note was made in the early summer of 1533)[16] reveals the parish struggling, probably unsuccessfully, to resist demands for the repair of Hukeley bridge triggered by a new piece of Tudor legislation. In its 1531/2 session, Henry VIII's Reformation Parliament passed 'A Generall Acte concernynge Commissions of Sewers', a statute designed to rectify the neglect of waterways and sea defences, and to ensure also the repair of ruinous bridges.[17] The Commissioners had power 'to taxe assesse charge distreyne and punysshe' those liable for the maintenance of neglected bridges and waterways. Liability was to be established by enquiry from 'honest and lawful men of the shire', and in the case of repairs charged on land, allocated 'after the quantity of ... landes, tenementes and rentes' held by those liable. The Commissioners were empowered to commandeer 'as manny cartes, horses oxen beastes and other instrumentes necessary ... and as many trees, woddes underwoodes and tymber' as were needed for the work; they could also requisition the services of local workmen.

The implementation of this statute evidently resulted in a claim against Morebath for Hukeley bridge. In attempting to resist it, Morebath's leading men became embroiled in an expensive and time-consuming series of visits to Bampton and Exeter. Both the Vicar and Thomas Norman, one of the Four Men, were involved in a series of negotiations at Bampton, while another of the Four Men, John at Courte, together with the Tithingman for that year, Thomas Borrage, and two more parish stalwarts, Harry Hurley and Richard Raw, rode backwards and forwards to Exeter 'at on tyme and at a nother', to make representations before the Commissioners. The Commissioners evidently found against the parish, however, and distrained parish property to pay for repairing the bridge, for Morebath now instructed a lawyer to take out a 'writ of replevin' in the county court to recover their goods. The lawyer in question, Roger Yorke, serjeant at law, was one of the most senior men in the profession. He was Exeter born, but since his marriage to Eleanor Lovell in c.1520 primarily based at Wellington in Somerset, only fifteen miles from Morebath. So distinguished a lawyer is most unlikely to have needed or sought the 12d Morebath paid him 'at the delyveryng of the replevy at Exeter for Hucly Brige' in the way of ordinary business, and his acting for them must reflect prior acquaintance from another context.[18] To discover the outcome, Harry Hurley was sent to consult the 'schere boke [shire book] at Exeter to kno whether the schere dyd passe a gayn us or noo for Hucly Bridge'. The result is unclear from Sir Christopher's record: Harry Hurley went yet again to Exeter to fetch 'a quyttance', but this need not mean that they won their case – it could well have followed admission of liability and settlement of the debt by the parish. However that may be, what is certain is that most of those involved in these transactions, including the vicar, ended up out of pocket. The sums concerned were a matter of shillings and pence, not pounds, but all the same the Four Men 'suryd' and repaid them a good deal less than their actual outlay, yet another example of the uncomfortable demands which the corporate life of the parish was liable to make on its members.[19]

This incident provides the first evidence in the accounts of the strain which the legislative action of the Tudor state might place on the internal workings of the parish: within five years the accelerating pace of Henry's religious revolution would begin to cut deep into the living tissue of Morebath's communal life. What is notable about these minor financial flurries in the early 1530s, however, is the language of moral responsibility and conscientious dispensation of justice in which the entry describing them is framed. Other Devon parishes entered setts and financial settlements into their records – there are lists of similar obligations at the beginning of the Kilmington churchwardens' book, for example[20] – but everywhere else, these lists are merely that – brief records of the liability of each parishioner, retained for practical purposes. At Morebath, Sir Christopher, who was paid sixpence for writing the whole thing up, ensured that this routine record of a piece of parish business becomes something more, an elaborate expression of the values on which the parish's moral unity was founded. He insists on the whole transaction being the parish's property, its remainders 'yn kepyng tyll the parysse doo call for hyt'. The transaction itself is of course reported with all his customary meticulous insistence on minute accountability, and special attention is paid to money gone astray in the tangle of business transacted by many hands. Characteristically, at this point Sir Christopher's reporting allows us to catch a momentary echo of the Four Men speaking:

> ys for the v^s [5/=] that Thomas Norman ressevyd of John at Courte...we can have no knolyge of how hyt ys bestowyd: and no more we can not of the xx^d [20d] that Harry Hurlye ressevyd of John at Courte savyng only they sayth that they be stowyd hyt but they can not tell where a pon.[21]

> *as for the 5/= that Thomas Norman received of John at Court ... we can have no knowledge of how it is bestowed: and no more we cannot of the 20d that Harry Hurley received of John at Court, saving only they say that they bestowed it but they cannot tell whereupon.*

But above all, the entry is framed in the language of communal morality, of oath-bound fidelity, of conscience. The sett for Exebridge, he notes, was authorised by the manor court 'the next court be fore medsomer day: s[w]orne a pon a boke'. Four parishioners were nominated

> to sett the parysse *connsonabylly* and to sure every man ys axcion and *to se every man content: by there oathe and after there consyens*: with the *advyssment of the vicar* Sir Christopher Trychay and William Tymewell at Wode: by mydsomer day every man to *be contentyd and payd after the conssiens of these for sayd men a pon a grett payne.*[22]

to sett the parish conscientiously and to ensure every man his exaction, and to see every man content by their oath and after their conscience: with the advice of the vicar Sir Christopher Trychay, and William Timewell at Wood; by midsummer day every man to be contented and paid after the conscience of these aforesaid men under a great penalty.

The not-so-subtle hint of menace there, with the Exebridge settlement made 'a pon a grett payne', alerts us to the fact that the peace of Morebath depended on more than the bonds of good will and good neighbourhood. However united the parish might be against external threat, its internal harmony was both fragile and in need of enforcement. Secular responsibilities needed the sanction of law as well as the moral and religious enhancement bestowed by the involvement of the priest – in itself a striking testimony to the interweaving at Morebath of material and spiritual values – and the deployment of the language of obligation and conscience. By the same token, religious responsibilities also needed all the secular reinforcement they could get. The boundaries between matters of the soul and of the body in Morebath were loosely drawn. This emerges from a poignant entry in the accounts for 1531, when Richard Hukeley completed a bequest made by his recently deceased daughter Joan for a candlestick of five lights to burn before the image of the Virgin. Joan Hukeley's bequest did not cover the full cost of the new candlestick, and so her father paid the rest. He did so, however, not simply out of paternal piety for a dead daughter, but with an additional ulterior motive which strikes the squeamish modern reader as shockingly mercenary. The parish, it seemed, owed Hukeley money for expenses incurred on their behalf for work on the railing of Exebridge, and he hoped that his bounty towards the altar of Our Lady might encourage the parishioners to settle this debt. And so, the priest explains, he gave this money in his daughter's memory, 'by cause you schuld se the soner that he mayth be contendyd for the rayling of Exbryge'.[23]

That characteristic Tudor interweaving of sentiment and savvy, the personal and the public, and the tendency for sacred and secular to converge at Morebath, emerge very clearly in the prolonged disputes surrounding the payment and duties of their parish clerk, which dribbled on through the 1530s and almost brought the parish to blows in the spring of 1537. The office of parish clerk was essential to the running of any parish church. The clerk was a paid official who assisted the priest in the liturgy by saying or singing the responses and by reading the epistle at Mass (so he needed a degree of Latin literacy, and some musical ability). He helped prepare vestments, vessels, books, lights and altars for services (a responsibility normally shared with the wardens). He brought the pax-brede round to be kissed at the peace ceremony of the mass, and he carried and distributed through the parish the holy water which was valued as a powerful and popular sacramental, capable of repelling evil and bringing blessing on men, beasts and crops. In many parishes the clerk was named for this aspect of his duties the 'holy water clerk', and payment of his wages was linked to particular occasions in the year, like Easter, when he came with holy water to parishioners' houses.[24]

Canon law required that the clerk should be paid by the parish but chosen by the priest, and though one aspect or another of this stipulation was often contested, it was in fact the arrangement followed at Morebath.[25] The clerk was thus a parish official, answerable to the people who paid his wages, often wearing a uniform, as he did at Morebath, the parish 'livery'. He was also, however, the priest's right-hand-man, and, since the priest appointed him, usually also the priest's client, whose job depended on the priest's good will. At Sir Christopher's death in 1574, the current clerk had a son called Christopher, to whom the priest left a small legacy. He was probably another godson, further indication of the close links between priest and clerk.[26] Appointment to the clerkship was therefore a valuable piece of clerical patronage. In the 1550s, the parish clerk of Morebath was Sir Christopher's own nephew, Lewis and Joan Trychay's son, a married man for whom the clerkship was presumably his main source of income, and, since the clerk was also called *Christopher* Trychay, once again very likely the priest's godson.[27]

In 1531, trouble arose at Morebath over the payment of the clerk's wages. Like so much else in Morebath's economy, those wages were calculated and paid in kind, the clerk collecting corn from every household, a lesser quantity from the cottagers, but no one exempt. The fluctuation in value that arises with any payment in kind was a potential source of conflict, and there seems to have been argument about a number of issues – how much the clerk was entitled to claim from each parishioner, when he could demand it, and what was to be done if the household concerned had had a bad or late harvest, or the grain was somehow spoiled. These disputes came to a head at Michaelmas 1531, when an unspecified number of parishioners reneged on the clerk's wages, and 'this parysse they coude not a gre for a clerke by cause the clerke cudde not have hys duty'.[28] Sir Christopher refused to appoint a clerk unless the parish would securely guarantee his wages, and it was decided to settle the matter by electing five men who with the Vicar would give a ruling on 'the order of this clerke scheppe'. When 'at laste the Vicar and the five men were … agreyd', the settlement was a comprehensive one, and the priest at his most expansive in recording it. In addition to his liturgical duties, too well understood to be specified, the clerk was to keep the church key and one of the church's chalices. He was to be responsible for locking the church. Evidently there had been trouble about security, with parishioners hanging about the building after

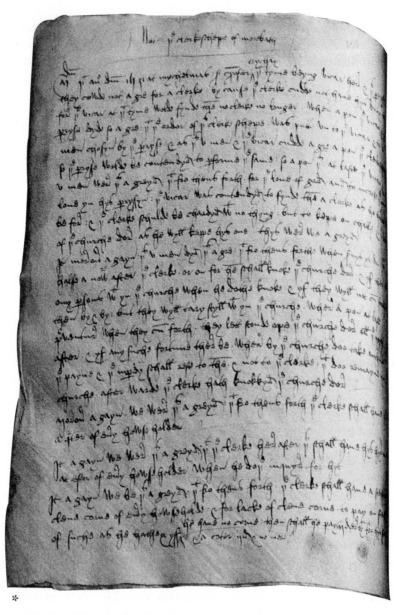

*

services and then leaving the door unlocked all night. Sir Christopher's note at this point becomes positively prolix, suggesting some degree of exasperation; in the process he allows us a fascinating glimpse of the use of their church building by the people of Morebath: are the lingerers he describes praying, gossiping, sleeping? The parish church belonged emphat-

---

* Sir Christopher's account of the beginning of the disputes over the wages of Morebath's parish clerk [Binney 33–4 / Ms 356–7]

ically to the parishioners, and so the clerk, it seems, had no power to evict anyone from the building. He must lock the church half an hour after the end of the last service of the day, when he was nevertheless to

> knoke the churche dore and yff there be any perssons with yn the churche … and yff they wyll not cum forthe then by and by but they wyll tary styll with yn the churche where a pon at laste perventure when they cum forthe they lett stond oppe the churche dore all the nyghth after and yff any suche fortune there be where by the churche doo take any hurte, the payne and the iupardy schall rest to them and not to the clerke that doo remayne yn the churche after warde the clerke hath knokkyd the church dore …

> *knock on the church door and if there be any persons within the church … and if they will not come forth then by and by, but they will tarry still within the church where-upon at last peradventure when they come forth they let stand open the church door all the night after and if any such fortune there be whereby the church do take any hurt, the penalty and the jeopardy shall rest to them and not to the clerk that do remain in the church afterward the clerk hath knocked the church door …*

In return for all this, the clerk was to be paid a penny a quarter by every household, and in addition was to have a 'steche' or bundle of sheaves from every householder, payable on demand. Cottagers or those with no corn could commute this obligation for a cash payment. The collection of the clerk's corn had been at the root of the previous disputes, 'because besenys hath byn oftyn tymys yn payment of the steche yn tymys paste'. The Five Men and the priest therefore laid down that the clerk was to have his 'hyr mete', the quarterly penny per household, at Easter, and that he should send for his corn when it was ready, presumably after harvest time. Parishioners whose corn was not ready when the clerk sent for it were to keep it for him until he came again: if the corn was damaged or diminished, the clerk could claim cash in its stead, to the value of half a bushel of rye. The Five Men agreed to underwrite the clerk's wages in case of any dis-pute: and so, as Sir Christopher recorded,

> now a pon all these poyntis ys the Vicar and these five men full a greyd and these five men have promyssed un to the Vicar substanssially that they wyll see the clerk truly payd of all such dutis as ys expryssyd before with out any trobyll or vexacion.

> *now upon all these points is the vicar and these Five Men full agreed and these Five Men have promised unto the vicar substantially that they will see the clerk truly paid of all such duties as is expressed before without any trouble or vexation.*

And there, Sir Christopher hoped, 'trobyll and vexacion' would cease. Entering the record into the church book, he headed it with a note which indicated that he believed that this settlement would outlast him: 'anno domini 1531 at Mychelmas, Sir Christofer Trychay *that tyme beyng Vicar here*'.[29]

In fact the harmony established by the 1531 order lasted precisely five years, and then, 1536, spectacularly fell apart. At Michaelmas that year, once again parishioners began to cut up rough about the clerk's wages.[30] William Leddon 'wolde not pay hys steche of corne', William Scely and the (unnamed) tenant at Brockhole refused to pay the 4d in cash prescribed for householders who had no corn for the clerk. Two cottagers at Exebridge, John Don and John Nicoll, were up to date with payment of the 2d prescribed for a cottager with no corn, but they were in arrears with their 1d quarterly payments.

There was very possibly an element of social tension in all this. At least four of the five recalcitrant parishioners were certainly poor men, all of them, except the tenant of Brockhole, being cottagers, on whom the prescribed cash payments to the clerk in lieu of corn may have fallen particularly heavily, and who may well have resented paying the same quarterly charge of a penny as the wealthier men of the parish. William Scely in particular was to have something of a history of awkwardness over the financial demands made by the parish. Three years on, when he was warden of the church sheep, he would antagonise the priest and delay the annual sheep count for six months because the parish owed him money he had laid out on the repair of Exebridge. Scely held on to 4s all but 1d from the funds of the sheep store, refusing to balance his books or present an account until he was reimbursed, 'and so keppt our mony tyll he was payd'.[31] 3/11d is a relatively small sum to warrant so large and aggressive a disruption of the parish calendar, and the priest quite evidently thought so: the incident probably tells us as much about Scely's personality as his poverty. At any rate, when he died in office as High Warden in the fraught year of Reformation 1548, his widow would continue the family tradition for awkwardness by unilaterally '[selling] away the church goods with out commission', thereby evoking from Sir Christopher one of his bitterest expressions of outrage.[32]

However that may be, with five out of Morebath's thirty-three householders in one way or another withholding the clerk's wages, the priest considered that something must be done. And so for

> lacke of tru payment the vicar that fownde the parysse a suffycyent clerke before that tyme wolde not mell [meddle] no more with the clerkscheppe by cawse he cowd not have hys duty truly payd with out dysplesir takyn of hys paryssyn.

> *lack of true payment the vicar, that found the parish a sufficient clerk before that time, would not meddle no more with the clerkship, because he could not have his dues paid without displeasure taken of his parishioners.*

At Christmas 1536 he gave the clerk three month's notice,

> desyryng the parysse hole to be contendyd to provyd him a new clerk agayn
> our Lady at lent then follyng for he wolde mell no more with hyt.

> *desiring the whole parish to be contented to provide him with a new clerk before Our*
> *Lady at Lent then following, for he would meddle no more with it.*

By dumping this problem in the parish's lap at Lady Day, Sir Christopher
was playing his cards skilfully. The deadline he had set, Lady Day (25
March 1537) was of course one of the quarter days, and a usual time for
starting or ending contracts. But it fell that year, as the priest must certainly
have known, on Palm Sunday, the day of the parish's annual commemoration of dead benefactors but also the start of Holy Week, and, he notes, 'the
besy tyme of Ester', inaugurating two weeks of the most elaborate liturgical
celebrations of the year, which made a clerk's services absolutely indispensable. The 'parysse universall' therefore begged him to continue the clerk's
services till 'lytyll Easter Day', that is, the Sunday after Easter, pending a
proper settlement. Trychay duly did so, but once more 'when that day was
come, communicacion was hadd, and they coude not a gre a bowt a clerk'.

An opportunity to bring outside pressure to bear on this fraught situation
now presented itself. By a coincidence, the parish was due to send its representatives to an episcopal visitation at Uplowman, near Tiverton, on
Thursday of that week. The Vicar, the senior warden Harry Hurley, and
Thomas Rumbelow, standing in for the village smith, John Hukeley, who
was second warden that year, together with John Norman at Court, one of
the Four Men, duly presented themselves before the bishop's official. The
parish, presumably at Sir Christopher's prompting, had already determined to
ask for authority for four 'honyst men chosyn by the hole parysse' (whom
they had already elected), to 'rule and governe the parysse yn all caussis concernyng the welthe of the churche'. With the added urgency of this new
complaint, the official granted the order. It was written on the back of the
loose-leaf copy of the High Wardens' account presented for routine inspection, and duly sealed with the official's seal, and later entered into the account
book (though it has not survived). The vicar and wardens were then authorised to 'goo home and take and desyre Mr John Sydenham un to them', so
that he and the duly elected four men could determine the matter of the
clerkship, which 'the vicar and the parysse schalbe contendyd withal'.

The inclusion in this group of John Sydenham, son of Sir Christopher's
friend Edward Sydenham of Dulverton, and so a gentleman from quite
another county and diocese, is striking. He was probably chosen not merely
as a representative of the nearest gentry household, and a friend of the
priest, but because two of the Exebridge cottagers refusing quarterage to
the clerk were Sydenham tenants. At any rate, he accepted the invitation,

and a 'fresse day ... of communicacion' was set for Sunday 22 April, the eve of St George, the parish's patronal festival.

Once again, however, the 'day of communication' did not resolve the dispute. Mr Sydenham duly appeared, as did the bishop's summoner, Matthew; together, like twin representatives of God and Mammon, Sydenham and the summoner quizzed the parishioners individually 'by name' whether they were contented to obey the official's ruling, elect four men to determine the matter with Sydenham, and abide by the outcome. Anxious to emphasize the thoroughness of the consultation, Sir Christopher notes their precise words – 'now how say ye to this, ye parysse, they sayd'. The parishioners duly elected William Timewell at Wood, John Norman at Court, Richard Hukeley and Robert Timewell at Hayne, parish heavyweights with a record of service in the stores, the high wardenship, and the government of the church stock. These were in fact the men already nominated in the official's mandate, 'the same selfe persons that were chosen a fore and admyttyd by the ordinary to rule and governe the churche gooddis as ys expressyd a pon the bake of a cownte and under the ordinaris auctorite'. The parishioners were then quizzed again, householder by householder, whether they would agree to be bound by whatever the Four Men and Sydenham decided. Twenty-six consented, but 'there was 5 men of the other parte that wolde not be orderyd by no man'. Sir Christopher names four of the five:[33] they were by no means parish marginals or malcontents, nor poor men smarting under excessive demands. They included parish leaders like Thomas Norman, one of the Five Men responsible for the original order upon the clerkship in 1531 and one of those elected to 'sett the parysse conssonabylly' for old debt in 1532.[34] Another of them, John Timewell at Burston, had recently served as both St Anthony's warden and Our Lady's warden, a third, Richard Webber, had been High Warden in 1533, and if, as seems likely, the unnamed fifth man was William Leddon, the dissidents also included one of the previous year's high wardens. The meeting therefore dissolved with no agreement, and at 'evensong follyng', first vespers of St George's day, there was no clerk to help the priest, 'nother the morrow that was sent iorge ys day'.

The lack of the clerk on the church's patronal festival was to poison an already harrowing human situation. One of the poorest men in the parish was the Exebridge cottager, Marke. His wife had just given birth to twins, both of whom however died soon after baptism. Such children were known as 'crysom children', from the holy oil of chrism used in the baptismal rite and the fact that at death they were still wearing the 'crysom' cloth bound round the child's brow over the spot anointed by the priest and worn for a week thereafter. Poignantly, the account of the Alms Light for 1537, kept that year by the priest's brother Lewis, includes the poor man's payment of a penny from Marke, 'for the occupyeng of the almys lyghth by the deth of hys 2 crisimmers'.[35]

As it happened, Sir Christopher had arranged to celebrate a requiem mass for Marke's children on the morning of St George's day. When he arrived at the church that morning with the grieving family, still raw from the recent deaths, however, they found the door locked, there was no chalice, and no one present was able to make the responses or serve the Mass. Marke therefore was obliged 'to goo to John at Courtis [one of the Four Men] to fett the churche dore key and the challys and also he fett the wolde John Waterus [a former parish clerk] to helppe the vicar to mas be fore he coud have any mas sayd for hys chyld: and all was for lacke of a clerke'.

Morebath church was dedicated to St George, and St George's day was in any case one of the *festa ferianda*, universally observed religious holidays when no work was done.[36] That year the whole parish was due to go to the house of William at Timewell for the betrothal of his daughter Margaret to William Taylor, the day presumably chosen because everyone would be at leisure to join the party. But the distressing scene at the church ensured that this was a doomed occasion. 'All that day', the priest reported, 'we resonyd schamfully a bout our clerkscheppe.' William Leddon, one of the men whose refusal to pay the clerk's corn had precipitated the crisis, was also at the betrothal, and the bereaved father, Marke, nerves raw from the fiasco over his children's requiem that morning, confronted Leddon, so that they 'ware a most by the eris [ears] for the same causse'. The resulting scene and the arguments that followed were spectacular enough to persuade everyone that something had to be done to resolve the situation, 'so yn conclusion the parysse hole concludyd there and sayd lett us have a fresse day of communicacion and we wolle be orderyd every on of us'.

The priest therefore re-appointed the clerk on a temporary basis, and a new parish meeting was fixed for the next Sunday but one, the Sunday before Rogation week. This date must have had a special resonance in the circumstances, and was perhaps chosen deliberately, since Rogationtide was a traditional time for the settlement of parish disputes. One of its principal ritual and symbolic themes was the restoration of charity and harmony in the community.[37]

In the meantime, the manorial court of Morebath met. Barlinch Priory had been dissolved the previous year,[38] and the manor, together with the rectorial tithes of Morebath and the right of presentation to the vicarage, would pass in May 1538 to a notable soldier and courtier, Sir John Wallop: from then on the priest refers to the tenants of the manor as 'Mr Wallop's tenants'. From March 1537, however, the manor and rectory of Morebath were let to the Somerset landowner Hugh Paulet,[39] whom the priest describes in several places as 'Master' to the manorial bailey, Hugh Dysse –

Paulet was, therefore, effectively the parish's principal landlord. In the week after the confrontation at poor Margaret Timewell's betrothal, 'Mr Hu Powlett kept courte at Morebath', accompanied by another gentleman with property in the parish, Mr Hugh Stucley, whose family owned the land grazed by the Sydenhams on Hawkridge Down.[40]

To the moral pressure of the parish and the ecclesiastical authority of the bishop's official and the summoner, Paulet now added a secular landlord's muscle and the weight of the manor court. He 'exortyd these for sayd 5 perssons and so dyde Mr Hugh Stycly also that they should be contendyd to be orderyd as the moste parte of the parysse ware: and yf they wolde not he wolde ordor them he sayd.' Paulet therefore issued a formal citation into the court, to be held in menace 'to cyte all such perssons as wold not be orderyd by Mr Sydenham and by the 4 men'.[41]

In the event, there was no need to implement this citation. On the appointed Sunday, Sydenham and three of the Four Men (Robert at Hayne was ill), backed by Hugh Dysse the bailey representing Paulet and Mathew the summoner on behalf of the diocese, were able to settle the dispute. Though two of the recalcitrant parishioners (the cottagers William Leddon and William Scely) had absented themselves and Margaret Timewell's father William was also missing, the rest of the parish were present and 'then was the parysse syngulerly demanndyd a gayn by name' whether they would 'bide by the ordor' of Sydenham and the Three Men, and 'they said ye[a] all that were yn the churche that tyme'.

The order made 'to this entent to have the more unite and pece a mongg us and to have the church the better served' spelled out in greater detail than ever the arrangements for the clerk's wages, and established a new machinery for recovering them if parishioners proved troublesome. The clerk was to have a steche of 'clene corn' from every household, or, where there was none, a steche of oats. Households with no corn to give paid three pence instead, cottagers paid two pence. If the clerk was dissatisfied with the quality of the grain offered, one of the Four Men would inspect it and decide whether it was 'sufficient'. If not, the clerk was to be allowed 'with out any besenys' to fetch a better from one of two guarantors or sureties, Richard Hukeley for the western part of the parish, John at Court for the eastern, appointed by the parish to see that the clerk should be paid 'without any trobyll or vexacion'. If any 'froward felow' should refuse payment, and the sureties had to pay the corn on their behalf, then the parish undertook to 'were them harmlis' and make good their loss.

In addition to his corn, the clerk was to have a penny quarterly from every household, and to be paid a fee of tuppence at every wedding, and every funeral and month's mind 'song by note'. Once a year he was to go about the parish with holy water 'when menne have schorne there scheppe', to gather wool from each household, 'to make him cotte to goo yn the paryssen ys livery'. His duties were briefly specified – to keep and hide the church door key 'as he wyll doo hys one', to keep the chalice, and to help the wardens make up the vestments and dress the altars. That year, to make good the 'losyn of hys duty yn tymys paste' the parish 'schall helppe to drenke him a cost of ale' at Trinity Sunday, at which it was stipulated that all the dissident parishioners must be present, and thereafter there was to be 'a cost of ale' drunk in the church house at Easter for the clerk's benefit. The settlement was duly noted 'here a pon this cownte boke to testyfy truly the clerke ys duty and our award to a voyd all other unconveniens'.[42]

1537 was a fraught year in Morebath, with signs in the accounts of ragged nerves and parish tensions, quite apart from the strains created by the clerkship. There was trouble over the Young Men's store, when one of the elected wardens, Edward Norman of Loyton, 'wolde not take this Wardyn scheppe a pon him', and a substitute had to be found. Later in the year Sir Christopher himself antagonised some of his parishioners by making an unauthorised payment of 20/= 'agaynst the parysse wyll' to John Paynter, then at work on a new High Cross for the church. The priest was to end up a pound out of pocket because 'some of you gurgyd [grudged] at hyt', and in that year of conflicts he thought it prudent to let the matter pass, accept that he had put himself in the wrong, and donate the money to one of the other church funds.[43]

But the affair of the clerkship brings into sharp focus the extraordinary complexity of the concept of community in Morebath, and the interweaving of religious and secular considerations in the pursuit of peace. It discloses to us a small rural community in which the non-cooperation of a handful of poor men could paralyse the parish's decision-making and smooth working, and in which consensus, however achieved, rather than majority rule, was felt to be the essential basis for collective action. It discloses, too, a community in which economic division, though present, was not the fundamental principle of social organisation or hierarchy. What may have begun as a protest by some of Morebath's poorer parishioners against a burden they perceived as falling harder on them than on others, had certainly broadened beyond any purely financial basis, to include some of the more substantial farmers. It had become a dispute about order, and the willingness of individuals to 'be orderyd as the moste parte of the parysse ware'. The dispute had begun within the parish church, and it focussed on the payment of a key figure in the liturgy of that church, the priest's right-hand man. But it invaded one of the most domestic moments of parochial sociability, Margaret Timewell's betrothal, and it extended itself first to the ecclesiastical and then to the manor court. Parochial disorder found its liturgical counterpart in the disastrous requiem for Marke's chrismers, and it was resolved by a formal meeting of the parish in the church between

Mass and evensong on Rogation Sunday, a settlement in which the parish's landlords and the representative of the bishop lent their weight. The restoration of 'unite and pece a mongg us' was celebrated in the church ale house, at a feast of reconciliation at which the dissident parishioners, those *froward fellows* whose action had disrupted the peace of the parish in the first place, were ordered to be present, and which doubled up as a fund-raising exercise to make reparation to the clerk for the financial loss inflicted on him by the dispute.

Like everything else at Morebath, we view the whole incident through the priest's eyes. His account of this 'fresse warde a pon the clerk scheppe', the longest single item in the book, is by no means a neutral document. The distress caused by the delays before the requiem for Marke's children and the father's frantic searching through the parish for key and chalice and someone to serve 'be fore he coud have any mas sayd for hys chyld', the acrimonious disruption of Margaret Timewell's betrothal, the shamefulness of division in a small community set 'a most by the eris' by its inability to resolve its differences – all are reflected to us through his sensibility, and it is Sir Christopher's dismay we feel. His narrative is marked by easily recognisable clerical concerns – his elaborate protestations that he will 'mell no more' with an issue which might incur the 'displeasure of his parishioners', his emphasis on the official's seal and the anxiety this represents to underpin the community's self-regulation with the authority of the bishop, the religious language of 'unite and pece a mongg us'. But the events he describes, and the community voices and relationships his account displays so circumstantially, bear all the marks of authenticity. 1537 was the last year in which Morebath's pre-Reformation pieties, and the complex social arrangements which underlay them, would remain comparatively undisturbed. Sir Christopher's account of the rise and resolution of these conflicts allows us to observe the dynamics of a world at the last possible moment before it underwent dramatic and far-reaching change. As a working model of the inter-penetration of secular and religious values and institutions in pre-Reformation England, the clerkship dispute at Morebath would be hard to better.

CHAPTER FOUR

The Piety of Morebath

We are forever shut out from all but the surface of Morebath's religion. Late medieval Christianity moved between distinct but complementary poles – public and private, the religion of the liturgy and the religion of the heart. But neither the solemnities of the liturgy nor the secrets of the heart leave much trace in churchwardens' accounts, even when kept by Sir Christopher Trychay. The annual cycle of the great festivals, and the daily and weekly round of ordinary worship, Matins, Mass and Evensong, went on at Morebath as everywhere else in early Tudor England, but only the barest outline of that pattern can be guessed at from entries in the accounts. The handing on from warden to warden of the foot of the parish's silver pax,[1] and the purchase of a box for holy bread, signal the presence, in this always close but sometimes tense community, of the equipment needed for the celebration of the central peace-rituals of the liturgy.[2] Extra wax, paid for by the Young Men and Maidens, was bought at Easter from the bee-keeping Morsses for the sepulchre lights round the ritual 'tomb' of Christ, and the great paschal taper was fetched from Slade the chandler at Bampton.[3] But these hints are poor equivalents for the intense social and religious resonances of the demanding liturgical cycle which made up what Sir Christopher once and only once describes as 'the besy time of ester'[4] – all of it looming large in lay consciousness: the barefoot 'creeping to the cross', the watching round the Sacrament in its sepulchre from Good Friday afternoon until dawn on Easter Day, or the hours spent in church in the weeks beforehand, while the priest heard the whole parish's annual confessions.[5] The celebration of Christmas is similarly invisible to us in the Morebath accounts, apart from an inconspicuous extra seasonal outlay on tallow candles. In towns, payments for holly and box and ivy alert us to the importance of the Christmas festivities in the church as in the home.[6] In a wooded rural parish, winter greenery for the decoration of the church could be pulled from every hedgerow, and was not a charge on the wardens' accounts: we hear nothing of it. A single reference to the 'wyven taper' is our only hint of the churching of Morebath's women, the ceremony with candle and veil which was an important rite of passage for women, marking the ritual end of a woman's 'confinement', and representing the religious sanctification of childbirth and its dangers.[7] And the more sombre aspects of the parish's experience of religion are similarly concealed. Payment for repairs to the 'oyle box', and the purchase of 'a new purse for to put the sacrament yn' are the solitary reminders of Sir Christopher's death-bed ministrations and the anointing and 'houselling' (communion) of the dying, one of the most crucial and most intimate aspects of the priest's work in this parish where death was so frequent a visitant.[8]

Even celebrations peculiar to Morebath, like those which presumably marked its patronal festival around the feast of St George, are shrouded in uncertainty. The churchyard was cleaned every year 'a gayn sent Jorge tyde'[9] and an unexplained expense of this sort is recorded just once for 'revyll Sunday'. Round these two facts, and the holding of the wardens' annual ales, the editor of the Devonshire volume of the Records of Early English Drama series has woven a charming picture of an 'annual revel Sunday... at St George's tide' or its nearest Sunday at Morebath, organised by a guild or store of St George, and possibly including a play, procession or tableau of St George.[10] In fact this is largely fantasy: while it is possible and even likely that there was some sort of fair at St George's tide, the churchyard was also cleansed at Lammas tide (1 August) and at 'wother times', there were no 'guilds' at Morebath, there is no concrete evidence of any annual celebration though its existence is likely enough, we do not know the dates of any of the ales, and the priest's circumstantial account of the events of St George's day 1537 make it clear that in that year at least there was no fair (though we know from elsewhere in the accounts that sheep were sold that day); there does not even appear to have been a special mass on the feast day itself.[11] Sir Christopher does indeed record the payment of a penny for the sweeping of the churchyard 'agaynst revyll Sonday' in 1538, but this is the first occurrence of the word, and he never uses it again. There was a vigorous royal campaign against the cult of the saints in progress in 1538, and Sir Christopher may have used the word 'revyll' as a neutral shorthand for the religious ceremonies of their patronal festival.[12] And despite the church's dedication to St George, if there was an annual parish 'revel' at Morebath, Lammas seems a likelier time for such an event than the chancy weather of late April.[13] The evidence is just too incomplete to say.

Nor have we any very clear notion of the mechanics of daily and weekly worship in early Tudor Morebath. Sir Christopher was the only priest in the parish, for Morebath was too poor and too small to support chantry foundations like those which employed three priests to say or sing masses for the dead in Bampton church in the 1520s.[14] Yet Morebath's worship sometimes rose to splendour. Payments for processional tapers[15] reveal candle-lit processions, and Sir Christopher and his father completed a parishioner's gift of a fine set of white vestments by donating the dalmatic and tunicle in which deacon and subdeacon were robed at high mass. We know that on feast days at Morebath there normally *was* a high mass, a service which requires the presence of at least one priest or deacon in addition to the celebrant (the role of the subdeacon could be played by a layman). Neighbouring clergy sometimes assisted at solemn diriges (dirges) for the Morebath dead, as the parson of the nearby Somerset village of Anstey did for Joan Rumbelow's obsequies.[16] Such diriges were usually sung 'by note', which would normally have required the assistance of a small choir capable of singing plainsong, though at a pinch the clerk alone could have sung the responses and psalms with the priest.[17] But the accounts tell us little or nothing about how any of this was managed, or where auxiliary clergy might have been found for these great occasions. Sir Christopher's priest friend Sir Edward Nicoll, who lived in Brushford but whose parents were probably Morebath parishioners,[18] may have helped,[19] and the fact that the Bampton chantry priests contributed in 1534 to a parish collection to replace a stolen chalice strongly suggests that they too sometimes officiated.[20] But since such priests were not always paid by the wardens, we hardly glimpse them. Routine, in any case, leaves few records, even though most of what is fundamental to ordinary existence is a matter of routine – undocumented, invisible and, as a consequence, far too easily discounted by the historian seeking to touch the texture of the life of the past.

If the detail of the public religious life of Morebath eludes us, how much more its private devotion. We learn from a payment for 'glovys to wasse the corporis' that whoever laundered the cloth on which the priest consecrated the bread and wine at Mass wore gloves, so as not to touch the cloth directly, part of the *cordon sanitaire* the medieval church threw around the sacred.[21] But account books and balance sheets have nothing to say about the devotional intensity, or lack of it, with which the ranks of stolid, weather-beaten moorland farmers and their wives regarded the Eucharistic Host Sir Christopher raised above his head at the climax of their worship every Sunday. We do not know what passed between him and them at the shriving stool when he heard their confessions, or how far their priest's sick-room ministrations, or the requiem masses and diriges he sang in their church, eased their dying or their grieving. Their Christianity, in all likelihood, was largely conventional, which is not to say that it was either insincere or superficial. But the conventions of the past, like its routines, are hard to penetrate, not least because for Tudor Devon some of the sources which historians have most relied on to assess the spiritual convictions of ordinary men and women, are almost wholly missing. A Luftwaffe bomb destroyed the Exeter Probate Office in 1942, reducing most of the wills of Tudor Devon to ashes. A few survive in the records of the Prerogative Court of Canterbury, and from them we can gather the unsurprising fact that Morebath parishioners shared the region's general aspiration to burial in 'hailie grave ... God willinge'. They tell us little else about Morebath's religion.[22]

It is as well to remind ourselves like this of the limitations of our source material, the difficulty in all attempts at close encounter with the people of the past, of grasping what it was that mattered most to them. Yet when all that is said, the distinctive character of the Christianity of early Tudor mid- and North Devon is not entirely invisible. It had its public monuments, and even public monuments can take us some way towards a grip of the convictions that inspired them. If Morebath itself preserves little concrete evidence outside the parish account-book for the religious hopes and fears of its people, enough survives from the surrounding region to offer us a route into these hidden places. Both the priest and leading parishioners of Morebath were frequent and regular visitors to Tiverton, ten miles southwards down the Exe valley: they went there to market, for ecclesiastical visitations and, especially in the stormy years of Edward VI's reign, to make repeated appearances before reforming Royal Commissions.[23] The Visitations will have been held in Tiverton's parish church of St Peter, and in the years immediately before and after Sir Christopher's arrival in Morebath, that parish church was being transformed by the bounty of Tiverton's richest citizen, the wool merchant John Greneway, patron of the explorer John Cabot, member of the Fellowship of Merchant Adventurers, and Warden of the London Drapers' Company.[24] Greneway's wealth was based on the wool of the flocks of the Exe Valley, Morebath's along with the rest, and in 1532 Morebath church was to be one of the lesser beneficiaries of the will of Greneway's widow Joan.[25]

In 1517 John Greneway built a chantry chapel on the south side of St Peter's church, and decorated it with his initials, merchant's mark and coat of arms. He also commissioned for it a programme of carvings which proclaimed with equal insistence his worldly success and his other-worldly aspirations. The chapel and porch are patently *expensive*, battlemented, elaborately pierced and emblazoned with heraldry, an exercise in conspicuous consumption, albeit of a sanctified sort. Round the string course above the windows are twenty superbly carved scenes from the life of Christ, begin-

ning with the Flight into Egypt and ending with the Ascension, but con-
centrating, as contemporary piety did, on the incidents of the Passion. Even
in the bright sunlight which sometimes bathes this south-facing wall, it is
difficult to do justice to them without binoculars, so it is hard to say what
Sir Christopher and his parishioners might have made of them. Below
them, and easier to see, in cheerful and mildly shocking contrast, a fleet of
Greneway's laden wool ships sail their cargo of kerseys jauntily over the
carved sea which runs rippling round the building. The new structure
included a handsome porch with pinnacled niches for the parish's and
Greneway's patron saints. This porch was itself a distinctive contribution to
parish worship, for the opening ceremonies of the baptismal rite were held
in the porch, and so too was the wedding service. Greneway's porch is
therefore not just a handsome entrance, but a sumptuously decorated ritual
space for marriages and christenings, the two special sacraments of ordinary
people, a deliberate exercise in lay piety. And above the inner door, the
parish was reminded of their benefactor, and the sacrament of matrimony
vividly represented, by the figures of Greneway and his wife Joan kneeling
at carved prayer-desks, united in veneration of the Virgin Mary assumed
into heaven. Marian piety was at the heart of late medieval religion, and the
Greneways' gesture towards the Virgin was no doubt heart-felt. But we
cannot help remembering also that the Virgin was the patron saint of the
Drapers' Company: there is just a whiff of the business logo and corporate
sponsorship about it all.

Carved inscriptions in the chantry itself reflected the same unself-con-
scious linking of commerce and christianity. Some of them announce
Greneway's devotional largesse, and his clientage to helper saints likely to
be specially useful to a married man who was also a merchant adventurer
and trader in cloth – St Christopher, protector of travel, St Blaise, patron of
wool carders, and St Anne, patron of married people and of childbirth:

> To the honour of St Christopher, St Blaze and St Anne
> This chapel by John Greneway was began.

Several are conventional *memento mori*, or appeals for prayers:

> Whilst we think well and think t'amend
> Time passeth away and death's the end.

And, more straightforwardly:

> Of your charite prey for the souls of John and Joan Greneway his wife,
> which died 1529. And for their faders and moders and for their friends and
> their lovers: on them Jesu have mercy: amen. Of your charite say Pater-
> noster and Ave.

But in some of these inscriptions, desire for heaven unmistakably, and rather endearingly, takes second place to solicitude about Greneway's worldly prosperity:

> O Lord of all grant John Greenway good fort'n and grace
> And in Heaven a place.
> God speed JG.[26]

Greneway's chantry was just one half of his religious provision in Tiverton. The other was his almshouse, built in 1529 to house five old men (in honour of the Wounds of Jesus) whose duty it was to pray daily for the founder, the prudent investment of a proportion of his riches in God's poor, whose prayers could powerfully assist him into heaven. The inscriptions on the almshouse chapel sound the characteristic Greneway note:

> Remember the poor
> Have grace ye men and ever pray
> For the sowls of John and Joan Greenway
> Rest a whyle ye that may
> Pray for me by nyite and day.[27]

Greneway's pragmatic piety, half wedded to the things of this world, yet conscious too of death and what came after death, was far from idiosyncratic. The tomb of Edward Courtenay Earl of Devon, who died in 1509, also stood in St Peter's, Tiverton, and it too had an English rhyme proclaiming these same intuitions – the high value of marriage, the transience of life and the contrasting permanence of charitable giving to the poor. Sir Christopher and his wardens must often have remarked it.

> Loe, loe, who lyes here?
> Tis I, the good Erle of Devonsheere
> With Kate my Wyfe, to mee full deere,
> We lyved togeather fyfty fyve yere.
> That wee spent, wee had;
> That wee lefte, wee loste;
> That we gave, wee have.[28]

The kneeling figures of John and Joan Greneway, frozen in their perpetual piety, have open books before them. These are books of hours, by the early sixteenth century an indispensable devotional accessory for even the moderately well to do.[29] All such books contained a simplified form of the standard devotions of the late medieval church – psalms, hymns and scripture passages arranged in seven daily 'hours' of prayer in honour of the Virgin, the text of the dirige or solemn office for the dead, and a small group of additional devotions and intercessions to Christ and the saints. But many also had handwritten additions inserted by their owners and reflecting their devotional preoccupations. Two such annotated books of hours from

North Devon survive, and their manuscript additions reflect much the same sort of domesticated piety on display in early Tudor Tiverton. One was from fifteenth-century Tawstock, near Barnstaple: its calendar has had a small group of extra saint's days added, including two of the most important saints' cults in late medieval North Devon, those of St Nectan and St Urith of Chittelhampton. Another addition is the feast of St Pancrace, and that entry has a characteristically this-worldly note – 'bonum pro pomis' ['Feast of Pancrace, good for apples'].[30] The other book was in use in the 1520s just fifteen miles from Morebath, in the Harewode family of South Molton, and it too has additions to the calendar – the feast days of Nectan and Urith again, the beginning and end dates of the 'dog days', notes of family anniversaries – 'my mother decessid upon this daye' – and the dedication festival of South Molton church. Both books also have prayers inserted by the owners, like these devotional rhymes to be repeated five times with the Lord's Prayer, the Hail Mary and the Creed, from the Tawstock book:

Ihesu for thy precious blod
Make my last endyng goodd.
Lady for thy ioyes five
Led me the rythe wey to leve.

There are also charms and medical remedies like 'a soverayne medsyn for the sietica', a system of devotional fasting to ensure a holy death, and a prayer-charm to St Peter designed to protect against worldly disgrace, storms at sea, 'the blode fluxe', or mishap in pregnancy.[31]

This is piety for practical people, attached to their families, their locality, their parish, centred on the sufferings of Christ and the joys of Mary, but devoted also to Devon pilgrimage saints like St Urith and the holy places of their own region, people for whom Christianity is about living right and dying well, but also about belonging, both to a place and to a lineage, about winning respectability, ensuring safe child-birth, about the best time to prune apples and the most effective way to ease sciatica or stop a diarrhoea. It is recognisably the religion of John and Joan Greneway, and it is the religion too of the people of Morebath and their priest.

For although we do not have access to the intimacies of Morebath's religion, we do have plentiful evidence of its external shell, its busy piety, a piety vigorously directed and urged on by their priest. Sir Christopher came to Morebath in the summer of 1520. He was probably in his late twenties, delighted to be there, young, energetic and eager. His predecessor, Sir Richard Bowden, had been vicar of Morebath for thirty years, and had died in office.[32] Perhaps Sir Richard had run out of steam before the end, and Sir Christopher saw himself as a much needed breath of fresh air for Morebath. At any rate, from the moment of his arrival he flung himself into a flurry of activity which, over the next fifteen years, would gather and grow until it

resembled not so much a breath as a gale, and which simultaneously transformed the interior of his church, and the devotional life of his parish.

The little church of Morebath in 1520 was already densely peopled with
saints, whose images filled the building. On either side of the high altar, as
required by canon law, were the principal statue of the Virgin, and the
patronal image of St George, each of them in decorated niches (called
'tabernacles') hung with curtains. Over the church's side-altar, where the
weekday masses were celebrated, was the image of Jesus, possibly an image
of the infant Jesus, but more likely a standing figure of Christ holding a
globe, the 'Salvator Mundi' which was probably the commonest early
Tudor 'Jesus' representation. The cult of the Holy Name of Jesus, spon-
sored by the Lady Margaret Beaufort, reflected in the spread of Jesus altars
and celebrations of the Jesus Mass in parish churches all over the country
and nourished by devotional texts and practices stressed the tenderness and
accessibility of the human Christ, was one of the growth areas in early sixteenth-century lay piety: Morebath's Jesus altar put them in the van of fashion.[33] Against pillars and walls round the church, as we have already noted,[34]
were half a dozen other niched and tabernacled figures: the Sunday Christ,
a 'Man of Sorrows' representation of Jesus pierced by tools and implements
of work;[35] St Loy or St Eligius, patron of smiths and carters and a West
Country favourite, usually portrayed holding a horseshoe, a hammer or a
horse's leg;[36] St Antony, healer of men and of farm animals, usually accompanied by one or more pigs;[37] and St Anne, often portrayed teaching the
young Virgin Mary to read, or with the adult Mary and her child Jesus.[38] St
Anne was a barren woman made miraculously fecund. She had, according
to legend, been married three times, and was not merely the grandmother
of Jesus but, by her other two daughters, of six of the twelve apostles. For
obvious reasons she was a devotional favourite with late medieval married
people, anxious in one way or another about childbirth and posterity.

In contrast to the obligatory statues of the Virgin and St George behind
the screen in the chancel, all these images represented devotional choices by
the parishioners of Morebath. They were located in the body of the small
church, close to the people who maintained lights before them, and to
whose anxieties and hopes they held up a devotional mirror. Included
among them was another representation of the Virgin, Our Lady of Pity,
the stricken figure of Mary at Calvary, weeping over the body of her dead
son laid in her lap. Once again, this was an image which appealed powerfully to late medieval people, both as a model of the appropriate devotional
response to the sufferings of Christ, the tears of Mary a symbol of the peni-
tent heart, and also as an objective correlative for their own predicament in
the universal experience of death and bereavement.[39]

These images and the cults they represent all have an immediate and obvious resonance in the lives of the people of a farming community like

Morebath. Though the figures of Jesus and Mary are essentially *devotional*, emblems of the central affirmations of the Christian faith, all the rest are Holy Helpers, embodiments of religion harnessed as much to the everyday material needs as to the spiritual longings of labouring and suffering men and women. Even the figure of Our Lady of Pity, though symbolic of the Passion, was also a Holy Helper in this more concrete sense, for Mary above all was the saint of the death bed, a resource against both its physical and its spiritual terrors. In the early sixteenth century the image of Our Lady of Pity was intimately associated with dying and death, bereavement and burial. It is not hard to see why the many Morebath parents who grieved over their own dead sons and daughters might respond to such an image.[40]

What was lacking among Morebath's intercessors in 1520 was any saint who might embody regional pride and sense of identity. These were universal saints, venerated not only in Devon but throughout England and indeed the whole of western Europe. But the more geographically specific dimension of the cult of the saints, the sanctifying of place, of the local, was also fundamental to its appeal.[41] It was clearly important, for example, to the owners of both the Books of Hours from Tawstock and South Molton, as the addition to their calendars of local dedication festivals and the feastdays of St Nectan and St Urith demonstrate. And it was important to Sir Christopher, too, the whole of whose long ministry in Morebath would reveal a passionate engagement with the parish and its people, a man rooted as few men are 'in one dear perpetual place'. Soon after his arrival in the parish, therefore, he set about remedying this lack in the pieties of Morebath. As he later noted,

> Dominus Christoferus Trychay condam istius eclesie vicarius the furst ere that he was made vicar here he gave yn Sent Sydwyll and payd for her makyn and gyltyng xxxiij^s & iiij^d [33/4d].[42]

> *Sir Christopher Trychay, onetime vicar of this church, the first year that he was made vicar here he gave in St Sidwell and paid for her making and gilding 33/4d.*

Saint Sidwell was an Exeter saint whose body lay in a church dedicated to her outside the east gate of the city. Travellers to Exeter from Culmstock, Sir Christopher's home village, would have had to pass it, and the more pious, or more needy, might have stopped to pray there, for from at least the fourteenth century her grave had been the site of a pilgrimage, noted for its healings. Sidwell or Sativola was a Saxon virgin, supposedly murdered by a jealous stepmother who had ordered her farm labourers to decapitate the maiden with a scythe; a well sprang up where the head fell, and later the saint herself carried her head to the site she had chosen for her shrine. The legend, and Sidwell's iconography, have close similarities with that of St Urith of Chittelhampton. By the early Tudor period her cult had spread well beyond the immediate locality of Exeter. There was a church dedicated to her at Laneast in Cornwall, and her image is still to be seen on twenty painted screens, bench-ends or stained glass windows in Cornwall, Devon and West Somerset. Exeter had no other 'native' saint, so Exeter men abroad felt patriotic about her: Roger Keyes, canon of Exeter, who oversaw the building of the chapels of both Eton College and All Souls, Oxford, saw to it that this obscure regional saint was represented in the stained glass and wall-painting of these prestigious institutions.[43]

We do not know the origins of Sir Christopher's devotion to Sidwell, though it strongly suggests that he had spent some key part of his life in Exeter. At any rate, he quickly set about transmitting his enthusiasm to his parishioners. Rather than consign Sidwell to a tabernacle on a wall or pillar, Sir Christopher had her strategically placed alongside the figure of Jesus over the altar where daily and requiem masses were said. The 'tabyllmentis' or base on which she stood were paid for 'by hys devocon *and the paryssyn*', which means that Sir Christopher had induced some of them at least to contribute to the new shrine.[44] A priest ministers to the dying, and in Tudor England often acted as the scribe and draughtsman of parishioners' wills. Sir Christopher was therefore well placed to encourage pious donations to the parish's new-found Devon intercessor. The first bequests begin in 1523, when Margery Lake bequeathed an altar cloth for 'Sent Sydwyll ys auter', and a basin of latten 'to sett lyghth on a fore St Sydwyll'.[45] The phrase 'St Sidwell's altar' is startling, for the altar certainly existed before Sir Christopher donated the statue, and it also supported the figure of Jesus: perhaps we catch here the priest's own determination to promote the cult of his patroness. But this note was written many years after the event, and maybe it simply reflects the way in which, little by little as her cult grew, the altar had in fact come to be thought of as Sidwell's special possession. At any rate, in the following year Jekyn at More bequeathed a pair of painted altar-cloths 'to dresse Sent Sydwyll ys auter', as well as another lamp basin for the saint, which was evidently surplus to requirement, for it was pressed into service for the alms light 'before the hye crosse'.[46] From now on donations to St Sidwell become routine, small gifts to maintain her light, larger gifts to adorn her altar. The existence of the light required a fund to maintain it. By 1526 there was a 'store' of St Sidwell, administered by the wardens and with its own small flock of sheep. By the late 1520s, these devotional gestures were becoming more imaginative and more intimate, indications that the parish had embraced and internalised the cult their priest had pressed on them. In 1528 William Potter at Poole left a hive of bees, which John Morsse had managed for him, to the altar of Jesus and Sidwell, the wax

> to mayntayn a lamppe burnyng a fore the fugar of Jhesu and a fore sent Sydwyll every princssipal feste yn the ere, to burne from the furst even song un tyll hye masse be done the morrow.[47]

to maintain a lamp burning before the figure of Jesus and before St Sidwell every principal feast in the year, to burn from the first evensong (i.e. first vespers of the feast) until high Mass be done the next day.

In the same year Joan Hyllyer of Bampton gave the parish a banner with St George on one side and St Sidwell on the other, a striking mark of the saint's growing place in the parish's devotional consciousness; she also donated a candlestick of latten to stand before St Sidwell, and there is no mistaking the delight with which Sir Christopher records the gift:

A pon the wyche canstycke sche dothe mayntayne a taper before sent syd-wyel trimyd with flouris to borne there every hye and prynscypall festis this sche dothe entende to mayntayne whyll sche lyvyth gracia divina.[48]

Upon which candlestick she doth maintain a taper before St Sidwell trimmed with flowers, to burn there every high and principal feast: this she doth intend to maintain while she liveth, by the grace of God.

Sir Christopher's own father Thomas died in 1529, and predictably, at his son's prompting, made an offering to St Sidwell, bequeathing a swarm of bees to the parish, once again to be looked after at 'half money' by John Morsse, the wax to maintain a light before Jesus and St Sidwell; an identical bequest fo a 'butt of beys' for Jesus and Sidwell was received from Sir Christopher's mother Joan when she died three years later.[49] These double gifts to Jesus and Sidwell on their shared altar had by now become commonplace, like Elenor Nicoll's 1529 bequest of a 'lytyll sylver cross parcel gylte' to Jhesu, and her wedding ring to St Sidwell 'the wyche ryng dyd helppe make sent sydwyll ys scowys': the wedding ring was of silver and was melted down to help make a silver shoe, attached to the feet of the statue as a mark of devotion.[50] The commissioning of this silver shoe coincided with a series of bequests from other parishioners for the painting of the image of Jesus, the gilding of St Sidwell, and the provision of painted cloths for their altar.[51]

The bequest of so personal a possession as a wedding ring to be melted to make shoes for an image suggests a more than conventional devotion, and by the late 1520s the cult of St Sidwell was eliciting from the people of Morebath many such gestures of intimacy and affection. Rosaries were among the most prized possessions of devout women in Tudor England. Worn at the waist and constantly fingered, they were often the costliest item a woman owned, and an important part of female status and identity. The bequest of one's rosary to an image, to be draped round it on high days and holidays or to hang on its surrounding shrine, or simply to be sold to help finance the cult, was a token of a special affection for a saint, and a sign of the donor's desire to be remembered in the saint's powerful intercession. Richard Hukeley's daughter Joan left her beads to St Sidwell in

1531, though, as the priest reported with irritation the same year, 'ys for the bedis that Joan Hucly be quevyd un to sent Sydwyll Richard Webber sayth that they be loste'.[52] With happier results Alison Zaer, dying the same year, also left 'a pere of bedis of gette [jet] and sylver pater nosters and a gurdyll with barris of sylver and a ryng of sylver and parsyll gylte' to St Sidwell,[53] though these handsome objects were later sold to help pay for the saint's silver shoe. There were many such gifts: kerchiefs, girdles and beads, all of them signs of the success of the priest's devotional initiative. More intimately still, by the mid-1530s at least two of the girls of the village had been given Sidwell as their Christian name.[54]

The steady growth of the cult of St Sidwell was just one aspect of Sir Christopher's successful impact on the devotional life of his parish. The adornment of the statues and altar of Jesus and Sidwell coincided with a more general campaign to renovate the rest of the church's imagery, and to renew its vestments, banners and altar-furnishings. From 1529 onwards, most of the imagery in the church was replaced or else revamped by being gilded, repainted and installed in new or redecorated tabernacles. This process began, once the cult of St Sidwell was securely established, with a new image of Our Lady, inaugurated with the bequest of her best gown by Christine Timewell and by the entire estate of 'wolde dame Rumbelow' to a new image of Our Lady, 'the wyche image was her exsector with us wardyns as ys expressyd be fore a pon her testament'.[55] The image of the Virgin was a special focus for piety in later medieval England, and appealed particularly to women. The language of that entry in the High Wardens' accounts for 1529, in which the statue features as an executor along with them, suggests a distinctive devotional personalising of the image, and a special sense of clientage to the Virgin on Joan Rumbelow's part. The phrasing may well be the priest's, but Sir Christopher was not falsifying the devotional intent: the symbolic force of gifts of kerchiefs, girdles, beads and gowns conveyed much the same sense of intimacy, as do bequests for flowers and lights to burn before specified images between first vespers and mass – that is, all night long – on feast-days. Together, they alert us to the special importance of the cult of images in the symbolic fabric of early Tudor Morebath's religion.

That importance found expression in expensive campaigns of replacement and renewal of the church's imagery up to the very moment of Reformation: the new statue of the Blessed Virgin, commissioned in 1529, delivered to the church in 1531 and gilded in 1532,[56] 'a nimage of the nativite of our Ladye with her purtenes [appurtenances]' in 1530,[57] a new tabernacle for St Sunday the same year,[58] the regilding of St Loy, the erection of new candle brackets before St Sunday and St George, and the commissioning of a new carving of St George in 1531, the gilding of our Lady's tabernacle and of the other image of Our Lady of Pity in 1533,[59] a new High Cross or crucifix over the entrance to the chancel, with Mary and John on either side, commissioned in 1535 and worked at for the next two years,[60] a new ceiling of honour over St Sidwell's altar in 1537 to stop drips from the tiling 'to the savyng of auter clotwhys'.[61]

Alongside all this attention to the images, the church building and its other furnishings were also being transformed – the erection of a new screen or 'enterclose' in 1529, and the reordering of the chancel area and the surroundings of the high altar, which was reconsecrated after the work in the same year by one of Bishop Vesey's suffragans,[62] new choir stalls in 1530, the entire church or 'the moste parte' of it re-pewed in 1533–4, and along with them the renewing of the timber work around the font and high altar.[63] And with the structural work, came an avalanche of smaller purchases and gifts, new palls for laying on the dead at funerals, new candlesticks of timber and brass and iron, a new set of white vestments, a new cope, a silken pillow, banners of silk, streamers for the rogationtide and other outdoor processions, painted altar-cloths, a new Easter Sepulchre of wood and iron for the Holy Week ceremonies, and the painted cloths to hang about it, a new Lent veil, a new gilt basin with a fringe to hang over the Blessed Sacrament in the chancel.[64]

This wave of activity, which has its parallels in parishes all over the county and all over the country, brought a stream of artisans to Morebath. Some of them make walk-on appearances just once or twice: Harry Dey who made the enterclose, the 'painter at Trebarrow' who gilded St Loy, or Stebbe the smith from Bampton who repaired the gear around the little bell in 1531 and the 'bonde of the vawnte' [lock for the font-cover] in 1539, or the tinker from Dulverton 'for the sawderyng of our latyng canstycks', or 'Mylbroke and his man' who mended the church house stairs and door in 1537, or 'Chylcote and his man' who repaired the trusses of the great bell and the second bell in 1538, or Quycke the mason and his men who did the stonework for the enterclose in 1529, and who lime-washed and pargetted the chancel, taking two days over it for 6/8d, in 1531.[65] Others move so frequently through the pages of the account book that they become familiars, like John Creche, the painter and gilder from Bampton who painted the screenwork, painted the imagery on the sepulchre cloths, gilded all the church's tabernacles, the ceilings of honour over the statues and the basin over the Sacrament, as well as all the images themselves, and who had a standing contract to wash the imagery and tabernacles every year.[66] He was sometimes paid in kind, given eightpence worth of 'flesse' for washing the tabernacles, or taking the church wool in part exchange for gilding Our Lady,[67] as other workmen were, like the plumber given lumps of solder or old pewter plates in part exchange for his work.[68] Another regular was Thomas Glasse the carver, who made the new George and the image of the

Nativity of the Virgin: his contracts with the parish were made publicly at the audit and circumstantially copied into the accounts: for carving the new George he was to have the old one in part exchange:

> so now we be at a clere powynte with him that he schall make us a new iorge and a new horsse to our dragon to hys one proper coste and charge...and for the makyn of this he schall have our iorge a gayn and xiii^s & iiij^d [13/4d] of mony and yff he doo well hys partye he schall have of us xv^s [15/=] when hyt ys done and sett up.[69]

> *so now we be at a clear point with him, that he shall make us a new George and a new horse to our dragon, at his own proper cost and charge...and for the making of this he shall have our George again and 13/4d of money, and if he do well his part he shall have of us 15/= when it is done and set up.*

The contract with William Popyll, the carver who made the new High Cross, was equally specific. Other West Country parishes ordering new Roods demanded a drawing in advance, like the Somerset parish of Banwell in 1521 which provided the carver with paper 'for to draw the draff of the rood lofte'.[70] Morebath dispensed with this nicety, and instead required Popyll simply to keep them ahead of the Joneses, in the form of the neighbouring village of Brushford. He was, they instructed him, to make them a crucifix, Mary and John 'a cordyng to the patent of Brussorde or better', he to provide all his own materials except for the great beam on which the cross would rest, which the parish was to put in place, 'he to spoyle hyt to hys costis'. As with all the parish's major projects, payment was carefully staged through the work, with an earnest penny at the making of the bargain, a substantial instalment when work commenced, and then successive payments at the quarter days until the crucifix was completed for St George's day 1536.[71] Most of these workmen were local, none of them coming further than from Tiverton, with the exception of Sir Thomas Shorcum, the priest who made and maintained the parish's vestments, who lived at Dunster in Somerset.[72]

This sustained devotional outlay can of course be paralleled in many other West Country parishes of the period: Sir Christopher's enthusiasms were widely shared by both priests and people. Ashburton, for example, painted Our Lady above the high altar in 1516–17, mended the statue of St Erasmus in 1520–21, St Roche in 1522–3, made a new tabernacle for St John in 1523–4: they commissioned a handsome new roodloft and seats in 1522–3, and a new image of St George in 1529–30, as well as a more or less continuous programme of gilding and repainting of images and tabernacles.[73] But the outlay on all this for so small and poor a community as Morebath was staggering. Between 1527 and 1537 the profit from the High Wardens' ale, the largest component of the parish's collective income, never exceeded £3/8/11 (1536) and was usually nearer £3. The Young Men's ale never brought in more than £2/7/2½ (1535) and was usually less than £2. Through these years the priest took to keeping a rough tally of the total income from all sources, including the Four Men's 'stock'. The peak year for this tally was 1537, when Sir Christopher noted that the 'resettis of all cowntis of this churche syns was the hye Wardyns a cownte laste with the maydens getheryng and with the geftis and bequestis hyt cumyth a moste to 20 mark', that is, £13/6/8d.[74] Most years, however, the total income from all sources was between £8 and £10, and sometimes less. Against these modest sums, the rising tide of devotional investment in the late 1520s and early 1530s is little short of staggering: William Popyll's crucifix cost £7, the new image of St George cost £5,[75] and the image of the Nativity of the Virgin also cost £5,[76] respectively more than two thirds and a half of an entire year's income. The first charge on that income, moreover, remained all the routine and not-so-routine running costs of the church and church house, both of them in apparently perpetual need of expensive roofing and repair, so that the additional outlay on pious fittings called for sustained effort and investment. There was some outside help: devout women from the surrounding villages of Devon and Somerset contributed occasional gifts to St Sidwell, Sir Edward Nicoll bequeathed the money which paid for the new sepulchre cloths, the Prior of Barlinch duly paid the patron's portion of the costs of re-roofing the chancel, and when the church had its new pews, Barlinch donated two oak trees for the work. The prior's largesse outmatched that of the leading men of the parish, John Morsse and John Norman at Court, who gave one oak apiece, as did Harry Hurley. The vicar however trumped them all, by donating four oak trees to the work, a fitting indication, as it was no doubt meant to be, of his own dominant role as mover and stirrer in the busy piety of Morebath.[77]

For in all this the priest was undoubtedly making most of the running, directing the death-bed bounty of parishioners to the currently favoured projects while emphasising to the parish that the money must thus be spent, 'a cordyng to the dedis wyll',[78] and often receiving money directly from testators for these purposes, thereby in effect circumventing the wardens. Sir Christopher was careful to emphasise that where he had received such direct donations, they were for him to spend at his discretion, to be 'bestowyd here yn this churche as hyt schall plesse M. Vicar', as when in 1531 he reported in the course of the High Wardens' account that:

William Robyns a yong man dyde be quesse unto this churche iij^s & iiij^d [3/4d] wyche money ressevyd the vicar and he hath payd a gayn of the same mony for ij [2] pere of tymber canstyckis: on pere afore the hye awter and the other pere a pon sent Sydwell ys awter xx^d [20d] and so the other xx^d resteth in the vicar ys hand: he to bestow hyt for the churche a vantage *sicut placuit ei*.[79]

William Robyns a young man did bequeath unto this church 3/4d which money received the vicar, and he hath paid again of the same money for two pair of timber

candlesticks: one pair before the high altar and the other pair upon St Sidwell's altar,
20d, and so the other 20d resteth in the vicar's hands; he to bestow it for the church's
advantage as it pleases him.

The project most nakedly espoused as his very own was the fund for the
black vestments to be worn at requiem masses for the parish dead, inaugurated by Sir Christopher with the public donation of his small tithes on the
church sheep in 1529, an emolument formerly kept for themselves by the
vicars of Morebath, as he was at pains to point out: 'for before Sir
Christopher tyme Sir Richard Bowdyn Vicar before hem hadd home ever
the tuthyng [tithing]'.[80] Characteristically, Sir Christopher punctiliously
exacted a token return for this benefaction of his, since he surrendered the
wool tithe only on condition that the honey and wax tithe from the church
bees should be given to him already 'made', separated from the comb and
cleaned, and from time to time he proprietorially reminded the parish that
the tithing money 'schall reste yn my hande tyll my hony be made'.[81]

There was a fine line here: Sir Christopher was the major contributor to
the black vestment fund, and was quite clear that his would be the determining say in how and when the money should be spent, 'when hyt schall
plese the vicar as sone as the mony wyll extend'.[82] But he wanted his parishioners to contribute also, which would only happen if they too were
allowed to feel some ownership of the project. The conflict this caused for
him can be sensed in the patently grudging formulae he devised in 1536 to
express this shared responsibility – the fund was, he declared 'to b[u]y a
schewte of blacke vestmentis with all to the vicar's pleasure *and sumwhat to*
the paryysyng' [somewhat to the parishioners' pleasure].[83]

He did not have it all his own way. The priest was certainly aware of the
pressure put on parish funds by these ongoing devotional projects, and he
often had to curb his own enthusiasm and tread carefully. He was at pains,
for example, to point out whenever some new item was acquired as a free
gift rather than a purchase, 'and hoo ys mony hyt was that payd for this …
now schall ye have knolyge of …', as he does with the cope bought in 1537
by a series of parishioners' bequests, no doubt orchestrated by himself.
Listing the bequests, he comments that 'under this maner was the cope
payd for *and the churche at no charge'*, a process repeated over the candlestick
of five lights placed before the figure of Jesus in 1531, 'of the be quest of
Christina Norman at Wode' completed by her husband John, so that *'thus*
the canstyck ys cum fre to this churche'.[84] Moreover, the sense of collective
responsibility was strong in Morebath, and the final say about expenditure
lay with the parish through its Wardens and the Five Men. Sir Christopher
could push his natural authority as their priest only up to a point, as he
found to his cost in 1537 during the work on the new High Cross. The
bargain was made for the work before the parish had carefully specified the
quarter days as the dates for successive payments to John Creche and his

subcontractors; in August 1537, however, 'John Paynter', the gilder working on the cross, was in desperate need of money, probably because of illness. The vicar, softheartedly, parted with 20/= , ostensibly on behalf of the
parish, 'at hys nede, before hys day'. The kindness, however, backfired, for
'a pon that he deyd', leaving the work unfinished and the 20/= gone. The
vicar duly claimed this money back from the parish, but to deep discontent,
for it was felt that the money had been lost because the priest had acted
'agaynst the parishe wyll'. Sir Christopher cut his losses by agreeing to
return the money to the parish, but salved the worst sting of this climb-
down – not to mention the very considerable financial loss – by stipulating
that it should be devoted to his own pet project – 'y said unto you that hyt
schuld goo to the blacke vestmentis and so hyt schall and y wylbe
cowntabyll unto you for this xx^s [20/=]'. It was a lesson he did not forget,
however: ten years on he was still smarting at the 'grudging' of 'sum of
you' over this twenty shillings.[85]

It would be a mistake, however, to imagine that this was a community
frog-marched into an alien piety by an overweening priest. Sir Christopher
was proud of the orchestration of all this devotional investment, secured, as
he would later boast about the black vestments, 'by my procurement to the
honor of God and the churche and to the worschyppe of this hole parysse'.[86]
This was a perception almost certainly shared by most of his parishioners, as
the competitive indenture for their new crucifix 'after the pattern of
Brussorde or better' indicates. The cult of images at Morebath provided the
parish with symbolic equivalents for their own conditions of life, not merely
in saints of agriculture and toil like Anthony and Loy, or of marriage and
childbearing like Anne, but in more general correspondences, rooted in age
and gender as well as work and marital status. The Young Men funded the
lights before St George, and in 1531 paid the first 40/= towards Thomas
Glasse's new carving of the saint, because George was celebrated widely in
Tudor England not only as the royal and national saint, but as a symbol of
youthful vigour and military prowess.[87] In the same way the Maidens maintained lights before the Virgin and before the maiden saint Sidwell.
Honouring the images, they celebrated themselves and their concerns.

And much of the devotional investment of Morebath was manifestly
rooted in domestic affections, or pride of family. Husbands commemorated
their wives, parents their children, wives or sons completed a husband's or
father's bequests, seeking by means of this investment in the public space of
the church an affirmation of the endurance and holiness of their private
fidelities. For all the parish, the 'worship' or honourable maintenance of
their church was an aspect of their sense of worth and integrity as individuals and as a community. This was of course implicit in the social organisation of the cult of the saints in Morebath, the demanding system of stores,
the management of the sheep whose wool serviced the lights and images,
the detailed procedure of audit and report. It was evident too in the

involvement of the Young Men and Maidens in parish finance, the activities and natural bonding of age and gender groups harnessed to the wider community of the parish.

That shared sense of community identity was on display in the remarkable response of the Young Men and Maidens to an act of sacreligious theft committed in Morebath in November 1534, recorded, as ever, with characteristic detail by Sir Christopher.[88] Friday 20 November was the feast of St Edmund King and Martyr; that night,

> by twyxte the fryday and the saterday a theffe with a ladder gate up a pon the churche and pullyd up the ladder after him and sette the ladder to the towre wyndow and brycke uppe that wyndoo and so gate yn to the bellis and fro the bellis came a downe yn to the churche.

> *betwixt the Friday and the Saturday, a thief with a ladder got up upon the church, and pulled up the ladder after him, and set the ladder to the tower window and broke up that window and so got into the bells, and from the bells came down into the church.*

It is not at all clear what a thief with a ladder was doing roaming one of the remoter fringes of Exmoor in the depths of winter, though the ladder may have been part of the lumber remaining around the church in the wake of the recently completed re-pewing; equally, the thief may have come from Bampton, or may, just possibly, have been a Morebath parishioner. Whoever he was, he had a tinder box with him, and, as the priest explained in his note with all the relish of an amateur detective,

> with a fyre box strake fyre and to proffe thys he left hys yre that he strake fyre with all by hynd hym and was fownd.

> *with a fire-box struck fire, and to prove this, he left his iron that he struck fire with behind him and it was found.*

The thief then broke open the church's two coffers: in the 'stock coffer' was one of the parish's two chalices, but no other valuables. He made his escape through the choir door (carefully pulling it to after him), taking with him the chalice and the silver shoe of Sir Christopher's beloved St Sidwell.

It was the response of his people to this outrage that caused the priest to insert the note in the church book, for, as he recorded with pride:

> so a pon this the yong men and maydens of this parysse dru themselffe to gethers and with there geftis and provyssyon the bofth yn a nother challis with out any chargis of the parysse.

> *so upon this, the young men and maidens of this parish drew themselves together, and with their gifts and provision they bought in another chalice without any charges of the parish.*

Both groups were used to fundraising, and a collection 'of devocion' was the normal way in which the Maidens paid for the tapers before the Virgin and St Sidwell. They now combined forces to collect from every unmarried man and woman in the parish, in sums ranging from 1d to 20d, with many brothers and sisters combining to make joint donations. Sir Christopher lists all 105 contributors to this collection, which raised 32/8½d, the new chalice eventually costing 28/8½d, with an additional 4d to have it blessed by the bishop, and the costs in 'horsse mett and mans mett' to Lewis Trychay the priest's brother and William Hurley for fetching it, with the promise that when everything was paid 'then they schall have sum what for their labour'.

This incident came at the end of the year in which the vicar and wardens had attended the first metropolitical visitation of Henry VIII's new Archbishop Thomas Cranmer, a cloud on their traditionalist horizon no bigger than a man's hand.[89] The response which the theft elicited tells us a good deal about the collective nature of 'devotion' in Morebath on the eve of the great changes which were about to sweep over it – and which were to take from the parish a great deal more than a silver chalice and the shoe of St Sidwell. The Young Men and Maidens' initiative attracted some outside donations, from men and women with family, professional or simply friendly connections to the parish – the chantry priests at Bampton, who each gave 4d, the price of a mass or dirige, 'Mr Coldasche', Elnor Gauteny of Milverton, John at Ven, Richard Raw of Bampton. The list included servants or labourers like John Jordyn, who gave a silver necklace worth 3½d, and artisans like 'Thomas Scely the work man' and William at Moore, 'a work man', who gave the surprisingly large sums of 6d and 1s respectively. Indeed all the trades of Morebath were represented – Richard Norman 'a husban man' (who gave a ring worth 10d), Jorge Smith, John Bocher. Members of three of Morebath's poorest families, Thomas Scely, John Leddon and Thomas Zaer, each gave 1d. But non-contribution, though an option, was clearly disapproved of. Richard Timewell gave nothing: the priest nevertheless included his name on the list, which was presumably read aloud when the chalice was brought home, and he wrote against it 'nil'. Shame, as well as pride, was an incentive in the pieties of pre-Reformation Morebath.

CHAPTER FIVE

Banishing Saint Sidwell

On 20 November 1534, while the Morebath burglar prepared his tinder-box and ladder for the raid on St Sidwell's shoe, the clerks of the House of Commons were copying and engrossing a short piece of legislation which had finally completed its slow way through parliament that same week. The Act of Supremacy declared that 'the king, our sovereign Lord, his heirs and successors, kings of this realm, shall be taken, accepted and reputed the only supreme head on earth of the Church of England, called *Anglicana Ecclesia*'.[1] This was the crowning moment of the revolution in religious affairs which had been gathering momentum over the previous five years. The Act translated into statute an already accomplished practical transfer of all the juris-dictional powers of the Pope to a layman, the King of England. By it, the liberties of the Church of England from secular interference that had been guaranteed by Magna Carta were repudiated in favour of total control by the Crown, and the English church's thousand-year-old allegiance to the Holy See was formally brought to an end.

The progress of the Reformation in England to this point had been by no means a foregone conclusion. When Martin Luther's attack on the Catholic Church and the authority of the Pope first began to spread outside Germany, the pious King of England had been one of the most determined and most organised opponents of the new teachings. Henry and his chief minister, Cardinal Wolsey, had mobilised the theologians of Oxford and Cambridge to preach and write against Luther. The reformer's books were publicly burned in London, and his English followers pursued and executed. William Tyndale's superb translation of the New Testament, with its pugnaciously anti-Catholic footnotes, was banned and burned, and Tyndale became a hunted man. Henry himself published a competent defence of the seven sacraments against Luther, for which in 1521 the grateful Pope Leo X granted him the title Defender of the Faith. The anti-Protestant treatises of England's leading theologian, John Fisher, bishop of Rochester and chaplain to Henry's formidable grandmother, Margaret Beaufort, carried Henry's arms on their title-page. When Wolsey fell from power in 1529, he was replaced as Lord Chancellor by the devout Catholic layman Thomas More, and over the next four years More was to write more than a million words in exhaustive, fierce and often funny defence of traditional Catholicism, and in denunciation of the reformers.[2]

But Wolsey's fall from favour was itself the by-product of a problem that was to take England from loyal defence of the papacy into the Protestant camp, namely, the king's divorce. Henry had succeeded to the throne because of the untimely death in 1502 of his elder brother, Prince Arthur. As Prince of Wales, Arthur had contracted a dynastic marriage to the Spanish princess Catherine of Aragon, and after Arthur's death King Henry VII had decided that in the interests of continued alliance with Spain, the young prince Henry should marry his brother's widow. Such a marriage, however, was forbidden by church law, and so a papal dispensation was needed: the warrior Pope Julius II duly obliged, and on becoming king in 1509 Henry proceeded with the marriage. A dynastic marriage, however, must above all things serve the dynasty. None of Henry and Catherine's male children survived, and Henry could not contemplate entrusting the still shaky future of the *parvenu* Tudor monarchy to a girl, their one living child, Princess Mary. He genuinely worried that his marriage to his brother's widow, despite the papal dispensation, might have broken the natural law and so have angered God: more to the point, he wanted a son, and knew now that his ageing Spanish queen would not provide one. By the mid-1520s, Henry's eye had lighted on a sprightly frenchified court lady named Anne Boleyn, and he decided to seek a divorce. This time, however, the pope (Clement VII) would not cooperate, and the failure of a special papal legation to deliver the desired result in 1529 led to Cardinal Wolsey's disgrace.

From 1529 Henry pursued two different but complementary strategies to secure his freedom from Catherine and the right to marry Anne. The first was suggested by an obscure Cambridge don named Thomas Cranmer, who proposed that the theologians of Europe should be consulted on the validity of the original dispensation: if the weight of scholarly opinion was that natural law forbade such a marriage, then the Pope's dispensation was invalid and the marriage to Catherine null and void. A campaign of bribery and intimidation began to secure the desired opinion from Oxford and Cambridge, and from a selection of European faculties of theology, presumably with the ultimate aim of using these to persuade or browbeat the pope. Simultaneously, Henry and his ministers set about stirring up anti-clerical feeling in the country and squeezing the English church in every way possible so as to bring pressure on Rome, which would naturally fear that this hitherto devoutly Catholic country was about to go over to the Reformation. At this stage Henry himself remained firmly Catholic, though increasingly hostile to the pope, but Anne Boleyn held genuinely Protestant opinions and was surrounded by Protestant clients.[3] The king himself needed the help of servants favourable to reform, above all Thomas Cromwell, who gradually came to fill the vacuum left by the fall of Wolsey and the refusal of Wolsey's successor as Chancellor, Thomas More, to support the divorce. While the increasingly impatient king smouldered, Cromwell encouraged a circle of radical writers and publicists, some of whom had been in danger of arrest and execution for heresy in the 1520s but who were now given their head. Protestant books were still being banned by proclamation in 1529, and occasionally thereafter. From then on, however, anti-clerical and anti-Catholic material began to appear under official auspices, 'cum privilegio regali' [with royal protection], and a stream of measures masterminded by Cromwell and aimed against church and clergy was pushed through parliament or established by proclamation. The clergy put up only a feeble resistance, and one by one the demands of the Crown were accepted. Appeals to Rome were forbidden, and the pope's right to issue dispensations in England denied; payment of any church taxes to the papacy was outlawed, and the Convocation of the Clergy agreed to submit all ecclesiastical legislation to the Crown for approval. Thomas More, unable to accept this dismantling of the church's authority and independence, resigned the Lord Chancellorship immediately after the 'Submission of the Clergy' on 15 May 1532.[4]

By the beginning of 1533 Anne was pregnant and Henry urgently needed his divorce. The archbishop of Canterbury, William Warham, who had watched the assault on the church with growing dismay but little effective resistance, had died in August 1532. Urged on by Anne, Henry nominated as Archbishop Thomas Cranmer, a cautious but convinced Protestant with a German wife, and the pope, desperately hoping to fend off an open breach with Henry, issued the Bulls needed for his consecration. Once safely in office, Cranmer pronounced the king's first marriage invalid, and Anne, who had already been secretly married to Henry, was crowned Queen in June 1533. Early in 1534 an Act of Succession was passed, repudiating Queen Catherine, bastardising the Princess Mary, and settling the succession on the children of Henry and Anne. Every man in England over the age of 14 was required to take an oath accepting the provisions of the Act. In April, Thomas More and John Fisher, who both refused the oath, were arrested and placed in the Tower: they were to emerge only for trial and execution.

Royal commissioners were appointed all over the country to administer the oath to the adult male population. Though not exhaustive, its enforcement was thorough, and Sir Christopher and his leading parishioners would have taken a break from clearing their church for the new pews to make their way to Bampton or Tiverton sometime in the early summer of 1534 to take this oath, their first direct encounter with the changes which were about to shatter their world.

But if this was the first time that the events unfolding at court and in London had impinged on them directly, it was certainly not the first they had heard of reformation. Devon was a solidly traditionalist county, in religion like everything else. The native English heresy, Lollardy, had made almost no inroads there, and though some of the Franciscan friars in Exeter flirted briefly with the new ideas from Germany, and one of them, their Warden John Cardmaker, was eventually to die for the Protestant faith under Queen Mary, the Lutheran message found very little support in the diocese at large. Protestantism had indeed surfaced in Exeter itself in 1531 in the person of Thomas Benet, a Cambridge graduate and former priest, who had fled with his wife to the anonymity of a post as a private schoolmaster in Butcher Row in the city. The exact extent of Benet's Protestantism is not clear, but he certainly believed the pope to be antichrist, and condemned the 'false traditions' of Catholicism, in particular the veneration of the saints.[5] In October 1531 Benet, who had hitherto prudently kept his opinions quiet, took to posting bills against the pope with sealing wax on the door of the cathedral. The anonymous bill-sticker was solemnly excommunicated in a show-piece ceremony in the cathedral, at which Benet gave himself away by laughing. He was eventually arrested, tried and, after debate with Gregory Basset, one of the Exeter Franciscans who had himself briefly favoured Luther, was found guilty of heresy, and on refusing to recant, burnt at the stake by the sheriff of Devon at Livery Dole, outside the city limits. Benet's refusal to invoke the Virgin before his execution antagonised the officials and the crowd who had come to watch, and who now surged forward to throw fuel on his pyre: as the Elizabethan Protestant chronicler John Hooker commented with justifiable bitterness, 'such was the devilish rage of the blind people, that well was he or she that could catch a stick or furze to cast into the fire'.[6]

Morebath will certainly have heard news of so notable a county event as the burning of a heretic, and despite the horror of his death, Benet's hostility to the cult of the saints was not calculated to appeal to the devotees of St Sidwell. Echoes of the remoter aspects of Henry's revolution must also have reached them. Their own bishop, John Vesey, one of Henry's favourite courtiers and a skilled diplomat, was also an absentee: his responsibilities as President of the Council of Wales from 1525 to 1534 meant he was rarely in Exeter, and from 1527 his permanent residence was in his native midland town of Sutton Coldfield. After 1534 Veysey came regularly to Exeter for ordinations and visitations, and the diocese was well enough administered by his officials and archdeacons. Like most of the rest of the Henrician episcopate, however, he was to acquiesce unresistingly in every one of Henry's moves against the church. But John Clerk, the bishop of the neighbouring diocese of Bath and Wells, whose borders were less than two miles from Morebath church, was a very different character. Sir Christopher's clerical friends in Brushford and Dulverton will have been agog in December 1530 at the news of the arrest of their bishop, along with Bishops Fisher of Rochester and West of Ely, for appealing to the pope against the anticlerical legislation of the early sessions of the Reformation parliament.[7] Bishop Clerk, moreover, was the only bishop who explicitly refused his assent to the Submission of the Clergy (other opponents, including John Fisher, absented themselves from the crucial session of Convocation on 15 May 1532).[8] One of Clerk's chaplains in 1533 let slip that 'he trusted to see the day that my Lord of Canterbury should be burned', and he was almost certainly speaking his Bishop's mind as well as his own.[9] In Morebath's immediate neighbourhood, therefore, as in most of the West Country, the ethos of religious reform fashionable at the court of Queen Anne was viewed with deep suspicion, by clergy 'not inclined to the fashion of the world as it goeth now'.[10]

But whatever their reservations, slowly the king's religious policies began to impinge on them, for while John Creche carved and the ailing John Painter prepared to gild Morebath's new crucifix, Cromwell pushed on with the extension of reform measures into the parishes. The best preacher in the West Country, the radical Protestant Hugh Latimer, was sent to Exeter in June 1534 to preach the king's supremacy over the church. He preached at the church of St Mary Major on its dedication day, to the annoyance of the clergy there who grumbled that the sermon would interfere with the processions and other ceremonies. The crowd which came to hear him was so great that 'glass wyndowes were broken open for people to hear the sermon'. Hooker, the Elizabethan Protestant historian of Exeter, considered that Latimer's preaching had been much appreciated – 'the more he was heard the more he was lyked';[11] this was wishful thinking, in fact. Despite the crowds, Latimer had a hostile reception, being resisted by the Franciscans who would not let him into their church, and he was denounced by some of his hearers as a 'heretic knave' and threatened with being pulled down by the ears. Latimer had to abandon one of his sermons because of a spectacular nosebleed, which was of course gleefully hailed as the judgement of God on his heresies.[12]

In June 1535 a proclamation spelled out the implications of the abolition of 'the abuses of the Bishop of Rome, his authority and jurisdiction'. Clergy were commanded to teach the Royal Supremacy to their people, and to 'cause all manner prayers, orisons, rubrics, canons in mass books, and all other books used in the churches, wherein the said Bishop of Rome is named or his presumptuous and proud pomp and authority preferred, utterly to be abolished, eradicated and erased out, and his name and memory to be nevermore (except to his contumely and reproach) remembered'.[13] It was for just such anti-papal language that Thomas Benet had been howled down by angry Exeter citizens at his arrest four years earlier, and which had made the people eager to bring sticks to hasten his burning. Now what had been rank heresy was royal and episcopal policy. In obedience to this proclamation, Sir Christopher, like the rest of the parish clergy of England, will have been required by the bishop's official to scrape or cut the pope's name out of the Canon of the Mass in his mass-book, and to cease to bid the parish to pray for him each Sunday. The list compiled for the collection of the Pope's Pence in Morebath in the very year of Benet's arrest, was now redundant, the relic of an outlawed allegiance.[14]

We have no way of knowing what the people of Devon and of Morebath made of this royal *volte-face*. The restoration of the pope's authority was perhaps implicit in the rebels' demands in 1549,[15] but may have been included at the prompting of papally minded priests. Generally speaking, the English laity seem to have taken the shedding of papal authority in their stride, something for princes and bishops to worry about, not the man in the pew. Sir Christopher did not record his feelings about any of these changes, but given his general religious conservativism, he is unlikely to have approved. He is even less likely to have liked the innovatory clerical tax of First Fruits and Tenths introduced in 1535, and designed to create a permanent new source of royal revenue by taking one tenth of every beneficed cleric's annual income. To implement it county commissioners carried out the most thorough survey of clerical incomes ever devised, the 'Valor Ecclesiasticus', a painfully concrete expression of Henry's understanding of his Headship of the church.[16]

The following year brought further radicalisation, in the form first of the dissolution of the smaller monasteries of England, and then, in August, of a series of measures directed against 'abuses' in the practice of religion in the parishes. The Dissolution was to end in the total abolition of the monastic life in England by 1540, though to begin with Henry probably had only a partial confiscation in mind, motivated mainly by the Crown's financial need. It was not popular in the West Country. In Exeter in the summer of 1535 the women of the city rallied to the priory of St Nicholas, the first of the city's religious houses to be dissolved, and, as it happened, one noted for its charity to the poor. The enraged women, 'some with spikes, some with shovels, some with pikes, and some with such tools as they could get', trapped the workmen who had been ordered by the royal commissioners to dismantle the roodloft of the priory church. Two of these workmen were Breton carpenters, evidently Huguenots (French Protestants) who had boasted that they would pull down the crucifix 'with all the saints there, naming them to be idols'. The women stoned one of the men, who leapt from a tower to escape, breaking a rib in the process. One of the city alder-men, John Blackaller, came to the workman's aid, 'thinking what with fair words and what with foul words to have stayed and pacified the women': he too, however, was set upon by the women, who 'gave him a blow and set him packing'. In the end, they had to be dispersed by the mayor at the head of an armed posse.[17]

There was no such rallying of the local population when Barlinch was dissolved, in February 1536, and it is impossible to say how the parish viewed the disappearance of the monastic community whose prior had been their Lord of the Manor for centuries, and the patron who had appointed Sir Christopher to his post. We have no way of telling whether the monks were good or bad landlords, though Barlinch was certainly not notable for its largesse to the parish. Its total contribution to the campaign of repairs and equipping of the building in the 1520s and 1530s was the piffling sum of 3/4d donated towards covering the chancel roof, though the prior did con-tribute two out of the ten oak trees used to make the new seating in 1534, which he was not obliged to do. Their other possible contribution to Morebath's amenities, Master Juyne's school, had very probably long since closed. Barlinch's disappearance did in fact bring one concrete benefit to the parish. By 1537, the year of the clerkship dispute, the monastic buildings had been acquired by the Somerset landowner Hugh Paulet, who was disman-tling them for their materials. In a friendly gesture to mark the transfer of the lordship, the manorial bailiff, John Dysse, offered the parish one of the stained glass windows from the priory church, worth, as Sir Christopher noted, 'with the yre gere and stone and all yn valure of £3, to pray for hys M[aster] (Hu Powlyth) and him'.[18] With the help of a glazier the window was removed from the unroofed priory, loaded on to five wains, and trun-dled down to Morebath church: its installation there (towards the cost of which Paulet contributed nothing) was not completed until 1538.[19]

It is perhaps unlikely that anyone in Morebath wept bitter tears over the disappearance of their local monastery, though some, including their priest, may have shaken their heads over the attack on religious life that it repre-sented. The attitudes of the man and woman in the pew towards the Dissolution are hard to assess, and must often have been ambivalent. But Morebath's acquisition of a window from the spoil of Barlinch should not be taken as a sign of approval. In the 1560s, a generation after the Dissolution, a Yorkshire yeoman who had been part of a syndicate which had bought up the timber and bells from the steeple of Roche Abbey was asked by his son 'whether he thought well of the religious persons and the religion that was then used'. When he replied that he had indeed thought well of the monks, having had no occasion to think otherwise, his son asked 'then how came it to pass you was so ready to destroy and spoil the thing you thought well of? What could I do, said He: might I not as well as others have some profit of the Spoil of the Abbey? For I did see all would away: and therefore I did as others did.'[20]

The reform measures of August 1536 touched parish life more closely, and were the clearest sign so far of the extent of the revolution represented by the Royal Supremacy. Henry had appointed Thomas Cromwell, a layman, his 'Vicegerent in spirituals', effectively chief executive of the Church. To the scandal of religious conservatives, Cromwell presided in Convocation, and the bishops found themselves subordinated to him. The Supremacy was now used to implement rationalising reforms of religious observance which struck at the heart of traditional religion. On 11 August Cromwell promulgated an act of Convocation abolishing all the holy days which fell in the Westminster law terms or during the harvest period from the beginning of July to the end of September, with the exceptions of the feasts of the Virgin and the Apostles, St George's Day, the nativity of St John the Baptist and All Saints Day. The abolished days, it was claimed, had been damaging to the country's economy, stopping vital work and impoverishing workers. Services might still be held on the abrogated days, but people were to go to work as usual, and the services were not to be solemnly rung, nor announced as days of obligation to the people beforehand.

This was a potentially explosive measure, which caused very widespread discontent throughout England. At a stroke, the act abolished or demoted most of the major regional festivals, many of which were the most important social events as well as religious celebrations of the year, focuses of local religious feeling and regional pride, and the occasions for fairs and markets crucial to local economies.[21] Cromwell went on to issue a set of injunctions requiring the clergy to preach the Supremacy, and to expound the recently approved 'Ten Articles'(a mildly Protestant formulary of faith agreed in Convocation). The injunctions also required parents and employers to catechise their children and servants on the Lord's Prayer, Creed and Ten Commandments in English rather than the traditional Latin, insisted on strict compliance with the act for abrogation of the feast days, and attacked the alleged superstitions surrounding the cult of pilgrimage and images, declaring that 'it shall profit more their soul's health, if they do bestow that on the poor and needy, which they would have bestowed upon the said images or relics'. Every parson or rector of a church was to provide a bible in Latin and English, to be placed in the church for anyone who wished to read.[22]

Once again, Sir Christopher's attitude to these measures was probably ambivalent. He was himself decently educated and, as his account book amply demonstrates, the hortatory mode came naturally to him. He is likely to have taken seriously the injunction to catechise the young people of Morebath. In the Elizabethan period, his bishop would note both his learning and his conscientious preaching, a rarity in that part of Devon at any point in the sixteenth century.[23] But he must certainly have looked askance at most of the other injunctions, which agitated conservative laity and clergy everywhere. Resentment was strongest in the north of England, where official endorsement of what had formerly been considered heresy was perceived as a prelude to an attack on the religion of the parishes. In October 1536 this discontent crystallised into the protest movement known as the Pilgrimage of Grace, which spread through much of northern and north-western England, an open rebellion that came close to toppling the Tudor monarchy before it was suppressed in the spring of 1537.[24] The very self-description of the protest, as a 'Pilgrimage of Grace for the Commonwealth', was a challenge to the hostility to pilgrimage and the cult of the saints enacted in the Royal Injunctions and elaborated in the propaganda emanating from Cromwell's circle. So one of the Pilgrim ballads prayed:

> Christ crucifyd!
> For they woundes wide
> Us commens guyde!
> Which pilgremes be
> Thru godes grace,
> For to purchace
> Olde welth and peax
> Of the Spiritualtie.[25]

The 'Pontefract articles' containing the rebels' demands called for the acknowledgement of the pope's supremacy in spirituals, the restoration of the monasteries, the abolition of first-fruits and tenths, a campaign to 'annul and destroy' the heresies of Luther and others, and the punishment of Cromwell as chief of the 'maynteners of the false sect of those heretiques and the first inventors and bryngands in of them'.[26]

There was a great deal of popular support for the cause of the 'Northern men' throughout England,[27] and not least in the West Country. Cromwell's monastic visitors for Cornwall reported widespread anger there about the suppression of local feastdays, and in April 1537 alarming reports came of a banner of the Five Wounds of Jesus, like those carried by the rebels in the Pilgrimage of Grace, which had been commissioned at St Keverne parish in Cornwall. It portrayed the people kneeling 'making this petition to the picture of Christ that it would please the King's grace that they might have their holydays'. And all this came close to Morebath too, for in the same month, Sir Thomas Denys, the sheriff of Devon who had presided at the burning of Thomas Benet, reported that rumours about the activities of the 'Northern Men' were rife in the Tiverton area.[28]

The summer of 1537 brought a new Protestant champion to the region in the person of the able but combative Dr Simon Heynes, the new Dean of the cathedral. Heynes was President of Queens' College, Cambridge, and a former vice-chancellor of the University. He was a vigorous and effective anti-papal preacher, well thought of at court, and in 1538 was to be sent by the king on an embassy to Charles V. He was also a convinced and eager reformer, whose appointment over the head of a popular local candidate ensured him a frosty reception in Exeter from the bishop downwards. Not in the least intimidated, Heynes at once set about antagonising his colleagues in the cathedral chapter by his blatant lack of respect for tradition and his ill-concealed contempt for their reactionary rejection of the 'new learning' of the Reformation. In part their dislike of him was rooted in the realisation that his appointment posed a threat to the cathedral itself. Like many Tudor Protestants, Heynes disapproved of the waste and superstition he thought implicit in the elaborate liturgical splendours of cathedral worship. He therefore proposed to the king a radical reduction of the cathedral staff, and the replacement of the dean and chapter by a college composed of a pastor and twelve preachers, all graduates in theology, who would expound the gospel in the cathedral and round the diocese: he wanted some of the cathedral resources ploughed into an almshouse for twenty-four old soldiers, a free grammar school and a song-school.[29]

Heynes was particularly dismayed by the backwardness of the cathedral chapter and the Devon clergy at large. He found the canons had utterly ignored the Injunctions of 1536, of which there was no copy to be found in the cathedral, and he reported to Cromwell that 'if I had them (it was said) … they imported nothing else but that we should do as we have done in times past, and live after the old fashion'. The people of Exeter, he told Cromwell 'I like … very well', but not the clergy: 'as far as I have yet seen, the priests of this country are a strange kind, very few of them well-persuaded or anything learned.' Behind this religious inertia he detected a general resistance to royal policy: Devon was 'a perilous country, for God's love let the King's grace look to it in time'.[30] And Heynes's reforming zeal was directed especially at the sort of observances which lay at the heart of the piety of Morebath. Among the aspects of traditional Catholicism which he most detested was the cult of images. In the course of a wide-ranging memorandum on reform composed in 1537, Heynes asked with particular urgency:

> If it may appear that the common people have a greater affiance or trust in outward rites or ceremonies than they ought to have, and that they esteem more virtue in images and adorning of them, kissing their feet or offering candles unto them, than they ought to esteem, and that yet the curates knowing the same, and fearing the loss of their offerings, do rather encour-

age the people to continue after this sort, than teach them the truth in the premises according to Scripture; what the king's highness and his parliament may do, and what they are bound in conscience to do, in such a case?[31]

Heynes's question, what the king was obliged in conscience to do to suppress the cult of the saints, was symptomatic of the agenda of both Cranmer and Cromwell and of the ascendant reform party at Court, with whom he was in close touch. They were clear that the flow of royal reform had now set definitively against what Cranmer called the 'phantasy of ceremonies, pilgrimage, purgatory, saints, images, works and such like, as hath these three or four hundred years been corruptly taught'.[32] The dismantling of shrines and pilgrimage sites therefore progressed through 1537 and the early part of 1538, and there were a series of elaborate ceremonies in London in which notable images were publicly 'humiliated' and burned.[33]

Morebath's bishop, Vesey of Exeter, was certainly no Protestant – he was still granting indulgences to the laity of his diocese for contributions to pious works as late as Christmas Day 1536, a fact which suggests not only an unblinkingly conservative understanding of Christianity, but also a certain lack of grip on the direction of official religious policy.[34] Nevertheless, in May 1538 Vesey too issued a set of injunctions for the diocese of Exeter, somewhat belatedly designed to endorse and enforce the royal injunctions of 1536 in the West Country. Accordingly, Vesey's document was partly aimed at specific abuses like the drunken all-night wakes held after funerals in Cornwall, but was mainly concerned with the local implementation of the more generally applicable provisions of the 1536 injunctions. Vesey therefore required his clergy to preach regularly in favour of the Royal Supremacy and 'to utterly abolish and extirpe the usurped power of the bishop of Rome'. His treatment of the cult of images was brief but emphatic in its claim that 'many of the unlearned people of my diocese have been much blinded, following many times their own superstitious fantasies': from now on the standard of teaching about images was to be the exposition of the Second Commandment (against worship of images) contained in the recently published 'Institution of a Christian Man', an official formulation of the Church of England's faith known as the 'Bishops' Book'.[35] Vesey here was acting in concert with the other bishops, but the requirement that the Bishops' Book become the standard of teaching on images was in fact a move in a decidedly Protestant direction. Though traditionalist bishops like Stokesley of London and Tunstall of Durham had a hand in its production, on this issue the Bishops' Book adopted a sternly reformed position, insisting that 'we be utterly forbidden to make or have any similitude or image, to the intent to bow down to it or worship it', and grudgingly allowing the existence of statues and pictures in church only as a regrettable concession to the dullness of men's wits and the persistence of 'gentility' or paganism within popular Christianity.[36]

The progress of reform can be measured by the fact that all the bishops, even so unreconstructed an establishment conservative as Vesey, found themselves obliged to enforce so dramatic a break with traditional pieties. Conservatives everywhere reacted to all this with outrage, and traditionalist clergy used the pulpit to advocate resistance to the new religious mood. The vicar of Tysehurst in Essex urged his parishioners to continue in the old ways, offering candles to St Loy for their horses and to St Antony for their pigs and cattle: the spirit of reformation and its emphasis on the bible 'is but trick and go, Lightly it came and lightly it will begone again'. Morebath, where candles burned still before the newly gilded statues of Loy and Anthony, would have cheered.[37] In September 1538, however, Cromwell swept aside conservative resentments by issuing his second set of royal injunctions, the most radical exercise of the Supremacy to date, and a further sharp move leftward for the English Reformation. Some of these injunctions essentially reiterated or strengthened the provisions of the royal injunctions of 1536, for example prescribing detailed regulations for regular catechising and examination of the laity in the fundamentals of the faith, and enjoining strict conformity to the royal abrogation of feast days. But the injunctions also included much that was new, requiring clergy and parishioners between them to provide and set up publicly in church 'one whole book of the whole bible of the largest volume', the newly approved 'Great Bible', which was not in fact published until the following year, and warning clergy to exhort the laity to read it. From now on also every incumbent was to maintain a register of weddings, christenings and burials. To keep this register-book safe, the parish was to provide a coffer with two locks and keys, one to be held by the wardens and the other by the priest, and the priest was to fill in the register every week in the presence of the wardens.

The most radical aspect of the new injunctions, however, was the heightened ferocity of their language against the cult of images. All parish clergy were now instructed to preach a sermon at least once a quarter declaring 'the very Gospel of Christ', in which they were to exhort their people to works of charity, mercy and faith prescribed in Scripture, 'and not to repose their trust and affiance in any other works devised by men's phantasies, besides Scripture; as in wandering to pilgrimages, offering of money, candles, or tapers to images or relics, or kissing or licking the same, saying over a number of beads, not understood or minded on, or in such-like superstition'. If there were in any church any 'feigned images' which had been abused in this way 'with pilgrimages or offerings of anything made therunto ... ye shall, for avoiding that most detestable sin of idolatry, forthwith take down and delay, and shall suffer from henceforth no candles, tapers or picture but only the light that commonly goeth across the church by the rood loft, the light before the sacrament of the altar, and the light about the sepulchre, which for the adorning of the church and divine service ye shall suffer to remain'.[38]

These directives against images were so many arrows aimed at the heart of Sir Christopher Trychay. Since his arrival in Morebath, he had coaxed the pieties of the parish into precisely those expresssions of the cult of the saints which the injunctions now denounced as 'mens phantasies', contrary to Scripture. Twenty years of pious investment and communal effort – Margery Lake's and Jekyn at Moore's altar cloths and basins, Joan Hillyer of Bampton's candlestick trimmed with flowers before St Sidwell, Elenor Nicoll's silver shoe and the beads donated to Our Lady and St Sidwell by Joan Rumbelow, Joan Hukeley, Alison Zaer and Richard Oblye, the hives of bees donated by William Potter and by the priest's own mother and father, not to mention the endless programme of renovation and maintenance of lights and statues – all those tokens of the tenderness and hope which Morebath had invested in its saints were now expressly declared unchristian, and placed outside the law. The compilers of the injunctions, moreover, clearly had priests like Sir Christopher firmly in their sights, and were determined that they should eat humble pie for their ignorance and blindness. Injunction ten insisted that:

> If ye have heretofore declared to your parishioners anything to the exalting or setting forth ... of images, or any such superstition, ye shall now openly afore the same recant and reprove the same, shewing them (as the truth is) that ye did the same upon no ground of scripture, but as one that being led and seduced by a common error and abuse crept into the church, through the sufferance and avarice of such as felt profit by the same.[39]

The injunctions were to become a battleground between reformers and their opponents. Conservatives argued that they merely banned abuse: images might remain as laymen's books, provided no pilgrimage was made to them nor candles burned before them. Only notorious images like those at the centre of shrines need be removed, and the conservative archbishop of York was careful to say that such images should merely be 'deposed and sequestered from the sight of man', which might mean no more than storing them safely in a cupboard, and a long way short of the burning or breaking which Protestants felt was the proper fate of graven idols, and which the use of the word 'delay' in the injunctions was probably intended to imply. Evangelicals like Archbishop Cranmer and Bishop Shaxton of Salisbury, by contrast, used the injunctions as an excuse for a wholesale assault on all images, and Cranmer antagonised the monks of Canterbury by removing and destroying statues which they claimed had never been 'abused' with pilgrimage or cult.[40]

These disputes were replicated in Devon, where Dean Heynes, armed with the injunctions, set zealously about cleansing his cathedral and the city from the sin of idolatry. According to his enemies he caused 20 marks worth of damage (£13/6/8d) to the choir books of the cathedral in his zeal to remove all mention of the pope and of St Thomas Becket, he deposed the image of Christ which dominated the exterior of the church of St Mary Major, and he destroyed handsome images in the Cathedral which the angry canons claimed had never been superstitiously abused. He rooted up £40 worth of brass and iron memorials (which presumably had images of saints) and stripped of its brass and inscriptions the tomb of Edmund Lacy, a medieval bishop of Exeter locally venerated as a saint, round whose burial-place pilgrims had left many wax votive offerings in gratitude for healings. He went beyond the injunctions too in extinguishing the light before the Blessed Sacrament, which at Exeter the Dean had traditionally paid for, and which the injunctions had explicitly commanded should be allowed to continue.[41] Nor was Heynes's radical action confined to the cathedral. He was appointed by Cromwell one of the Royal Commissioners charged with enforcing the injunctions in the diocese of Exeter, and in the spring of 1539 gained further weight as a member of the Council of the West under Lord Russell. Unsurprisingly he found himself 'marvelous hated and maligned at' as he set about carrying his unpopular campaign against the idols into the parishes.[42]

Morebath must have been one of the first communities in the West Country to be affected by these moves; indeed, mysteriously, their impact was felt there even before the injunctions were in the public domain. Cromwell had the text of the injunctions in something like their final form by the beginning of September 1538 – a note on the draft says that they were 'exhibited' on 5 September, which may be the date on which he showed them to the king in Kent, though it is hard to be sure. They were sent to Archbishop Cranmer on 30 September 1538, and the Archbishop issued his mandate for their publication on 11 October.[43] Almost a month earlier, however, on Sunday 15 September, Sir Christopher had presented the annual accounts of St Anthony's store and Our Lady's store to the parish, with the usual elaborate sheep-count: it is plain from both accounts that Morebath had already been informed about the content of the injunctions, and had begun a damage limitation exercise in response to them.

We can be sure of this because both accounts reveal that for the first time ever, the lights in front of the images of Morebath church had been extinguished, and the devotional ornaments hung about Our Lady's statue had been stripped away. Up until 1538, Saint Anthony's wardens invariably report their chief expense for each year as being 'for wex for the hole ere and for makyn be fore Sent Antoni'.[44] The maintenance of the light was of course the principal *raison d'être* of this and all the other stores. In this September account of 1538, however, John Smyth and Richard Raw reported that 'for wex and wyk and makyn for the hole ere' they had spent 'nil'.[45] This does not mean that there had been no light before St Anthony all that year. The wardens of the stores normally bought the new year's supply of wax shortly before the accounting date, when all their receipts were in: what we learn here, therefore, is that no new candles had been bought that September for the coming year, 1538–9. In the same way, John Tayler and Thomas Rumbelow, Our Lady's wardens, reported that they too had spent nothing 'for the makyn of the taper a fore our Lady and wyke and wex for this ere'.[46] They also reported that the beads of coral and silver presented by Katherine Robbyns to Our Lady's statue had been sold for 4/10d, and bought by Christian, the wife of Katherine's executor and residuary legatee, John Tutlake. 'Tutlackis wyffe' had evidently long coveted 'our Lady's bedis', and now she had them. The money from the sale of the beads was given to Harry Hurley in trust for the black vestments 'and so to have ... Kateryn Robyns [name] in these vestmentis for the gefth'.[47]

There can be no question that these moves, the reversal of the whole direction of Morebath's devotional activity over the previous eighteen years, can only have been a response to the Injunctions' prohibition of lights before images, and their further attack on the 'saying over of a number of beads'. But how did the parishioners of Morebath know what had yet to be formally published by Cranmer and his suffragans, and why did they act so promptly on them? The date of the account, 15 September 1538, almost a month before the promulgation of the Injunctions, is not in doubt, for on 9 March 1539 the Four Men referred back to this account as having been presented 'at Rowdemas', that is, around the feast of the Exaltation of the Holy Cross, which falls on 14 September.[48] There is only one plausible explanation, and that is that Dean Heynes, whose 1537 memorandum on reform had so vehemently targeted the popular cult of images, and who was a trusted lieutenant of Cranmer and Cromwell, must have had a hand in the drafting and finalising of the 1538 Injunctions, or at any rate have been aware of their contents. If so, he must then have hurried back to Devon in the first or second week of September, armed with an as yet unpromulgated reforming instrument for the rooting out of 'idolatry': the ink can scarcely have been dry before they were imposed on Morebath.

The probability that the extinguishing of the lights of Morebath church in September 1538 represents some limited initiative against the cult of the saints by Dean Heynes is strengthened when we consider the High Wardens' account read to the parish on 24 November 1538.[49] This account, made in the name of the wardens Thomas Norman and Richard Hukeley, barely registers the currents of reform which were stirring the diocese and the whole of England that winter. The wardens busy themselves with routine expenditure – the money owed to the plumber for maintenance work 'to a mend all fawtis a pon the church', to Chylcote and his man for work on the bells, to John Creche for washing the tabernacles. There are no expenses whatever in implementation of the positive provisions of the Injunctions – the buying of the bible or the register book and its coffer, for example. But the specifically negative aspect of the Injunctions, their attack on the cult of the saints, is registered. The wardens make a final report on the sheep of St Sidwell and of Jesus 'that the hye wardyng ys charged with all a fore this', but also note that 'ys for the wolle of the store of Jhesu and of Sent Sydwyll ... our Wardyn of the churche scheppe schall make a reconyng son at hys a cownte'. Our Lady's sheep, St Sidwell's sheep, and all the sheep of the other stores are from henceforth 'the church sheep', and this demotion of the saints as proprieters of the animals whose wool maintained their lights is the only aspect of the 1538 injunctions to have been absorbed by the end of the year. In the main body of the account, the priest busily pursues projects for the adornment of the altars and images inaugurated in previous years: the implications of the attack on images have clearly not yet fully dawned on him. So he upbraids parishioners who have not yet honoured promises made in previous years for donations to pay for paintings around the church's altars, painting which may have included scenes from the life and legends of Sidwell and George, but which at any rate were now destined never to be completed. John Waters had promised to complete his wife's bequest to the adornment of St Sidwell's altar, 'to this yntent to have hys wyfe ys name a pon the church boke to be prayd for every Palme Sonday ut ceter', and William Timewell at Wood had promised to pay for the painting of the ceiling over the high altar: so the priest reminds them testily,

> Item John Waterus remember yor promysse to the syde auter as ys expressyd the ere be fore a pon Harry Hurlys cownte.
> Item Willam at Wode remember your paynter for the hye auter in yor v^s [5/=] a cordyng to you promysse of the laste ere a pon Harry Hurlys a cownte.[50]

> *Item John Waters remember your promise to the side altar as is expressed the year before upon Harry Hurley's account.*
> *Item, William at Wood remember your painter for the high altar in your 5/= according to your promise of the last year, upon Harry Hurley's account.*

In early Tudor England the year ran not from 1 January to 31 December, but from 25 March to 24 March of the year following. The last accounts of the year 1538, therefore, were made on Sunday 9 March 1539, when the Maiden Wardens, the warden of St Sunday, and the Four Men presented their reports to the parish. The Maiden account once more reveals the new situation: the usual gathering is simply 'of devocion', not as the account routinely stated 'of devocion to Our Laydy lyght': they are said to have spent their money not, as previously, 'for the taper be fore our Lady and a nother a fore the hye crosse and a nother a fore sent Sydwyll', but merely on 'wex and wyk and makyn for the hole ere (with the taper a fore the hye crosse)'.[51] John Norman presented his account for the store of St Sunday: alone of all the stores, he was still spending money on wax before a statue. Possibly the account was in arrear, or possibly the fact that St Sunday was a figure of Christ, not an ordinary saint, meant that the parish had not been clear whether the provisions of the injunctions applied here also. By the time his account was presented, however, they knew that this lamp too must be extinguished. St Sunday's store was wound up, and noting that the store was 6/1d in credit, the priest added that,

> for this mony the iiij men schall cownt here after and our lady wardyn schall cownte for these scheppe and all wother scheppe concernyng the churche in future.
> Not[e]: Lett all the churche scheppe in future be put yn our Lady merke full what store so ever they be of.[52]

> *for this money the Four Men shall account hereafter and Our Lady's Warden shall account for these sheep and all other sheep concerning the church in future.*
> *Note: Let all the church sheep in future be put in Our Lady's mark, full what store soever they be of.*

It is however in the account of the Four Men, presented the same day, that the full impact of the 1538 Injunctions is to be seen. Much of the account was concerned with the never-ending process of repair and renewal of the building – the last payments to Creche for the work on the High Cross and the scaffolding that had required, the complete retiling of the church floor, with all the expenses involved in quarrying and carrying and dressing and laying of stone, the installation or repair of several windows including the one 'by the figar of Jhesu', the repair of the church house. But the Four Men had also paid out for the systematic equipping of the church in accordance with the injunctions: they spent 13/4d on 'the churche boke callyd the bybyll', and paid 16d for its carriage from Exeter. The string and canvas wrapping in which the book came was thriftily sold again. This was Cranmer's Great Bible 'of the largest volume', but they also paid three shillings for 'the boke of the new testament in inglis and yn latyn … the wyche we ware cumawndyd to by at Mychelmas laste paste by the kynggis injuncion', actually stipulated in the 1536 not the 1538 Injunctions, but which Vesey had only recently reminded his clergy they must provide. They paid 12d for 'a boke to wrytt there namys yn that be crystenyd and wedded or buryed a cordyng to the kynggis injuncions'. They bought six boards for 14d 'to make our churche coffer with all', to keep the register book in, bought nails and hinges for it for 10d, they paid Lousemore and his man 12d to make up the coffer, and paid Stebbe 18d for setting in the two locks required by the injunctions.[53]

Morebath's obedience in all this was strikingly prompt. Many Devon parishes dragged their feet over one aspect or another of the 1538 Injunctions. Bishop Vesey complained bitterly in October 1539 of the persistence in the diocese of the celebration of abrogated feastdays and of 'superstitious' observances surrounding the cult of the saints, for example the refusal of carters and smiths to work on the feast of St Loy.[34] The positive reform provisions of the Injunctions were also widely ignored, with many parishes making no attempt to provide an English bible. The villages of Camborne and Stratton, and even the large and bustling town of Ashburton, did not acquire their copies of the Great Bible until 1541, and probably only then under pressure from a Royal Proclamation of 6 May that year, which threatened the 'many towns and parishes within this realm' which have 'negligently omitted their duties' with a fine of 40/= for every month they were without the Bible after the feast of All Saints.[55]

By contrast, from mid-September 1538 Morebath seems obediently and completely to have abandoned the active promotion of the cult of the saints which had hitherto been the most striking feature of its devotional life, and in the year that followed the parish dutifully equipped itself with all the books and other items required by the Injunctions. The accounts for 1539 reveal the systematic working out of the implications of the Injunctions, and the drastic modification of the parish's internal structures to accommodate itself to them. This involved the disappearance of most of Morebath's stores, and the alteration of those that remained so that they could not be accused of illegality. The first casualty of this process had been the absorption of the sheep of the stores of Sidwell, Jesus and St Sunday into a single church flock administered by Our Lady's wardens: after their last accounts in 1538, all these stores simply disappeared. The Alms Light, the candle burned before the High Cross in memory of the parish dead, particularly the impoverished dead who had no other memorial, was abolished on 18 May 1539, when its last warden, the widow Joan Goodman, paid 19d for the previous year's wax and handed the 2/8d that remained in the stock to the Three Men to help to pay for a theologically unexceptional project, the purchase of a new cope.[56] The next to go was St Anthony's store, whose wardens accounted for the last time on 21 September, reporting that they had spent nothing that year, indicating the extinguishing of St Anthony's light. Once again the wardens handed over all the funds remaining in the stock to the Three Men, and the Vicar noted 'and sic [thus] ys this store dyschargyd'.[57]

Two of the three stores that remained, the Young Men and the Maidens, were not of course dedicated to any saint, but even they were modified to remove any reference to the cult of the saints. The Young Men had maintained three lights, two tapers before the High Cross and one before St George: in 1539 they paid only for two tapers before the cross: from the following year they resumed payment for three tapers, but all now before the cross.[58] The Maidens had also maintained three tapers, before St Sidwell, Our Lady, and the High Cross: they now switched their main provision to the Sepulchre light in honour of the Blessed Sacrament at Easter, and to maintaining two tapers before the High Cross, like the Young Men.[59] But this deliberate process of adaptation was at its most explicit in the store of Our Lady, dedicated of course to the chief of all saints, the Virgin Mary, but too central in the parish's financial and spiritual economy simply to be abolished. Instead, it was secularised by the removal of Our Lady's patronage. The Wardens for 1539, William Leddon and Robert at Hayne, accounted to the parish on Sunday 26 October. The priest headed the transcript in the book 'Our Ladis store' as usual, and duly wrote out, for the last time, the internally rhymed devotional hexameter with which he always began Our Lady's account: '*Auxilium nos fer pia nunc Sancta Virgo Maria*', [bring us help now, o tender Blessed Virgin Mary]. He immediately signalled the new situation, however, by adding 'et deinceps sent iorge', literally 'and next, St George', but in this context implying rather *deinde*, 'from now on', a momentous transfer of patronage from the Virgin to the parish saint, and the symbolic equivalent of the transition from 'Our Lady's sheep' to 'the church sheep'.[60] That transition was spelled out in the heading which named the wardens 'beyng wardyns of the churche scheppe (quod in praeteritis esset de stanzo beate marie)' [which (were) formerly of the store of the blessed Mary].

The High Wardens' accounts for that year, presented to the parish on 2 November, reflect the same process of adaptation, reminding the parishioners 'that ys for the scheppe of the store of Jhesu and of Sent Sydwyll the Wardyns of the churche scheppe doth answer for', and redirecting benefactions which had been earmarked for now outlawed and therefore abandoned projects, like the paintings for St Sidwell's altar. The purchase of a new cope had become the central parish project, alongside the slowly growing Black Vestment fund, and all the benefactions of that year, whatever their original object, were channelled into one or other of these two funds. So the priest told the parish that although 'Waterus promysse to the syde auter ys all loste and gon', yet 'ys for Richard Webber for the bequest of hys son John towardes our cope the 4 Men schall answer for a pon there a cownte ij^s [2/=] the wyche he had thofth [thought] to bestow hyt a pon the payntyyng of the syde auter'.[61] We can measure the extent of Sir Christopher's deliberation, in the apparently innocent reiterated phrase 'the syde auter' here, which had first made its appearance in the accounts of the previous year. Behind its use lies not merely caution but a deafening silence, for this of course was the altar on which he had placed the gilded image of his beloved St Sidwell, on which his parishioners and family had lavished their devotional giving, and which largely by his agency over the previous twenty years had been transformed from 'the altar of Jhesu' into 'Sent Sydwyll's auter'. What he thought of the retrospective outlawing and disparagement of so much that had seemed tender and important to him and his people, we can only guess. His carefully neutral phrase 'the syde auter' certainly reflected no instantaneous conversion to reformed views, but he was not to speak publicly of St Sidwell before the parish, except to record the sale of her altar's ornaments,[62] for another fifteen years.

We can be quite sure that Sir Christopher had not lost his belief in the intercession of the saints. The final account of each of the stores is headed with the usual pious invocation of the patron, and for the rest of Henry's reign, the priest would go on writing at the head of each year's High Wardens' accounts 'Sancte Iorge ora pro nobis' [St George pray for us].[63] Over the next two years he was to display some of his old enthusiasm for new projects in encouraging bequests to pay William Hurley 'the next tyme that he goeth to London' to buy 'a banner of sylke of sent iorge', which he expected the parish at large to underwrite – 'and yff yt coste more mony ye must be content to ley more to hyt and yff hyt coste lesse ye schall have that ys lefte'.[64] This new banner was itself an intriguing monument to the priest's cautious exploration of the geography of the new devotional landscape after the passing of the royal bulldozer of the 1538 Injunctions – the banner was needed presumably because the existing parish banner had an image of St Sidwell on one side in addition to that of St George on the other.[65] As his invocations at the head of the High Wardens' account each year show, Sir Christopher clearly thought pious deference towards the parish patron was still permitted, even if overt demonstrations of devotion to other saints were not.

Yet precisely because it is clear that Sir Christopher remained a firm believer in the intercession of the saints, the extent and promptness of Morebath's conformity to the letter of the 1538 Injunctions becomes all the more striking. Elsewhere in Devon many parishes made no such wholesale attempts at accommodation. Though the lights were almost certainly extinguished before all the statues in the county within a year or two of their outlawing, in many communities the stores founded to maintain those lights went on functioning, their resources now being channelled into the general needs of the parish. The stores of Our Lady, St Julian and the High Cross were all still functioning at Ashburton in 1546, the stores of St Catherine, St Michael and the High Cross at Chagford till at least the same year, the stores of St Peter, Holy Rood and the High Cross were still operating at Broadhempston in 1547, the stores of Our Lady and St John survived at Woodland as late as 1549, and at South Tawton the stores of Jhesu, St Mary, St George and St Andrew were operating into the early 1550s.[66] These examples all come from the south of the county, and there may have been local differences in the process of visitation and enforcement. At Morebath there is another possible hint of externally imposed compliance. In 1539, the year of all these other major realignments in the parish's piety, the wardens sold off the rood loft cloth, presumably the cloth used to veil the images on the roodloft in Lent.[67] The ceremonies of Lent and Holy Week in which this cloth was used remained part of the official worship of the English church for the remainder of Henry's reign, and went on being celebrated everywhere. If the disposal of the cloth at Morebath was connected to the implementation of the Injunctions, therefore, which is by no means certain, it must have been because it was decorated in a way which was thought to infringe them. It was common for such cloths to have texts painted on them as well as images, and the Morebath cloth may have been painted or embroidered with lines in praise of the saints, or from one of the liturgical hymns in honour of the cross used in Holy Week, such as the Vexilla Regis. This hymn in praise of the image of the cross would certainly have been considered a manifestation of superstitious cult by a zealot like Heynes, who had used the Injunctions as his warrant for ripping funeral brasses out of the floor of Exeter cathedral, precisely because they had images or inscriptions honouring the saints.

But all this is speculation. Though the parish's pre-emptive extinguishing of the tapers before its saints in September 1538 strongly suggests some such intervention by Heynes or one of his associates, indeed is hard to explain on any other hypothesis, we cannot be sure that Morebath was in fact under greater pressure than any other north Devon parish. And the subsequent prompt and wholesale character of its compliance may well lie not in outside interference but in the priest's habitual punctilious and clear-sighted attention to detail and in the parish's equally habitual law-abidingness. Both were to be sorely tried in the years ahead.

Whatever their source, the attempt to establish some sort of normality in the wake of the Injunctions and the drastic reduction of Morebath's stores was only partially successful. The Maidens could now in theory continue to organise 'the getheryng of the sepulture lyghth with wother lyghth a fore the hye crosse', but this activity was now without any intrinsic devotional rationale. There had been an obvious symbolic congruence in the gathering of the girls of Morebath 'of devotion' to provide lights before virginal patrons like Our Lady and St Sidwell: by contrast, the allocation of responsibility for the sepulchre light to them was purely arbitrary, and it did not work. Free-will offerings to the Maiden store dry up, leaving only meagre obligatory contributions to a parish expense. The Maiden's annual collection 'of devocion' had raised 7/6d on average through the 1530s.[68] In stark contrast, the Maiden Wardens raised just 22d in 1540 for the sepulchre light, and only a miserable 2d 'of devocion'. The following year they raised a mere 16d for the sepulchre light, but nothing at all 'of devocion', and the parish faced facts by appointing no new wardens for the following year.[69] The store was wound up, part of its small stock being handed over to help pay for a streamer of silk for use in parish processions, the remainder of the gathering for the sepulchre money being put aside to relieve the needs of a poor woman, Margaret Isak.[70]

This petering out of the Maiden store, not with a bang but a whimper, is symptomatic of a process of cooling and disenchantment within the devotional life of Morebath in the remaining years of Henry's reign. With the extinguishing of the lights and the abandonment of the patronage of the saints over the two remaining stores, a dimension of warmth and humanity evident in the accounts up to that point, fades a little. The statues of the saints remained in their tabernacles and were decently maintained, for through the early 1540s John Creche was paid 8d a year 'for clensyng of the imagery of the churche', a task for which in 1542 he was offered payment in kind, in the form of the old statues of Mary and John from the High Cross which had been replaced in 1538 (he declined the offer and took cash).[71] But with the ending of their cult, the offering to the images of candles and flowers, the gifts of beads and kerchiefs and wedding-rings, they had dwindled from presences to not much more than furniture. The very phrase, 'the imagery of the churche', at one level of course simply a convenient collective abstraction, is itself a measure of that process of disenchantment. The images recede, paraphernalia to be referred to in bulk, not loved individuals invoked by name, as they routinely were when in the 1520s and 30s workmen had been paid for 'settyng yn of a borde about Jhesu', 'for the new gyltyng of sent Sydwyll', 'to sett up the canstyck a fore sent iorge and a nother a fore sent sonday', 'for the gyltyng of sent loy', 'for dressyng of the stondyng of Sent Anne'.[72] With the injunctions of 1538, the images lose not only their power to charm or comfort, but even their names.

And as with the images, so with the people. For now an extraordinary change comes over the accounts in Sir Christopher's book. With the single exception of the Maiden Wardens' accounts, he had to this point invariably presented the accounts of all the stores of Morebath, as well as those of the High Wardens and the Four Men, in the person of the accounting warden. Each of the accounts, therefore, was an exercise in symbolic ventriloquism in which the priest, whose distinctive tone of voice is never for a moment in abeyance, and who certainly read the accounts aloud on the wardens' behalf, nevertheless effaces himself within the phrasing of the accounts themselves in order to allow the wardens to seem to speak in their own right. 'Item we ressevyd of the wolde wardyns ye laste ere at the begynnyng of our a cownte … ij^s ij^d [2/2d]' … 'Memorandum that y William at Pole ressevyd at the begynning of my wardynscheppe of the wolde wardyns xxij^s j^d ob [22/1½d]'…. 'I Thomas Rumbelow have ressevyd ….'[73]

From 1540 onwards, however, all the accounts are presented in the third person: 'yn the begynning of *there* ere *they* ressevyd of the wolde Wardyns xiij^s & x^d [13/4d] Item *they* made frely of there ale all cost quytte lvs & vjd ob [55/6½d].'[74] It is hard to put one's finger on the exact significance of this shift, and there is a danger of reading too much into it. At one level, certainly, nothing much had happened, since Sir Christopher had been no less responsible for the drafting and presentation of the old accounts than he was for the new, in which his authorship is more frankly acknowledged. Yet his parishioners must have been acutely conscious of it, and it can hardly be doubted that the change is somehow related to the upheavals which had flowed from the Injunction of 1538, or that the shift in phrasing reflects some subtler shift in relationships. To put the matter at its lowest, far fewer parishioners in Morebath now shouldered responsibility for the community's affairs. The number of those elected annually to office and responsibility in the parish had dwindled from twelve to six, and there were no longer any girls or young women among them. That meant fewer chores, but also fewer opportunities for influence, and a narrowing of the number of those in charge of parish business. It is as if with the disappearance of the stores and the receding of the saints, the community of the parish also reconfigured itself, and was less broadly and less personally conceived.

From 1540, however, the pressure for religious change in the country at large and in Devon in particular, eased, as conservative influences gained the King's ear at court. Henry, having taken as his fifth queen the voluptuous Catherine Howard, a member of one of the most conservative of aristocratic clans, distanced himself from the evangelical cause. Morebath continued its careful conformity, replacing its first version of the Great Bible in 1542 with a grander copy, bound with bosses to protect its cover as it lay, available for public reading, chained to its desk in the church.[75] Yet the passage of the Act of Six Articles in the summer of 1539, with its reaffirmation of the doctrine of transubstantiation, its veto on clerical marriage and its ferocious and quite new provision for the mandatory burning of heretics without the option of recantation, represented a disastrous setback for the reformed cause. In its wake the leading evangelical bishops, Shaxton and Latimer, resigned their sees, and within a year the chief promoter of reformation, Thomas Cromwell, had been disgraced and beheaded. The roller-coaster of faction would continue to rise and fall, Henry would toy with reform again in a fresh campaign against images and shrines, and the king would play Evangelicals and Catholics off against each other for the rest of his reign. Cranmer, despite an unsuccessful plot designed to compromise him as a heretic in 1543, remained high in Henry's favour at Canterbury. On the whole, however, the early 1540s were a time of conservative regrouping and optimism.[76] In Morebath, Sir Christopher sat down early in 1541 with the account book and his own notes, and compiled an exhaustive list of every gift given to the church since his arrival twenty-years before, so that 'here after schall ye see and knoo how this churche was prevaylyd by the dethe of all these persons that here after ys expressyd by name'.[77] This striking piece of stocktaking has an element of the elegiac about it, and was certainly a potent gesture of pietas to a past so recently and so rudely shaken. But despite the uncertainties through which the parish was still passing, it was also a sign of some confidence in a future in which the bounty of the dead would continue to evoke gratitude and prayer, and hence was worth recording.

For as Sir Christopher's gesture suggests, the national slackening of the pressure for reform was amply reflected in Devon, where Simon Heynes's influence had peaked and was now rapidly waning. From July 1540 the fiery Dean was on the defensive in his perennial struggles against the canons of the cathedral, who charged him with vandalism and malicious damage because of his iconoclastic activities. The outcome of that case is unknown, but Heynes was clearly rattled and withdrew from Exeter. His enemies there pursued him, and with Cromwell his patron dead, and given the increasingly conservative climate at court, they had him on the run. In March 1543 he was hauled before the Privy Council, accused of 'lewde and seditious preaching and the sowing otherwise of many erronious opinions', and clapped in the Fleet Prison, where he remained until July, when he was released but bound over to keep the peace for the vast sum of 5000 marks.[78] As the historian of Exeter Cathedral has commented, 'How they must have gloated over the news in Exeter: the dean in prison for heresy!'[79] They may have gloated a little in Morebath too: at any rate, conservatives all round the county will have slept easier for the knowledge that the chief local activist in the upheavals which followed the injunctions had been routed, at least for the present. Morebath bought a chain for its Great Bible that year, to prevent its removal from the church: the chain might have been symbolic of the restraint now set upon the Reformation, for in May 1543 Parliament passed an 'Act for the Advancement of True Religion' aimed at heretical preaching and unauthorised translations of the scripture. In addition, however, it forbade bible-reading altogether by 'women ... artificers, prentices, journeymen, serving men of the degrees of yeomen or under, husbandmen or labourers', a prohibition which would have included most of the inhabitants of Morebath.[80] Evangelicals were understandably bitter at this assault on the popular base of the Reformation: 'Died not Christ as well for craftsmen and poor men as for gentlemen and rich men, and would not Christ that the poor labouring men should have wherewith they might comfort their souls ...?'[81]

In this cooler atmosphere, parochial solidarities reasserted themselves at Morebath, and in 1542 found an expression as demanding as any of the major projects of the 1530s. Among the casualties of the 1538 Injunctions were the many small non-parochial chapels, especially common in the West Country and usually housing a venerated image, visited in pilgrimage on feast days or as a rogation-tide 'station' for the ceremony of beating the bounds.[82] There had been a chapel of this sort, dedicated to the Virgin Mary, at Bury, the hamlet immediately north of Morebath across the Somerset border, and which was now of course redundant. In 1542 Morebath bought this chapel, dismantled it, and used its materials for a total rebuilding of the church house, together with the window from the church replaced by Hugh Paulet's stained glass from Barlinch. In the course of this work, the ale-house was equipped with an entirely new chimney and fireplace, new doors and new windows, new tables and cupboards, and was completely re-thatched. The project took up most of the summer, and required the help not merely of a carpenter from Brushford and Quycke the mason from Bampton, but of most of the householders of the parish, who donated money, building materials or labour, spent days delving stone in one or other of the three local quarries, Lodvin, Black Pool (Blackpole) or Grants (Grownte), felled oak trees at Hukeley to act as buttresses and dragged them to Morebath town, fetched shingle or sand or sacks of lime, and ferried stone in panniers on the backs of horses during harvest time, when labour was especially precious and hard to come by. It was the sort of cooperative venture which warmed the cockles of Sir Christopher's heart, and he lovingly documented every detail of it in the account of the Three Men presented on 29 October 1542.[83] He names twenty-five householders who contributed money, materials or service to the project, specifies minutely the nature of their contribution, sets a price on the materials or work they gave, and finally notes that they donated this freely – he uses the Latin words 'dedit', 'he gave', or 'hoc' or 'omnia dedit', he gave this or gave it all, to make this point. The sequence the list follows is essentially the same as the sheep counts, and as in the sheep counts, the effect is like a litany in which the unity of the parish is displayed and celebrated. The list, which notes the gift of labour made by poor men like Marke of Exbridge as well as the larger gifts of the strong farmers, is prefaced with a rubric which explains its significance: in it 'ye schall se furder devocion of diversse perssons of this parysse to the churche howsse with out the wyche devocion we hadd not been abyll to pay and redd men clenely as they ofth to be':

Richard Hucly fownd a man at Lowdven quare and a nother to Blackpole quare and payd for the fettyng of a sack of lyme sum xiiijd [14d] quod dedit.
Jone Morsse caryd ij [2] lowde of stone fro Grownte quare for the wyche sche askyd xvj^d [16d] and omnia dedit.
Mark gave halfe a days work at Blackpole quare j^d [1d] quod dedit. ...
John Tymwell at Borston was a hole day at Blackpole quare for the wyche was countyd in iiij^d [4d] and that he gave.
Thomas Borrage caryd 3 lowde of stone fro Blackpole and fett the jame stone for the chimny at Courte and for this he demawndyd xvj^d [16d] and omnia dedit. ...
Thomas Norman fett 2 lowde of stone at Blackpole quare and was at Bere [Bury] to se the chapyll with William at Wode and for this he askyd x^d [10d] and all he gave ...
Willaim Leddon fett a sack of lyme (iiij^d) [4d] and that he gave.

Richard Hukeley found a man at Lodvin quarry and another to Black Pool quarry and paid for the fetching of a sack of lime sum 14d which he gave.

Joan Morsse carried two loads of stone from Grants quarry for the which she asked 16d and gave it all.

Marke gave half a day's work at Black Pool quarry 1d, which he gave.

John Timewell at Burston was a whole day at Black Pool quarry for the which was counted in 4d and that he gave.

Thomas Borrage caryd 3 load of stone from Black Pool and fetched the jamb stone for the chimney at Court, and for this he demanded 16d, and gave it all.

Thomas Norman fetched 2 loads of stone at Black Pool quarry and was at Bury to see the chapel with William at Wood, and for this he asked 10d, and all that he gave

...

William Leddon fetched a sack of lime (4d) and that he gave.

But the list was also punctuated, as the sheep counts always were, by the names of five householders who had refused to join in this communal enterprise. Sir Christopher names and shames: 'Jone Goodman nothyng. Richard Don nil ... Robert at Hayne nothyng ... Richard Raw nothyng. William at Combe nil'.

The church house was the centre of conviviality and shared feasting in the parish, the place where the parish sat down together to drink and unwind.[84] Since the abolition of the stores, the ales organised there were now, along with the church sheep, the major surviving element in the church's reduced finances. One might consider it the secular equivalent of the church, except that to apply the notion of secularity at all to such a building in a community where the spiritual and the material intertwined so tightly as they did at Morebath, is itself perhaps to commit a category error. The high moral and religious charge which the rebuilding of the church house carried for Sir Christopher, as an exercise of communal charity and mutuality, is implicit in his repeated use of the technical religious term 'devocion' to describe their generosity. It is most clearly on display in his opening description of the contributions of two of the Three Men, the moving spirits in the project:

William Tymwell at Wode fett ij [2] lowd of tymber at Hucly and on with Jone Morsse and fownde a man iij [3] days at Blackpole quare and fett ij sackis of lyme and for all this he demanndyd iij^s & iiij^d [3/4d] and all he gave: and a gayn he was at Bere [Bury] to se the chapyll on day and a nother day he went to Grownte quare to se work goo forth and also went to Brussard [Brushford] for the carpynter and many tymes went a bout the parysse for horssis and sackis to cary lyme and for all that he taketh never j^d by sydis wother days and halffe days ....

John Norman at Courte caryd on lowd of tymber fro Courte wode to make the clavell with all and ij lowd of scaffoll timber and gave hyt and fellyd hyt and fett ij sackis of lyme and was iij days at Blackpole quare and fownde hem selfe and for all this he askyd iij^s & iiij^d [3/4d] and all he gave: by sydis many wother days and halffe days that he was here yn hervyste tyme to helppe to provyd stuff that the worke mayth goo forthe: and takyth not jd for his labor

But yff they schuld y don this for mony they wold not y don hyt and gevyn such atendans not for a angyll and nobyll[85] a pece of them and yff hyt hadd not byn to the churche.

William Timewell at Wood fetched two loads of timber at Hukeley and one with Joan Morsse and found a man three days at Black Pool quarry and fetched two sacks of lime and for all this he demanded 3/4d and all he gave: and again he was at Bury to see the chapel one day and another day he went to Grants quarry to see work go forth, and also went to Brushford for the carpenter and many times went about the parish for horses and sacks to carry lime and for all that he taketh never a penny besides other days and half days ...

John Norman at Court carried one load of timber from Court wood to make the lintel withal, and two loads of scaffold timber, and gave it, and felled it, and fetched two sacks of lime and was three days at Black Pool quarry and provided his own food and for all this he asked 3/4d, and he gave it all: besides many other days and half days that he was· here in harvest time to help to provide stuff that the work might go forward: and taketh not a penny for his labour.

But if they should have done this for money, they would not have done it, and given such attendance, not for an angel and a noble apiece for them, if it had not been to the church.

Morebath's saints were gone: but for a little longer, its harmonies held.

CHAPTER SIX

Morebath Dismantled

I SWAN SONG

The last years of Henry's reign must have seemed, to begin with, calm after storm for Morebath. The so-called 'King's Book', published in 1543 to be the doctrinal norm for the English church, was in most respects far more conservative than its predecessor, the Bishop's Book.[1] The Henrician Reformation, a tiger in the late 1530s, seemed now a reassuringly torpid tabby-cat. Its public manifestations, like the English Litany of 1544 and the King's Primer of 1545, were cautious further steps in a protestant direction, certainly, but they barely impinged on the parish, though Morebath dutifully and with its usual speed equipped itself with the Litany.[2] Despite the loss of so many of its stores, the parish had accommodated itself to the prohibition on the cult of images, and was finding fresh outlets for devotional spending in neutral projects which the evangelically inspired legislation of the 1530s had not touched – the black vestments, banners and streamers. Gifts to the church were prone now to be left strategically vague, like the bequest of Richard Webber which, the priest told the parish in 1544, his widow Mary 'wyll bryng ... yn a fore Cristmas and wyll be stow hyt yn the churche for the welthe of her husbans sowle as hyt schall plese her and her rulers'.[3] Though the annual parish income was now closer to £5 than the £8–10 common before 1538, Morebath had regained sufficient confidence by 1546 to undertake an ambitious and expensive new reordering of the nave, with an elaborate 'enterclose' or screenwork carved by Thomas Glasse, the whole thing to involve extensive reflooring, and costing £9 for the woodwork alone.[4]

The calm, however, was deceptive: within three years of entering into their contract with Thomas Glasse, the parish was to be to all intents and purposes bankrupt, the interior of its church gutted, its ornaments defaced or confiscated, and its remaining social institutions in disarray. Morebath itself was to be implicated in the folk protest known as the Prayer Book Rebellion, which would end with the butchering of thousands of the men of Devon and Cornwall by foreign mercenaries under a royal flag. At the root of it all was religion, and the social impact of rapid religious change, implicit in the advance of a Protestantism more radical than anything Morebath or any other parish in Devon had ever contemplated, even in nightmare. But, at the start, Morebath's slide towards disaster began with money.

When princes go to war, their subjects bleed. In the last years of Henry VIII's reign, the haemorrhage was financial as well as literal, for after 1542 the frenetic campaigning of Henry's barren wars with Scotland and with France was increasingly ruinous, in less than five years draining away a stupefying £2,000,000, money the king simply did not have. The result for the people of England was a period of the heaviest taxation they had experienced for centuries, with an unprecedented stream of enforced 'loans', grants, benevolences and subsidies exacted from both laity and clergy. Henry was also forced into an avalanche of sales of confiscated monastic lands, which swept away much of the permanent advantage the Crown might have hoped to gain from the dissolution of the monasteries.[5] More and more frequent crown demands for money were accompanied by a mounting need for manpower, as a monarchy without a standing army struggled to raise forces large enough for its aggressive foreign policy. In the summer of 1543 Morebath's landlord, Sir John Wallop, led an army of 5,000 men across the channel bound for Calais, and all over England local communities were increasingly obliged to organise themselves to provide men, weapons, harness [armour], and money to keep the armies marching.[6]

This mounting pressure was felt in Morebath. The West Country, with its long and vulnerable seaboard, was considered front-line territory: even inland Devon parishes were required to pay towards the maintenance of the county's coastal defences, and about this time Morebath began to make contributions for the 'bole wark' [bulwark] at Seaton, in the south-east of the county.[7] The parish also paid to make and maintain a 'vyre-bykyn' [fire-beacon] and from 1545 the accounts are increasingly concerned with raising money not merely for ongoing parish projects like the black vestments, but to service the escalating military needs of the Crown. Part of the proceeds from the sale of the wool of the church sheep in 1545, supplemented by the profits from the Young Men's ale, was used to satisfy these new royal demands: 20/= was lodged 'yn William at Tymwyll ys handis to serve the kyng at all tymys'. From now on references to substantial proportions of the parish's annual receipts set aside 'yn redeneys to serve the kyng' becomes a familiar refrain.[8] The Three Men in February 1546 reported paying 'Wyett', one of the parish poor men, 'to be the parysse man to serve the kyng this ere', and successive parish tax-officials, the 'tithing-men', busied themselves about collecting the last royal levy of the reign, the subsidy with two fifteenths and tenths voted in November 1545, and collectable over the next two years.[9]

The king's need for money led in December 1545 to the passing of the first Chantry Act,[10] authorising Henry to confiscate maladministered funds left in trust for prayers for the dead, to pension off the priests whose job it was to say the prayers, and to retain the capital to fund the war. The Act was not implemented, and was in no sense a protestant measure, for it made no theological criticism of the legitimacy or virtue of prayer for the dead. In its wake in February 1546, nevertheless, Henry appointed commissioners to survey the wealth and personnel of the chantries on a county basis, and though Morebath had no chantries, they had to send John Taylor to meet the commissioners at Exeter with Sir Christopher's account book to prove it.[11] There were however still two functioning chantries at Bampton, one of whose priests, Sir Thomas Tristram, probably had close contacts with Morebath, since he was a member of the wealthy Bampton family which had acquired a share in the rectory of Morebath, becoming in the process one of Sir Christopher's patrons.[12] And the commissioners' enquiries will certainly have been unwelcome to everyone, whether directly concerned or not, ominously reminding them of previous commissions, like the one whose work had preceded the dissolution of the monasteries, or of Dean Heynes's 1538/9 commission, which had put out the lights before all the saints of the region and ended the practice of pilgrimage. It must all have added to a growing sense of jumpiness and unease.

Henry's military involvements were meanwhile forcing Morebath itself to uncomfortably drastic expedients. By 1546 the parish was launched on its last major building project, Thomas Glasse's new screenwork. In September 1546 the Three Men reported that they had paid Glasse £3 'for hys furst payment', which the receipts of that year from all sources, a little over £5, comfortably covered: for future payments they would draw on the money from the Young Men's ales and the proceeds from the wool of the church sheep. However, they had also had to pay out more than £5 the same year for the parish's military obligations to the crown, in 'coat and conduct' money for equipping and manning the army: '5 dublyttis to serve the kyng ... 5 cappis ... harnys for a man and for halfe a harnys ... for the makyn of 6 cotis. ... To Thomas Sexton for a dagger and a sworde', and so on. For the first time in

Sir Christopher's ministry therefore, Morebath was in danger of running seriously into the red. To balance the books, the Three Men drew heavily on the parish's accumulated stock, but they were also forced to sell off the silver cruets bought a few years before to hold the water and wine for the Mass, and the foot of the parish's silver-gilt pax-brede.[13] The disposal of church plate to meet parochial or national emergencies was nothing new, nor in itself of much religious significance: it was to prove, however, a portent of the spoliation which was soon to devastate Morebath's life.

The death of Henry VIII on 28 January 1547 did nothing to stem the financial pressure on the parish communities of England. Sir Christopher duly sang requiem mass and dirige for the old king, for which the parish paid him 4d, and they sent Harry Hayle and Lewis Trychay to represent them at the 'knyghthyng spendyng' [knighting spending] at Exeter, the assembly which marked the knighting of the boy-king Edward by his uncle, Protector Somerset, in February 1547.[14] By the second Sunday in March, however, they had turned to more mundane matters, and a special parish meeting was held at which six men, including the priest's brother Lewis, were elected to adjudicate the payments outstanding in the parish for a range of obligations to the county and the crown, from the mending of Exebridge to the payment of arrears of the 'Five Dole', as the last Henrician Fifteenth and Tenth tax was known (because of the £5 worth of goods which was the minimum level for liability).[15] William Hurley, one of the six, was paid 20d for 'sarchyng of the bokis of the cheker [exchequer] for the a lowans of the v dole', as part of the research needed before they could decide fairly on each parishioner's liability. The 'sett' or 'order to gether the 5 dole ever here after by this boke' made 'by the consent of the courte' represented a realistic acceptance by the parish and the manor that the Crown's mounting fiscal demands were now an established fact of life, for which they must provide. It was however set out with Sir Christopher's usual insistent moral spin on any matter concerning 'the welthe of the parysse': the Six Men had been elected, he declared,

> to se a order takyn after there consciens for the getheryng of the x and xv
> for ever here after: what every man schuld pay for hys part and a gayn they
> schuld se that every man ware consyonabylly payd of all suche dutis as hadd
> byn payd for the welthe of the parysse be fore this day and these for sayd
> men to make a sett after there consciens that may pay suche demanndis ...
> (deliberacion takyn).

> *to see an order taken after their conscience for the gathering of the Tenth and Fifteenth*
> *for ever hereafter: what every man should pay for his part and again they should see*
> *every man was conscientiously paid of all such duties as had been paid for the wellbe-*
> *ing of the parish before this day and these aforesaid men to make a sett after their con-*
> *science that may pay such demands ... (deliberation taken).*

The summer of 1547 provided the priest with one last set-piece occasion in which to display and celebrate the values by which his parish had conducted itself for a generation. The boy king was an ardent protestant, surrounded by protestant advisers and guardians. The evangelical party was now triumphant in Court and Capital, and a floodtide of religious revolution was about to be loosed on England. The nation knew it. Rumour was rife, 'secretly spread abroad by uncertain authors, in markets, fairs and alehouses … of innovations and changes in religion and ceremonies of the Church feigned to be done and appointed by the king's highness'. Protector Somerset and the Privy Council indignantly denied it all, but got on with planning precisely what they denied.[16] In May, a Royal Visitation on the model established by Cromwell was announced, the first since his fall, and the regional panels of Commissioners, handpicked by Cranmer, and protestants to a man, made it abundantly clear what its character was to be: inevitably, Dean Heynes of Exeter was prominent among those chosen for the West Country.[17] But then, mysteriously, preparations for the Visitation stalled, and the weeks went by with no further action. In an atmosphere poisoned by local confrontations between conservatives and evangelicals, England held its breath.[18]

In Morebath, however, a more expansive air prevailed, if only briefly, for in July 1547 a twenty-year wait had come to a joyful end. Twenty years of painfully slow saving, the dribbling in of the priest's meagre wool-tithe, the sixpences and shillings coaxed from dying parishioners, the negotiations with executors and widows to divert bequests to this project above others, the formulaic reporting at every year's sheep-count of the snail-like progress of the fund: after all that, the priest now had enough money to buy the black vestments he had coveted for the whole of his time in the parish. He was beside himself with pleasure. Harry Hurley, who had been elected by the parish in 1528 to keep the black vestment fund, had died the previous year, a Moses destined never to see the promised land. He donated the 6/8d for his burial in the church to the fund he had kept so long, and Sir Christopher himself took charge. He travelled the twenty-five miles around the edge of the Moor to Dunster, on the Somerset coast, to the workshop of Sir Thomas Schorcum, the priest who made the vestments, then sent them by carrier twenty-five miles in the opposite direction to Exeter to be blessed by the bishop. By mid-July they had been 'recaryd' to Morebath, and everything was ready. On 17 July, the Sunday before the Feast of St Mary Magdalene,[19] he presented the annual sheep count, with its usual extraordinary itemising of the church sheep and their passage round the parish: 'how many of the churche scheppe be dede and gon and sold and how many there be as yett a lyffe and not solde and yn hoys kepyn they be now wyll y schow you.'[20]

But for once, the litany of the sheep and their custodians was not the highlight of the account. Along with the usual bales of wool and 'lamb-tow' were displayed the chasuble, fannon, stole and cope of black 'fustian knapis', a form of velvet, which would now dignify the parish's funerals and the annual Palm Sunday dirige for all the benefactors of the church. At the end of the sheep account, Sir Christopher launched into an elaborate speech in which he recounted the whole history of the black vestment project, from its 'furst fundacion' in 1528, when the parish had agreed on the deal about his honey and wax tithe and had appointed a warden 'to kepe this [wool] tuthyng tyll hyt came to a sum the wyche was Harry Hurly, whylle he levyd, God reste hys sowle', down to its successful conclusion in the accumulation of £6/2/4d, 'quod recepi [which I received] furst and laste'. The speech itself sandwiched an elaborate and exhaustive account which, for the only time in the book, was made throughout in Sir Christopher's own name; it was also the first account since 1540 to speak in the first person:

> and what this hathe incressyd unto this present day ye schall have knolyge of and also what geftis there hath been gevyn un to the vestmentis (and yff any man can say or prove that there hath byn any moo geftis to the vestmentis then thes that y wyll rehersse un to you lett hem aske me and y wyll make hem answere and so now this ys the recettis furst that Harry Hurlye resevyd to wardis these vestmentis ...

> *and what this hath increased unto this present day ye shall have knowledge of and also what gifts there hath been given unto the vestments (and if any man can say or prove that there hath been any more gifts to the vestments than these that I will rehearse unto you, let them ask me and I will make them answer and so now this is the receipts first that Harry Hurley received towards these vestments.*

The detailed account reveals that less than £2 of the final total had been accumulated by the time of Harry Hurley's death and the bulk of the money had in fact been raised subsequently, much of it in the form of bequests or commemorative gifts from devout women, a testimony both to the pastoral activity of the priest and the absence after 1538 of rival projects. Sir Christopher dwelt on his own input into the fund – the gift of the tithes in the first place '(for before Sir Christopher tyme Sir Richard Bowdyn vicar before hem hadd home ever the tuthyng)', as well as the money he had donated for Edward Sydenham's knell and to have his name 'sett a pon the ludger' [placed on the church bede-roll to be prayed for], which 'y wylbe countabyll unto you here now in my resetis that y have ressvyd hyt'. He recalled, with awakened resentment, the row over his action when 'y payd xxˢ [20/=] for you to John Paynter at hys nede before hys day and a pon that he deyd', and how 'sum of you gurgyd at hyt' and how as a result he had donated the 20/= to the fund. And the account concluded with Sir Christopher's inimitable and endearing blend of financial punctiliousness, self-importance, parochial pride and old-fashioned piety:

Thys costis a lowyd y have payd ij^s & iiij^d [2/4d] more than y have ressevyd (bysydis all my rydyng and sendyng to Donster) and yn case ye wyll a low me ij^s & iiij^d in future in the cownte of the churche scheppe (ut placeth vobis) and now lok ye a pon these vestmentis and the cope and take them at a worthe with all there fawtis for y have don the best that y can doo yn getheryng of the small pensse to gethers y pray God that hyt may be for there sawelis helthe that gave any gefth un to hyt for this ys cum with owt any charge of any store by my procurement to the honor of God and this churche and to the worschyppe of all this hole parysse as y pray God hyt may soo be. Amen.[21]

These costs allowed, I have paid 2/4d more than I have received (besides all my riding and sending to Dunster) and in case you will allow me 2/4d in future in the account of the church sheep (as you please) ... and now look upon these vestments and the cope and take them for what they are worth with all their faults, for I have done the best that I can do in gathering of the small pence together, I pray God that it may be for their soul's health that gave any gift unto it for this is come without any charge of any store, by my procurement to the honour of this church and to the worship of this whole parish as I pray God it may be so. Amen.

To the reader possessed of hindsight, there is an autumnal tone to this count of the black vestments. It was to prove Catholic Morebath's swan-song, the last untroubled expression of its pre-Reformation piety. On 31 July, exactly a fortnight after Sir Christopher's speech, Somerset published a new set of Injunctions for Religious Reform,[22] and the country was launched on the floodtide of religious change which had been expected for months, and which would leave not a stone upon a stone of the religious practices represented by the vestments.

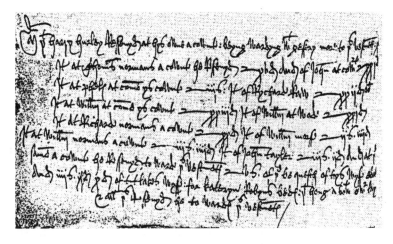

The 'count of the black vestments' in July 1547 [Binney 153 / Ms 364]

The Injunctions of 1547 looked like a somewhat expanded reissue of those of 1538: in reality they were a charter for revolution. They did incorporate the 1538 material, but in their new form all the qualifications and ambiguities that might give shelter to traditionalist religious practices were systematically edited out. Whereas in 1538 the recitation of the rosary was condemned if done superstitiously or without understanding, 'saying over a number of beads not understood or minded upon', now 'praying upon beads', the most basic form of lay Catholic piety, represented by the beads at the girdle of every matron in Morebath, was rejected absolutely, along with all 'suchlike superstition'. All processions were now forbidden, rendering redundant at a stroke the banners and streamers which Morebath had been investing in since the 1538 Injunctions had halted their spending on images. The new Injunctions ordered the destruction not only of all abused statues and shrines, but even of such images in stained glass windows, an advance towards an absolute ban on imagery almost without parallel in protestant Europe. The 1538 Injunctions had permitted lights before the Rood and the Sepulchre, and the Young Men and Maidens at Morebath had accordingly transferred their lights from the tabernacles of the saints to the basins and candlesticks before the High Cross and Sepulchre. But for convinced Protestants, lights about the Sepulchre or the Crucifix were if anything grosser manifestations of idolatry than lights before the lesser images of saints. The 1547 Injunctions now banned all lights or candles anywhere in the church except the two on the high altar. Every church was now to provide a triple-locked coffer with a hole in the top to serve as a poor man's box, and the priest at the death-bed was to urge parishioners to leave their money not to ornaments like Sir Christopher's black vestments, but to the poor. All stocks and funds designed to support lamps and candles were now to be put into this poor man's box, though a proportion of them might be used for the maintenance of the church building itself.[23]

Ardent Protestants now had the mandate they needed for an all-out onslaught on the forms of traditional religion. In London, evangelicals began a wholesale purge of all the images in the city churches and in St Paul's. Initially the Council, worried about the dangers of unrest in the city, tried to halt such action, but in November the Commissioners accepted these radical initiatives, and supervised the removal of all the images in St Paul's, including the great crucifix. In February 1548 Somerset and the Privy Council extended the total ban on all images to the country at large, on the tongue-in-cheek pretext that this would calm 'strife and contention' in the parishes.[24] And in case anyone was in doubt about the doctrinal revolution which underlay all this, in December 1547 Somerset pushed a new Chantry Act through parliament. Like its Henrician predecessor, the measure was intended to fund the war with Scotland from the revenues of the chantries, but this time what was planned was not a reform but a total confiscation, and the chantries were condemned root and branch as based in 'blindness and ignorance', all of them founded 'by devising and phantasising vain opinions of purgatory and masses'.[25]

Meanwhile, in the early autumn, Commissioners, armed with a draconian set of enquiries based on the Injunctions, had moved into the regions, and the process of enforcement began. By the time Morebath's High Wardens presented their annual account to the parish on Sunday 30 October, four parishioners had been to Exeter to present themselves before the Commissioners. As yet, the parish had not implemented any of the measures commanded by the Injunctions – there had scarcely been time – but in the light of the encounter with the Commissioners, a momentous decision had been taken. With Heynes in charge, it was likely that the Injunctions would be interpreted as radically as possible. The Commissioners must have emphasised the provisions of Injunction 28, ordering the redeployment to the poor man's box or the church repairs of all money 'which ariseth of fraternities guilds and other stocks of the church ... and money given or bequethed to the finding of torches, lights, tapers and lamps'.[26] The Morebath church sheep no longer belonged formally to a store designed to maintain a light, but that had been their original purpose, and it must have seemed possible that they might be confiscated. Did Heynes threaten the assembled wardens and clergy, or did Sir Christopher, ever alert to the implications of words and the drift of events, draw his own conclusions? At any rate, the count of the church sheep was presented to the parish on the same Sunday, but now for the last time. The wardens reported the sale of the entire church flock (to Harry Hayle for forty-two shillings, a bargain for seventeen animals). Sir Christopher bought the church bees, which the wardens of the church sheep also administered, perhaps because a sweet tooth and a special fondness for honey underlay the original deal he had struck with the parish in 1528 over the swap of his wool tithe for the 'making' of his wax and honey, or perhaps because his parents had donated the hives to St Sidwell in the first place. The entire profits and stock were handed over to the parish, to pay the expenses of the Visitation, to help pay Thomas Glasse for the enterclose [screen], to equip soldiers for the king, and to make the poor man's chest. 'Et sic' [and thus], reported the priest, 'under this sort ys this wardynscheppe dyschargyd as now.'[27]

It is worth pausing over the significance of this ending for Morebath. The church sheep were an important source of income, whose abolition was to contribute to the calamitous financial crisis shortly to engulf the parish. But there was more to their disappearance than mere finance. Morebath's curious system of parochial custodianship had regularly involved virtually every farmer and cottager in a very direct expression of support for and involvement in the community of the parish. Until very recently that practical involvement had been explicitly linked to a collective Marian piety (maintaining Our Lady's light), and to devotion to lesser saints like St Sidwell. The decision to wind up the store suggests that for the parish at large that connection was still thought to be a living and therefore a compromising one. However that may be, the yearly sheep account, so lovingly itemised and elaborated by their priest, was the parish's single most extended ritual of belonging, an annual register of who was and who was not pulling their weight. All of them had looked after church sheep, many of them had acted as wardens of the store. Both the wardenships and the lesser burden of keeping the sheep were sometimes perceived as a chore, and occasionally refused. It is very doubtful, however, whether this sudden amputation of so central a parish institution was perceived as an uncomplicated blessing even by those who had grumbled about it or resisted its obligations. Religious reform here touched and tampered not only with the parish's economy, but with its sense of itself. More and worse was to follow.

Two days after this Morebath meeting, on All Saints day and the eve of All Souls, Simon Heynes and the other Commissioners for the West issued a new set of directives, partly matched to the season, and partly the product of the mounting impetus of reform. They forbade clergy to wear black copes over their surplices 'because yt ys thought to be a kynde of monkery': this was explicitly aimed at the canons and vicars choral of the cathedrals of Exeter and Wells, but it had the side-effect of making Sir Christopher's precious black fustian cope dubiously legal. The Commissioners also forbade the ringing of knells, the 'immeasurable ringing for ded persones at their buriall, and at the feast of All Sowles', which in Morebath as in most West Country parishes was a much-valued expression of regard for the dead. Most devastatingly of all, the Commissioners ordered the archdeacons and officials 'to give commandment unto the churche wardeans and other the parishioners from henceforth to surcease from kepinge any churche ales, because it hath byn declared unto us that many inconveniencies hath come by them'. Despite which, churchwardens were ordered to go on raising funds, by making 'yearly collection for reparacion of their churches, and for the sustencion of other commune charges of the parish'.[28]

The prohibition of church ales was the first blast in what was to become an ongoing puritan campaign against popular disorder, destined to stretch well into the next century;[29] it was also a body-blow to the parishes of the West Country, for in many, perhaps in most, ales were an indispensable source of revenue. But once again much more than money was at stake. The ales were also a lynchpin of social life, the *raison d'être* of the church houses. Theirs was a religious as well as a social reality, since, in their shared feasting linked to religious festivals and the parish dedication, the ales were one of the most practical expressions possible of the life of charity which the parish existed to support and foster. And, more mundanely, in many communities, as at Morebath, the abolition of the stores had in fact left the church ales as the only reliable source of parish funding. The Commissioners' *blasé* instruction to churchwardens to go on raising just as much money without the ales must have added insult to injury, a rewording of Pharaoh's order to the Israelites to go on making bricks without straw.[30]

While Morebath reeled from this new requirement, the Chantry Act passed through Parliament, and the suppression began. The Commissioners for this latest instalment of reform set about their work promptly in the West Country. Every parish was required to send representatives with a certificate declaring whether or not they had anything liable to confiscation under the Act, which included the property of all guilds, lamps and obits as well as chantries proper.[31] Sometime in February or early March Morebath's High Wardens and the Three Men rode to Tiverton 'to make a nownswer for chantery grownd'. The effects of the dissolution of the chantries were of course indirect at Morebath, but were visible all around them nonetheless: the clerical staff of Bampton church was reduced from three to one, and Sir Thomas Tristram and Sir Thomas Vigours pensioned off and sent packing.

Morebath had its own deepening troubles. On 18 March the Three Men called an extraordinary meeting of the parish, six months ahead of the High Wardens' account at which they normally reported. The meeting dealt with some routine business, including payments to Thomas Glasse for the new enterclose and for relaying the floor which that work had necessitated. The Three Men also accounted to the parish for more expenses connected with the two Visitations, that of Heynes and his colleagues to enforce the Injunctions, and the Chantry Commission. There were payments for making 'the cheste aliter the powre men boxe', and 'to the summoner for warnyng of the kyngis visitacion and for warnyng of the paryssyng of wother iniuncions concernyng the kyng'.[32] These 'wother iniuncions' must have included the prohibition of church ales, for the main business transacted that day was the dissolution of the last of Morebath's pre-Reformation institutions, the Young Men's store. The Chantry Act's provision for the confiscation of obits and lights may have played a part in this decision, but its essential cause must have been the prohibition of ales. The 'grooming Ale' was the main activity of the Young Men, and without it their store had no rationale, and their wardens no work. Their funds were therefore handed over to the Three Men, part to pay Glasse for the enterclose, and part 'for the dressyng of 2 mens harnys': no new wardens were elected, and the store came to an end.[33] This dissolution of the last of its organisations was a bleak moment for the parish, made bleaker still by the fact that the expenses of the Visitation on top of the continuing payments to Thomas Glasse had exhausted all the accumulated stock of the parish, and the banning of ales left them with no discernible way of replenishing them. Completing the account, the priest noted tersely 'Thys costs a lowyd and never 1d lefth, and thus be the 3 men dyschargyd'.[34]

The Young Men's store was dissolved at Morebath on 18 March, Passion Sunday, two weeks before Easter. All over western England, the radical implications of the Royal Visitation and the dissolution of the chantries were now unfolding. Archbishop Cranmer had forbidden the imposition of ashes on Ash Wednesday and the bearing of palms on Palm Sunday, now just a week away. The ban on processions in the Injunctions had in any case deprived Palm Sunday of its central liturgical feature, the elaborate mimetic 'entry into Jerusalem', half religious ceremony, half pageant, which characterised the solemn mass of that day.[35] The Commissioners everywhere were now enforcing the removal of all images, and, where they could secure it, their destruction: at Ashburton the parish paid 2/4d for taking down 'le image called le George' and another 3/4d for removing the rood and other images: at Stratton in Cornwall it cost 8d to take down 'the horse of the ymage of seynt George', and another 8d to dismantle the rood.[36] It is not clear whether Morebath's images were removed now, or whether the parish managed to keep them a little longer: mention of the 'bolt of yre' on which St George had stood, and of the 'yre gere of the crosse' in November 1549 suggest that their destruction did not occur until the aftermath of the fateful events of the summer of 1549.[37] Meanwhile, however, many of the most distinctive features of Catholic cult were being suppressed, including the solemn veneration of the Easter Sepulchre containing the crucifix and the consecrated Host in Holy Week. From Easter Sunday, which in 1548 fell on 1 April, a new 'Order of Communion' was ordered to be inserted into the Mass after the end of the canon, containing long English devotions derived from continental Protestant sources. In place of annual reception of the consecrated bread only at Easter-time, the 'order' required that lay people receive communion often, in the form of both bread and wine.[38]

To the agitation these measures aroused was added the fear of further raids by the Crown on the resources of local communities. The regime now ordered the compilation of inventories of the church goods of every parish, ostensibly 'for the preservation of the church juelles', a protestation of benign intent that few sensible people believed. It seemed to many that the dissolution of the chantries was a mere prelude to the rape and pillage of the parishes, and many began a pre-emptive sale of their treasures to forestall confiscation.[39] Tudor parishes were remarkably docile in the face of increasing government intrusion, but all this was too much for some West Country communities, especially where the abolition of the chantries seriously undermined their communal life. At Ashburton, where the guild of

St Lawrence was effectively the town council and governed the local market, hospital and water supply, the dissolution of the chantries and stores not only reduced the staff of the parish church from seven priests to one, but also threatened the infrastructure of the town. Twenty parishioners, including three farmers, a pewterer, a tinner, a mercer and a smith, set about the commissioners' servants in the market square.[40] But the most notorious outbreak was at Helston in Cornwall, where in Easter week an angry crowd dragged out and murdered the odious and overbearing William Body, a layman who had purchased the right to 'farm' the archdeaconry of Cornwall from Cardinal Wolsey's bastard son Thomas Winter, and who was exploiting his investment by vigorous confiscations. The leaders of the mob included a local chantry-priest and a group of farmers from St Keverne, and the incident snowballed until it was alleged that more than 3,000 men had assembled in a full-scale rebellion designed to raise the kingdom. Loyalist gentry mobilised some east Cornish parishes to provide troops to oppose the rebellion, and some places, as impoverished by recent events as Morebath, were obliged to sell church plate to finance these musters, but there was almost certainly widespread sympathy for the Helston cause. It was reported that the rebels wanted a halt to any religious innovation until the king achieved his majority: until then, 'they would have all such laws as was made by the late Henry VIII and none other'.[41]

The Helston rising seriously alarmed Somerset's regime, as well it might, and the ringleaders were taken to London for trial: in the event only the priest, Martin Jeffery, was executed there (though there were ten hangings at Helston). This was a characteristic outcome, for the regime refused to acknowledge that popular loyalty to Catholicism might be rooted in anything deeper than the work of obscurantist and crafty priests leading an ignorant and gullible laity astray. On 24 April the Privy Council issued a proclamation denouncing 'divers unlearned and indiscreet preachers and other priests' who have 'of a devilish mind and intent' incited the people to disobedience, with tales of fresh confiscations and a tax on baptisms, weddings and funerals. The laity had thereby been seduced 'and brought to much disorder of late, and in some parts, in manner to insurrection and rebellion'. Parish clergy were therefore forbidden to preach at all unless specifically licensed to do so, instead being ordered to read to their people from the Archbishop's new official *Book of Homilies*.[42] On 17 May another proclamation was issued, pardoning all but the ringleaders, and enjoining the Cornishmen to abandon 'rebellions, unlawful assemblies, riots, routs and conspiracies' and 'from henceforth like true and faithful subjects use yourself in God's peace'. These warnings against sedition hawked around the West Country are as likely to have reminded their hearers of the discontents of their region as to have deterred them from further complaint. The parishioners of Morebath probably listened to them, but local upheavals were increasingly played out against a wider background of crisis. They paid 6d that year to the summoner 'for a copy of the kyngis commandment, and for the oracion of the pece'. The 'king's commandment' must be either the instruction to use the order of communion at Easter, or this ban on preaching. The 'oracion of the pece' was almost certainly the 'Prayer for Victorie and Peace' issued on 10 May 1548 for peace with or victory over Scotland, and for a marriage between Edward and Mary Queen of Scots. In the agitated West Country, the words of this supplication by Archbishop Cranmer for the eradication of 'warre and hostilitie' and the growth of 'perpetuall amitie and concord' in 'the small porcion of yearth, which professeth thy holy name', 'this Isle of Britaigne' may have had an ironic ring.[43]

We can trace the impact of the Royal Visitation on Morebath in the summer of 1548. The parish had hung the Lent cloth as usual on Ash Wednesday to conceal the altar until Holy Week, and had again celebrated the 'generall dirige of the churche' for dead benefactors on Palm Sunday. But that was probably Sir Christopher's last chance to wear the black vestments. By the time the High Warden reported on Michaelmas day, at the end of September, much of the church's ritual equipment had been disposed of, and its liturgical life drastically simplified. Only one warden reported, the widow Lucy Scely, or Luce at Myll. Lucy had not been elected: she had taken on the office because of the death of her husband William Scely, appointed senior warden the previous year, along with Robert Isac. Isac had been elected as the ale warden, but since ales were now forbidden, he was redundant, and simply stood down: for the rest of the reign Morebath elected a single warden each year.

Lucy Scely's was an unenviable job, for she inherited all the traditional responsibilities of the wardenship without any source of income to meet them, except the 2/8½d inherited from her predecessors in office; she was herself a poor woman. The Three Men had 'not a penny' in hand, and there were continuing expenses to meet the requirements of the royal visitation, like the setting in order and repair of the register and its box, 'the cofer with the boke of the names'. There were also the usual round of minor repairs and maintenance of bells and roofing lead, and the parish's continuing liability for the costs of regional defence, such as its payments for the fire-beacon. To meet all these demands, Lucy decided to dispose of the liturgical equipment recently made redundant by the Archbishop's directives and by the actions of the Commissioners. Sometime before the end of September 1548 she sold off the Lent cloth, the painted hangings for the Easter Sepulchre, the frontals for the high altar and St Sidwell's altar, the painted cloth which veiled the High Cross in Holy Week, some of the church's streamers and banners, the basins in which tapers had burned before the high cross, and a quantity of brass candlesticks.[44]

The widow Scely evidently took this action without consultation with the parish, so that the priest could later report that 'by her tyme the churche gooddis was sold a way with out commission': Sir Christopher clearly deeply disapproved.[45] He cannot have been the only one. Many of the items sold by Lucy Scely were gifts in commemoration of the dead. The Sepulchre cloths had been paid for with a bequest given to Sir Christopher as he stood at the death-bed of his priest-friend Sir Edward Nicoll, and he himself had commissioned them from John Creche. The altar cloths came from John Smyth and Christina Taylor, the basins came from Margery Lake and Jekyn at Moore; the silk streamer, for which Lucy got only 8d with a banner thrown in for good measure, however, was probably not the 'best stremer of sylk' which had cost 20/= only six years before, and had been paid for by bequests from three parishioners, Elizabeth Hukeley, William Norman and Joan at Quartley.[46] Nevertheless, 19/6d, the total takings from the sale, cannot have seemed much of a price to place on so large a tract of the parish's memory and the parish's mourning.

By the spring of 1549, Morebath's financial crisis had deepened to desperation. The Vicar, Lucy Scely and the Three Men were summoned once more to Tiverton to appear before the King's Commissioners and to deliver to them an inventory of the church goods. William Hurley, Harry's son and now the parish's chief man of business, was paid 3/8d for the costs of making the official inventory on parchment and having it formally agreed and sealed – the whole business involved Hurley riding twice to Tiverton and once even further afield to Hollacombe. The parish had evidently been prodded by the Commissioners to complete the·equipment required by the Injunctions, for they now bought 'the bok of erassamus', the *Paraphrases on the New Testament* by the great humanist scholar Desiderius Erasmus, which every church was required to possess.[47]

All of this cost almost £1, which Morebath now simply did not have: Hurley advanced the money himself, taking the parish's best crimson velvet cope as a pledge at pawn for security. To repay him, another sale was decided on, this time however 'by the consent of the hole parysse'. On St George's eve 1549 (22 April), which was also Easter Monday, Hurley and five other men acting as feoffees [trustees] on the parish's behalf sold off the entire contents of the church house – the table and planks, the greater and lesser spits, the fireplace hangings for the pots, the 'wolde cobord', the dishes of treen and pewter. They raised 46/2d by the sales, paid Hurley his 20/=, and reclaimed the pawned cope – as the priest noted 'and so this cope [is] our own (under the king) as our invitory dothe record being in Pole ys hand'.[48] Another pound was handed over to William at Timewell for future needs, 'the wyche ye schall have at all tymys', and the remaining 6/2d was put in the new poor man's box.[49] The worn linen from the church-house and the church was distributed to some of the poor men of the parish, board or table-cloths given openly ('palam') to William Bicner, Marke of Exebridge and to 'Holcumbe' and, secretly, the font cloth was given to the parish clerk, an altar-cloth to Richard Cruce, and an old surplice divided between John Wood and Thomas Sexton (given Morebath's preference for occupational names, almost certainly the parish gravedigger). The church-house, formerly the parish meeting-place but essentially redundant since the abolition of ales, was now stripped of all the equipment needed for its communal use, and effectively privatised. From 1552 and possibly earlier, it would be let out as a private dwelling – the priest's nephew, Christopher Trychay, the parish clerk, became the tenant, renting it for 6/= a year.[50]

The closure and disposal of the church house, devastating as its implications must have been for Morebath's corporate life, was not their only trouble. The order to compile and certify to the Commissioners an inventory of church goods clearly alarmed the parish, and we possess a vivid documentary snapshot of their attempt to fend off the confiscations which they feared it foreboded. Early in 1549 Sir Christopher compiled a list of the vestments owned by the church, which reveals that they had been distributed round the farms of the parish for safe-keeping – the black vestments to John at Court, the red velvet vestments and their matching altar-cloth of satin to Nicholas at Hayne, the Lenten vestments of blue to Thomas Rumbelow, the cope of blue satin to William at Timewell. The best silk streamer and the new banner were rolled in a table-cloth, and together with the best blue vestments they were entrusted to John Norman at Poole. The parish's satin pall for funerals and the white vestments which Sir Christopher and his father had paid for were placed with William at Combe.[51]

For once, Binney's admirable edition of the Morebath accounts lets us down here, for its neat editing obscures the ramshackle nature of this list, quite unlike Sir Christopher's usual meticulous entries. Though it is clearly in his handwriting, it is cramped and disfigured by crossings-out which indicate changed locations for the vestments. In a way which most of the entries in the book are not, this is manifestly a working record, the trace of action still in progress. None of these (perfectly legible) crossings out, however, were reproduced or even hinted at in Binney's printed version. The manuscript at this point positively breathes a sense of crisis: the list was not included as part of the 1549 accounts, but crammed into a blank space at the foot of a previous page with a cross reference back to it, and it had clearly been compiled before William Hurley had agreed to lend the parish money and take the crimson cope as security. As the deletions indicate, this cope had originally been placed with Robert at Moore, and Hurley had been entrusted with the blue velvet vestments. The funeral pall had at first been with Joan Morsse, and the white vestments were originally placed with John at Court. It is not at all clear why, apart from the pawned cope, it was subsequently thought necessary to move so many of the vestments around the parish in this way,

but there can be little doubt that their removal from the church and place-
ment with the farmers of the parish represented a deliberate act of concealment, designed to foil the Commissioners in the event of any confiscation.
Up till now the vestments had certainly been kept in the church, and the
handful which Morebath did eventually hand over to royal confiscation in
1552 – two copes and two tunicles – excluded most of the items listed here,
which silently vanished, some at least of them to reappear in Mary's reign.[52]
All over England, parishes were reacting to the increasing pressure from the
Crown in the same way, hiding or selling their treasures to prevent their confiscation. And all over England, too, the atmosphere of uncertainty and confusion, and the flood of church goods coming on to the market, led to an
opportunistic surge in sacreligious thefts.[53] Morebath, too, fell victim. As if to
underline the general bleakness, a thief broke one of the church windows,
and stole the clerk's rochet and the best surplice. It was St George's day, and
their patronal festival.[54]

III COMMOCION TYME

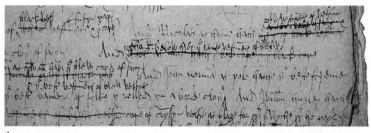

*

By the early summer of 1549, therefore, the parish of Morebath had been
stripped to the bone. Its images and many of its ritual furnishings were
gone, its vestments concealed, its social life was suspended as the church
house lay locked and empty, and every one of its parish organisations had
been dissolved. A decade before there had been a minimum of twelve
elected parish officials active in Morebath, frequently involving women and
always including two teenage youths and two girls. Between them all, they
raised and managed a total annual income of up to £10, deployed about a
multitude of parish projects. There was now a single warden, operating
with a balance in hand of less than 2/=, and, as a result of the sale of the
church flock, the outlawing of ales and the consequent disappearance of
parish feasting, without any regular source of income to meet the mounting
costs of reformation. The concealment of the vestments and the sale of the
church house goods in the spring of 1549 are a measure of the desperate

---

* Sir Christopher's note of the concealment of the vestments in 1549. The deletions
represent the movement of items from one farm to another [Binney 160 / Ms 371]

by the course of reform over the previous twelve months. At this low ebb, the parish's local problems, which were replicated across the county, were swept decisively into greater upheavals. The smouldering grievances of rural England erupted.

It was clear from the very start of 1549 that it was going to be a bad year everywhere for conservative country communities caught in a tightening vice of government fund-raising and the rush of religious change. On 21 January Parliament had passed the Act of Uniformity, abolishing the medieval liturgy lock, stock and barrel, and substituting for its elaborate and regionally varied cycle a radically slimmed down English book designed to impose a centralising uniformity of worship across the land. The new Book of Common Prayer, prepared by a panel headed by Archbishop Cranmer and including Dean Simon Heynes, was to be introduced everywhere by Whitsun at the latest.[55] For the West Country this was deeply unwelcome news. Scarcely less disturbing was the legislation of 12 March, when Somerset forced through Parliament a new financial grant to the Crown, the so-called 'Relief of Sheep', essentially a poll-tax on sheep designed to finance the war. This new Act levied a charge of 3d per ewe and 2d for other shearling sheep on flocks of 11–20 kept on enclosed ground, or 1d a head for animals grazed on commons: the levy was halved for smaller flocks. Liability was to be assessed by Commissioners working through local panels consisting of the priest, the tithingman and three other 'honest and discrete persones' of 'every parish, village and hamlet': the first assessment was to start on 1 May and to be completed by 25 June, just a fortnight after the last day for the introduction of the new Prayer Book.[56] Along with the Relief of Sheep went the 'Relief of Cloth', a tax of 8d in the pound on every piece of woollen cloth made after 24 June, a provision which Morebath parishioners would have felt the weight of every time they took their wool to market. And one can only imagine the feelings of the priest and the Three Men of Morebath at the prospect of being empanelled to collect the data for a further mulcting of themselves and their neighbours, by the regime which had already forced the dismantling of almost every institution of their common life. The Relief of Sheep and of Wool caused deep dismay in Devon, and it was rumoured that 'they should be made to pay, first for their sheep, then for their pigs and geese also, and other like things: and whatsoever they had in store, or should put in their mouths, they must fine therefore to the king'.[57]

But there was popular unrest everywhere, in eastern and southern England largely directed against grasping landlords, whose enclosure of common land and engrossing of farms into large holdings was perceived as the root cause of growing peasant landlessness, and of the hardship and dearth many of the rural poor were experiencing. From April onwards the Council was disturbed by frequent reports of agrarian discontent, riot, and the rooting up of enclosure hedges. Angry men with pitchforks and flails were out in minor displays of force from Norfolk in the east to Frome in Somerset in the West.[58] These disturbances were to climax in the most turbulent months of the Tudor century. Discontent simmered during a long hot summer, to erupt first in Cornwall, at Bodmin on 6 June, three days before the new Book of Common Prayer was due to come into use, and a few days later in Devon, at Sampford Courtney, on the northern fringe of Dartmoor. The causes of the outbreak at Bodmin are uncertain, though the imminent enforcement of the Prayer Book was probably the main trigger. It was certainly so in Devon. On Whit Monday, 10 June, the parishioners of Sampford forced their priest William Harper to put aside the Book of Common Prayer, which he had used for the first time the previous day, in favour of the old Latin Missal; he 'yielded to their wills and forthwith ravessheth himself in his old popish attire and sayeth mass and all such services as in times past accustomed'.[59] The protestors from Bodmin joined forces with those from Sampford Courtney, and commotion spread through the villages of Devon and Cornwall. By the start of July a peasant army was encamped outside the city of Exeter, and the city was under siege. Similar but much smaller religiously-motivated outbreaks followed in Oxfordshire, Yorkshire and Hampshire, where the banner of the Five Wounds, emblem of the 'Northern men' in the Pilgrimage of Grace, was seen again.

In the second week of July the Eastern commotions came to a head at Wymondham, where the local inhabitants threw down enclosure hedges and then, under the leadership of Robert Kett, encamped themselves outside the walls of Norwich on Mousehold Heath: the county rallied to them, and by 12 July there were said to be 16,000 people outside the city walls.[60] Commotion spread now across southern and eastern England, and camps were established across East Anglia, the Thames valley and the home counties, so that the summer of 1549 was ever after known as 'the camping time', and the insurgent protestors as 'camping men'.

It is routine now to draw a very hard and sharp distinction between the western 'rebellion', as historians have come to call it, and these East Anglian and Home Counties 'commotions'. The western protest was religiously conservative, its major demands, as we shall see, being for a wholesale reversal of the Edwardine Reformation. By contrast, the leaders of the eastern camps deployed a biblical rhetoric, designed to ally them with the reform aspirations of Somerset's regime. We now know that Somerset, to the horror of some of his colleagues and rivals in the Council, sought to conciliate the protestors, offering to hear and consider their grievances. Professor Diarmaid MacCulloch, the most perceptive interpreter of the East Anglian commotions, has laid particular stress on the contrasts between the disturbances in eastern and western England, claiming the camps in Norfolk, Suffolk and Essex as the expression of a 'vigorous popular protestantism', and stressing the recognition by Somerset's regime that the men of East Anglia 'do acknowledge the Gospel which ye say ye greatly hunger for'. These were, he thinks, 'evangelicals arguing with each other in evangelical terms'.[61] He has highlighted the crucial role of known Protestants among the leadership of the East Anglian disturbances, and has emphasised the settling of the eastern protestors into camps, in pursuit of a policy which they saw as the rescue of the commonwealth, not as rebellion, in contrast to the more menacing advance of the western rebels towards London.

These contrasts are real, but it would be a mistake to make too much of them. The men of the West also encamped themselves, indeed they issued their demands as 'The articles of us Commoners of Devonshire and Cornwall in Divers Campes by East and West of Excettor'. They too were 'camping men', and in Devon as everywhere else these events were referred to not as rebellion, the label Somerset and the Council immediately fixed on them, but as 'the comocyon tyme'. The Devon rebels too thought of themselves as rallying to communal values, not challenging the monarchy or legitimate government. Certainly the eastern protestors, in absolute contrast to the men of the West, ostentatiously secured Prayer Book worship and reformed preaching in their camp at Mousehold Heath, in which, famously, the future Archbishop Matthew Parker played a part. But Parker came within a whisker of being lynched by the rebels, who resented his reiteration of the regime's propagandist claim that the chief commandment of scripture was unresisting obedience to lawful authority. According to the contemporary chronicler Nicholas Sotherton, this Prayer Book conformity was a matter of policy rather than piety or conviction, adopted 'in order to have a fayre shew and a similitude of well doinge'. This was also suspected by Somerset, who told the Essex rebels that he wondered whether their protestations of hunger for the gospel 'proceade not from the harte and that there is in yow only a recyttal of textes to make for your present purpose'.[62] The notion that rural Norfolk and Suffolk by 1549 were populated by tens of thousands of peasant Protestants contradicts almost everything else we know about the religion of the region in the 1540s. Protestantism certainly played a part in the formation of the official programme of the East Anglian commotions, but it would be naïve to conclude that therefore all or most of those participating were convinced evangelicals. Far too little attention has been paid, for example, to the perfectly astonishing fact that the Norfolk disturbances erupted in the first place at an assembly of hundreds of local people gathered for a two-day jamboree and a play, celebrating the abrogated and doubly illegal feast of the translation of St Thomas Becket's relics [7 July], absolute anathema to any self-respecting Protestant.[63] We know very little indeed about the rank-and-file members of the East Anglian camps, but we catch a glimpse of some of them, the men of the mid-Norfolk village of Heydon, marching to Mousehold Heath behind the banner from their parish church. This was a strongly traditionalist (and illegal) gesture, once again inconceivable from convinced evangelicals, and reminiscent of the Pilgrimage of Grace and the revived Five Wounds banners even then being redeployed in Hampshire.[64] Somerset's regime was prone to see traitorous popish priests under every bed: nevertheless, it is not entirely without significance that they purported to believe that the outbreaks in Norfolk were being fomented by 'some naughtie papists priests that seeke to bringe in the olde abuses and bloodie laws whereof this realme is by God's sufferaunce well delivered'.[65]

But whether or not we ought to place the Eastern and Western Commotions within a single broad explanatory framework, 'olde abuses and bloodie laws' in the shape of the return of the Latin Mass and the revival of the laws against heresy were certainly high on the agenda of the men of the West. When William Hellyons, a local gentleman, tried to defuse the disturbances at Sampford Courtney, he was hacked to death by the Devon mob on the steps of the church house. Significantly, his body was buried lying north and south, not east and west, an easily recognisable piece of symbolism indicating that he was considered a heretic and an outcast from the Catholic church.[66] Economic and social discontent and class antagonism now converged with religious outrage to stir the whole of the West Country 'and the comon people so well allowed and lyked thereof that they clapped their handes for ioye; and agreed in one mynde to have the same in everie of their severall parishes'.[67] Revealingly, the villagers of Clyst St Mary near Exeter, destined to be the scene of the bloody massacre which would end the rebellion, first joined the revolt when the Protestant gentleman Walter Raleigh tried to stop an old woman saying the rosary as she walked to Mass there in Whit week, on the grounds that beads were now illegal. The old woman roused the parish, 'sayinge she was threatened by the gentleman, that except shee woulde leave her beades and geve over holie breade and water the gentlemen woulde burne theyme out of theire howses and spoyle theim'; the enraged commons swarmed from the church 'like wasps' and fortified the village.[68] When, later in the month, royalist forces under the Evangelical adventurer Sir Peter Carew burned the barns of the rebel-held town of Crediton, 'the common people noised and spread it abroad that the gentlemen were altogether bent to overrun, spoil and destroy them'.[69] By 2 July, a peasant army several thousand strong had advanced to Exeter, captured the suburbs and laid a siege, establishing camps in a ring round the city from St David's Down on the north-west, round St Sidwell's to the north, and down the Southernhay to the Westgate.

In Devon as in East Anglia, there was a strong undertow of hostility towards the gentry, which manifested itself in a rebel demand for the limitation of the right of gentlemen to keep servants. The 'Relief of Sheep' also undoubtedly contributed to the discontents of the commons of Devon. But the declared grievances of the rebels were predominantly religious, and focussed on rejection of the Prayer Book. Cranmer's new liturgy not only undermined medieval Catholic belief in the real presence and the eucharistic sacrifice, it abolished daily Mass unless there were communicants to receive along with the priest, it put an end to sacramentals like holy water and holy bread (formerly distributed to the congregation at the end of Mass every Sunday, and much valued for healing and as a defence against evil spirits). It discouraged the baptism of infants on weekdays, establishing public baptism on Sundays as the norm: confirmation, formerly administered whenever a bishop was available to infants up to the age of three, was henceforth to be confined to children and young people old enough to memorise and recite the catechism.

All of these innovations were rejected by the rebels. In a world where one child in ten was dead before it was a year old, and in which ten percent of infant mortality occurred in the baby's first week, the provisions for the delay of public baptism until the Sunday seemed to put their children's souls in jeopardy; they demanded that the old practice of same or next-day baptism be continued, and, likewise, that children be confirmed whenever a bishop was available. The Mass they wanted celebrated 'as it hath bene in tymes past, without any man communicatyng with the Priestes', and they demanded the restoration of the sacramentals of holy bread and holy water. They wanted the blessed sacrament reserved in the churches as it had universally been before the recent Visitation, and they demanded the retention of the rule of clerical celibacy.[70] By late July, these demands had been elaborated, clericalised and made fiercer, to include the re-enactment of the Act of Six Articles and the execution of heretics, to have all bibles and books of scripture in English 'called in agayne' so that heretics might not triumph over priests in argument, and to have the Holy Week ceremonies, images and 'all other auncient ceremonyes used heretofore, by our Mother the holy Church', restored. In this sharpened form, the demands seemed even to envisage the rolling back of much of the Henrician Reformation. They called for the reinstatement of the doctrine of purgatory, and the reestablishment of two monastic houses in every county. They demanded that Cardinal Pole, the king's aristocratic cousin living in exile in Italy for his opposition to the Reformation, be recalled and made a member of the Privy Council. This is a demand which has puzzled commentators, since Pole had lived in Italy for almost a generation and was hardly a household name. He had however been deposed as Dean of Exeter in 1537, when Simon Heynes was installed in his place, and the demand for his return may reflect animosity to Heynes's Protestant activism and a desire for a new balance in the county, or jostlings for local influence among the region's aristocracy, rather than any special admiration for Pole himself.[71] One memorable common feature of all versions of the rebels demands is the claim that the new English liturgy was 'but lyke a Christmas game': this seems to be linked to an earlier claim by the rebels that the new communion service encouraged promiscuity and gave 'authoritee and lycence to whoredome'. Both complaints probably derive from the provision in the new Communion service that communicants should file into the quire, men on one side and women on the other, which evidently struck the men of Devon as being like the start of a country dance.[72]

In faraway London and with a rash of other disturbances on his hands, Protector Somerset was slow to register the seriousness of the Western Rebellion. Lord Russell, the Lord Privy Seal, was despatched to deal with it on 24 June, but found it hard going, since the gentry and commons of the county sullenly refused to put down a rebellion with which most of them were in essential if ingloriously passive sympathy. Demands to the Justices of Peace of Devon to 'putt your selfs with such of yor tenants and servants as you best trust, secretely ordered to attend' fell on largely deaf ears.[73] By 10 July even London was aware that the Devon gentry professing loyalty were not lightly to be trusted; by the third week of July Russell was at his wits' end for lack of adequate numbers of troops.[74] Foreign mercenaries were sent, and the Privy Council ordered Russell to levy foot soldiers from the neighbouring counties of Somerset and Dorset. If they proved reluctant he was to issue proclamations threatening that if they did not show themselves ready 'to fight against the rank rebells and papists of Devon ... they shalbe both demed and for trators and forfeit theyr landes, Copiholds and goods without redempcion to themselves, wyfes and children, and be without all hope of pardon'. It was thought that this threat about 'the matyr of Copiholds' would infallibly galvanize the reluctant into action, though in fact in Somerset there was little response because of the 'evill inclynation of the people', some of whom 'do not styck openly to speak rash traterous words agaynst the kyng and in favor of the trayterous rebells'. Russell was instructed to hang two or three, *pour encourager les autres*. It was hardly worth doing, for even those who did join up would prove to fight 'most fayntly' against their Devonshire neighbours, and they were disbanded at the earliest opportunity.[75]

The rebellion, however, ended in overthrow for the men of Devon and Cornwall. Reinforced by foreign mercenaries, Lord Russell confronted the rebel army at Clyst St Mary, west of Exeter, on 5 August: the peasant force was no match for the professionals, and the rebels were routed. When news of the ensuing blood-bath reached the besiegers, they recognised defeat, and melted away, leaving their camps deserted. The largest contingent, containing most of the Cornishmen, was pursued westwards to Sampford Courtney, while the rebels who fled up the Exe valley into Somerset were chased by Morebath's steward, Sir Hugh Paulet, knight marshall in the royal army, the last remnants being butchered at King's Weston.[76]

Contemporaries estimated that the total rebel losses were around 4,000 men. Once again the regime singled out priests for special punishment, and half a dozen were executed. The most famous case was that of the vicar of St Thomas' church, by Exbridge to the south of the city. He was a Cornishman named Robert Welshe, a man of respectable parentage, a notable wrestler and archer with both longbow and crossbow, and a good shot with a gun. He was also a fiery preacher and a devoted Catholic, who had refused any truck with the new Prayer Book and had been 'an Archcaptain and principle doer' in the rebellion. He had also, however, restrained the wilder spirits among the rebels from torching the city, and even his enemies acknowledged his honourable behaviour. Lord Russell now condemned him to the grotesque and terrible death of hanging in chains as an example to others. A gallows was erected on the tower of his church, and he was left to die from exposure dangling from it by a chain around his waist, 'in his popishe apparrell and having a holye water buket, a sprinckle, a sacringe bell, a payre of beddes and such other lyke popyshe trash hangued about hym'. John Hooker, an eye witness, commented that he hung there a long time, and 'made a verie smale or no confession but verie patientlie toke his dethe'. His courage elicited a grudging accolade from the staunchly protestant chronicler: 'he hadd benne a good member in his commonwelthe had not the weedes overgrowne the good corne and his foule vices overcomed his vertewes.'[77] Welshe's foul vices, of course, boiled down to no more than steadfastness in his faith, and a militant refusal to acquiesce in its suppression. His terrible end was designed to send a strong and clear message to conservative priests everywhere, and spectators who watched his corpse stiffen above his church in its mass-vestments and beads were left in no doubt just what it was that had been defeated in the overthrow of the Western Rebellion.

Morebath's part in all this is hidden in ambiguity; indeed, until 1997 none of those who used Sir Christopher's accounts, myself included, appear to have noticed that the parish had any part in it at all. It is clear that there were no protestants in Morebath, and as we have seen, the Edwardine reforms had pushed its social and religious structures to the point of collapse and beyond. It can hardly be doubted that the traitorous speeches being voiced just over the county boundary in Somerset must have had a fervent echo among Sir Christopher's parishioners. An astonishing entry by the priest in the parish accounts reveals, however, that the men of Morebath did more than murmur. We know now for certain that the patience of this most law-abiding of villages snapped in mid-July 1549, and that they equipped and financed a group of five young men to join the rebels in the camp outside Exeter at St David's Down.

On 18 July Russell complained to Somerset and the Council of the 'dayly encrease of the rebells numbers'. The Morebath entry gives details of 'another rekenyng … about sent iamys day' (25 July), for money laid out sometime in the days or weeks before. The entry does not allow us to be precise about dating – it commences, for example, with the payment of 4/4d for the purchase of the Book of Common Prayer, which must have been made nearly two months before, since the book came into use on Whitsun, 9 June. But this special 'reckoning' had become necessary because the main transaction it records put the parish in the red. It is likely therefore that the reckoning was made soon after that happened, which suggests that we are dealing with an event in mid-July at the earliest. The bulk of the entry is devoted to a series of payments to five parishioners – William Hurley 'the yong man', Thomas Borrage 'the yonger', John Timewell, Christopher Morsse and Robert Zaer, 'at their goyng forthe to sent davys down ys camppe'.[78] Of these men only Morsse and Timewell occur as Morebath tax-payers in the subsidy returns of 1543, and so far as can be deduced from the accounts, none at this point were householders, except perhaps Robert Zaer, who had been sheep warden in 1547: all of which suggests that the group as a whole was made up of unmarried 'Young Men', the group directly undermined and disenfranchised by Simon Heynes's ban on church ales eighteen months before. John Timewell had been one of the two Young Men's Wardens in the year that the Young Men's store had been dissolved. There were so many John Timewells in mid-Tudor Morebath that it is impossible to be certain whether this was the same young man, but it seems likely. I have found no unambiguous subsequent references to Morsse, Borrage and Hurley: it may well be that they never returned to the village, because they lay among the dead at Clyst St Mary. They had been by no means marginal men: the fathers of two of them, William Hurley and Thomas Borrage, were among the most active and responsible of Morebath's parish officials, and Borrage senior had been High Warden just two years before. Zaer himself, who did return, was to serve as High Warden twice in Elizabeth's reign. The parish, it seems, sent their brightest and best to fight on their behalf.

Whatever their precise identity and standing, they certainly went with the parish's blessing and support. William Timewell and William Hurley senior had the parish's remaining stock from the sale of the church house goods, 15/8d after the purchase of the Book of Common Prayer, in their keeping. They disposed of it in providing each of the young men with 6/8d 'at hys goyng forthe' and in providing them with arms – swords for all but Zaer, who was paid 2/= for his bow. There was a shortfall of 9/10d, made good by two parishioners, William at Combe and John at Poole, and the tithing man, William Leddon, later levied an official sett on the parish to recompense them. 2/6d towards the cost of Christopher Morsse's sword was raised by a collection made by John at Courte 'at the churche style, of viij [8] persons viij groats' [a groat = 4d].[79]

This is, on the face of it, a baffling, almost an incredible, incident, and its very existence was masked from earlier users of the accounts by Binney's mistranscription of 'sent davys down' as 'sent denys down'. W.G. Hoskins, in his splendid history of Devon, cited the payment for the Prayer Book from this very page of the accounts in the course of his portrayal of Morebath as the archetypical conformist Devon parish, not noticing that the rest of the page actually documented the parish's participation in armed rebellion and high treason.[80] On first consulting the Morebath manuscript in 1995 I noticed Binney's mistranscription, and grasped at once that the entry must refer to the siege of Exeter, but I simply could not credit that Sir Christopher could have documented in detail the parish's involvement in armed rebellion, naming not only the men who had directly participated, but the parishioners who provided the money for their arms and maintenance money. In an essay published in 1997, I aired those doubts, and the enormous problems implicit in the notion of a parish equipping its sons for rebellion and then solemnly recording the proceedings in the churchwardens' accounts. I concluded that the entry must refer to the pressing of the young men of Morebath into a government militia presided over by Paulet, their Manorial Steward. Other West Country parishes recorded parochial expenses in connection with the 1548 Cornish 'commotions', incurred in support of the Royal forces who had put down the rebellion, as part of the secular obligations of the parishes.[81] In 1549 too, many Devon parishes were required to provide men and money to combat the rebels – Ashburton, where many must have been sympathetic to their cause, nevertheless sold £10 worth of plate 'with the whiche money they served the kings majestie against rebells ...', and Tavistock paid £13/6/8d from sales of plate and vestments 'to serve the kynges majestie in the comocion tyme'.[82] The 6/8d given to each of Morebath's young men looks at first sight as if the Morebath entry might be another of these enforced levies for royal troops – 6/8d, known in the sixteenth century as 'a noble', looks like an officially fixed sum, the wage given to a militia man, and it is clear that the parishioners believed each man must have just so much and no less; when the parish stock was exhausted, enabling only 3/4d to be given to John Timewell, Willam at Combe gave him another 3/4d 'to make up his nobyll'.

And we know that musters of this sort were in fact being raised at just this point. In the midst of general lamentation about the reluctance and failure of the West Country gentry to mobilise their tenants on behalf of the crown, the Privy Council instructed Russell on 22 July 1549 to convey the King's special thanks to the gentry who had responded to his appeals and done the King 'good, faythfull and paynefull' service. Among them was almost certainly Sir Hugh Paulet, who knew Morebath parish well, and

who had been, if he was not still, the Steward of their Manor, acting on behalf of Sir John Wallop, their landlord. After the collapse of the rebellion, Paulet would be rewarded for his services to the Crown with the governorship of Jersey.[83] A hawkish professional soldier, he was one of the key figures in the Royalist counter-attack against the rebels, and within weeks of the Morebath account on St James's day would chase the retreating remnants of the rebel forces up the Exe valley, almost to Bampton itself. It seems plausible that Paulet might have pressed Morebath into service in his troops, and required them to help in the bloody suppression of a rebellion they must certainly have approved of in their hearts.[84]

None of this, however, will do. In the first place, the standard allowance to a man pressed into a royal muster was not 6/8d, but 13/4d, the sum paid to each of their twenty men by Tavistock parish, and found in other entries relating to the militia from the period.[85] There is precedent for the sum of 6/8d as a payment by parishes to soldiers in time of crisis, but not for royal troops – during the Pilgrimage of Grace in the north of England in 1536, many communities paid for the costs of rebellion by official levies, and some seem to have paid their men £1 for three days' service in the rebel hosts, i.e. 6/8d.[86] More to the point, we have seen already that Morebath had by 1549 become accustomed to making payments to equip soldiers for royal armies. In all such payments, Sir Christopher invariably notes that such money 'to the settyng forthe of sawders' was paid '*to serve the king*' (or queen) – the same formula used at Ashburton and Tavistock about their payments to men in the commotion time.[87] The absence of any such formula in Morebath's 1549 entry, where one might most expect protestations

---

* Sir Christopher's indiscreet record of the parish's involvement in the Prayer-book rebellion with his subsequent attempts to blot out references to the rebel 'camppe' [Binney 163 / Ms 375]

of loyalty, is very eloquent. Moreover, the destination of the young men is three times repeated – 'to sent davys downe ys campe'. This cannot be a description of a departure for a royal militia camp, though I mistakenly argued in 1997 that this phrase might have been a intended as a shorthand reference to just that. The priest, I suggested, writing in retrospect after the defeat of the rebels, knew that the royal forces had ended up at Exeter, and so had expressed their entry into the royal forces in that form.

Once again, however, this simply will not account for the known facts. No royal army *ever* came anywhere near the camp on St David's Down, in July or later, for when Russell overthrew the rebel forces he did so at St Mary Clyst, to the east of the city. He then entered Exeter in triumph, not from the north-west, where St David's Down lay, but from the south. By the time he arrived, St David's Down was no longer a rebel encampment. And in any case, the very repetition of the word 'camp' three times in the entry is a sure signal that the men were joining the insurgents, not setting out to suppress them. The commotions of this summer were described then and subsequently by both their friends and their foes as the '*camping* time': on 19 July Sir Thomas Smith could talk of the rebels in Essex as 'Runabouts … or *Camp*-men'.[88] The same usage was applied to the Devon rebels, by themselves as a self-description – when they dated their demands from 'divers *campes* by est and west of Excettor' – and by their opponents as a term of abuse. The Devon Protestant polemicist, Philip Nichols, in one of the best of the official replies to the Devon rebels, reproached them for '*encamping* themselves and rebelling against their natural prince': he urged them to 'leave off … your *camping* at your own doors'.[89] The word 'camp' therefore was an incriminating one, with inescapable overtones of rebellion against royal authority: it simply would not be used to describe joining a loyalist militia, least of all by someone as alert to the nuance of words as Sir Christopher. And, with hindsight, Sir Christopher knew the words were incriminating. At some point he revisited this entry, and rather ineffectively blotted and scratched out the word 'campe' on each of its three occurrences. The words remain clearly legible, perhaps because the ink has thinned and faded with the years, but the attempt to cover them up tells its own story, inexplicable if the entry was made long after the event or was merely an innocent reference to the equipping of royalist militia. Once again, Binney's edition gives no hint of this blatant but botched attempt at concealment, and so helped mask the extraordinary indiscretion of the original entry.

The chief reason for doubting the plain evidence of the Morebath accounts that the parish had joined the rebels at the siege of Exeter is of course precisely the apparent implausibility of such an indiscretion. How could any man in his right mind, much less one so intelligent and alert to the value and permanence of the written record as Sir Christopher, have been so idiotic as to compile so incriminating an account? The first thing to be said is that he was not alone. On the other side of the country, Harry Ruston, churchwarden of the Norfolk parish of North Elmham, also documented in detail his parish's (and his own) involvement in rebellion. The Elmham accounts for 1550 have pages of detail about 'the summes of money payed and delyvered by me the seyd Herry Ruston in the tyme of the campe at Mussolde with the Assent and consent of the ynhabytance of the Townschype of Elmham'. These payments include the provision and carriage of food and supplies to the rebel camp, outdoor relief to the wives of the poor men of the parish who were in arms at Mousehold, and expenses for the treatment of men wounded in skirmishes with the royal forces, and for beer given to demobbed rebels on their way home after the collapse of the protest and the bloodbath at Dussindale which ended their hopes.[90]

We are here confronted with two distinct aspects of Tudor parish awareness. The first is the principle of accountability, whereby every penny spent must be declared, whatever its purpose. By the time that Harry Ruston presented his accounts at Elmham, the Norfolk camping men had been massacred at Dussindale, their leaders had been executed as traitors, and the whole episode had been branded as treason. Yet the same pages which record rebellion at Elmham, record without any sense of incongruity the dutiful removal of the altars from Elmham church, the conversion of the wooden retable from above the high altar into a white-painted 'ministering table' placed in the midst of the quire for the 1549 Prayer Book communion service, and the surrender of the old books of the Latin service to the archdeacon. Legal or illegal, money spent was money to be accounted for. We need not doubt that Sir Christopher's punctilious insistence on accurate record-keeping dictated the same degree of incriminating accountability at Morebath.

But secondly, we need to register that at the time of the parish's involvement in the siege of Exeter, the men of Morebath are most unlikely to have considered themselves to be rebels at all. The county was in arms to defend its ancient traditions against the king's bad counsellors, not the king. The regime might damn the men of the West as rebels and traitors, but that was not their self-description. Had not the Privy Council deliberately instructed Russell to mount a propaganda effort 'by spredyng abrode rumors of theyr develyshe behavours, crueltye, abhomynable levings, robberies, murders and such lyke'. This had duly been done, and Philip Nicholls had told the rebels that 'youre houses falle into ruin, your wives are ravished, your daughters deflouered before your own faces, your goods that ye have many long years laboured for lost in an hour and spent upon vagabonds and idle loiterers'.[91] The men of Morebath, equipping their sons to defend their traditional values, and conscious of the way in which the policies of the regime had plundered their resources, will have taken all such fulmination with a pinch of salt, for they knew the men they were sending to be neither rapists nor vagabonds. They considered themselves to be defenders of the right, not rebels in arms, and with the whole county in arms, they will not have considered it incongruous to use the normal machinery of parish management to equip and arm their representatives. John Hooker acknowledged the prevalence of this mentality when he observed that the majority even of the citizens of besieged Exeter 'were of the olde stampe and of the Romysh religion': they shared the religious outrage of the besiegers, and were sympathetic to their cause, and Hooker records their anger at the handful of protestants whom they considered had provoked the righteous indignation of the county – 'Come out theise Heretiques and two penye booke men, where be theye, by Goddes Woundes and bloode we will not be pynned in to serve theire turne; we will go oute and have in our Neighbours they be honest good and godlie men'.[92] This shared sense of righteous indignation was the explanation of the 'peremptory and vengefull' tone of the rebels' demands, which so antagonised the regime and its apologists at the time, and which has aroused the comment of historians ever since:

> Fyrst we wyll have all the generall counsell and holy decrees of our forfathers observed, kept and performed, and who so ever shal agayne saye them, we holde them as Heretikes.
> Item we will have the Lawes of our Soverayne Lord Kyng Henry the VIII concernynge the syxe articles, to be in use agayne, as in hys tyme they were.
> Item we wyll have the Sacrament hange over the hyeghe aulter, and there to be worshypped as it was wount to be, and they whiche will not therto consent, we wyl have them dye lyke heretykes agaynst the holy Cathlyque fayth.[93]

These were men certain of the righteousness of their cause, convinced they had been pushed beyond endurance, determined to set their world right again. In joining the siege of Exeter, therefore, the men of Morebath believed that they too were behaving like 'honest good and godlie men' defending the traditions of their fathers and the well-being of their community and their region, which had been assailed beyond toleration by an alien regime in London. For that reason their tithing-man could levy setts to pay the costs of war, and their priest, as he always did, could write everything down.

The involvement of Morebath in the Prayer Book rebellion not only adds five new names to the fifty or so identifiable rebels, it throws a good deal of light, too, on the motivation for the whole revolt. The articles of the rebels in their final form doubtless represented clerical as well as lay priorities, but there is a consistency about the fundamental grievances of the protestors from the very beginning of the commotions in the West, and the men besieging Exeter quite certainly saw themselves as defending their inherited faith. The strongly religious and ecclesiastical tone of their demands must of course reflect clerical input, but if Morebath is anything to judge by, clerical input was a normal part of opinion formation in the West Country. The religious terms in which the demands are framed reminds us that the conservatism of communities like Morebath was more than a matter of the rejection of sheep taxes or the preservation of church furnishing and church funds. They were angry not only that the Reformation had doused the lights and destroyed the statues, but that it threatened the Mass and silenced their prayers for the departed, that it had emptied the religious houses, perhaps even that it had put the king in the place of the pope.

There has been a tendency for historians to try to assign either religious or secular motives for Tudor rebellions, as if they could be neatly separated. The Devon economic historian Professor Joyce Youings was incredulous that anything so trivial as religious change could have driven hard-headed Devonians into such reckless folly. 'Are we really to believe', she asked, 'that men and women who had used vernacular prayers as long as they could remember ... and some of whom had seen English bibles in their churches for more than a decade, now took up arms and left their homes just before the harvest to protest about the new English prayer book? or for religious causes alone?'[94]

But there was no such thing in Tudor England as 'religious causes alone', for religion was inextricably woven into the social fabric, and a change in the doctrinal definitions was more than a slight adjustment in the way people prayed: apart from anything else, it had just smashed all the best statues in England. For many in Tudor England, the Reformation spelt liberty and truth, the casting off of man-made complication, the dazzling light shed by the bible. To hear the scriptures, to worship in one's own tongue, these were things which made many among the Eastern camping men 'acknowledge the Gospel which ye say ye greatly hunger for'. But in the West, religious change could not be separated from the other mounting demands of Tudor government on Tudor people. The suppression of the saints at Morebath negated twenty years of the parish's collective fund-raising, it had put out all the lights in the church, it had dispersed the Young Men and Maidens and dissolved the parish's other organisations, it had bankrupted the parish church. The new Prayer Book to them did not look like new light: it spelled an end to the daily Mass and prayer for the dead, it was of a piece with the forces which had sealed up their church house and outlawed their ales. Was Sir Christopher one of those 'unlearned and indiscreet preachers and other priests' so much detested by the regime who, 'of a devilish mind and intent' had brought the people of the West 'to much disorder of late, and in some parts, in manner to insurrection and rebellion'?[95] Who can say, though it is hard to imagine his parish acting in this matter without his advice and counsel. All we know is that the parishioners of Morebath, so prompt in obedience, so law-abiding, had at last come to see in the Edwardine reforms a force which threatened the foundations of their world. Vainly, belatedly, they had tried to call a halt.

By the time the parish assembled for the High Wardens' annual account at All Saints 1549 the Prayer Book rebellion had been suppressed, and Morebath was obliged to come to terms with defeat. Robert Zaer and John Timewell had returned, perhaps along the route of defeated rebels chased to Bampton by Sir Peter Carew and Sir Hugh Paulet. Morebath may well have been mourning the violent death of the rest of the young men – Christopher Morsse, William Hurley's son, Thomas Borrage's son. If any knells were rung for them, however, Sir Christopher did not record them in his book, for knells, like the Mass, had been vanquished at the siege of Exeter. Morebath was certainly obliged to pay now for its mistaken gamble in the summer. The German reformer Martin Bucer, established in Cambridge as Regius Professor of Divinity, reported that during the commotions the rebels had gathered all the copies they could find of the Book of Common Prayer, the root of all the trouble, and had burned them in the camps.[96] Morebath's copy, bought by William at Timewell in the early summer for 4/4d, was almost certainly one of these burned books. Recording its original purchase, the priest described it as 'the *furst* communion boke' and the parish now had to buy a second, paid for by collecting donations from prominent parishioners, since the parish had insufficient funds even for so modest a purchase.[97] Indeed, in the wake of the defeat of 1549, Morebath's normal processes of accounting and the central role of the High Warden broke down. Richard Cruce, the High Warden for 1549, inherited the sum of 15d from his predecessor, Lucy Scely. He in turn passed a paltry 3½d to his successor Richard Hukeley, and Hukeley had nothing at all left to pass to Richard Robyns in 1551.[98] With no income beyond the few pence to be got from selling the ends of old bell-ropes, and some small legacies from dying parishioners, the effective financial management of the parish had to be taken over by the more prosperous parishioners, grouped as the Six Men, who were now obliged to meet urgent parish needs from their own resources. The transfer of responsibility for the expenses of reformation from the warden to the Six Men, and the episodic nature of the Six Men's accounting, means that the precise sequence of events in these years becomes hard to reconstruct.

Inch by inch, however, the parish met the continuing requirements of the Edwardine reform. Cost as much as conservatism kept their compliance slow. In addition to the Prayer Book, they were now required to have a psalter for the recitation of the psalms in English. This too was bought by a collection of groats extracted from nine of the parishioners assembled for morning service, some time in 1550: as the priest reported, 'the sawter boke was bofth a god whyle after the boke of communion wherefore we stayed to have money by twyxt masse and matyns for the sawter boke ....'[99] The images were taken down and some were destroyed in 1549 (as they were at Ashburton),[100] and like other Devon parishes Morebath surrendered their Mass book and the great breviary used for the sung Latin offices 'accordyng to the command-ment', recouping 18d by selling the leather 'skynnys' which had covered them.[101] A selection of the hidden vestments, including the black set, were returned to the church for use in the new English liturgy.

Sir Christopher says nothing at all about the destruction of Morebath's images, though it must have been for him, even after the years of cooling of devotion to them since 1538, a peculiarly painful moment. William Popyll's gilded crucifix, completed so expensively on the eve of the 1538 Injunctions, was certainly burned, for it had to be replaced in Mary's reign. But, as would later emerge, a crowd of spectators attended the removal of the church's statues, and many took something home with them. William Morsse at Loyton rescued the figure of John from the crucifix, John Williams from Bury took the matching figure of the weeping Virgin Mary, and the figures of the king and queen from the carved scene of St George and the Dragon. The rood-loft had been decorated with 'pageants', painted scenes or, more likely, carved alabaster plaques placed along the loft front: many parishioners took one or more of these away, and others took some of the church books: these were to resurface in the safety of Mary's reign. It is not clear whether these were good Catholics rescuing what they could, or looters, or souvenir hunters. When he brought his swag back in Mary's reign, John Williams of Bury, not a parishioner of course, expected to be paid for doing so, and the matter was referred to the bishop. Sir Christopher himself saved what he could: St Sidwell's statue was destroyed, but he took back to the vicarage a cloth painted with her image, and the basin in which her light had burned.[102]

But Sir Christopher's silence in the face of what must have been a trau-matic event is not in fact so very surprising. All over England, conservative priests and parish officials in Edward's reign recorded successive stages of the religious reforms in private memoranda or notes in church books, but they almost never expressed an opinion or commented on in any way that which might disclose dissent or invite official retaliation. Commenting on this phase of the Reformation in the parishes, the Elizabethan Anglican cleric Michael Sherbrook shrewdly remarked that the authorities 'by the colour of those words Superstition and Idolatry' made 'the ignorant churchwardens and such other like of the Parishioners ... afraid to speak any word against their doings, contrary to the Law (least they should have been taken up for hawks meat as all Papists were)'.[103] In the aftermath of 1549 Morebath had every reason to keep quiet, but even perfectly law-abiding priests and parishes gave no hint of the dismay they must often have felt. In the Midland parish of Much Wenlock another conservative cleric, Sir Thomas Butler, had recorded the holocaust in 1547 of his town's greatest treasure, the bones of the local patron saint, St Milburga, burnt at the church gate on a pyre made of four local pilgrimage images. Like Sir Christopher, Sir Thomas was an inveterate notetaker and record-keeper, and he entered a brief account of what he must certainly have thought of as this act of sacrilege into the parish register. The note is in the clipped Latin he generally chose for his notes of momentous religious changes, and he allowed himself no comment except that 'hoc fuit ex percepto et injunctione visitator sive Commissio'r in visitaci'oe Regia ...' [this was done by the command and injunction of the Visitor or rather Commissioner during the Royal Visitation'].[104]

And still the commands and Injunctions went on. In November 1550 the reluctant Bishop Vesey was ordered by the Privy Council to bring the Exeter diocese into line with the rest of the country by seeing to it that the altars in every church and chapel were removed 'and yn lyeu of them a table sett up in some convenyent part of the chaunsell ... for the administracion of the blessid Communion'.[105] In 1551 Morebath duly complied, John Lowsmore being paid 3/= for taking away the altars and the rood loft, and John Darche 4d for iron gear to hang up the pulpit.[106] The warden sold off the six great altar candlesticks of brass, 80 pounds weight of them, for which 'the braser of Exceter' gave them 3½d the pound, scrap metal prices: the money was swallowed up in the debts the parish owed the Six Men, and the brass no doubt found its way into the casting of guns for Scotland.

But however his church might be reordered, Sir Christopher himself was totally unreconstructed. He continues to call the new communion table, set east and west in the people's part of the church, the 'altar'. The parish at large, however, was clearly treating the table as a desacralised object, in a way inconceivable for the old stone altar in the chancel. The table was being used as the counting table for the parish audit, for Sir Christopher refers explicitly to transactions carried out upon it. Twice in 1551 he reported that 'y ressevyd of William at Combe on[e] of the groats *that he toke up here a pon the auter* that was left of the byeng of the sawter boke': this usage of 'taking up' money *here upon the altar* would disappear in Mary's reign, when the stone altars were restored, but it would be resumed when there was a table once more in Elizabeth's reign.[107] The placing of parish money on the table for the next warden or the priest to take it up, is not, of course, entirely without its own symbolic resonance, and even solemnity. The combination of the old sacral language of altars, alongside the quite new use of the table as a suitable surface for the solemn transfer of parochial resources and responsibilities, is instructive, and full of significance for the future. Already, however unwillingly, however tentatively, a new ceremonial sensibility was in formation.

In all this the parish was being policed by the continuing process of visitation and inspection. Morebath was in trouble over its 'cooked' inventory of church goods, from which it had excluded so much that had been concealed around the parish. The Commissioners realised that the parish was witholding items, and the vicar and some of the parishioners had to make four expensive visits to Exeter to answer queries. When the final Edwardine inventories were eventually ordered prior to total confiscation in 1553, the parish surrendered two copes, two tunicles, a silver pax and a small patten, which they certified 'was all the churche gooddis that they hadd'. This certainly tallies with the pathetic little list of religious bric-a-brac in the church chest by 1553 – worn-out towels and napkins, pieces of ironwork, the foot of the processional cross, a holy-water bucket, the sanctus and lych bells.[108] But it was certainly not the whole truth: it is notable that there were no chasubles (the main Mass vestment) among the surrendered items, and no word of the other vestments concealed round the parish.[109]

The commotion time itself had hit the parish's tottering finances, for in its wake the Privy Council ordered the removal of all but a single small bell from every church tower in Devon, since it was by the bells the people had been summoned to rebellion. In practice, this meant the removal of the clappers, and the committal of the bells to the notional custody of selected 'honest men' of the parish. In 1550 the Council granted the clappers and bell furniture as a perquisite to Sir Arthur Champernon and John Chichester, a move which, like so much else in Tudor policy, proved self-defeating, since they promptly cashed in on this grant by allowing parishes to redeem the bells, for a price. Morebath bought its clappers back on 27 June 1551, at a cost of 26/8d loaned by three parishioners – John Norman, Edward Rumbelow and Thomas Borrage: Borrage was still waiting for the parish to repay his money in 1554.[110]

But not all the church's financial difficulties were attributable to the enforcement of reform or the aftermath of the Commotions. Mundane as well as religious concerns demanded the parish's collective attention. The whole region was in the grip of a depression, the poor of the neighbouring towns multiplying and suffering.[111] The most substantial outlay during these years was for repairs to the roof of the church, costing a huge £4/10/9d, 'for coveryng of the church for led, sawder mette and drynke', all of which had to be borrowed from the Six Men.[112] But the parish was also involved in a running series of expenses in attempting to get exemption from the obligations of 'the Sherowe towrne' – the feudal duty to send representatives to wait upon the sheriff during his biennial 'turn' through the county.[113] This was a chore which many parishes resented, and sought to free themselves from. Most of Morebath's notables were drawn into this effort – John Norman and William Hurley rode to see the sheriff Sir Thomas Denys 'for our fredom', and there were endless ridings backwards and forwards, often with costly overnight stays, by Lewis Trychay, Nicholas at Hayne, John at Court, William Hurley and Thomas Borrage, to fetch bills and other documents at Uffculme and Bradninch, and 'to kno the baylis plesure whether he wold have on man of the parysse to ryde with him to Sir Thomas Denys or no to dyscharge us of the scherowe torne by our fredome'. Roger Borrage bore a goose worth 8d to the Bayley of Bradninch as a sweetener 'for our liberty', and Lewis Trychay gave a capon worth 10d to Mr Sydenham to help with Hukeley bridge, for the parish was involved once again in disputes about their responsibility for the maintenance of the bridge. They continued to pay for the sea defences at Seaton, for the maintenance of tithing harness for the militia, and to provide arrows for soldiers bound for France.[114]

These costs were met in part from the sale of the ten-shillings'-worth of gold rescued from the destruction of the images, and from the sale of the church ale, which began again in 1551, since the authorities had come to realise that parishes simply could not survive without this resource.[115] Morebath's church house was still let out as a dwelling and no longer available for parish feasts, so the ale seems to have been hawked round the parish. Reporting the proceeds, Sir Christopher does not use the customary 'they made freely of their ale' but the distinctive phrase 'the … men that sold the parysse ale', suggesting a commodity rather than an event – another aspect of the privatising impact of the Edwardine reforms on the parish.[116] The ale nevertheless realised the substantial sum of £4/5/= in 1551, maybe an indication that parishioners were rallying round their church in its difficulties. But England was now in the grip of galloping inflation, the consequence of devastating harvest failures in 1550 and 1551, the ruinous costs of war, and the debasement of the coinage which had been the nearest successive regimes since the mid-1540s could get to a coherent monetary response to crisis. The 'fall of money' drastically undermined this effort. Sir Christopher reported that 'the batyng of this money' had reduced the ale money to two-thirds of its face value, and had halved the value of the 10/= received for the gold from the imagery.[117] For the whole of Edward's reign, therefore, a sense of financial crisis runs through every account, and the priest makes clear the value of every penny and groat, as when in 1551 he reported that William Hurley had 21d in hand 'cowntyng William at Combe ys xijd [12d] savyd of the xs [10/=] and besydis the sawter boke, and that must be tornyd in to a nother thyng to helppe pay our dettis'. By 1553 the parish had outstanding debts of over £6, and no obvious way of meeting them.[118]

The continuing crisis had the effect of moving the management of the parish's affairs out of the hands of the elected wardens, all of them in these difficult years men of modest means, and more and more into those of the Six Men and the priest. Sir Christopher, in alliance with one or other of these men, was constantly having to take executive action, as when he and John at Court organised the collections to buy the prayer book and the psalter in 1549–50. The result was sometimes confusion – on at least one occasion the Six Men were unable to balance the books, 'they cowd not make there cownte perfytt that day nother they cowd not agre a pon there ressettis and paymentis tyll candyllemas day follyng as here after ys declaryd ...': the priest turned in two attempts that year at getting the sums straight.[119] In the immediate aftermath of the Commotion, the parish, with plenty to hide, had to scramble to acquire the books and furnishings needed to avert the hostile scrutiny of the authorities, but these expenses, handled by the Six Men not the Warden, were not accounted for until 1551. By that time, no one could remember what some of the money had been spent on, or where it had come from, so the priest reported that 'we payd to vij [7] men for a nother boke (the wyche boke nescio [I know not]) vij groats and the wother grote ys reservyd to the parysse use for hyt ys not knowyn to whome that grote schuld be payd'. Sir Christopher did eventually work out what the money had gone on and, ever punctilious, added a note to an earlier version of this account 'for the boke of communion and the sawter boke ut puto [as I suppose]'.[120]

The priest was uneasily aware of the drift of responsibility from the wardens, and took elaborate precautions to reassure the parish about the shift. The accounts he presented in these years of crisis bristle with phrases designed to emphasise the answerability of the Vicar and Six Men to the parishioners at large:

Sum of the hole that we be yn dette as yett ys vere (as hyt stondyth here in wrytyng) xj [11] nobyllis and iiij[s] & vij[d] [4/7d] ... thus have y certyfyed you now of the troth of every thyng as y have byn informyd
We do you to knolyge that ...
More over a gayn *we doo yow to knolyge* that at the last hye Wardyns a cownte *you ware yn Richard Hucly ys dett* iiij[s] & vj[d] [4/6d], where of now furder *more ye schall have knolyge by this a cownte* of thes men that solde the parysse ale what there ys payd of this forsayd dette and what ther ys to pay.
they payd of dette to these ix [9] men xij[d] [12d] a pece ... and y bofth the boke of communion and the sawter boke *as y schowyd you be fore*
and for the clappers these men wyll answer for them at all tymys *they sayth.*[121]

Sum of the whole that we be in debt as yet is truly (as it standeth here in writing)

eleven nobles and 4/7d ... thus have I certified you now of the truth of everything as
I have been informed ...
We do you to knowledge that ...
Moreover, again we do you to knowledge that at the last High Wardens' account you
were in Richard Hukeley's debt 4/6d, whereof now furthermore you shall have
knowledge by this account of these men that sold the parish ale, what there is paid of
this aforesaid debt, and what there is to pay.
They paid of debt to these nine men twelve pence apiece ... and I bought the book of
communion and the psalter book as I showed you before.
And for the clappers these men will answer for them at all times, they saith.

Morebath's stagger from crisis to crisis reflected that of the diocese as a
whole. Vesey's last years as bishop were marked by the enforced surrender of
the bulk of his episcopal lands to the Crown. In these years, the diocese is
said to have lost up to two-thirds of its revenues and Exeter, one of England's
wealthier sees in the late Middle Ages, now became one of its poorest.[122]
Vesey himself was forced to resign in August 1551, ostensibly on the (not
unreasonable) grounds of his great age – he was then in his eighties – but in
fact because he was felt to be dragging his feet over reform, for which he had
a notable lack of enthusiasm. The old man took his pension and settled down
to rebuild his home town of Sutton Coldfield. Vesey was instantly replaced
by Miles Coverdale, the great biblical translator responsible for one of the
glories of Tudor religious writing, the version of the psalms used in the Book
of Common Prayer. But Coverdale's religious radicalism did not endear him
to his conservative diocese. His reforming ideals were borrowed from
Switzerland, he was a married man, and the lifetime dispensation from fasting
in Lent he at once secured from the King for himself, his household and the
guests at his table, scandalised his clergy, who cared nothing for his biblical
labours and saw only an anarchist in the seat of judgement. Despite conscientious preaching and residence, Coverdale was also widely despised by the laity
in this bastion of traditionalism, not least because he had been first drafted
into the diocese to preach against the Commotions, and the bishopric was
seen by some as his purse of thirty pieces of silver. His brief episcopate was to
be dogged by 'open railings and false libels and secret backbitings' among the
common people.[123] It was also marked by a visible collapse of clerical confidence in the church's future, signalled by the virtual drying up of vocations to
the priesthood. This was in fact a national phenomenon, triggered initially by
the flood of clerical labour released on to the market by the dissolution first
of the monasteries and then of the chantries, but it was very marked in
Exeter. In Vesey's first fifteen years as bishop, an average of forty-eight men a
year were made priests. Between 1535 and 1543 there were only sixty ordinations; only five men in all were ordained to the priesthood during
Coverdale's three years in post.[124] Sir Christopher, ordained in the halcyon

days of Bishop Hugh Oldham, when clerical recruitment in the Exeter diocese was at its highest for two hundred years and an average of sixty-five men a year presented themelves for the priesthood, must have felt that he was living in the last days, when it had been predicted that faith would fail.[125]

Edward's reign ended for Morebath as it had begun, with confiscation. Bishop Vesey and even Bishop Coverdale were rebuked by the Council because of the stubborn retention by many parishes of forbidden Catholic ornaments and practices. But a combination of Protestant zeal and the continuing urgency of war-funding now brought that issue to a head. At the beginning of 1552 the regime ordered the delivery of all inventories of church goods into the hands of the King, and on 16 May a fresh commission was issued for new inventories. On 16 January 1553 the order was given for the confiscation of all church valuables except the minimum required for its reformed rites. These rites had been further simplified in the summer of 1552 by the publication of a new Book of Common Prayer, markedly more Protestant than that of 1549. The Communion service now was to be celebrated not in the traditional vestment, or even the cope permitted by the 1549 Book, but in a simple surplice, like that worn by the parish clerk. Morebath had duly organised another whip-round of parishioners to raise the 5/= needed to acquire the book. But the new rules for celebration meant that the copes and vestments returned to the church under licence in 1550 for use with the 1549 book could no longer be used, and so were no longer safe. They had already prepared their new inventory on 1 April 1552, listing the cope of blue satin and the red velvet cope with spread-eagles which William Hurley had held at pledge in 1549, together with two tunicles, the silver-gilt pax and 'the patent of the lesse challis', these being, so they claimed, 'all the churche gooddis that they hadd'. Later that year, Lewis Trychay and three other parishioners travelled to Exeter to hand everything over to the Royal Commissioners. Harry Hayle bought the odds and ends of velvet left for 2/=, the warden's only income that year.[126] When the Five Men reported to the parish on the Sunday before Whitsunday 1553, they itemised all the remaining goods in the church chest, which that year's warden, Lewis Trychay, had handed over to them. A pitiful litany of dilapidation, it was surely intended by Sir Christopher, who placed a high value on the material expression of religion, and who knew the weight of words better than most, as a comment on the pass to which Edward's government had brought the parish. Of all the lists compiled by Sir Christopher, it is by far the most poignant and the most telling: notice in the midst of the dead-pan itemising, the flash of feeling revealed by the phrase 'poure lytyll towle'.

They ressevyd on[e] auter clothe and ij wother auter clothers with ryngis that servyd for curtyngis, a nold auter cloth that came fro Pole, a diaper towle and a nother poure lytyll towle, a nackyn for the priestis handis, a nolde sylkyn banner, a black herse cloth of bockaram, ij tapers, a lytyll pece of say with a frange, 2 sacryn bellis, 2 lyche bellis, the fotte of the crosse and on length of brasse of the staffe that bare the crosse, the holly water bockytt (de brasse) 2 pecis of led, a coller of a bell with 2 yris a bout (quod pertenet to Court and Borrage) the hyer part of the sens [censer] and the schyppe [the container for incense] a payntyd paper, ij boltis of yre and a hoppe of yre, the wyche hoppe of yre was delyveryd to the clerke to make a new twyste with all for the churche howsse dore and all the reste of these for sayd restyth yn the cheste as they say …[127]

They received one altar cloth and two other altar cloths with rings that served for curtains, an old altar cloth that came from Poole, a diaper towel and another poor little towel, a napkin for the priest's hands, an old silken banner, a black hearse-cloth of buckram, two tapers, a little piece of say [silk] with a fringe, two sacring bells, two lych-bells, the foot of the cross and one length of brass of the staff that bore the cross, the holy water bucket (of brass), two pieces of lead, a collar of a bell with two irons about (which belongs to Court and Borrage), the higher part of the censer and the ship, a painted paper, two bolts of iron and a hoop of iron, the which hoop of iron was delivered to the clerk to make a new twist withal for the church house door, and all the rest of these aforesaid resteth in the chest, as they say …

The Five Men's accounts for this year, made on 14 May, nevertheless, mark another very significant stage in Morebath's accommodation to the realities of the Reformation. For the first time anywhere in the accounts, the monarch is described in the heading as 'defender of the fayth and yn yerthe of the churche of inglonde and also of yerlonde the supreme hedd'. Sir Christopher had copied this striking and distinctive form from the inventory drawn up by John Scely a month earlier on 1 April, when the parish had delivered the church goods to the Commissioners in Exeter. Scely was presumably following a pattern provided by the Commissioners or copied from other parishes. The priest was intensely interested in this title: he did not bother to copy the inventory itself into the account book, just the heading with the royal titles as far as Scely's 'y John Scely made this wrytyng', tailing off thereafter with an 'etc.'. Under this truncated entry he recorded the surrender of the vestments, and headed the whole double-entry with the memorandum, 'Not[e] the style of the kyng', round which he drew a box. It was clearly the title, and not the inventory itself, which he thought worth recording. He himself duly followed this style exactly in compiling the Five Men's account six weeks later, and in the account of his brother Lewis as High Warden in 1553, by which time Edward had died and it is the Catholic Mary whom Sir Christopher described as 'supreme hedd' of the Church.[128]

The claim of Edward VI to be, like his father, Supreme Head of the Church in England, was not of course new to Sir Christopher in 1553. He himself, like every other beneficed clergyman, had taken the oath of supremacy in the 1530s, he was required to explain it to his parishioners four times a year, and it had been endlessly asserted in proclamations and injunctions ever since. But it had made no documentary impact in the Morebath records until now. His careful note of it and subsequent use in the accounts must therefore represent his acceptance, reluctant or complaisant, of a direct order from the authorities, or perhaps of pressure from his parishioners, or internal conviction. The last possibility is unlikely in the extreme, and was to be belied by Sir Christopher's manifest enthusiasm for the restoration of Catholicism in Mary's reign. Not everyone in Morebath may have been as resistant as he was to the new opinions. John Scely was Lucy's and William's son: maybe John's use of the royal title, like his mother's unauthorised sale of the church goods, represents his acceptance of Protestantism. This, however, is to read a great deal into uncertain evidence. It is just as plausible that the Commissioners for Church goods were leaning on parish officials and scribes to get their communities to tow the line in formal documentation like inventories and accounts. For obvious reasons, Morebath may have been specially anxious to protest its loyalty – from 1551 onwards the priest had taken to ending the accounts of the Five Men with a patriotic 'God save the kyng',[129] and the emphasis on the ecclesiastical title may have represented more of the same. For whatever cause, however, by 1553 Morebath and Sir Christopher had shifted into granting the foundational claim of the English Reformation, the Crown's headship of the church. They had travelled a long way from St David's Down.

But the Crown itself was about to call a halt to that process of accommodation. Within two months of Morebath's adoption of Edward's title to Supremacy, the young king was dead, and his Catholic sister Mary had become queen. Her reign would bring back to Cranmer's chair at Canterbury Cardinal Reginald Pole, the one-time dean of Exeter whose return had been demanded by the men of the West in 1549. With him would come the restoration of England, and Morebath, to Catholic communion, and the revival of some at least of the practices of their old faith. Sir Christopher's heart was about to lift.

CHAPTER SEVEN

Under Two Queens

I MOREBATH RESTORED

When news of the accession of Queen Mary reached Exeter at the end of the third week in July 1553, Bishop Coverdale was preaching to the citizens in the cathedral. As the whisper that England now had a Catholic monarch travelled round the building, the congregation stood up one by one and walked out, until none but a 'a few Godly men' were left to listen.[1] It was a foreshadowing of the imminent evaporation of the gains which the Reformation had made in the West Country over the previous six years. There were by now, of course, many convinced Protestants in the region – among the gentry of Devon, like Peter Carew and Walter Raleigh, among the citizens of the city and market towns, like John Midwinter, who was to serve as Mayor of Exeter in 1554–5 despite having been a committed and active 'proffessor of the ghosple' under Edward; he was one of several such in Exeter.[2] There were even Protestants among the peasantry. Only one heretic was burned in the diocese in Mary's reign, a Cornish woman from Launceston, Agnes Priest. She was a labourer's wife who had left her husband and family because of their proselytising enthusiasm for the Marian restoration of the old religion. Stocky, blunt and fatally outspoken, she was illiterate, and 'that I have learned was of Godly preachers and of godly books that I have heard read' – testimony in itself to the spread in the West of a Protestant culture. Agnes

Priest was by her own admission an isolated figure, moving from place to place to avoid detection, inventing excuses not to go to Mass on Sunday, but in Exeter at least 'divers had delight to talk with her': she could argue persuasively the nature of the presence in the eucharist, and knew the names of all the books of the Bible by heart.[3]

As the reign progressed, West Country Protestants in general found themselves members of a small and increasingly beleaguered minority, and even the convinced did not prove stout-hearted. The reformed cause in Devon was compromised almost from the start by the involvement of its principal leader, Sir Peter Carew, in a West Country conspiracy against the Queen and her Spanish marriage, one of the manifestations of patriotic Protestant disaffection of which the Kent-based 'Wyatt's Rebellion' was the most serious manifestation. Carew, detested by the conservative peasantry for his role in the bloody suppression of the 1549 rising, fled to France at the end of January 1554, and with him went any hopes of Protestant resistance in the diocese.[4] Nor did Protestant clerical leadership prove much more enduring. The Exeter parish of St Petroc housed most of the city's elite. William Herne, their priest since 1528, had been sincerely converted to the new learning, and his parish led the rest in adopting the teaching and practices of Protestantism. A close friend of Alderman Midwinter's, Herne told him in Edward's reign that he would rather be torn apart by wild horses than say the Mass again. Yet when the Mass was reintroduced in December 1553, Herne promptly conformed. Midwinter, entering the church and seeing his friend robed and ready for the old service, 'poynted unto him with his fynger, remembringe as it were his olde protestations that he wold never singe masse agayne; but parson herne openly yn the churche spak alowde unto hym. It is no remedye man, it is no remedy.'[5]

Herne was no isolated figure: about seventy clergy, 15% of the total number in the diocese, had married in Edward's reign: these men must have subscribed to some at least of the teachings of the Reformation. All of them were now ejected from their livings by the diocesan authorities, but a third put away their wives, did public penance and found another benefice, where they functioned once more as Catholic priests (though at least half of those who did so were reported to be secretly consorting with their wives).[6]

Nevertheless, even in so conservative a region and in the face of so decisive a collapse of Protestantism, it was, to begin with at least, a time of confusion and mixed opinions. On Christmas Eve 1553, neighbours gathered for the festivities at the house of John Combe of Linkinhorne in Cornwall. One of them asked Combe whether he had been to church, and he replied that he had 'one hour agone; and that he had heard and seen that thing he saw not in four year before, for I have, thanked be God, heard mass and received holy bread and holy water'. One of the company, Sampson Jackman, cried out that he wished all priests were dead, and when reminded that the Mass was now restored by the Queen's command denounced the Queen, 'a vengeance take her': he expressed his fear that 'before twelve months you shall see all houses of religion up again, with the Pope's laws'. He deplored the very notion that a woman should bear rule, but if there was to be a queen, he wished it might be the lady Elizabeth, who was at least a Protestant.[7] This rash conversation led to denunciations and an official investigation, but everyone concerned was bailed, and no action taken against them. It was the same elsewhere in the diocese, men and women being by and large willing to turn a blind eye to their Protestant neighbours' heterodoxies, as Walter Steplehill, the Catholic mayor of Exeter did to his Protestant fellow-citizens during his spell of office in 1556, when he 'did friendly and lovingly bear with them and wink at them'.[8] And even Morebath can have been no stranger to divided opinions over religion. Whatever the religious solidarities of their own small and conservative community, whatever the bitter legacy of 1549, a market town like Bampton must certainly have had converts to the new faith among its 600 adult inhabitants. The gentry household of Thomas Southcott at Shillingford, just outside the parish boundaries, was praised by the first Elizabethan bishop of Exeter as soundly Protestant by 1564, and may well have been so already at the start of Mary's reign: Southcott's father had married a Sydenham, but Thomas Southcott himself had married a niece of Peter Carew's.[9]

Indeed, in Morebath itself the accession of Mary found the warden, Sir Christopher's brother Lewis, dutifully providing for the long-term future of Protestant worship in the parish. There had recently been an episcopal or archidiaconal visitation, and the tablecloth used for the communion, in need of repair, had evidently been judged unworthy. A parishioner, Roger Bagbere, was commissioned by Lewis Trychay to make a new one out of the church's depleted store of redundant vestments. With the parish running on deficit, nothing could be wasted: the 'scredis' of red velvet left over from Bagbere's work were delivered to William at Combe, who promptly lost them.[10] But these were the last consequences of a regime which Morebath, in common with the rest of conservative rural England, recognised at once was gone, and rejoiced at the going. The Queen issued a proclamation on 18 August enjoining charity and mutual tolerance in religion, but permitting the reintroduction of the old Latin liturgy alongside the still legal Book of Common Prayer, until 'such time as further order by common assent may be taken therein'.[11] It was a signal for the restoration of Catholicism eagerly taken up all over the country. Robert Parkyn, the conservative curate of Adwick near Doncaster, reported that by the beginning of September 'there was veray few paryishe churches in Yorke shire but masse was songe or saide in Lattin'.[12] At Much Wenlock, Sir Thomas Butler recommended saying Mass in Latin 'more antiquo et secundum usum Sarum' [in the ancient way and according to the Use of Sarum'] on Sunday 3 September.[13]

We have no indication when Sir Christopher resumed saying the Latin Mass 'more antiquo', but there is no doubt that the parish saw Mary's accession as bringing to a decisive end the chaos and financial disaster which had marked the preceding six years. Two months into the Queen's reign, the Manor Court of Morebath met for a 'law day', at Michaelmas 1553, presided over by a new landlord. Sir John Wallop had died of the sweating sickness in 1551, leaving the Manor of Morebath to his nephew, Harry Wallop. Still in his early twenties, Harry Wallop presided himself at the Morebath law day, and authorised the Four Men and the Vicar 'with the consent of the hole parysse as the byll of recorde doth testifye' to make a grand settlement of all the debts incurred during Edward's reign 'with all wother contraversy a mong us'. Acting under solemn oath, they were to investigate every claim on the parish resources, levy a collection to meet them, and having 'qualifyed and passifyed ... all the dettis and demaundis', re-establish harmony and order in the parish's life.[14]

This settlement was plainly seen as part and parcel of the restoration of Catholicism, a social and economic reordering to match the liturgical and doctrinal one. Lewis Trychay presented his account as High Warden just a fortnight after the swearing-in of his brother and the Four Men to carry out this settlement. The account was written as usual by Sir Christopher, and listed a number of recent deaths in the parish and the legacies owing to the church as a result. The priest's unmistakable accents are audible in his reminder to the parish that although Thomas Rumbelow's widow owed them 6/8d for his burial in the church, Rumbelow had been one of the men who had bailed the parish out of difficulty during Edward's reign with his own money, and so Mistress Rumbelow 'sayth that ye are more yn here dett then [the cost of the grave] cometh unto where a pon when yow and sche hath recovyd [recovered] sche wyll pay you for the grave *lyke a nonyst woman*'. And the exultation in that familiar voice is palpable in Lewis's report that 'as for the iij[s] & iiij[d] [3/4d] of the bequysth of Rycharde Robyns and v[s] [5/=] of William Tymwell at Wode the wyche ys viij[s] & iiij[s] [8/4d] in the hole, this sum of mony are the sectoris and the rulers of these for sayd perssons *utterly determynd* to bestow hyt a pon a new patent for the lytyll challis as sone as may be yn ony wysse a cordyng to the dedis wyll'.[15] There is not much doubt that this 'utter determination' on the part of the executors to replace liturgical equipment lost to the reform owes as much to the priorities of their priest as to 'the dedis [dead man's] wyll'.

The grand settlement made by the Four Men and Sir Christopher took six months to complete, and was not finally presented to the parish until Easter Tuesday, 27 March 1554. In an account framed throughout in the language of disinterested conscience and accountability not heard since the 1542 rebuilding of the church house, the priest presented an immense reckoning, which must have taken the best part of an hour to read. In it, the fore said iiij men [William at Timewell, William Timewell at Combe, John Norman at Poole and William Hurley] with the vicar doo make yow a cownte of all the dettis and demaundis that we have qualifyed and passifyed and of all the ressetis that we have ressevyd and what order that we have taken yn hyt after our conssiens by the othe that we dyd take ye schall hyre for we have no[t] taken wother tax of yow then we have takyn of ourselfis.[16]

the aforesaid Four Men with the vicar do make you an account of all the debts and demands that we have qualified and pacified and of all the receipts that we have received and what order that we have taken in it after our conscience by the oath that we did take ye shall hear, for we have not taken other tax of you than we have taken of ourselves.

The reckoning was in effect a resumé of all the disasters and demands of the reign of Edward for which there remained outstanding debts. Since the costs connected with the Commotion and St David's Down had been settled by a levy made by the tithing-man at the end of 1549, there is no allusion to that traumatic episode, but most of the subsequent problems and involvements of the parish feature in Sir Christopher's reckoning. The account falls into two parts – a circumstantial itemising of all the money laid out on the parish's behalf since 1549, with the names of those who had provided it, and then an account of how the Four Men and the vicar had settled the debt. These two wings of the account are placed on either side of a list of free-will donations to the church made by every household in the parish. The listing of debts and repayments follows the clockwise spiral circuit of the parish used in the old sheep counts, starting from the church and Morebath Town, and the whole document represents the most extended of all Sir Christopher's celebrations of the unity and social geography of his parish. We travel from the vicarage itself to Town to Black Pool to Exebridge to Burston to Warmore to Hayne to Timewell to Rill to Court to Combe to Hukeley to Moore and back to Town, ending at Lewis Trychay's cottage there. En route, we are circumstantially informed how each parishioner had rallied to the community in its hour of need:

Thomas at Tymwell askyd for arrows that ware sent to Bullyn [Boulogne] xij^d [12d] ...
John at Courte askyth for hys parte for payng for the clappers xv^s & viij^d [15/8d]. Agayn he asketh viij^d [8d] that he payd for hys parte of the iij^s & iiij^d [3/4d] that the bayly of Brodnynch schuld have to cum to Ufcolme to the scherow torne. Agayn he askyth ij^d [2d] that he payd to Leuys and Hurley when they rode to Brodnynche and j^d [1d] to a man to fett Dabbe at Brusford to cum to Bawnton for evydens of Hucly bryge. Agayn he askyth for expenssis ij tymys at Exeter for the invitory of the churche gooddis xxiij^d [23d]. Agayn he askyth for hys expenssis ij tymys to Mr Ford to have a

byll of hys owne hande whatt there was payd for the clappers xvj^d [16d].
Sum in toto xxj^s & iiij^d [21/4d].
William Tymwell at Combe askyth of wolde dettis for hys parte of the iiij
[4] nobyllis that yow dyde owe him for the reparacion of the churche vs &
iiij^d [5/4d]. And ij^d [2d] to Hurly when he rode to Brodnynche with Leuys
he askyth (and for the capon that Mr Sydenham had for Hucly Bryge he
askyth x^d [10d]) and xij^d [12d] he askyth for hys parte for the communion
boke and xvj^s [16d] that he payd for wrytyng of the laste invitory. And
agayn he askyth for expenssis for horse and man for iiij tymys rydyng at
Exceter for the invitory of the churche gooddis vs [5/=].
Sum xiij^s & viij^d [13/8d] in toto sibi
William Leddon askyth for expenssis for fettyng of the tuthyng harnys at
Exceter xij^d [12d].
… Robert at More [High Warden 1552] askyd of yow a pon hys last a
cownte for the reparacyon of the churche ij^s & viij^d [2/8d] and the wother
ij^s [2/=] a pon hys a cownte was for hys expenssis ij tymys at Exceter for the
invitory of the churche.
Sum sibi in toto viij^s & viij^d [8/8d].[17]

Thomas at Timewell asked for arrows that were sent to Boulogne 12d …
John at Court asketh for his part for paying for the clappers 15/6d. Again he asketh
8d that he paid for his part of the 3/4d that the bailiff of Bradninch should have, to
come to Uffculme for the sheriff's turn. Again he asketh 2d that he paid to Lewis and
Hurley when they rode to Bradninch and 1d to a man to fetch Dabbe at Brushford to
come to Bampton for evidence of Hukeley Bridge. Again he asketh for expenses two
times at Exeter for the inventory of the church goods, 23d. Again he asketh for his
expenses two times to Mr Ford to have a bill of his own hand what there was paid for
the clappers, 16d.
Sum in all 21/4d.
William Timewell at Combe asketh of old debts for his part of the four nobles that
you did owe him for the reparation of the church 5/4d. And 2d to Hurley when he
rode to Bradninch with Lewis he asketh (and for the capon that Mr Sydenham had
for Hukeley Bridge he asketh 10d) and 12d he asketh for his part for the communion
book and 16d that he payd for writing of the last inventory. And again he asketh for
expenses for horse and man for four times riding to Exeter for the inventory of the
church goods, 5/=.
Sum in all to him, 13/8d.
William Leddon asketh for expenses for fetching of the tithing harness at Exeter, 12d.
… Robert at More asked of you upon his last account for the reparation of the church
2/8d and the other 2/= upon his account was for his expenses two times at Exeter for
the inventory of the church.
Sum to him in total 8/8d.

Seventeen parishioners in all are listed as having incurred expenses on
behalf of the parish, or having loaned money to it in Edward's reign, from

Thomas Borrage's 27/10d to William Leddon's 12d, to a grand total of £6/5/8½d. The priest then announced the donations which he and the Four Men had just received from every household in the parish (thirty-two names, but thirty-three households in all, since Nicholas at Hayne held two farms and made a double donation 'consyderinge hys bothe bargayns'). These gifts ranged from 5/= or more from the strong farmers like Joan Morsse, Richard Hukeley, William at Timewell and William Timewell at Combe, down to single shillings from cottagers like John Skinner and James Goodman, or sixpences from the poorest households, like those of John Wood or Marke's widow at Exebridge. Sir Christopher introduces the account of the collection in emphatically religious terms, stressing that the money was donated freely 'of devocion', not by a sett or compulsory tax. Sir Christopher is deploying here an important distinction in medieval Catholic theology, indicating that these donations were what is technically known as a 'work of supererogation', considered specially meritorious because done over and above any obligation in law or duty: 'Now to pay these forsayd dettis and demawndis ye schall hyre of all our ressettis that we have ressevyd and how gentylly for the most parte men have paid of there owne devocion with out ony taxyn or ratyng as ye schall hyre [hear] here after more playner declaryd'.[18] There then follows a second full recitation of the details of the indebtedness of the parish to the seventeen parishioners, in which the priest reports how each debt was settled. In some cases the parishioner was paid the full sum outstanding. In most, however, they received only part payment, and the priest records their ready acceptance of this loss, on top of which he reminds the parish about their additional free donation. He starts with himself, then proceeds on his walk around the parish :

> Whereas the Vicar demandyd ix^s & viij^d [9/8d] of dett as hyt aperyth yn the begynnyng of this for sayd a cownte for the reparacion of the churche and other expenssis and of all this he takyth not j^d ...
> And whereas John Norman at Pole askyd yn the begynnyng of this a cownte for a bossyl of lyme when Robyn at More was wardyn now have we payd hym viij^d [8d] and ys content agayn whereas he askyd for hys expenssis viij^d for on tyme at Brodnynche and a nother time at Uffculme now have we payd him vj^d [6d] and ys plesyd ... (And ys for the viij^d that he callyd for hys expenssis at Seton and the xvj^d [16d] for caryng tymber at Exebryge of this he takyth not 1d and yett he gave hole hys gefth by sydis)
> ...
> And whereas William at Combe dyd ask of wolde dette yn the begynnyng of this a cownte v^s & iiij^d [5/4d] for the reparacion of the churche that have we payd him. And for the communion boke we have payd him hys xij^d [12d] and ij^d [2d] that he payd to William Hurley when he rode of Brodnynche. And xvj^d [16d] we have payd him for the wrytyng of the last

invitory. Sum vij^s & x^d [7/1od] thus ys he payd. And for hys expenssis iiij tymys to Exeter for the invitory with wother chargis the valure of a crone [crown= 5/=] of this he takyth not j^d and gave hys v^s [5/=] bysydis and ys plesed.[19]

Whereas the vicar demanded 9/8d of debt as it appeareth in the beginning of this aforesaid account for the reparation of the church and other expenses, and of all this he taketh not a penny.

And whereas John Norman at Poole asked 9d in the beginning of this account for a bushel of lime when Robin at More was warden, now have we paid him 8d and he is content. Again, whereas he asked for his expenses 8d for one time at Bradninch and another time at Uffculme, now have we paid him 6d and he is pleased ... (and as for the 8d that he called for his expenses at Seaton and the 16d for carrying timber at Exebridge, of this he taketh not a penny and yet he gave whole his gift besides) ...

And whereas William at Combe did aske of old debt in the beginning of this account 5/4d for the reparation of the church, that have we paid him. And for the communion book we have paid him his 12d, and 2d that he paid to William Hurley when he rode to Bradninch. And 16d we have paid him for the writing of the last inventory. Sum 7/10d thus is he paid. And for his expenses four times to Exeter for the inventory with other charges to the value of a crown, of this he taketh not a penny and gave his 5/= besides, and he is pleased.

This 1554 Easter Week reckoning at Morebath, therefore, was a formal celebration of the restoration of parochial life, not merely its replacement on a viable financial footing, but the recovery of its pre-Edwardine spirit of 'devotion'. That 'devotion', the practical expression of the charity existing between parishioners, was represented by their free service and gifts to the community, furthering both its secular concerns and the dignity and upkeep of its church building. As always when Sir Christopher addresses the question of parish loyalty, there is a strong moral charge in his commendation of 'how gentylly *for the moste parte* men have payd of their own devocion', perhaps a tacit rebuke to those who have insisted on the full payment of their debts. As the clerkship dispute demonstrates, disputes and their painful resolution were nothing new in Morebath, but the rhetoric of this whole passage, with its insistence on the peaceable and gentle settlement of debts, is in deliberate contrast to the opening evocation of 'all wother contraversy among us', the strife and dislocation which, Sir Christopher implies, had been the legacy of the Edwardine episode.

Revival of devotion was on display again in the High Wardens' account for that year, presented on Sunday 28 October. Mary had issued a fresh set of Royal Injunctions for the Church on 4 March, repudiating the Royal Supremacy, commanding the suppression of heresy and the deprivation of married priests, and restoring the Latin liturgy, the calendar as reformed in Henry VIII's reign, and the use of 'the laudable and honest ceremonies which were wont to be used, frequented and observed in the Church'.[20]

Morebath was clearly keeping pace with all this: it paid 4d to the summoner to have this proclamation read to it, and set about implementing its provisions. Though the start of the reign had found them without a Mass book, they paid a local priest, 'Sir John of Cousse', 2/= for the loan of his Mass book, until Thomas Borrage presented the parish with a new missal as a gift. The high altar was rebuilt and the communion table banished. The Palm Sunday 'generall dirige of this churche' had once more been sung for the parish dead, and for the Holy Week celebrations the parish unearthed and repaired the Easter Sepulchre, concealed during the Edwardine destructions after Lucy Scely had sold its painted cloth coverings. It cannot have been in need of much work, for the whole repair, including some attention to the 'standings' for the tapers ranged around it, cost only 2d. Another parishioner, Richard Timewell, presented a box to keep the Blessed Sacrament in, and the parish paid 4d for wire and cord to hang the canopy over it. William Hurley was paid 2/8d to bring a processional from Exeter or London, and 19d to fetch a new silver paten for the little chalice, which cost 7/11d (replacing the one confiscated by the Commissioners in 1553). Payments resume 'for makyn clene of the churche yerde', suggesting the revival of whatever celebrations had surrounded their patronal festival. Morebath also now revived the custom of ringing – and paying for – knells for the newly dead.

Above all, the wives of the parish, twenty-seven of them led by Alison Norman at Court and her daughter-in-law Tamsin, had taken a collection, 2d from the better-off women, 1d from the poor, 'the getheryng of the wyvis devocion', to pay for a manual. Both Joan Trychay, Lewis's wife (and hence called here 'Jone Leuys') and Christina Trychay, her daughter-in-law, wife of the priest's nephew and parish clerk, Christopher, paid 2d each. Lewis and his family had come up in the world since they had first arrived in the wake of the priest in the 1520s, among the poorest cottagers. The 'manuell' this collection paid for was the book used for all the services directly associated with the domestic intimacies of the Christian life, and the great rites of passage – baptism, churching of women, the marriage service, funerals – all the special concern of women.[21] The wives' collection was therefore a striking revival of feminine symbolic gifts, like the former Maiden Store's maintenance of lights before virgin saints, or the donations of wedding rings, beads and girdles to their images, which had been common in Morebath church before the watershed of Reformation.

As usual, the priest made the most of it, reading out all the names: 'how and of whome this money was gevyn and getheryd ye schall hyre', and for once there were no recalcitrant non-contributors to name and shame. Indeed, the collection raised more than was spent on the book: interestingly, the wives did not hand the surplus over to the High Wardens, even though, as it happened, the senior warden that year was a woman, the widow Joan Morsse, who had herself contributed to the fund. Instead they kept the money at their own disposal, in the hands of their own organiser, a flexing of collective female muscle which had not been felt in the parish since the dissolution of the Maiden Store a dozen years before: 'and so there restyth as yet of this forsayd gefth yn Alsyn at Courtis ys handis that ys lefth xv^d [15d] whyche xv^d these forsayd wyvis wylbe stow yn thyngis concernyng the churche as hyt schall plesse them'.[22]

As all that suggests, along with the reconstruction of Morebath's worship went the gradual recovery of some of its pre-Edwardine organisations. As they had done every year since the suppression of church ales by Heynes and his fellow Commissioners in 1548, the parish had elected only one warden for 1553–4, the widow Joan Morsse. By the time she presented her account in late October, however, she had been joined by Thomas at Timewell acting as ale warden, and they had 'ressevyd for sellyng the church ale' four marks, or £2/13/4d. As that form of words suggests, the ale was still a commodity, not an event, since the clerk's lease on the church house did not run out until 1556, and there was as yet nowhere to hold a parish feast. His nephew's tenancy of a parish resource may by now have been something of an embarrassment to Sir Christopher. Christopher junior was sometimes in arrears with his rent, and the priest quite evidently found reporting that fact uncomfortable. In a strikingly tortuous entry, he is careful to distance himself by calling his nephew 'the tenant', and makes it more than usually clear that he is merely reporting business conducted by others:

Item received about sent Andrew ys day laste paste for the churche howsse rent for an hole yere then paste vj^s [6/=] and ys for the viij^d [8d] hyt was payd for the lordis rent for ij [2] yere then paste [the ground rent due to the Lord of the Manor]. And at ester last past received for the halfe ere ys rent of the church howse iij^s & iiij^d [3/4d] and now for the wother halfe ere ys rente at Mychaelmas laste past the wardyng hathe demawnd hyt of the tenot and answer ys maden that he wyll pay the faythfeys as the wardyng says and so he hath now as the faythfes says.[23]

Item, received about St Andrew's day last past for the church house rent for a whole year then past, 6/=, and as for the 8d, it was paid for the lord's rent for two years then past. And at Easter last past received for the half year's rent of the church house, 3/4d, and now for the other half year's rent at Michaelmas last past the Warden hath demanded it of the tenant, and answer is made that he will pay the feoffees, as the warden says, and so he hath now, as the feoffees say.

In 1555, following the lead of the wives, another of Morebath's gender groups reappeared. For the first time since 1548 the Young Men met, chose themselves two wardens, and threw themselves into the general reconstruction of the parish. They gave the High Wardens 20/=, and made a separate collection for books for the church, which, like the wives, they kept in their own hands. On Sunday 5 July 1556 they made their first account, a red-letter day for the parish which the priest noted with the heading 'Begynnyng of the young men wardyns a gayn that stayd 8 yere and hadde no wardyngis': their ale that year had raised 48/5d, only 5d less than the High Wardens ale.[24] Most of the proceeds of this Young Men's ale were handed over to the parish for the repair of religious equipment and ornaments and the purchase of the books required by the Marian authorities. The Young Men's accounts in these years were presented at the beginning of July on the Sunday nearest the summer feast of St Thomas Becket, that special target of reformed animosity: in 1557 the priest makes a point of calling St Thomas 'the martyr'. In the previous year he had discontinued his recent practice of ending the accounts with 'God save the Kyng and the Quynes grace', and had begun once more to open them with 'Sent George ora pro nobis'.[25]

The parish was by now working at full stretch to meet the stringent requirements of the official Catholic restoration.[26] The Vicar and Wardens trooped off to Exeter in 1555 to present a new inventory of their church goods to the Royal Commissioners, this time not as a prelude to confiscation but to establish what was still missing and in need of provision. Ten yards of canvas were bought to make a new Lent cloth, Cecily at Moore was paid seven groats for making up a new surplice, and allowed to keep the seven-pence-worth of linen she had left over. From a series of business trips William Hurley brought back a new pyx for the Sacrament and, separately, the winter and summer volumes of a new breviary 'of the largest volumen' for Sir Christopher to say his service. Two sets of vestments (long since out of hiding) were being repaired, and the wardens paid Mr Huys at Bampton 4/2d for a makeshift crucifix while a better one was carved. It was a prudent sale-and-return arrangement, pending procurement of a better carving, 'and yn case we bryng home a gayn the crucifix un to him a fore candylmas next commyng we schall have ij^s [2/=] of our money a gayn'. They also packed up their English Bible and their copy of Erasmus' *Paraphrases*, and sent it by carrier to Exeter to be handed over to the authorities there. To help with all these expenses, dying parishioners were once more being encouraged to make bequests to the church, like the 5/= from John at Court which 'ye schall have as sone as the wydow and her rulers can see where a pon to be stow hyt here yn the churche conveniently as hyt may be to the honor of God and for the welth of hys sowle a cordyng to hys wyll'.[27]

Best of all, confident that the Marian restoration was here to stay, parishioners and neighbours now brought out of hiding the flotsam rescued from the Edwardine purge of imagery. Sir Christopher himself gave back the painted cloth with the picture of his patroness St Sidwell, John Williams of Bury produced 'a image of Mary and the kyng and the quyne concernyng

Sent iorge'. William Morsse at Loyton returned the figure of John from the Rood group, the widow Jordan gave 'tralis and Knottis', and 'of diverse wother perssons here was rescevyd pagynttis and bokis and diversse wother thyngis concernyng our rowde lowfth'. The vicar was enchanted: 'lyke tru and faythefull crystyn pepyll this was restoreyd to this churche by the wyche doyngis hyt schowyth that they dyd lyke good catholyke men'.[28]

Here Sir Christopher was perhaps idealising. Not everyone who returned goods to Morebath church was motivated by pure zeal for the Catholic truth. Edward Rumbelow, executor for small legacies to the church from his father and from Roger Budd, donated a valuable tunicle (not necessarily originally belonging to Morebath), which more than covered those legacies, but he wanted the church to reimburse him for the difference – 'and the overplus of that tunakyll ys referred to the parysse discrescion'. John Williams of Bury expected to be paid for having kept safe so many of the parish's endangered images: he nagged on about this, and seems to have threatened to pursue the matter in the episcopal courts. For the next two years the priest reminded the parish 'lett John Williams at Bery be payd for the kepyn of Mary and the kynge and the quyne *etc vel saltem vult dicere episcopo* [or anyhow (does Sir Christopher mean 'or else'?) he wants to speak to the bishop]'.[29]

But there were plenty of less mercenary gifts to maintain the priest's sense of a returning tide of piety: the legacy of a coat from Roger Don at Exebridge 'to be prayed for', 6/8d from Thomas Stevyn of Clotworthy towards the altar crucifix and for painting the ceiling over the Sacrament, a pair of altar cloths from John Norman at Court, another altar cloth from Elizabeth Yondyll of Bampton, all in 1556.[30] In the following year the Young Men and the Maidens (though the maidens did not revive their store) once more collected round the parish to paint the ceiling of honour above the high altar.[31] Recording it all, Sir Christopher is careful to underline the pious motives behind these benefactions: the young men and the wives have money in store 'of devocion', the wives buy a manual 'of there benevolence', the young men paint the ceiling over the altar 'of there owne frewyll', John Norman makes up a shortfall of 9d for a mended censer 'of his owne devocion'. And alongside the giving, the continuing scramble to keep pace with the pressure from the diocesan and crown authorities to hurry the restoration of full Catholic worship.

1556 was a demanding year, with visitations both by the archdeacon and by the new bishop, James Turberville, and the wardens had to pay 8d to the bishop's officers in Exeter 'to have respytt to make our certificath', since so much work was still in progress. Both church stiles were rebuilt (two trees were used in the process), Yowans was paid for sawing a stock (whole tree trunk) in Court wood for the rebuilding of the roodloft, and Wynesor and his man spent a fortnight on that work, suggesting that its destruction in

Edward's reign had been pretty complete. Their board and lodgings at William Taylor's house cost the parish 10/8d, their wages 16/8d. The Marian authorities required every church to have two altars, the high altar and at least one side altar, a provision designed to re-establish the cult of the saints. So at Morebath that year St Sidwell's altar was rebuilt, and bequests from Joan Morsse and her son John, both dead that year, were used to paint a ceiling of honour over it.[32] Progress was slower than Sir Christopher had hoped or the archdeacon cared to tolerate: in 1558 the wardens once more paid 1/= 'at the visitation to have a lycense to have a longer day to se such thyngis redressyd as was in payne in the court'.[33] The trouble was in large part a labour shortage: with every church in the deanery and diocese engaged in the same process of reconstruction, craftsmen were at a premium. The cathedral authorities in Exeter, where even the reformed parish of St Petroc's was engaged in energetic Catholic reconstruction,[34] hired themselves 'a cunning Dutchman' to put the noses back on the 'fine images' disfigured as a result of Protestant zeal in King Edward's days.[35] There were no cunning Dutchmen to be had in north Devon, and in 1557 Sir Christopher explained to the parish that Joan Scely had left them 3/4d,

> the wyche schuld y byn bystowyd or now yn the churche yn case the payn-ter hadd kept hys promysse and so schuld William at Tymwell ys iij^s & iiij^d [3/4d] and the ij^s & v^d [2/5d] that was ressevyd for the basyn ... that hong over the sacrament also but not with stondyng hyt schalbe bestowyd in this churche as sone as we can gette a workman paynter *gracia divina*.[36]

> *the which should have been bestowed before now in the church in case the painter had kept his promise, and so should William at Timewell's 3/4d and the 2/5d that was received for the basin ... that hung over the sacrament also, but notwithstanding, it shall be bestowed in this church as soon as we can get a workman painter, by the grace of God.*

There were bitter experiences along with all this sweetness. On St Clement's Eve 1554 yet another burglar broke into Morebath church by the south quire window, and stole linen, silk, and velvet altar cloths, a surplice, and one of the parish's two sets of vestments, the white ones which Sir Christopher and his father had paid for,[37] and which had survived the Edwardine regime, a tin bottle with the altar wine, the corporasses on which the Host and chalice were consecrated in the Mass and, worst of all, the pyx and the Blessed Sacrament it contained. The haul also included five chrysom bands, recent baptismal bindings cloths which had to be returned to the priest since they were soaked with holy oil, their number a sign both of the parish's fertility, and of the restored use of the Sarum baptismal rite.[38]

Nevertheless, by the end of 1558 Sir Christopher was able to look back over the previous five years as a period of triumphant rebuilding, a restoration not merely of the church's ornaments and building, but of the parish's

Catholic spirit. Thumbing through the church book, he read again the list of benefactors and benefactions he had compiled for the twenty years up to 1540, and he determined to bring it up to date. Once more he listed the wardens, year by year, and under each set of wardens recorded all donations to the church in their time 'what there was gevyn to this churche by there tyme now schall ye have knolyge of'.[39] The list was a good deal thinnner than the one compiled for the 1520s and 1530s, because the onset of the Henrician Reformation had drastically curtailed the willingness of the laity to put hard-earned money where the crown might well confiscate it: most of the gifts recorded for the 1540s are to the black vestments. But the heart of the list was the entry for the reign of Edward, and the start of Mary's reign:

> Anno Domini 1548 was hye warden of this churche Lucy Scely and by her tyme the church gooddis was sold away with out commission ut patet postea and no gefth gevyn to the church but all fro the churche and thus hyt con-tinyd fro Luce ys time un to Richard Cruce and from Cruce un to Richard Hucly and fro Hucly un to Richard Robyns and fro Robyns un to Robyn at More and by al these mens tyme the wyche was by tyme of Kyng Edward the vi the church ever dekeyd and then deyd the Kyng and Quyne Maris grace dyd succed and how the church was restoryd a gayn by her tyme here after ye schall have knolyge of hyt and yn this last ere of the Kyng and in the furst yere of the Quyne was Levys Trychay hye wardyn.

> Anno domini 1554 was hye wardyng of the churche Jone Morsse wydow and Thomas at Tymwell and how this churche was comforted a gayn by these tyme and what geftis was gevyn to the churche now ye schall have knolyge of.[40]

> *Anno Domini 1548 was High Warden of this church Lucy Scely, and in her time the church goods were sold away without commission, as afterwards appears, and no gift given to the church but all from the church, and thus it continued from Lucy's time unto Richard Cruce, and from Cruce unto Richard Hukeley, and from Hukeley unto Richard Robyns, and from Robyns unto Robin at More, and in all these men's time, the which was in the time of King Edward VI, the church ever decayed: and then died the King, and Queen Mary's Grace did succeed, and how the church was restored again by her time hereafter ye shall have knowledge of it and in this last year of the King and in the first year of the Queen was Lewis Trychay High Warden.*

> *Anno Domini 1554 was High Warden of the church Joan Morsse widow and Thomas Timewell, and how this church was comforted again in their time and what gifts were given to the church now ye shall have knowledge of.*

This passage has become familiar recently, through its quotation in widely read histories of the Reformation.[41] What has been insufficiently noticed, however, is its formal character, not as a spontaneous response to the events of the early 1550s, but as part of a larger retrospect of the

Reformation, a mini parish-history written after five years of the Marian restoration. Historians of the Reformation, newly sensitive to the broad ground-swell of conservative religious feeling in Tudor England, have perhaps worked too hard the few unguardedly Catholic voices who dared to articulate explicit anti-reforming opinions in the mid-century. Robert Parkyn, curate of Adwick-le-Street in the deanery of Doncaster, is the best-known of these, and his vivid and highly coloured narrative of the Reformation, first published by A.G. Dickens in the *English Historical Review* fifty years ago, features prominently in every recent treatment of the period.[42] In fact, however, it is a most unusual document. Composed, like Sir Christopher's retrospective, with the benefit of hindsight provided by Mary's reign, it offers a rare Catholic overview of the process of Reformation, in this case viewed from Yorkshire rather than Devon. Its point of view is announced in its epigraph from the Book of Proverbs, *Regnantibus impiis: ruina hominum* (when the wicked are in charge, humankind goes to wrack and ruin). Its opening paragraph develops this theme by tracing from 1532 the emergence and progress of the Reformation movement 'to the grett discomforth of all suche as was trew Christians'. Throughout Parkyn's account we are never left for a second in doubt about his feelings, as in his account of the suppression of the religious houses in 1539, when

> all was suppressed furiusly under footte (even as tholly temple of Hierusalem was handled when the Chaldees had dominion therof) and many abbottes & other vertus religius persons was shamfully put to deathe in diversse places of this realme. And all this ungratiusnes cam thrughe cowncell of one wretche and hereticke Thomas Crumwell, and such other of his affinitie, wich Crumwell was headyde for highe treasson in the yeare after.

His glee in recounting the Marian restoration is equally unbridled, especially in the passages on the discomforture of those of his colleagues among the clergy – not least the Archbishop of York – who had dared to marry:

> Hoo it was ioye to here and see howe thes carnall preestes (whiche had ledde ther lyffes in fornication with ther whores & harlotts) dyd lowre and looke downe, when they were cammandyde to leave & forsake the concubyns and harlotts and to do oppen penance accordynge to the Canon Law, which then toyke effectt.[43]

The pedigree of Parkyn's rhetoric in such passages is easy enough to identify: it owes a good deal to the vivid invective of Thomas More's controversial writings against Luther, the married friar, and against Tyndale and the early English reformers, but just as much perhaps to the petitions and articles of the rebels in the Pilgrimage of Grace, and those of the western rebels of 1549, with the denunciations by the former of low-born heretical bishops and councillors like Cromwell, and the 'abhominable actes by them comytted and done', and the demands of the latter for the return of 'all … auncient olde Ceremonyes used heretofore, by our mother the holy Church'.[44]

But such a pedigree of course is sufficient indication of the problems that conservatives had experienced in articulating their view of the Reformation process as it unfolded. Criticism of Crown religious policy had been rapidly identified with treason in Henry's reign: under Cromwell it was indeed true that careless talk cost lives.[45] In the years that followed, it was rebels who publicly articulated criticism of Henry's and Edward's religious policies. There is an important connection between public rhetoric and private dissent, a connection which has been insufficently remarked by historians seeking to account for the comparative docility and silence of the Tudor populace in the face of reform. So, without any recognised or established anti-reforming rhetoric to legitimate or serve as an example for humbler comment, conservative chroniclers in their narratives, or churchwardens in their parochial accounts, might note successive stages of the religious reforms of Henry and Edward's reign, as Sir Christopher or Sir Thomas Butler did, but they rarely ventured an explicit opinion, or commented in any way which might disclose dissent or invite official retaliation.

The advent of Mary changed all this, because there now emerged a public rhetoric of criticism of the Reformation, legitimating and giving form to conservative popular opinion. From the beginning, the Marian regime was extremely sensitive to the role of such official utterance in forming public opinion and a shared public 'voice'. One of the key publications of Mary's reign was Edmund Bonner's *Profitable and Necessary Doctrine* with its attached *Homilies*, which every parish priest was required to have and read to his people: Morebath paid 2/9d for their copy in 1556.[46] The preface to this work puts its finger on precisely this point, in a remarkable account of the role of propaganda in shaping public support for the Reformation. Bonner wrote that:

> Where as in the tyme of the late outragious and pestiferous scisme … al godlynes & godnes was dyspysed, and in maner banyshed, and the Catholique trade and doctryne of the churche (wyth a newe envyouse and odious terme) called and named papistrye, like also as devoute religion and honest behavioure of men was accounted and taken for superstitioune and hypocrisye. And thereupon (by sondry ways and wiles) pernicious and evil doctryne was sowen, planted and set forth, sometyme by the procedyng prechers sermons, sometymes by theyr prynted treatises, sugred all over with a lose lybertye … sometymes by readyng, playynge, singinge and other like meanes, and new devises, by reason whereof great insolency disorder, contention and much unconvenience, dayly more and more dyd ensue … to the notable reproach, rebuke and sclaunder of the hole realme. The people wherof, by sondry wicked persons, were borne in hande that they had got-

ten God by the fote, and that they were brought out of tirranie, darknesse and ignoraunce ynto lybertie, lyght, and perfytte knowledge, wher in very dede they were broughte from the gode to the bad.[47]

It is not long before we catch the echoes of this official rhetoric taken up in the local sources – the fierce comments of the churchwardens of Stanford in Berkshire, for example, on the Edwardine period, which they characterised as 'the wicked time of schism … when all godly ceremonies and good usys were taken out of the church'.[48] For the first time, conservative Catholicism could invoke the language of peaceable obedience and good citizenship in defence of inherited religion: in Mary's reign Catholics, not Protestants, appear as the upholders of law, so that Protestants who spoke out against Catholic doctrine were liable to be denounced not merely as heretics, but as traitors and rebels, impugners of the Queen's procedings.[49]

Sir Christopher's outburst, therefore, is not just an expression of personal opinion, though it was certainly heartfelt, and distilled the anger he had clearly felt at seeing so much of his life's work and so many of his enthusiasms rubbished and undone under Edward. It is itself a sign of the endorsement in Morebath, or at any rate in Morebath's vicarage, of the wider values of the new regime, the perception of the Reformation as arrogant, destructive and un-English, a disastrous rebellion against God and the faith of our fathers. Sir Christopher's version of this story is small-scale, quite literally parochial, but in it too, the church 'ever dekeyed' under Edward, and was 'comforted' and 'restoryd' again by the advent of the Queen and her Spanish consort: the story he tells is one in which tragedy is turned to comedy by the advent of a good ruler. His obvious commitment to that version of events makes its Elizabethan sequel more poignant, and his own part in that sequel more ironic.

For even as he wrote his celebratory retrospect, news was on its way to Morebath that Sir Christopher's five-year idyll was at an end. Queen Mary was dead, and the accession of her Protestant step-sister Elizabeth, for Morebath and everywhere else, would halt the process of reconstruction in its tracks. For those with an eye to life's ironies, the timing is remarkable. Sir Christopher must have composed his retrospect immediately after the election of John Norman and William Timewell as High Wardens for 1558–9, for the list ends abruptly with the announcement of their wardenship and the statement that 'what this churche was prevaylyd by there tyme now schall ye se'. But the list of benefits received 'by there tyme' was never to be written. They were elected at the High Wardens' account made on the Sunday before St Catherine's day, 20 November 1558. Queen Mary had died and Elizabeth had been proclaimed Queen in London, just three days before, on the 17th. The news, however, had not yet reached Devon, and so Sir Christopher dated the account 'yn the 5th and 6th yere of the rayne of Kyng Phelippe and quyne Maryes gracyus mageste'.[50]

As it happens, Sir Thomas Butler, Sir Christopher's alter-ego at Much Wenlock in Shropshire, provides us with a vivid glimpse of the arrival of this news in another conservative community five days later. On 25 November the parishioners of Much Wenlock were gathered in their parish church of Holy Trinity for Mass, it being St Catherine's day. As the vicar made his way to the altar he was intercepted by the sheriff of Shropshire, Mr Richard Newport, newly arrived from London with the news of Queen Mary's death. At the sheriff's command, the vicar came down into the body of the church at the offertory where, as he later noted down in the parish register, he declared in a loud voice 'Friends ye shall pray for the prosperous estate of our most noble Queen Elizabeth, by the Grace of God Queen of England, France and Ireland, defender of the faith, and for this I desire you every man and woman to say the Pater Noster with the Ave Maria'. And then, we in the choir sang the canticle *Te Deum Laudamus, pater noster, ave maria, cum collecta pro statu Regni prout stat in processionale in adventu Regis vel Regine mutatio aliquibus verbis ad Reginam* [the Te Deum, the Our Father, the Hail Mary, with the collects for the welfare of the kingdom as it is set out in the Processional for the accession of a King or Queen, adapting the words as appropriate for the Queen]. And then went I to the altar and said out the Mass of St Catherine.

On the following Sunday, 27 November, the first in Advent, the vicar put on the parish's best cope, called St Milburga's cope, which despite its association with an outlawed cult had somehow survived the depredations of Edward's reign. Accompanied by the leading men of the town he processed once more into the nave to proclaim the new queen. Once more the congregation recited the Our Father and the Hail Mary for the Queen's prosperity, the choir sang the Latin litanies and collects for a Catholic ruler, Mass began with the festive processional *Salve festa dies*, and afterwards there was a bonfire at the church gate with a dole of bread, cheese and beer for the poor folks. If Sir Thomas remembered the burning of pilgrimage images and St Milburga's bones on that very spot eleven years before, or realised that those Edwardine bonfires were about to be re-enacted throughout the land with the images so expensively and laboriously replaced in the reign just ended, he does not say.[51]

And so, with impeccably Catholic ceremonial, all over the country parishes celebrated what were to be in fact the funeral rites of Catholic England. Sir Christopher does not record how Morebath inaugurated the new reign, but the accounts for the transitional year 1558–9 tell their own story. Those accounts were presented on 8 December. In July Queen Elizabeth had issued a fresh set of Injunctions for the 'suppression of superstition' and 'to plant true religion', to all intents and purposes a rerun of the Edwardine articles, reimposing a revised English Prayer Book and ordering the suppression of Catholic ceremonial, and the destruction of altars and images.[52] The Visitors for the West Country included John Jewel, a Devonian who had fled abroad under Mary, and who was a radical Protestant in the stamp of the recently deceased Dean Heynes. The Visitation began at Exeter in September with a peremptory ban on 'any more masses or popish services', and the Four Men of Morebath and Sir Christopher duly presented themselves there before the Commissioners. Like all the other parishes of the diocese, they were sent away to prepare a document containing an 'invitory of the churche gooddis' together with 'all the names of all the howsellyng pepyll in the parysse and all the namys of all them that ware buryed here syns mydsumer was twelfmonth cristenyd and weddyd'. Lewis Trychay and William at Combe had to ride back to Exeter with the completed return, the two trips costing the parish 10/6d.[53] Once more, the parish set about equipping itself for Protestant worship: 4/4d for the new Book of Common Prayer, and 1/= to John Skynner to fetch it, 4d for drawing down the two altars, 2/1d for a copy of the English Litany and a Psalter; John Norman at Pole was given 20/= to buy a Bible and a copy of Erasmus' *Paraphrases*.[54]

This was all very prompt, and indeed Jewel, writing to his friend Peter Martyr, commented on the ready obedience of the whole region: 'We found every where the people sufficiently well disposed towards religion … even in those quarters where we expected most difficulty.' The exception, predictably, was the response of the clergy, for 'if inveterate obstinacy was found anywhere, it was altogether among the priests, those especially who had once been on our side'. Jewel did however comment on the extraordinary extent of the Marian reconstruction in the West Country: 'It is however hardly credible what a harvest, or rather what a wilderness of superstition had sprung up in the darkness of the Marian times.'[55]

He would have thought Morebath a rank enough corner of that wilderness had he been able to scrutinise their accounts for that year. Alongside the expenses of the Visitation, they are packed with evidence that the Marian reconstruction had been in full flow there up to the very point at which the Royal Visitation intervened to stop it. The wardens had paid Agnes at Court 3d to mend the purse to carry the sacrament to the sick, and they had received gifts of girdles and gowns from Joan Rumbelow and Thomas Borrage's wife, money for a month's ringing of the great bell every night for the soul of Nicholas at Hayne, who had just died, a painted banner from Thomas at Timewell, and money 'bestowyd a pon the hye auter and a pon the syd auter for a remembrans for them to be prayed for'. It is not clear whether the parish had actually got round to spending this money in beautifying the altars before they had to be taken down.[56]

In Morebath's case, therefore, the prompt obedience which Jewel found so surprising was certainly not born out of enthusiasm for Protestantism, and their obedience was, to begin with at least, strictly external. They neither surrendered nor destroyed their chasuble and their Mass book, as they were supposed to do. The missal was returned to Thomas Borrage who had donated it, the chasuble was entrusted to Edward Rumbelow, pending further developments. Morebath, like many parishes in the West Country,[57] was hedging its bets. Every year for the next three years the priest would carefully remind the parish of the whereabouts of these two essentials for the Mass, in case they were needed again: 'Thomas Borrage hath our masse boke … Edward Rumbelow hath the chesapyll.'[58] There were subtler forms of persisting conservative sentiment too: Sir Christopher baptised Sidwell Webber in March 1559, and would baptise Sidwell Hill as late as 1570.[59] But compliance was hard to withold. The drying up of reminders about the chasuble and Mass-book after 1562 is probably due to firmer action by Bishop Alley and his officials. Morebath had to destroy its roodloft that year, and parishes elsewhere in the diocese who were slow to do likewise were soon in trouble. The churchwardens of South Tawton were excommunicated in 1563 because their roodloft was still in place: they rapidly complied. Excommunication proved a formidable tool in enforcing conformity in the 1560s, and several Devon parishes were brought to heel by it – Stratton, Dartington, Kilmington as well as South Tawton. At Cornwood, where the leading inhabitants were excommunicated because the loft was still up, the parish assembled the next day and removed it: 'Forasmuch as we be excommunicate for not plucking down the rood-loft let us agree together and have it down, that we may be like Christian men again of holy time.'[60] As that suggests, the enforcement of the Elizabethan settlement was strict in Exeter diocese, and though for an increasing number excommunication was essentially no more than 'a money matter', the authorities were also able to draw on pre-Reformation sentiments about the nature of Christian community to effect the work of reform.

And they were thorough. There had been not one but three visitations in 1559 – the Royal Visitation, and separate visitations by bishop and archdeacon. Morebath's wardens, unable to keep up with all the demands these visitations placed upon them, found themselves once again having to pay for the parish's non-compliance or tardiness, 12d to the bishop's official 'to strycke out the payns of the courte'.[61] There were three visitations again in 1561, the archdeacon after Easter, the bishop at Midsummer,[62] and Archbishop Parker's metropolitical visitation at Michaelmas. The widow Alison Perry was High Warden that year, and got so confused by this frenetic wave of inspection that at the end of her wardenship she claimed expenses for only two of the three visitations, with a consequent shortfall in her accounts which she could not account for and which was to continue to baffle the parish and Sir Christopher for ten years.[63] Under this degree of regular scrutiny, the parish had little option but to conform. The Young Men went on presenting their accounts in July, but in 1561 their account is dated not 'Sent Thomas's day' but the carefully neutral 'a pon Thomas Becottis day'.[64] And slowly the refurnishing of the church for Prayer Book worship went ahead. In 1561 a 'table' was placed above the communion table, which the priest went on calling the 'high altar': this was presumably a painted board hung on the wall with the Lord's Prayer, Creed and Commandments written on it.[65] The parish had not yet secured a copy of Erasmus' *Paraphrases*, and was in trouble at the visitation of 1562 as a result, but this delay was not in fact their fault. The rectorial tithe and advowson of Morebath belonged to a layman, Mr Stephen Tristram of Bampton. He had only just entered his majority, having been since 1544 a ward of the Crown.[66] As lay rector of Morebath, he was obliged to pay half the costs of the *Paraphrases*, the parish to pay the rest: in 1562 they duly sent 8/8d to Tristram 'for the parysse part to by the hole paraphrase and the parsson schuld pay the rest' but, as the priest tersely reported, 'bok have we non as yett'; they were still without the paraphrases in 1571, when the bishop fined them 2/= for the omission.[67]

Tristram's long period as a ward of the Crown cost the parish dear in other ways, too. During his minority, the rectorial tithes of the parish went to the Crown, but he had evidently resumed them at the start of Elizabeth's reign, and by 1562 local Crown officials were pursuing him for debts connected to his assumption of his majority. This was in itself always an expensive business: it involved proving one's age, to begin with, no easy matter before parish registers had become universal. Tristram may have been liable for distraint of knighthood – a demand at the start of a new reign on landowners worth more than £40 to assume the status and duty of knighthood or pay a fine in lieu. He may also have been liable for payment of the first subsidy granted by Parliament to Elizabeth in 1559, and he may well have owed the Crown substantial sums of money in administrative costs in the Court of Wards itself: in some cases such charges had been known to exceed the annual value of the lands actually held in wardship.[68] Or he may have resumed collection of his tithes from Morebath before the legal end of his majority, thus depriving the Crown of income. For whatever reason, by 1562 Crown officials had resorted to a process of distraint to recover these 'dutis lost the Quene', not on Tristram's own goods, but on the goods of those liable to pay the tithe in the first place, the parishioners of Morebath. Those whose goods were seized included Sir Christopher's brother Lewis. The parish rallied round to meet the Crown's demands, hastily organising a voluntary collection of sums ranging from 10/= to 3/4d from ten parishioners, the Young Men contributed £3, and the church stock was raided for another £4/17/=. To recover this very large sum of money – well over £10 in all – Lewis , John Scely and William at Pole rode to Exeter to get legal advice from counsel and to have Tristram bound over at the assizes to repay the money they had lost. The matter rumbled on until 1564, when Sir Christopher, in a carefully understated account that betrays his anxiety to stay on good terms with his patron, reminded the parish that 'hyt ys not unknown to you but here was a lytyll contraversye by twixt Mr Stevyn Tristram and thys parysse'. As he records, the matter was in fact settled amicably enough out of court, in a familiar Morebath way, with Tristram and the parish agreeing to accept the adjudication of John Sydenham of Dulverton. As a result of Sydenham's intervention, Tristram repaid 'all manner of axcions by twyxt hym and the parysse', the money being duly handed over before the parishioners on the Sunday before All Saints that year: Tristram's servant Moggrige, who brought the cash to Morebath church, was given a tip of 4d.[69]

Elizabethan Morebath did not always manage to avoid litigation. In 1560 there was a discrepancy of 10/4d in the accounts of the High Warden, John at Burston, which the parish refused to accept: the matter was referred to Bishop Alley at his primary visitation at Oakford. The warden was ordered to repay the parish its 10/=, but at the bishop's pacific insistence, the parish contributed 21d towards Burston's legal expenses, on top of their own costs of 3/3d.[70] The incident highlights the fact that the genial and conscientious Bishop Alley, a fine hand at bowls but also learned in Hebrew, made a point of getting round the county to see wardens and clergy for himself. This took him often within reach of Morebath at Tiverton, Oakford and Bampton, a proximity which no doubt made for better relations, but also for closer scrutiny. For all his geniality Alley was a determined reformer, deeply anti-Catholic, and during his incumbency of the see almost 10% of the clergy were deprived, in most cases for excessive attachment to the old ways.[71]

Sir Christopher, however, seems to have feared very little from such scrutiny. If anyone knew of his parish's involvement in the PrayerBook rebellion in 1549, they had by now forgotten it, and he himself, however much he disliked the new theology and the new worship, clearly felt able to function and even to flourish despite them. One of the consequences of the Reformation almost everywhere in England was a plunge in clerical numbers, and early Elizabethan bishops were often in desperate straits to fill livings. In the Exeter diocese there were many vacant parsonages in the early 1560s, one of them the joint living of Knowstone with Molland, fifteen miles from Morebath, the principal church of Molland set in a 'miserable-looking village' in what one Devon antiquary later called 'the most remote, dreary and primitive corner of North Devon'. Dreary or not, though, the living was valued at nearly £24, three times the value of Morebath. The advowson of this living in 1560 was theoretically in the hands of a minor, Hugh Culme, whose father had left him the Manor of Molland, and with it the right to present the living. In fact, his mother Agnes, recently widowed by the death of her second husband John Willoughby, had secured administration of Hugh Culme's estates and was acting for her son.[72] Agnes had also inherited the advowson of Seaton from her second husband John Willoughby and in that same year of 1560 had appointed another priest, Richard Gumley, to the living of Seaton.

No evidence survives of how Sir Christopher gained Agnes Willoughby's patronage. Her own religious views are unknown. Hugh Culme, her first husband, seems to have been an unexceptionable Catholic, and had presented a staunch conservative, Walter Mugg, to Knowston and Molland in 1554.[73] She and John Willoughby had presented a more ambiguous figure in succession to Mugg, when he resigned for another living in 1558: Anthony Hunt, instituted to Knowstone and Molland in Febuary 1558, had been deprived of the Devon living of Chawleigh and the Cornish living of Calstock in 1554, presumably because he had married – evidently he put away his wife, or she had died in the meantime, since otherwise he would not have been instituted to another living in the diocese. He was to recover Calstock in Elizabeth's reign and, in the light of his marriage and deprivation, he was presumably some sort of Protestant.[74] But we have no way of determining whether Agnes Willoughby was sympathetic to Hunt's views, or even whether she was aware either of them or of his marriage. Her patronage therefore offers us very little clue as to Sir Christopher's standing in 1560, except that he had sufficient support to secure presentation to a financially desirable second living.

So, late in 1560, Sir Christopher was presented by Agnes Willoughby to the living of Knowstone with Molland, and he had been instituted as Vicar there by July the following year.[75] Sir Christopher had to compound for the First Fruits and Tenths of this new benefice to the Crown, which involved having two sureties to guarantee payment of this tax on his first year's income. His guarantors were Thomas Govar, a clothier of Tiverton, and James Farr, a yeoman of Sampford Peverell, substantial men from farming and cloth-working communities far enough away from Morebath to remind us that the parish, its priest and its people, for all their remoteness, played an active part and had a wide acquaintance in the county community.[76]

His new living was a source of income for Sir Christopher, not a rival focus of attention. He did not move there, and discharged his responsibility to his new flock by a succession of curates, John Chaplyn and Tristram Lyd.[77] But taking a new living meant that Sir Christopher had to subscribe again to the Royal Supremacy and the Act of Uniformity imposing the Prayer Book and all the iconoclastic austerities of Protestant worship. Given his hostility to the 'decay' of the church under Edward, his delight when it was 'comforted' again under Mary, and the warmth of his commendation of the 'good catholyke men' of his parish who had concealed images and books, we are confronted here with one of the most puzzling aspects of Tudor religious history, the conformity of the overwhelming majority of clergy, despite their conservative opinions.

For Sir Christopher's conformity was more than a grudging minimalism. When Bishop Alley conducted a survey of his clergy in December 1561 for the information of Archbishop Parker, he noted that Sir Christopher was unmarried and celibate, not a graduate but well educated [non graduatus, satis doctus], resident at Morebath, and, though not licensed to do so, a regular preacher there.[78] It is of course no surprise to learn that Sir Christopher never stopped talking even when confronted with a pulpit, but we need to register that in preaching at all he was in fact highly unusual. Alley listed 252 priests and three deacons holding benefices in his diocese. Only twenty-eight of them were licensed preachers: no other clergyman in the deanery of Tiverton preached at all, indeed virtually no one else in North Devon.[79] Even Parson Herne in fashionable St Petroc's in Exeter was a non-preacher. What Sir Christopher preached we can never know, of course, but it must have passed muster with the reformed authorities, and Alley was certainly thorough enough to assure himself that none of his clergy were preaching popery. We have to assume that Sir Christopher, his mass-book still within reach, was teaching his people something recognisable to his superiors as Protestant Christianity. There is no easy accounting for it, though Tudor men had the habit of obedience, and Morebath's one venture into resistance had ended badly.

And when all was said and done, most of what he found in the Prayer Book he would have thought godly enough. Elizabethan Anglicanism used Edward's Prayer Book, rejected images, detested the pope. Nevertheless, after a draconian beginning, in most places it was far less abrasive than the Edwardine 'Tudor Church Militant' on which it was modelled. Elizabeth was a sincere Protestant, but she had none of her brother's precocious reforming zeal, and in her reign some of the deep rhythms of pre-Reformation religion, outlawed or suspect under Edward, were allowed to reassert themselves. Women were churched, parish ales were drunk, roga-tion-tide processions visited the old boundaries. Church accounts are not the place to look for strong doctrinal convictions, but it is perhaps signifi-cant that Sir Christopher's sternest condemnation of the Edwardine experi-ment was not that it had been born in schism and ended in heresy, but that under it Morebath church and its contents had 'ever decayed'. His tradi-tionalism must of course have had a doctrinal content, of the kind spelled out in the rebel demands of 1549 – loyalty to the Mass, the ancient faith, the sacraments – but it was before everything else informed by the genius of place, his religion in the end was the religion of Morebath. The strength and the weakness of such a religion were the same – the local character of its conservatism, the binding of its practitioners to a place, whatever change befall. Not for priests like Sir Christopher the walk away from the protect-ing known into the wilderness, undertaken by Protestant separatist and Catholic recusant alike, men and women in pursuit of principle at the cost of the dear and familiar. The unthinkable alternative to conformity was to leave his vicarage and the people he had baptised, married and buried for forty years. It was a course few took, for in 1559 there must have seemed very little he or anyone else could do if the Queen chose to stay out of the Pope's communion, even supposing the Pope figured very much at any time on Morebath's horizon. No doubt Sir Christopher had his own stoical version of Parson Herne's 'it is no remedy man, it is no remedy'.

There are respectable parallels, and it would be quite mistaken to think of Sir Christopher as an unscrupulous Vicar of Bray. Even the ferociously Catholic Robert Parkyn continued to serve in Elizabeth's church as curate of Adwick-le-Street. Dr Mark Byford has documented the remarkable career of another admirable conservative priest, functioning happily and effectively in the Elizabethan Church. This was William Shepherd, a former monk of the

Augustinian house, Leeds Priory in Kent, who became vicar of the tiny Essex parish of Heydon, an impoverished place of thirty-five households to Morebath's thirty-three, where he functioned from 1541 to 1586 as a model parish priest, generous to the poor and unfailingly dedicated to the welfare and unity of his parish. Retaining, at least to begin with, traditional beliefs and pieties, like the doctrine of purgatory or devotion to the holy name of Jesus, Shepherd gradually came to absorb also some of the concerns we associate with mainstream Protestantism, even puritanism. These included his campaign against the local fairs and sabbath-day games which kept 'people of the yonger sort' from 'heryng any one word of the ghospell of Christ preched, or part of any other dyvyne sirvice, contrary to the commanement of god and the quens maiestys Inniunctyons and decyent Rits of the church of Christ'.[80] That such a man could come to place so high a premium on preaching, and to see in the worship of the Prayer Book the 'decent Rits of the church of Christ' is a reminder that sharp distinctions between Catholic and Protestant, traditionalist and reformed, may look more straightforward and clear-cut to the historian than they did to those immersed in the press of events. And that men like Parkyn and Shepherd and Sir Christopher could accept and function within the Elizabethan church goes further towards explaining the success of the English Reformation than do the careers of radicals like Simon Heynes, who alienated as many of the unconvinced as they converted. There can be little doubt that the country people of Heydon felt easier about the Reformation because Mr Shepherd, whom they trusted, thought there was nothing in it to fear or to reject. The accommodating traditionalism of men like William Shepherd and Christopher Trychay had its own integrity, making possible the marriage of the old ways and the new, offering their congregations some preliminary gleams of the mellow light that plays over the church of George Herbert.

And so in Morebath the Reformation came to be, quite literally, part of the furniture. A seat was built by the quire door in 1564 for Sir Christopher to sit in while he read the services, a new and handsomer pair of tables of the Commandments placed 'by every syde of the auter' in 1568. This was evidently a county-wide phenomenon, rather than a spontaneous act of piety, for they had been up before the bishop at Tiverton at another visitation that summer, and that year the wardens were putting new Commandment boards in the choir at Sir Christopher's other benefice at Molland, too.[81] By the end of the 1560s, the authorities were pressing harder than ever for churches to be rid of all relics of popery, and properly ordered after a reformed pattern. During the 1569 rebellion in the north of England altar-stones and holy-water pots reappeared from the dung-hills and barns where they had been hidden, and the Mass was sung again in Durham cathedral.[82] These reappearances served to sharpen government awareness that the material instruments of Catholic piety were dangerous in themselves, encoded memories, which might erupt and disrupt at any time. In 1570 Morebath paid the summoner 14d for the 'declaration against rebellion' issued in the wake of the northern Rising; in the same year the Bishop summoned them to Tiverton and they were required to make a new and better communion table and to set in order all 'the ornamentis about the tabyll'. By stages, that was done. In the same year a covering for the table was made out of a silken tunicle presented to the church by Edward Rumbelow in memory of his wife, Catholic ornaments transformed into Protestant ones. A year later the 'timber of the churche a bout the syd auter', the last relic of St Sidwell, was finally dismantled and sold, along with the bolt of iron 'that stode in the hedd of the palme crosse'.[83]

The most concrete remaining relic of popery was the chalice with which Sir Christopher still ministered the communion. Archbishop Parker thought that where there was a chalice, there the people would imagine the Mass. All over the West Country in the early 1570s there was an episcopal campaign to call in and melt down the pre-Reformation chalices, and to replace them with respectable purpose-made Protestant communion cups. The Crown, never slow to capitalise on religious reform, insisted on its cut. Morebath was summoned to bring its chalice before Royal Commissioners at South Molton in March 1571: they were required to sell the chalice, for which they got 53/2d, of which the Commissioners took 20/= 'to the quenes mageste use'. Morebath in fact did not immediately buy a communion cup, as they were supposed to do: they had another small chalice, without a paten, with which they made do for the rest of Sir Christopher's life.[84]

By now the interior of Morebath church looked like a reformed place of worship. Old habits died hard for Sir Christopher. He went on calling Sunday evening prayer 'Second evenyng prayer', a hangover from the observance of First and Second Vespers in the old Latin rite.[85] In the same way, he almost invariably referred to the communion table as 'the auter' or 'the hye auter'. It was in fact a table of wood, standing not at the east end where the old altar had been, but at the lower end of the chancel or even in the nave: Sir Christopher would ask in his will to be buried 'above it', that is, to the east of it, and from 1565 there are references in the accounts to its prominent role at the parish audits. Outgoing wardens placed their surplus stock on it, for the incoming wardens to take up, a harking back to Edwardine practice. So in 1564 'the wold yong men wardyns layd a down a pon the hye auter all cost quytt 50/3d' from their ale and the High Wardens 'toke up' 40/=. Two years later the Young Men wardens 'ressevyd and toke up here a pon the auter 47/=' from their predecessors.[86] Near the table was the 'sett [seat] at the quyre dore for the priest' before the dismantled roodloft, which had cost the parish 6d to make in 1564 (they must certainly have been reusing older woodwork).[87] At Morebath as everywhere else, this seat in fact rivalled the pulpit as the main focus of reformed worship. The Elizabethan chronicler William Harrison tells us how it was used:

> whereas there was wont to be a great partition between the choir and the body of the church, now it is either very small or none at all, and, to say the truth, altogether needless, sith the minister saith his service commonly in the body of the church with his face toward the people, in a little tabernacle of wainscot provided for the purpose; by which means the ignorant do not only learn divers of the Psalms and usual prayers by heart, but also such as can read do pray together with him, so that the whole congregation at one instant pour out their petitions unto the living God for the whole estate of His church in most earnest and fervent manner.[88]

From this seat, therefore, Sir Christopher schooled Morebath in the ways of Protestantism, not merely the 'Psalms and usual prayers', but the occasional forms issued by government for special occasions, designed to inculcate appropriately Protestant sentiments to people receptively upon their knees. These included prayers of support for the suffering French Huguenots, prayers against the plague, prayers against the northern Catholic Lords in the 1569 rebellion, 'all those which be common enemies as well to the truth of thy eternal word, as to their own natural prince and country, and manifestly to this crown and realm of England'. They also included the two forms of prayer against the Turks for which Morebath paid 6d apiece in 1566. Sir Christopher will have summoned his people on six successive weeks to pray for the delivery of Malta and Hungary from the threat of Islam. In the process they will have heard him warn against the temptations of 'false religion and horrible idolatries', for popery was never far from the concerns of the Elizabethan Church of England.[89]

By the early 1570s, then, the priest and parishioners of Morebath had all the accoutrements of reformed worship, their chalice excepted. After the visitation of 1571 they not only fetched at last from London their copy of the *Paraphrases*, but they acquired the newly issued *Seconde Tome of Homelyes* and the *Thirty-Nine Articles;*[90] in 1573, on the bishop's instructions, they paid 10/= for 'doctor jule ys boke', John Jewel's *An apologie or answer in defence of the Churche of Englande*, the standard defence of the new church against its Catholic critics, and they spent 3d for a chain to keep it in the church.[91] They had a church chest, a register of baptisms, weddings and burials, they had a book of the poor. They had a communion table decently covered with a silk carpet made from part of a set of old High Mass vestments, they had a pulpit which their vicar used regularly to preach to them, they had a decent surplice and a prayer desk at the choir door. They had achieved this high state of conformity slowly, and with a good deal of prodding, endless appearances before archdeacon and bishop, endless traipsing to Tiverton or Exeter with the register book or their inventories, the occasional payment of fines for tardy or non-compliance. As well as the regular machinery of visitation they had been several times troubled by Commissioners searching out concealed chantry lands,[92] though Morebath had nothing to conceal in that respect. To the machinery of the church were added other less tangible pressures, the presence nearby of Protestant gentry like the Southcotts of Shillingford, and the more tangible pressure of their landlord, Henry Wallop. Wallop had inherited Morebath Manor from his uncle Sir John, a staunch conservative who had come close to disaster in Henry's reign for his religious traditionalism. But Harry Wallop was altogether different, by the mid-1560s a pillar of the Protestant cause in Hampshire, where he lived. Given the close interweaving of manorial and parochial concerns in Morebath, Wallop's ardent Protestantism must at least have nudged and perhaps helped to frogmarch his tenants into loyal conformity to the new order.[93]

By the end of his life, even Sir Christopher's conformity had more than mere prudence or resignation about it. He was not unaffected by the prayers he recited, the sermons he preached, the homilies he read. We catch just a single but poignant glimpse of his internalisation of the religion of communion table and prayer desk, just a year before his death. In 1573 William Hurley and his wife Eylon [Helen] gave the church of Morebath a gift. This was in fact a posthumous donation, the bequest from Eylon of the long witheld burial fee of 6/8d for her husband's grave, augmented to 10/= when she joined him there in 1573, and at last delivered to the parish.[94] William Hurley, who had been such a moving spirit in Morebath affairs in the fraught days of Edward and Mary, had died fifteen years before in 1558. His wife Eylon was one of the twenty-seven parish wives who had bought the new Sarum Manual for the parish when Catholicism was being reconstructed there in 1554. She was also the mother of William Hurley, 'the yong man' who had marched away to St David's Down, carrying Morebath's Prayer Book to the burning, and who had never returned.[95] But that, now, was all so long ago. Eylon's long-delayed gift to the parish was used to buy a Prayer Book and a psalter, sent for from London. Gifts of this size were a comparative rarity now, for giving to the church more often than not was simply the standard 6/8d for a burial place inside, which might anyway be divided between the fabric and the poor.[96] Whose idea it was to spend the money on a Prayer Book, of all things, the account does not say, but it is likely to have been the priest. Perhaps Sir Christopher had forgotten the part played by William Hurley the 'yong man' in the events of 1549, when another Prayer Book was burned. At any rate, recording the gift, he was moved to an expression of pious gratitude.

Item they ressevyd a communion bok and a sawter boke of the gefth of Willm Hurley and of Eylone hys wyffe prisse of x[s] [10/=] by sydis the caryge from London – *deo gracias*.[97]

Item, they received a communion book and a psalter book of the gift of William

Hurley and of Ellen his wife price of 10/= besides carriage from London – thanks be to God.

With the old priest's 'thanks be to God' for this addition to Morebath's Prayer Book worship, received from so painfully ironic a source, a door closes in the memory of Morebath.

III TALKING TO THE END

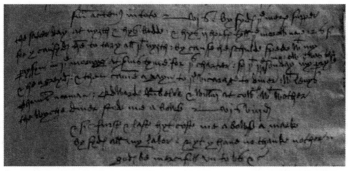

*

We have to glean Sir Christopher's changing attitude to religion from such hints, because the accounts he wrote and read to the parish throughout the first twenty-five years of Elizabeth's reign become steadily and strikingly less religious, more and more dominated by secular concerns: taxation, the equipping of armies, the upkeep of bridges and beacons and bulwarks, the relief of the poor, the maintenance of law and order, and the marketing of Morebath's livestock and wool. In this, Morebath was in no way unusual, and much the same concerns are to be found in other West County parish account books, whether from towns like Chagford or villages like Kilmington.[98] The institution of the parish was itself changing, as the Tudor state laid on it more and more fiscal, military and administrative responsibilities.[99] This was not directly an outcome of the Reformation, except in the sense that the settlement of religion under Elizabeth after twenty hectic years of reform and counter-reformation meant that churchwardens' accounts cease to provide the material for an unfolding narrative of doctrinal and ritual change. Humdrum management, repointing the tower or buying a new shovel for the sexton, replace the excitement of iconoclasm, the drawing down of altars or the burning of prayer books and bibles. In Morebath, however, the shift towards the secular may also have reflected a shift towards Protestantism, spontaneous or enforced, and registered in Sir Christopher's way of dating accounts. For almost forty years he had done so exclusively by the church calendar, by saints days – 'Sent Jamis day', 'In die

---

* Sir Christopher complains of his thankless labours on behalf of the parish, 1572 [Binney 249 / Ms 17]

Sanct Joahannis Baptiste', 'The Sonday a pon All Hallow day'. He does as usual in 1568, the Young Men's account 'a pon the visitacion of our Ladye', the High Wardens' 'the sonday a fore sent clementis day'.[100] Thereafter, with the exception of the High Wardens' accounts for 1571, made on Ss. Simon and Jude's day, which happened to be a Prayer Book 'red letter day', the accounts are dated by secular time, 'the xxii day of Marche', 'the xv of Julii', 'the ix day of November'.

In one other respect religious change did contribute to the growing secularism of church accounts. Morebath's accounts before the reign of Edward are dominated by devotional concerns, the maintenance of lights, the adornment of images and altars, the enrichment of the church building. There was merit in such things, they were the visible trace of love of God and neighbour, they pleased the saints and won their intercession, and they left behind a standing reminder to one's fellow Christians to pray for the repose of one's soul. The Reformation removed the rationale for all such giving – negatively, by denying the virtue of any pious acts for salvation, by outlawing prayer for the dead, by identifying this piety of externals with the worship of pagan idols – but also positively, by suggesting, on impeccable biblical warrants, that there was more virtue in generosity to the poor than in the gilding or girding of stocks and stones. The English Reformation also established the rule of thumb that anything given to the glory of God was liable to end up, sooner rather than later, being confiscated by the Crown and turned into a gun or a soldier's coat. This did not mean that all pride and generosity towards the parish church was at an end. Tudor men and women had always valued the element of display in such giving: a gift to the parish church declared that one had the means to give, it was a form of conspicuous consumption. That motive remained, and so too did the more amiable pride in one's familiar place, the desire to add dignity and decency to the worship of God, the concern for the comfort of one's neighbours. Elizabethan and Jacobean Protestant churches too, attracted their benefactors. All the same, there were limits to the outlets for such giving. Reformed churches had no use for donations of women's girdles, or kerchiefs or beads, disapproved of painting, whitewashed their walls, banned lights and candlesticks and crosses, robed their ministers in black serge or plain white linen. Everywhere, the streams of money and goods poured into the parish churches up to the mid-1530s, and in places like Morebath into the 1540s, dwindled and dried to a trickle.

But the process of secularisation of the parish was more than all this: it was in train before the break with Rome, and it was already marked at Morebath in Mary's reign, for it owes as much to the extension of strong government, and the multiplication of responsibility within local community, as to any ideological shift. Mary reversed her brother's religious policies, but she too fought France, and the costs of government did not diminish. So, in the midst of its scramble to restore Catholic worship, Morebath under Mary was also much preoccupied with temporal matters: the setting of levies to meet the costs of repairs to Exebridge 'of all Master Wallopis tenotis',[101] the carriage of stuff to Hukeley bridge and the tithing-man's levies to pay for its repair,[102] 'a sett for the bulwark at Seaton'.[103] In 1558 the Four Men exhausted the church stock in payments 'a bowt tem-porall maters', all of it spent on money, arrows, daggers, shooting-gloves and the like 'for settyng forthe of a man to serve the kyng'.[104]

These 'temporal matters' loom larger as ecclesiastical expenses dwindle in Elizabeth's reign: the endless 'new makyn of Exebrige',[105] the subsidies voted to the Queen,[106] and a growing focus on 'dett led out for sowders', the buying of coats and bows and caps, the scouring and carrying of harness to Cullompton, Tiverton, Halverton, the purchase of 'a gon wother wysse callyd a moryng',[107] emergency collections in 1562 and 1563 for money demanded by the Constable at Bampton 'to serve the Queen'. The Young Men's stock could be drawn on for these military expenses,[108] but in 1562 once again leading parishioners had to dig into their pockets to meet these demands, and it was ordered that they should be recompensed

> out of the churche stock by order of the vicar where a pon the vicar tok order at this a cownte and payd them of this mony that was lefthe as fare as hyt wolde extende as ye schall hyre.[109]

> *out of the church stock by order of the vicar whereupon the vicar took order at this account and paid them of this money that was left as far as it would extend, as ye shall hear.*

Such a direct raid on the church stock was a rarity, but year upon year Morebath, like all the other parishes of Devon and of England, was called on to set aside money 'for the settyng of sawders vj [6] men of the hun-dred', 'for sowders to be sett furthe to the new havyn', 'to serve the quene for sawders yn to erlonde', or simply 'for sawders cotis'.[110]

These were not the only secular concerns: the parish organised an inquest on a death by misadventure at Exebridge, 'the ladd that deyd with the prickyn of his owne knyffe when he leppyd to hys horsse',[111] paid men to rid them of a nuisance at lambing-time by catching rooks in a net, or to root furze out from their rough grazing.[112] Crime and poverty loom larger than ever before in the accounts, as parish officials pay the Constable of Bampton for 'rogis' [rogues]. In 1563 John Lambert spent 12d riding to see 'Mr Collis' 'for the thevis', while Edward Rumbelow and John at Poole travel to Chard in Somerset 'for the thevis', at the considerable cost to the parish of 14/8d.[113] Sir Christopher does not explain these expenses, but they were part of 'Robyn at Wode ys besenes', the arrest in 1563 of Robert at Wood, younger brother of John Wood, who was a householder but one of the poor men of the parish. The parish paid John Scely and John Wood, the culprit's own brother, another 12d for 'bryngyn of Robert at Wode to the quenes iaylye [gaol]', and paid Robert Zaer 12d for fetching the 'Mittimus', the receipt for his delivery. We hear no more details of this story until 1571 when Sir Christopher reports, perhaps in reference to 'old debt' that 'ys for the knell of Wode ys brother, John Wode hadd that grote for kepyn of a powr man'. From this we learn that Robert at Wood was dead and the parish had rung a knell for him at some stage, but was waiving the 4d fee due from his brother, who had given an equivalent amount of food or shelter to one of the parish poor instead – perhaps as a work of supererogation on behalf of his brother's soul.[114] Whether the thefts of 1563 and the knell mentioned in 1571 were connected is impossible to say, and we know nothing more of the circumstances of Robert at Wood's death. The hanging of a poor man for theft would have been no novelty in Elizabethan England, but whatever the nature of the Wood family's tribulations in 1571, they stirred Morebath to compassion, and not just in remitting the cost of the dead man's knell to his brother. For over a dozen years the parish had held this same John Wood accountable for some of the petty cash returned to the parish after the expenses of the stabbed boy's inquest had been paid, in the year when he had been ale warden. In the light of his family's misfortune, they decided now that enough was enough. Next year the priest added to the count of the Four Men 'a not[e] of wold dette that dependyth a pon the cownte bok to be answered', and itemised this debt among them. He observed that 'the bok of a cownte doth schow that John Wode was yn dett to thys churche 18d ... for 14 yere agon for cronyg [coronering] of the ladd that deyd ...'. Wood persisted in denial of this debt but 'not with standyng they iiij [4] men think that hyt ys more cherite to geve hyt hem then to take hyt frome hem *et sic finis*'.[115]

Perhaps however, Sir Christopher's '*finis*' was not quite the end of this sad and sour little affair. In 1573 William, John Wood's son, was elected one of the Young Men's wardens. He and his elected partner John Skynner the younger, another lad from the huddle of poor cottages at Exebridge, refused to serve: as the priest wrote testily 'they wolde not doo there diligens'. Instead, two adult members of the Timewell clan, Richard Timewell and Thomas Timewell at Leddons, had to undertake the job for their young sons (in characteristic Morebath fashion both boys were called William Timewell).[116] Thomas Timewell's economic standing is uncertain, but Richard was well-to-do, the son of Nicholas at Hayne, farming two 'bargains' in the parish. In the refusal of these poor men's sons to serve, and the stepping in of the better-heeled to replace them, perhaps we have a sign of the deepening gap between rich and poor which marked and darkened the hungry later years of Elizabeth.

But we need to beware of easy generalisations here. Mid-Elizabethan

Morebath shows signs of concern for poor parishioners, evident in the parish's handling of the financial and medical decline of Robyn Isac in the 1560s. Isac appears in the 1545 subsidy return as one of fifteen parishioners assessed at £2 (to Lewis Trychay's £4): since eight tax-payers were assessed at just £1, and since those assessed like Isac at £2 included Harry Hayle, who was in a position three years later to buy the whole flock of the church sheep, Isac was not among the poorest of the parish. He was elected senior High Warden for 1562, and the outgoing wardens handed over 13/4d stock to him. On the audit day in late October 1562, however, he had 'gon outt of the parish', and one of the Four Men had to stand in for him. The parish determined that he must account for the missing 13/4d, but two years later Isac had still not repaid it, and was clearly in difficulties. At the parish audit that year 'hyt was a greyd by the consent of the parysse' that Robyn 'schuld have forgevyn hem vj^s & viiij^d [6/8d], and the wother vj^s & viiij^d he schuld pay where of now we have ressevyd xx^d'.[117] They had to settle for the 20d, however, for they never received any more of the money. By 1568 Isac was seriously ill, and the Four Men were laying out significant sums of money, including 6/= from that year's High Wardens and 10/= from the Young Men's stock, for 'Isac's leche': by 1572 he was listed among 'the poure of the parysse' to whom the priest was giving handouts.[118] If the parish could still look after its own, however, the spread of responsibility within the parish was undoubtedly narrowing. Despite the fact that now four, not twelve, parishioners were called to office each year, Wardens were having to be elected to a second term of office with greater frequency than before. Morebath was becoming a less cooperative place, where power was less evenly distributed than had once been the case.[119]

There were other signs of a coarsening of social fibre. In 1557, while Philip and Mary still ruled, Morebath had made itself a cucking-stool. This was an instrument for the ritual humiliation of women, normally in punishment for the social offence of scolding or back-biting, but also for sexual offences like whoredom or bastardy. Cucking-stools were sometimes, though rarely, designed as *ducking*-stools, to plunge the unfortunate women condemned to them into cold water, and as a matter of fact Morebath's stool was made as part of the reparations of Exebridge.[120] But more often the stools were simply a form of tumbril, a chair mounted on wheels or a small cart in which the scold could be tied and dragged round the parish, or displayed at her door or the door of the person she had maligned: Morebath's stool may well have been of this sort. They had existed in the middle ages, and were becoming increasingly common in towns in the south-west in the late sixteenth century, but were something of a rarity in villages, though that may be defect of evidence rather than social reality. For whatever reasons, Morebath's cucking-stool, introduced in 1557, repaired in 1569 and remade at the cost of the Young Men in 1570,[121] is a sinister curiosity. Professor David Underdown has suggested that the spread of the use of the cucking-stool was a symptom of something amiss in the social order, evidence of strained gender relations and the decline of the status of women under the impact of patriarchy. He considered them to be more common in woodland and pasture villages (like Morebath), where farming was more individualistic, less cooperative than in arable country, and where manorial institutions were generally weak.[122] Such an analysis does not fit Morebath's comparatively tight-knit community structure, and women in fact played a major role in Morebath's public life. There were many women High Wardens in Sir Christopher's half-century as vicar of Morebath, there would be another, Grace Timewell, the year after his death, and his sister-in-law Joan, Lewis's widow, would serve as High Warden in 1578. But we hear nothing in the Morebath accounts of any stocks, the male equivalent of the cucking-stool, and it may be that their cucking-stool is indeed an ugly hint of developing animosity towards women, a hint strengthened by the fact that the Young Men took charge when it needed rebuilding in 1570. Though it was introduced under a Catholic Queen, maybe here is one area where the Reformation made a palpable difference for the worse. It is hard to say whether a community which still venerated the Virgin and St Sidwell, and which had a Maiden store functioning alongside the Young Men, would have employed a cucking-stool.

If the sacred was receding at Morebath in favour of an increasing engagement with such 'temporal matters', its priest remained central to all its activities. One consequence of the Elizabethan settlement was the reduction of business passing through the hands of the Four Men. They were still essential to the working of the parish, not least in times of unexpected financial strain. But the narrowing of the surplus between the parish's average income of £5 or £6, most of it from ales, and all these growing demands, meant that the stock held by the Four Men was small, and frequently exhausted. When in 1567 the parish had a substantial surplus, the priest thought it worthy of special note: 'Thus ye see in toto now that we have spend xx [20] nobyllis this yere etc and yett we have xl^s [40/=] in store *deo gracias*'.[123] The ales themselves were changing, as for every church in the region they became the principal source of funding. In neighbouring Dulverton by the end of Elizabeth's reign the warden's ales might involve the sale of hundreds of gallons of ale, and could raise up to £50 or £60 when benefit or 'bidding' ales were organised for special causes, when clergy in all the surrounding parishes were asked 'openly in their Churches at the tyme of devine service ... to signify and ... to make proclamacion unto his parishioners' about the ales, and urge them to go and spend their money.[124] Ales in communities like Dulverton were big business by the end of the reign. Early Elizabethan Morebath was not in the same league: it rarely raised much more than a total of £5 from the combined proceeds of

High Wardens' and Young Men's ales, but it was clearly involved in formal attendance at the ales of other parishes in the area as a matter of obligation, and not merely out of courtesy. Parishioners with 'bargains' or farms extending into neighbouring parishes were apparently obliged to attend those parish's ales, as honorary parishioners. Since, however, those parishioners owed primary allegiance to Morebath, and were expected to serve in office and contribute to Morebath setts and obligations when required, the Morebath wardens paid their ale fees, and these become a familiar item in the accounts. Presumably reciprocal arrangements operated for parishioners from adjoining parishes with land in Morebath.[125]

Morebath's parochial life now was increasingly reactive, responding to external demands and stimuli rather than initiating projects, and the bulk of the parish business passes through the High Wardens' rather than the Four Men's accounts. This relative marginalising of the Four Men was due to the fact that a high percentage of the church stock was actually an accounting fiction, since it remained in parishioners' hands. Most of the small legacies left to the parish were not actually handed over, but retained by relatives and executors instead. A good deal of space in the accounts year after year is taken up by reminders to the parish of these debts owed to the church by executors, often running on for years:

> Item Alsyn at Pery ys yn your debtte of here laste a cownte xx^d [20d]
> Item John Wode ys yn yor dette of hys laste a cownte xx^d
> Item there restyth in Rychard Tymwells hands of the bequeste of hys faders to this churche iij^s & iiij^d [3/4d]
> Item there restythe yn Cristyn morsse ys hande (wother wyse Tymwell) of the bequesthe of William Morsse her brother to this churche iij^s & iiij^d.[126]

> *Item, Alison at Perry is in your debt of her last account 20d*
> *Item John Wood is in your debt of his last account 20d.*
> *Item there resteth in Richard Timewell's hands of the bequest of his father to this church 3/4d.*
> *Item there resteth in Christine Morsse's hands (otherwise Timewell) of the bequest of William Morsse her brother to this church 3/4d.*

Keeping track of these debts and obligations was increasingly important to Sir Christopher, now very self-consciously custodian of the parish memory, keeping 'not[e] of wold dette that dependyth a pon the cownte bok to be answeryd'. The widow Perry's debt was a case in point. She had owed the parish '3 shillings and odd mony' ever since the end of her term of office as High Warden in 1561, a debt she admitted but could not explain. Her widowed status earned her respite, year after year, until in 1572, because she still 'cowd not ... fynd hyt how hyt schould be lost', she asked Sir Christopher to recast her account to find the mistake. He did so, but could not balance her books, tyll yn conclucion when the Vicar had well puruysed her a cownte he fownde that she was a lowyd for 2 visitacions and no more but the Vicar knew well when he hadd well consyderyd the yere that there was 3 visitacions that yere, that was the officialis visitacion after ester, the byschoppis visitacion then at medsumer then followyng, and my lord of Conterberye at michelmas the same yere. Thys beyng found out now for lack of remembrans of here partye by cause sche hadde forgotyng hyt to sett hyt yn a pon here a cownt the iiij men do fynd hyt now that hyt ys resonabyll to a low here the mony for the wother visitacion and thus sche ys dischargyd.[127]

till in conclusion when the vicar had well perused her account, he found that she was allowed for two visitations and no more, but the vicar knew well when he had well considered the year that there were three visitations that year, that was the official's visitation after Easter, the bishop's visitation at midsummer then following, and my Lord of Canterbury's visitation at Michaelmas the same year. This being found out now for lack of remembrance on her part, because she had forgotten it, to set it in upon her account, the Four Men do find it now that it is reasonable to allow her the money for the other visitation, and thus she is discharged.

He was getting crusty in his old age: always emphatic and prone to self-pity, he could be touchy about his right to take executive action. That same year William Wyott of Langford left 1/= to the poor of the parish. Sir Christopher distributed the pence to Roger Bagbere and Robert Isac 'quod esset ad meam discressionem' [because it was left to my discretion].[128] The crustiness and self-pity were on full display in a special account he added that year to the Four Men's account, for

a certayne debt to the Vicar for expenssis that he hath ledde forth for the parysse at sondre tymes by sydis all hys paynes rydyng and goyng at the parysse request and for there comoditye be fore the present daye and can have no pay a gayn for hys expenssis …[129]

a certain debt to the vicar for expenses that he hath laid forth for the parish at sundry times, besides all his pains riding and going at the parish request and for their commodity before the present day, and can have no pay again for his expenses …

Since 1568 Morebath had been seeking market privileges at Bradninch, a market town eight miles to the north-east of Exeter. It is not clear why they wanted the right to sell their beasts and produce there rather than at Bampton or Tiverton, which were much nearer, except that Bradninch offered better access to eastward trade to Somerset, Hampshire and onwards to London. Between then and 1572, when the matter was brought to a successful conclusion, most of the leading parishioners and the Vicar were involved in negotiating 'the charter of our privilege', riding to the market court at Bradninch, arranging a series of interviews with the Clerk of the Market, riding to Sampford Peverell where Hugh Paulet had a house to secure his help in the matter (they had to go back because he was away from home on their first call), squaring the Mayor of Bradninch to speak to the Clerk of the Market on their behalf. Sir Christopher rode to Tiverton where the legal papers were being drawn up, to examine the draft: the clerk he had hired found four mistakes and the whole thing had to be rewritten. Sir Christopher stood the clerk a well-earned dinner. He had, he complained, spent 6/= on all that,

> by sydis the meris supper the saterday at nyth and hys bedd and hys horssis tyll the morow none ij^s [2/=] for y caussyd hym to tary all that nyth by causse he schuld speke with my paryssyn in the mornyng at servis tyme for the charter so that the morow that was the sonday my parysse and he a greyd and then came agayn to the vicarage to diner with Levys, Thomas Norman, Edward Rumbelow and William at Courte with wother the wyche diner stode me a boutt vj^s & viij^d and sic furst and last hyt cost me a bowtt a mark by sydis all my labor and yet y have no thank nother. God be merciful unto us.

> *besides the mayor's supper the Saturday at night, and his bed and his horse's till the morrow noon, 2/=, for I caused him to tarry all the night, because he should speak with my parishioners in the morning at service time for the charter, so that the morrow that was the Sunday, my parish and he agreed and then came again at the vicarage to dinner with Lewis, Thomas Norman, Edward Rumbelow amd William at Courte, with others, the which dinner stood me about 6/8d , and so first and last it cost me about a mark, besides all my labour, and yet I have no thanks neither. God be merciful unto us.*

Sir Christopher presented the accounts of the High Wardens, Richard Raw and John Scely, and of the Four Men for the last time on 15 November 1573. There is nothing distinctive about them, except that having read out first the High Wardens' and then the Four Men's account, and ended with his customary 'God save the quene', he added, for the first and only time, 'Amen'. Punctiliously, he returned the wardens' draft account, and noted at the end of the file version 'And Richard habeth hys byll a gayn'. The old man, now in his eighties, made it through the winter, but in April he sickened, and on 14 April he made his will. That will was one of those destroyed by the enemy bombing of the Exeter Probate Office in 1942, but as luck would have it the Exeter antiquary Sir Oswyn Murray had read and noted it. Murray was a genealogist, with little interest in the substance or the flavour of wills. His normal practice was simply to extract and note the names mentioned. On this occasion, however, he was caught by that inimitable, slightly self-pitying voice, talking to the end. He copied this sentence:

> Item, at the making of this will I have but little money and but one quick beast and that the Lord of the Manor must have and I paid £4 of debt within four days before the making of this.[130]

Sir Christopher left his best gown to his brother Lewys, his worsted gown, his silver hook and all his books to his nephew Christopher. The clerk's son was also called Christopher, almost certainly a godson: to him, to Henry Butler his servant, to all the women-folk of his poor friend Roger Bagbere, and to Bagbere's son Christopher, doubtless another godchild, there were small legacies. There was no gift to the church, other than the fee for his grave. He asked to be buried in the chancel, above the communion table. So on 27 May 1574 they laid him there, between the site of the altar where he had sung the Mass, and the table where he had celebrated the Supper. The following year, the parish finally bought their Protestant communion cup, at a cost of 29/2d. With the 6/8d Sir Christopher had left for his burial, they bought a cover of silver, the kind with a foot which served as a standing paten for the bread. It cost 8/=, and a bequest from his brother Lewis, not long for life himself, made up the extra 16d.[131]

He had been their priest, Catholic and Protestant, for fifty-four years, for fifty-four years the heart and voice, above everything the voice, of all their enterprises. He had been the spirit of Morebath, the chronicler of its dramatic and sometimes tragic share in the religious revolutions of that turbulent age, and the custodian of its blunt attitudes and salt speech. He had baptised their children, buried their dead, married every one of them. He had been the guide of their pieties, he had almost certainly encouraged their sons into rebellion, and, when the time came, he had eased them into a slow and settled conformity to a new order of things. For a little while they would remember him. The late Elizabethan scribe who copied the register knew that this was a man of note. Against the burial record for 27 May 1574 he drew a hand with a pointing finger, the only entry distinguished in this way. Perhaps Morebath knew that with Sir Christopher Trychay they had lost something unique and irrecoverable, and that there, between the altar and the table, they had buried something of themselves.

THE WARDENS OF MOREBATH 1520–75

× indicates information has not survived

YEAR	HIGH WARDENS	ALE RECEIPTS	YOUNG MEN WARDENS	ALE RECEIPTS	OUR LADY (FROM 1538 'CHURCH SHEEP')	MAIDENS	ALMS LIGHT	ST ANTHONY	ST SUNDAY
1520	John Hukeley Richard Webber	×	×	×	×	×	×	×	×
1521	Richard Hukeley Wylmett at Timewell	×	×	×	×	×	×	×	×
1522	Williams Robbyns Thomas Borrage	×	×	×	×	×	×	×	×
1523	Jekyn at Moore Jack Timewell	×	×	×	×	×	×	×	×
1524	John Morsse Harry Hurley	×	×	×	×	×	×	×	×
1525	John Goodman Thomas Norman	×	×	×	×	×	×	×	×
1526	John Waters John Norman at Court	×	×	×	×	×	×	×	×

Continued

YEAR	HIGH WARDENS	ALE RECEIPTS	YOUNG MEN WARDENS	ALE RECEIPTS	OUR LADY (FROM 1538 'CHURCH SHEEP')	MAIDENS	ALMS LIGHT	ST ANTHONY	ST SUNDAY
1527	William at Poole Geoffrey Smyth	×	×	×	Robert at More Jac Timewell (presumably acting for young daughters or sisters)	John Timewell John Rumbelow	John at Wood	Richard Hukeley William Robbyns	×
1528	Margaret at Borston Richard Raw	×	×	×	Geoffrey Moore Harry Hukeley	Mary at Court Margaret at Poole	William Morsse	Robert at Moore Geoffrey Moore	×
1529	Thomas Borrage Thomas Timewell at Combe	£2/14/5	Richard Timewell John Taylor	34/4d	John Morsse Thomas Norman	Elizabeth Waters Agnes Rumbelow	William at Loyton	John Morsse John Goodman	×
1530	Jekyn Isac William Timewell at Wood	£3/7/=	John Timewell John Morsse	£2/9/=	John at Court John Goodman	Joanna Don Alison Hukeley	John Tyler	John Waters John Nicholl	×
1531	Thomas Rumbelow John Norman at Wood	£3/4/0$^{1/2d}$	Christopher Borrage William Taylor	£1/2/0$^{1/2d}$	John Waters Phelys at Combe	Agnes Timewell Christina Morsse at Town	William Leddon	John Don Joan at Poole	×
1532	Robert at Hayne William Morsse	£3/2/4$^{1/2d}$	John Timewell (son of William at Wood minimus) John Webber	£1/7/2	Richard Raw John Nicholl	Christina Norman at Court Mary Rumbelow	William Scely	Thomas Borrage John Timewell at Borston	×

Year											
1533	Richard Webber / William Norman at Loyton	£2/13/11	×	×	William Timewell at Combe / John Don at Exebridge 'beyng ded'	×	John Hukeley	Jekyn Isac / Thomas Rumbelow	John at Court
1534	William at Timewell / John Taylor	£3/6/9d	Richard Timewell (son of William at Timwell) / John Morsse (son of William Morsse)	£1/7/=	William Timewell at Wood / Joan at Poole	Margaret Timewell / Joan at Moore	Richard Hukeley	Robert at Hayne / Richard Webber	John at Court, 'yerly Wardyng'
1535	Thomas Borrage / William Leddon	£3/1/1	William Morsse (son of John Morsse) / William at Court (son of John at Court)	£2/7/2 ¹/²d	Richard Norman at Wood / John Timewell at Borston	Christna Norman at Court the younger / Joan Isac	Richard Robyns	William at Timewell / Thomas Borrage	John at Court
1536	Thomas Timewell / William Scely	£3/8/11	Thomas Timewell at Combe / Edward Norman at Wood	£2/0/8	Thomas Borrage / William Morsse	Christina Morsse daughter of William Morsse / Elizabeth Rumbelow	Robert at Moore	Thomas at Timewell / Harry Hurley	John at Court
1537	Harry Hurley / John Hukeley	£3/2/2	John Borrage / Edward Norman at Loyton (refused office, Thomas Borrage served)	£1/15/7d	Jekyn Isac / William Norman at Loyton	Joan Taylor / Katherine Borrgae		Thomas Norman / John at Court	John at Court
1538	Thomas Norman / Richard Hukeley	£2/9/2	Edward at Timewell / Thomas Webber	11/11d	John Taylor / Thomas Rumbelow	Joan, daugher of William at Combe / Elizabeth Robbyns	Joan Morsse widow	John Smyth / Richard Raw	John at Court

Continued

YEAR	HIGH WARDENS	ALE RECEIPTS	YOUNG MEN WARDENS	ALE RECEIPTS	OUR LADY (FROM 1538 'CHURCH SHEEP')	MAIDENS	ALMS LIGHT	ST ANTHONY	ST SUNDAY
1539	John Normat at Court Richard Robbyns	£3/-/=	Christopher at Court Christopher at Combe	18/3d	William Leddon Robert at Hayne	Joan Webber Agnes at Moore	Joan Goodman **Store dissolved**	William Timewell at Combe William Timewell at Wood **Store dissolved**	John at Court **Store dissolved**
1540	William Leddon (for the widows at Combe) Robert at Moore	£2/15/6½d	Christopher Morsse William Morsse at Loyton	£1/4/4½d	William Scely Richard Webber	Joan at Court Joan Borrage **Store dissolved**			
1541	Richard Raw Lewis Trychay	£2/2/2½d	Roger Borrage William Timewell (son of Thomas at Timewell)	£1/3/9½d	William at Timewell James Pester at Hukeley				
1542	William Timewell at Combe Joan Morsse	£2/4/4	John Scely John Timewell at Combe, (son of William at Combe, in place of Nicholas Timewell who refused office)	×	George Morsse William Robbyns				
1543	William Timewell at Wood Joan Goodman	£2/1/4	×	×	Thomas Borrage Richard Hukeley				

1544	Harry Hayle John Gupworthy	£2/2/1$^{1/2d}$	William at Moore Nicholas Timewell	£1/3/3	Thomas at Timewell Richard Robbyns
1545	William Morsse John Norman at Poole	£2/9/8	John Trychay ('John Lewis at Morebath') John Norman at Pole	£1/7/8$^{1/2d}$	Robert at Moore William Hurley
1546	John Taylor John Timewell at Borston	£2/-/=	Thomas at Timewell Edward Norman at Court	£1/7/6	Thomas Norman Lewis Trychay
1547	William Leddon Thomas Borrgae	£2/7/10	Christopher Timewell at Hayne John Hurley at Rumbelow's (son of William Hurley) John Leddon	£1.11.10$^{1/2d}$	John Norman at Court Joan Morsse at Town
1548	Lucy Scely (serving in place of William Scely her husband, died in office) Ale warden Robert Isac did not serve because ales abolished	No ale	Christopher Hayle (serving in place of John Timewell son of Thomas Timewell at Timewell and John Raw son of Richard Raw junior)	No ale	Robert Zaer Joan Goodman **Store dissolved**
1549	Richard Cruce	No ale	No wardens	No ale	
1550	Richard Hukeley	No ale	No wardens	No ale	
1551	Richard Robyns	£2/18/1$^{1/2d}$	No wardens	No ale	
1552	Robert at Moore	×	No wardens	No ale	

Continued

YEAR	HIGH WARDENS	ALE RECEIPTS	YOUNG MEN WARDENS	ALE RECEIPTS	OUR LADY (FROM 1538 'CHURCH SHEEP')	MAIDENS	ALMS LIGHT	ST ANTHONY	ST SUNDAY
1553	Lewis Trychay	×	No wardens	No ale					
1554	Joan Morsse Thomas at Timewell	£2/13/4d	No wardens	No ale					
1555	John Skynner Robert Isac	£2/8/10d	No wardens	No ale					
1556	James Goodman Nicholas Timewell at Hayne (in place of Joan Rumbelow)	£3/7/11d	No wardens	No ale					
1557	William Taylor (in place of George Smyth) Joan Rumbelow (in place of Nicholas at Hayne)	£4/0/2¹/²ᵈ	John Raw at Combe Thomas Hurley	£3/6/8d					
1558	John Wood Nicholas Timewell at Hayne	£4/14/4d	William Taylor John Timewell at Borston	£2/2/10d					
1559	John Norman at Poole Richard Timewell at Timewell (on his father William's death in office)	£5/6/8d	Christopher Hurley Thomas Borrage	£2/0/10d					

1560	John Timewell at Borston John Borrage at Brockhole	£3/2/9d (sum disputed: first account had £4/1/=)	John Timewell at Hayne William Leddon	£2/6/8d
1561	Alison Perry Eylond (Ellen) Hurley	£3/15/10d	Thomas Parson Robert Norman (son of Edward Norman at Wood)	£2/13/8d
1562	John Norman at Rill Robin Isac	£3/16/4d	John Taylor John Morsse	£2/1/8d
1563	Edward Rumbelow Alison Norman at Court	£3/13/9d	John the son of Richard at Timewell Thomas the son of William at Timewell	££2/2/10d
1564	John Lambert at Hayne Robert Zaer	£2/13/4d	Richard Leddon William Cruce	£2/12/2d
1565	John Lambert at Hayne ('for Webber's bargain') Richard Raw	£2/14/10^{12d}	Thomas Perry William Scely	£2/14/5d
1566	Richard Timewell William Timewell at Combe	£3/0/4d	Oliver Rumbelow Johnn Norman (son of Christopher Norman at Wood)	£2/2/5d

Continued

YEAR	HIGH WARDENS	ALE RECEIPTS	YOUNG MEN WARDENS	ALE RECEIPTS	OUR LADY (FROM 1538 'CHURCH SHEEP')	MAIDENS	ALMS LIGHT	ST ANTHONY	ST SUNDAY
1567	John Borrage at Brockhole / John Raw (in place of John Timewell at Wood)	£2/14/4d	Christopher Radford / William Timewell (son of William Timewell at Timewell)	£2/7/=					
1568	William at Timewell / Edward Norman at Wood	£2/16/4d	Robert Cruce / William Norman (son of Edward Norman at Wood)	£2/10/=					
1569	Eylon Hurley (she appointed William at Timewell to speak for her) / William Morsse	×	John Scely son of William Scely / John Farthyng the servant of William at Combe	×					
1570	Joan Norman at Rill / William Scely	£4/0/6d	Christopher Norman, the son of Christopher Norman / John Goodman, son of James Goodman	£1/14/9d					
1571	William Norman at Court (acting for his mother Alison Norman at Court) / Margaret Taylor	£3/3/8d	John Borrage son of John Borrage / John Raw son of John Raw	£1/10/=					

1572	Robert Zaer Thomas Timewell (in place of Susan Leddon)	£2/17/4d	James Goodman Edward Norman at Wood	£1/7/6d
1573	John Raw John Scely	£2/15/=	Silvester Norman, son of Thomas Norman at Hollwell George, son of Christopher Norman at Wood	£2/8/8d
1574	William Timewell at Combe Richard Cruce	£3/5/4d	William Timewell the son of Richard Timewell at Timewell William Timewell son of Agnes Timewell at Leddons	£1.13.4d
1575	Grace Timewell Robert Stone	£3/18/=	William Morsse, son of William Morsse Nicholas Scely son of John Scely	×

Bibliography

MANUSCRIPT SOURCES

CORPUS CHRISTI COLLEGE CAMBRIDGE

Parker Library, Ms 97

DEVON RECORD OFFICE, EXETER

Ashburton CWA: 2141A/PW1
Broadhempton CWA: 2659A/PW1
Chagford CWA: 1429A/PW1–4
Chudleigh CWA: 3944A/PW1–3
Coldridge CWA: 272A/PW1–2 (Microfiche)
Crediton CWA: 1660A/1–33
Dartington CWA: EDRO/PW1–2 (V)
Exeter St John CWA: EDRO DD 36765–75 (G13)
Exeter St Mary Major CWA: EDRO PW1 (V)
Exeter St Mary Steps CWA: EDRO PW1–6
Exeter St Petrock CWA: EDRO PW1–3 G13 (V)
Iddesleigh CWA (Microfiche)
Kilmington CWA: 3047A/PW1
Morebath CWA: 2983/PW1–2, PZ1
Morebath parish registers 1558– , microfiche
Northam CWA (Microfiche): MFK 2–4
Okehampton CWA 3210A/ PW1, 3–9
Plymstock CWA (Microfiche): MFC 92/1–21
Shobrooke CWA: 1048A/PW1–78
South Tawton CWA: 2915A/PW1
Tavistock CWA: 482 A/PW1–20 (Box 670)
Woodland CWA : 2660A/PW1 (B)
Woodberry CWA: EDRO PW1 (V)
Chanter 775–81, 854
DRO 96M/86/11, 13

EXETER CATHEDRAL LIBRARY

Exeter Cathedral Library D&C 4951, Court Roll 1508–9

PUBLIC RECORD OFFICE, LONDON

Prob 11/10
Prob 11/14
Prob 11/16
Prob 11/27
Prob 11/28
Prob 11/30
Prob 11/32
Prob 11/33
Prob 11/37
Prob 11/48
Prob 11/53
Prob 11/56
Prob 11/59
Prob 11/62
E 334/7 (Composition Book)

SOMERSET RECORD OFFICE, TAUNTON

A/AHT 1/1–10
A/AHT 10/1–7 (Sydenham of Dulverton papers)
Banwell Churchwardens' Accounts D/P/ ban /4/1/1
Ilminster Churchwardens' Accounts D/P/ ilm 4/1/1
Langford Budville Churchwardens' Accounts DD/X/ THR 9
Yatton Churchwardens' Accounts D/P/ yat 4/1/1–3.

WEST COUNTRY STUDIES LIBRARY, EXETER

Beatrix Cresswell, Notes on Devon Churches
Moger abstracts of Wills
Oswyn Murray Abstracts of Wills
Hennesey's Notes on Incumbents

PRINTED PRIMARY SOURCES

Robert J. Alexander (ed.), *Records of Early English Drama: Somerset* (Toronto and London, 1996)

M. Bateson (ed.), *Letters of Bishops to the Privy Council 1564*, Camden Society, NS 53 (1895)

J. Erskine Binney (ed.), *The Accounts of the Wardens of the Parish of Morebath, Devon. 1520–1573* (Exeter 1904 – Devon Notes and Queries, supplementary volume, 1903–4)

W. J. Blake (ed.), 'Hooker's Synopsis Chorographical of Devonshire' in *Reports and Transactions of the Devonshire Association*, vol. 47 (Plymouth, 1915), pp.334–48

Gerald Bray (ed.), *Documents of the English Reformation* (Cambridge, 1994)

J.S. Brewer and H. Bullen (eds), *Calendar of the Carew Manuscripts in Lambeth 1515–1574*, vol. 1 (London, 1867); (Hooker's life of Carew)

Clive Burgess (ed.), *The Pre–Reformation Records of All Saints Bristol*: Part 1 (Bristol Record Society, 1995)

Gilbert Burnet, *The History of the Reformation of the Church of England*, 2 vols (London, 1850)

Calendar of the Patent Rolls Preserved in the Public Record Office, Philip and Mary 1553–1558, 4 vols (HMSO, 1937–9)

C.R. Cheney and Michael Jones, *A Handbook of Dates for Students of British History* (Cambridge, 2000)

R. Pearse Chope (ed.), *Early Tours in Devon and Cornwall* (Exeter, 1918)

W. Keatinge Clay (ed.), *Liturgies and Occasional Forms of Prayer set forth in the reign of Queen Elizabeth* (Cambridge, 1847)

F.T. Colby, *Visitation of the County of Devon 1564* (Exeter, 1881)

Robert Cornish (ed.), *Kilmington Church Wardens' Accounts* (Exeter, 1901)

J.E. Cox (ed.), *Miscellaneous Writings and Letters of Thomas Cranmer* (Cambridge, 1846)

Beatrix F. Cresswell, 'The Church Goods Commission in Devon 1549–1552', *Reports and Transactions of the Devon Association*, vol. 43 (1911), pp.237–55

F.A. Crisp (ed.), *Abstracts of Somersetshire Wills*, 6 vols (London 1887)

J.R. Dasent (ed.), *Acts of the Privy Council*, NS vol. 1 (1542–7), (London, 1890)

A.G. Dickens (ed.), *Tudor Treatises*, Yorkshire Archaeological Society, Record Series CXXV (1959)

T.B. Dilks (ed.), *Bridgewater Borough Archives 1200–1485*, 5 vols (Somerset Record Society, 1933–71)

R. Dymond (ed.), 'The History of the Parish of St Petrock Exeter, as shown by its churchwardens account', *Reports and Transactions of the Devonshire Association*, vol. 14 (1882), pp.402–92

W.H. Frere and W.M. Kennedy (eds), *Visitation Articles and Injunctions of the Period of the Reformation*, vol. 2 *1536–1558* (London, 1910)

W. H. Frere (ed.), *Visitation Articles and Injunctions of the Period of the Reformation*, vol. 3 *1559–1575* (London, 1910)

J.E.B Gover, A. Mawer and F.M. Stenton, *The Place Names of Devon* (Cambridge, 1931)

E.A. Green, *The Survey and Rental of the Chantries Colleges and Free Chapels ... in the County of Somerset* (Somerset Record Society, 1888)

W. Haines (ed.), 'Stanford Churchwardens Accounts 1552–1602', *The Antiquary* XVII (1888), pp.70–72, 117–20, 168–72, 209–13

Alison Hanham (ed.), *Churchwardens' Accounts of Ashburton 1479–1580*, Devon and Cornwall Record Society N.S. 15 (1970)

William Harrison, *The Description of England*, ed. G. Edelen (Washington, 1994)

W.J. Harte, J.W. Schapp and H. Tapley–Soper (eds), *The Description of the Citie of Excester by John Vowell alias Hoker* (Exeter, 1919)

P.W. Hasler, *The House of Commons 1558–1603* (London, 1981), vol. 3

R.H. Helmholz (ed.), *Select Cases of Defamation to 1600* (Selden Society, 1960)

Historical Manuscripts Commission: Calendar of the Manuscripts of the Dean and Chapter of Wells, vol. 2 (HMCO, 1914)

Historical Manuscripts Commission: Reports and Records of the City of Exeter (London, 1916)

E. Hobhouse (ed.), *Churchwardens Accounts of Croscombe, Pilton, Yatton, Tintinhull, Morebath and St Michael's Bath* (Somerset Record Society, 1890)

Edward Hodnett, *English Woodcuts 1488–1535* (Oxford, 1973)

A.J. Howard and T.L. Stoate (eds), *The Devon Muster Roll for 1569* (Bristol, 1977)

M. Jurkowski, C.L. Smith, D. Crook (eds), *Lay Taxes in England and Wales 1188–1688* (Public Record Office Kew, 1998)

P.L. Hughes and J.F. Larkin (eds), *Tudor Royal Proclamations* vols 1 & 2 (New Haven and London, 1964–9)

A.L. Humphries, *Somersetshire Parishes: a Handbook of Historical Reference to all places in the County* (London, 1905)

C.S. Knighton (ed.), *Calendar of State Papers, Domestic series of the Reign of Edward VI, 1547–1553, preserved in the Public Record Office* (rev. edn, HMSO, 1992)

—— *Calendar of State Papers, Domestic series of the reign Mary I, 1553–1558, preserved in the Public Record Office*, (rev. edn, Public Record Office, 1998)

I.S. Leadam (ed.), *Select Cases in the Court of Requests 1497–1569* (Selden Society, 1898)

A.G. Legge (ed.), *Ancient Churchwardens' Accounts of the Parish of North Elmham 1539–1577* (Norwich, 1891)

Letters and Papers Foreign and Domestic, of the Reign of Henry VIII, 1509–1547, ed. J.S. Brewer *et al*, 21 vols (HMSO, 1862–1932)

F.W. Maitland (ed.), *Select Pleas in Manorial Courts* (Selden Society, 1889)

G. Oliver, *Ecclesiastical Antiquities of Devon* (London, 1840)

—— *Monasticon Diocesis Exoniensis* (Exeter, 1846)

—— *Lives of the Bishops of Exeter and a History of the Cathedral* (Exeter, 1861)

—— (ed), *A View of Devonshire in 1630 with a Pedigree of its Gentry by Thomas Westcote Gent* (Exeter, 1845)

Nicholas Orme (ed.), *Nicholas Roscarrock's Lives of the Saints of Cornwall and Devon* (Exeter, 1992)

F.M. Osborne (ed.), *The Churchwardens' Accounts of St Michael's Church, Chagford, 1480–1600* (Chagford, 1979)

Sir John Phear (ed.), 'Molland Accounts', *Reports and Transactions of the Devonshire Association*, vol. 35 (1902), pp.198–238

N. Pocock (ed.), *Troubles Connected with the Prayer–Book of 1549*, Camden Society, NS vol. 37 (1884)

Sir William Pole, *Collections towards a description of the County of Devon* (London, 1791)

Richard Polwhele, *The History of Devonshire* (London, 1797)

A Profitable and necessary doctryne, with certeyne homelies adioyned thereunto set forth by the reverende father in God, Edmonde byshop of London, London 1555 (RSTC 3238)

O.J. Reichel and W. Mugford (eds), *An Old Exeter Manuscript* (Exeter, 1907)

Tristram Risden, *The Chorographical Description or Survey of the County of Devon* (London, 1811)

H.E. Salter (ed.), *The Triennial Chapters of the Augustinian Canons* (Oxford Historical Society 74, 1920)

L.S. Snell (ed.), *The Suppression of the Religious Foundations of Devon and Cornwall* (Marazion, 1967)

—— (ed), *The Chantry Certificates for Devon and the City of Exeter* (Exeter, 1960)

The Statutes of the Realm, ed. A Luters *et al.*, 11 vols (1810–28)

T.L. Stoate (ed.), *Devon Lay Subsidy Rolls 1524–7* (Bristol, 1979)

—— *Devon Lay Subsidy Rolls 1543–5* (Bristol, 1986)

—— *Devon Taxes 1581–1660* (Bristol, 1988)

John Strype, *Ecclesiastical Memorials relating chiefly to religion and the reformation of it*, 3 vols (Oxford, 1816–28)

—— *Memorials of the life of Archbishop Thomas Cranmer* (London, 1812)

George Townsend and Stephen Cattley (eds), *The Acts and Monuments of John Foxe*, 8 vols (London, 1837–41)

P.F. Tytler (ed.), *England under the reign of Edward VI and Mary*, 2 vols (London, 1839)

Valor Ecclesiasticus Temp. Henry VIII (1814)

J.L. Vivian, *Visitations of the County of Devon* (Exeter, 1895)

J.W. Wasson (ed.), *Records of Early English Drama, Devon* (Toronto, 1990)

F.W. Weaver, *Somerset Medieval Wills, 3rd Series, 1531–58*, Somerset Record Society XXI (1905)

—— *Somerset Incumbents* (Bristol, 1889)

—— *Wells Wills* (London, 1890)

E. Lega Weekes (ed.), 'The Churchwardens Accounts of South Tawton' (transcript of the subsidiary store wardens' accounts), *Reports and Transactions of the Devonshire Association*, vol. 38 (1906), pp.522–8

D. Wilkins (ed.), *Conciliae Magnae Britanniae* (London, 1737)

J.F. Williams (ed.), *The Early Churchwardens Accounts of Hampshire* (Winchester, 1913)

R.N. Worth (ed.), *Calendar of the Tavistock Parish Records* (Plymouth, 1887)

C. Worth (ed.), *Devonshire Wills* (London, 1896)

Peter Wyatt (ed.), *The Uffcolme Wills and Inventories*, Devon and Cornwall Record Society, NS vol. 40 (1997)

Joyce Youings (ed.), *Devon Monastic Lands: Calendars of Particulars for Grants 1536–1558*, Devon and Cornwall Record Society, NS vol. 1 (1955)

BIBLIOGRAPHY OF PRINTED SECONDARY WORKS AND THESES CITED IN THE NOTES

Ian Arthurson, 'Fear and Loathing in West Cornwall: seven new letters on the 1548 Rising', *Journal of the Royal Instituion of Cornwall*, New Series II, vol. 3, pp.68–96

Kathleen Ashley and Pamela Sheingorn (eds), *Interpreting cultural symbols: Saint Anne in late medieval society* (Athens, Georgia, and London, 1990)

Margaret Aston, *England's Iconoclasts*, vol. 1: *Laws against Images* (Oxford, 1988)

W.O. Ault, 'Manor Court and Parish Church in Fifteenth–Century England', *Speculum* 42 (1967), pp.53–67

—— 'The Village Church and the Village Community in Medieval England', *Speculum* 45 (1970), pp.197–215

J. Baker, *Order of Serjeants at Law, a chronicle of creations* (Selden Society, 1984)

T.G. Barnes, 'County Politics and a Puritan *cause célèbre*: Somerset Church Ales 1633', *Transactions of the Royal Historical Society* 5th Series (1959), pp.103–22

M.W. Beresford, 'The Poll Tax and Census of Sheep 1549', *Agricultural History Review* 1 (1953), pp.9–15, 2 (1954), pp.15–29

G.W. Bernard, 'Anne Boleyn's Religion', *Historical Journal* 36 (1993), pp.1–20

—— 'The making of religious policy, 1533–1456: Henry VIII and the search for the middle way', *Historical Journal* 41 (1998), pp.321–49

R.J.E. Boggis, *A History of the Diocese of Exeter* (Exeter, 1922)

B. Bradshaw, 'The Controversial Thomas More', *Journal of Ecclesiastical History* 36 (1985), pp.535–69

Susan Brigden, *London and the Reformation* (Oxford, 1989)

—— *New Worlds, Lost Worlds: the rule of the Tudors, 1485–1603* (Harmondsworth, 2000)

A. D. Brown, *Popular Piety in Late Medieval England* (Oxford, 1995)

Clive Burgess, 'Pre–Reformation Churchwardens' Accounts and Parish Government: lessons from London and Bristol', *English Historical Review*, forthcoming

M.L. Bush, *The Government Policy of Protector Somerset* (London, 1975)

—— *The Pilgrimage of Grace: a study of the rebel armies of October 1536* (Manchester, 1996)

M.L. Bush and D. Bownes, *The Defeat of the Pilgrimage of Grace* (Hull, 1999)

M.S. Byford, 'The Price of Protestantism: Assessing the Impact of Religious Change on Elizabethan Essex, the cases of Heydon and Colchester 1558–1594', unpublished Oxford D Phil. thesis, 1988

Patrick Carter, 'Royal Taxation of the Parish Clergy 1535–58', unpublished Cambridge University PhD, 1995

Bridget Cherry and Nikolaus Pevsner, *Devon* (Harmondsworth, 1989)

Andrew A. Chibi, *Henry VIII's Conservative Scholar: Bishop John Stokesley and the Divorce, Royal Supremacy and Doctrinal Reform* (Bern, 1997)

G.W. Copeland, 'Devonshire Church Houses', *Reports and Transactions of the Devonshire Association*, vols 92 (1960), pp.116–41; 93 (1961), pp.250–65; 94 (1962), pp.427–39; 95 (1963), pp.135–55; 96 (1964), pp.202–7; 98 (1966), pp.157–68:

J. Cornwall, *Revolt of the Peasantry 1549* (London, 1977)

J.C. Cox, *The Parish Registers of England* (London, 1910)

A.G. Dickens, *The English Reformation* (2 edn, London, 1989)

—— *Reformation Studies* (London, 1982)

F.G. Dietz, *English Government Finance 1485–1558* (Illinois, 1920)

M.H. and R. Dodds, *The Pilgrimage of Grace 1536–7 and the Exeter Conspiracy 1538* (Cambridge, 1915)

M. Dowling, 'Anne Boleyn and the Reform', *Journal of Ecclesiastical History*, vol. 35 (1984), pp.30–45

E. Duffy, *The Stripping of the Altars: Traditional Religion in England c1400–1570* (New Haven and London, 1992)

—— 'Morebath 1520–1570: a rural parish in the Reformation', in J. Devlin and R. Fanning (eds), *Religion and Rebellion* (Dublin, 1997), pp.17–39

R. Dunning, *Christianity in Somerset* (Taunton, 1976)

Christopher Dyer, 'The English Medieval Village Community and its decline', *Journal of British Studies*, vol. 33 (1994), pp.407–29

C.R. Elrington (ed.), *Victoria County History of Somerset*, vol. 6 (Oxford, 1985)

G.R. Elton, *Policy and Police: The Enforcement of the Reformation in the Age of Thomas Cromwell* (Cambridge, 1972)

D.H. Farmer, *The Oxford Dictionary of Saints* (3rd edn, Oxford, 1992)

Ken Farnhill, 'Religious policy and parish "conformity": Cratfield's lands in the sixteenth century', in K.L. French, G.G. Gibbs and B.A. Kumin (eds), *The Parish in English Life 1400–1600* (Manchester, 1997), pp.217–29

A. Fletcher and D. MacCulloch, *Tudor Rebellions* (4 edn, London, 1997)

K.L. French, *The People of the Parish: Community Life in a Late Medieval English Diocese* (Philadelphia, 2001)

—— 'Local Identity and the Late Medieval Parish: the communities of Bath and Wells', unpublished University of Minnesota PhD dissertation, 1993

—— 'To free them from binding: women in the late medieval parish', *Journal of Interdisciplinary History* XXVII (1996–7), pp.387–412

—— 'Maiden's lights and Wives stores', *16th Century Journal* XXIX (1998), pp.399–421

K.L. French, Gary G. Gibbs and Beat Kumin (eds), *The Parish in English Life 1400–1600* (Manchester, 1997)

C. Haigh, *English Reformations: Religion, Politics and Society Under the Tudors* (Oxford, 1993)

—— (ed.), *The English Reformation Revised* (Cambridge, 1987)

W.P. Haugaard, *Elizabeth and the English Reformation* (Cambridge, 1968)

Peter Heath, *The English Parish Clergy on the Eve of the Reformation* (London, 1969)

W.G. Hoskins, *Devon* (Tiverton ,1992)

—— *Old Devon* (Newton Abbot, 1966)

R. Hoyle, 'War and Public Finance', in D. MacCulloch (ed.), *The Reign of Henry VIII* (London, 1995), pp.92–9

William Hunt, *The Somerset Diocese: Bath and Wells* (London, 1885)

Ronald Hutton, 'The local impact of the Tudor Reformations', in C. Haigh (ed.), *The English Reformation Revised* (Cambridge, 1987), pp.114–38

—— *The Rise and Fall of Merry England, the Ritual Year 1400–1700* (Oxford, 1994)

—— *The Stations of the Sun* (Oxford, 1996)

E.W. Ives, *Anne Boleyn* (Oxford, 1986)

—— 'Anne Boleyn and the early Reformation in England', *Historical Journal*, vol. 37 (1994). pp.389–400

W.K. Jordan, *Edward VI, the Young King* (London, 1968)

R. Kain and W. Ravenhill (eds), *Historical Atlas of South–West England* (Exeter, 1999)

C.J. Kitching, 'The quest for concealed lands in the reign of Elizabeth I', *Transactions of the Royal Historical Society*, 5th Series 24 (1974), pp.63–78

Beat Kumin, *The Shaping of a Community: the Rise and Reformation of the English Parish c.1400–1560* (Aldershot, 1996)

—— 'Parishioners in Court: Litigations and the Local Community', in S. Wabuda and C. Litzenberger (eds), *Belief and Practice in Reformation England* (Aldershot, 1998), pp. 20–39

S.E. Lehmberg, *The Later Parliaments of Henry VIII* (London, 1977)

Ethel Lega–Weekes, 'County armaments in Devon in the Sixteenth Century', *Reports and Transaction of the Devonshire Association*, vol. 61 (1909), pp.339–55

David Loades, *Two Tudor Conspiracies* (2 edn, Bangor, 1992)

Wallace T. MacCaffrey, *Exeter 1540–1640* (Cambridge Mass., 1975)

Diarmaid MacCulloch, *Thomas Cranmer, A Life* (New Haven and London, 1996)

—— *Tudor Church Militant* (Harmondsworth, 1999)

—— 'Kett's Rebellion in Context', *Past and Present* 84 (1979), pp.39–62

E.T. MacDermot, *History of the Great Western Railway* (London, 1931)

Marjorie McIntosh, *Controlling Misbehaviour in Early Modern England 1370–1600* (Cambridge, 1998)

R. Marius, *Thomas More* (London, 1993)

Peter Marshall, *The Catholic Priesthood and the English Reformation* (Oxford, 1994)

E. Miller (ed.), *The Agrarian History of England and Wales*, vol. 3, *1348–1500* (Cambridge, 1991)

C.E. Moreton, 'The Walsingham Conspiracy of 1537', *Historical Research* 63 (1990), pp.29–43

—— *The Townsends and their World: Gentry, Law and Land in Norfolk c1451–1551* (Oxford, 1992)

A.A. Mumford , *Hugh Oldham 1452–1519* (London, 1936)

Nicholas Orme, 'The Dissolution of the Chantries in Devon, 1546–8', *Reports and Transactions of the Devon Association*, vol. 111 (1979), pp.75–123

—— *Exeter Cathedral as it was, 1050–1550* (Exeter, 1986)

—— 'Indulgences in the Diocese of Exeter 1100–1536', *Reports and Transactions of the Devonshire Association*, vol. 120 (1988), pp.15–32

——— *Education and Society in Medieval and Renaissance England* (Hambledon Press, 1989)

——— 'Two Early Prayer–Books from North Devon', *Devon and Cornwall Notes and Queries*, vol. 36 (1991), pp.345–50

——— 'Church and chapel in Medieval England', *Transactions of the Royal Historical Society*, 5th Series vol. 47 (1996), pp.75–102

C. Oswald, 'Epidemics in Tudor Devon', *Reports and Transactions of the Devon Association*, vol. 109 (1977), pp.73–116

D.H. Pill, 'The Diocese of Exeter under Bishop Vesey', unpublished Exeter MA dissertation, 1963

——— 'The administration of the diocese of Exeter under Bishop Vesey', *Reports and Transactions of the Devonshire Association*, vol. 98 (1966), pp.262–8

——— 'Exeter Diocesan Courts in the early 16th century', *Reports and Transactions of the Devonshire Association*, vol. 100 (1968), pp.45–53

Sir Frederick Pollock and Frederick W. Maitland, *The History of English Law*, vol. 1 (Cambridge, 1968)

Athene Reiss, *The Sunday Christ: Sabbatarianism in English Medieval Wall Painting* (Oxford, 2000)

Richard Rex, *Henry VIII and the English Reformation* (London, 1993)

——— 'The English campaign against Luther in the 1520s', *Transactions of the Royal Historical Society*, 5th Series vol. 39 (1989), pp.85–106

F. Rose–Troup, *The Western Rebellion of 1549* (London, 1913)

Gervase Rosser, 'Going to the Fraternity Feast: Commensality and Social Relations in Late Medieval England', *Journal of British Studies*, vol. 33 (1994), pp.430–46

A.L. Rowse, *Tudor Cornwall, Portrait of a Society* (London, 1941)

F.W. Russell, *Kett's Rebellion in Norfolk* (London, 1859)

J.J. Scarisbrick, *Henry VIII* (New Haven and London, 1997)

Ethan Shagan, 'Protector Somerset and the 1549 Rebellions: new sources and new perspectives', *English Historical Review*, vol. 144 (1999), pp.34–63

W.B. Stephens, *Seventeenth Century Exeter* (Exeter, 1958)

L. Stone, *The Family, Sex and Marriage: England 1500–1800* (Harmondsworth, 1979)

M. Swanton, *St Sidwell, an Exeter Legend* (Exeter, 1986)

G.F. Sydenham, *The History of the Sydenham Family* (East Molesey, 1928)

R.N. Swanson, 'Titles to Orders in Medieval English Episcopal Registers', in H.M.E. Mayr–Harting and R.I. Moore (eds), *Studies in Medieval History presented to R.H.C. Davis* (London, 1985), pp.233–45

Joan Thirsk (ed.), *The Agrarian History of England and Wales*, vol. 4 *1500–1640* (Cambridge, 1967)

J.A.F. Thompson, *The Early Tudor Church and Society 1485–1529* (London, 1993)

D.E. Underdown, 'The Taming of the Scold: the Enforcement of Patriarchal Authority in Early Modern England', in A. Fletcher and J. Stephenson (eds), *Order and Disorder in Early Modern England* (Cambridge, 1985), pp.16–36

David Underdown, *Revel, Riot and Rebelliom: Popular Politics and Culture in England 1603–1660* (Oxford, 1985)

Jonathan Vage, 'The Diocese of Exeter 1519–1641', unpublished Cambridge PhD thesis, 1991

F.W. Weaver, 'Barlinch Priory', *Proceedings of the Somersetshire Archaeological and Natural History Society* LIV (1909), pp.79–106

S. and B. Webb, *The Story of the King's Highway* (London, 1913)

A.E. Welsford, *John Greenway 1460–1529, Merchant of Tiverton and London, a Devon Worthy* (Tiverton, 1984)

R. Whiting, *The Blind Devotion of the People* (Cambridge, 1989)

Penry Williams, *The Tudor Regime* (Oxford, 1979)

J.A.H. Wylie and I.J. Linn, 'Observations on the Distribution and Spread of the English Sweating Sickness in Devon in 1551', *Reports and Transactions of the Devon Association*, vol. 112 (1980), pp.101–115

J. Youings (ed.), *The Dissolution of the Monasteries* (London, 1971)

—— 'The South West Rebellion of 1549', *Southern History*, vol. 1 (1979), pp.99–12

Notes

CHAPTER ONE

1. E.T. MacDermot, *History of the Great Western Railway*, vol. 2 (London, 1931), p.172.
2. Richard Polwhele, *The History of Devonshire* (London, 1797), vol. 3, p.375.
3. J. Erskine Binney (ed.), *The Accounts of the Wardens of the Parish of Morebath, Devon, 1520–1573* (Exeter, 1904 – Devon Notes and Queries, supplementary volume 1903–4), hereafter cited as Binney, 2/Ms 64–5; 15/Ms 331; 56/Ms 198; 88/Ms 98;108/Ms 125.
4. Tristram Risden, *The Chorographical Description or Survey of the County of Devon* (London, 1811), p.5.
5. E. Miller (ed.), *The Agrarian History of England and Wales*, vol. 3, *1348–1500* (Cambridge, 1991), p.305; Joan Thirsk (ed.), *The Agrarian History of England and Wales*, vol. 4, *1500–1640* (Cambridge, 1967), pp.76–7.
6. Polwhele, *History of Devonshire*, p.375.
7. Binney 34–5/Ms 357.
8. For Barlinch, F.W. Weaver, 'Barlinch Priory', *Proceedings of the Somersetshire Archaeological and Natural History Society*, LIV (1908) pp.79–106; W. Page (ed.), *Victoria County History, Somerset*, vol. 2, pp.132–4; Nicholas Orme, *Education and Society in Medieval and Renaissance England* (Hambledon Press, 1989), quotation from p.113. For the disposal of the manor, Joyce Youings (ed.), *Devon Monastic Lands: Calendars of Particulars for Grants 1536–1558*, Devon and Cornwall Record Society, NS vol. I (1955), pp.3, 43–4; for the Sydenhams, G.F. Sydenham, *The History of the Sydenham Family* (East Molesey, 1928), pp.75, 79–81 and pedigree opposite p.50.
9. I have used the Ordnance Survey Explorer 2½-inch map, sheet 114, 'Exeter and the Exe Valley', and have established the ecclesiastical parish boundaries by reference to the Morebath tithe-map (dating from the 1840s) in the DRO.
10. Mill sites indicated on Mudge Map of Devon, published 1809.
11. Binney 38/s 181; field sizes: Polwhele, *History of Devon*, p.375 and information from Mr Jim Vellacott, formerly of the 'wester wode'.
12. Binney 83/Ms 93.
13. Binney 35/Ms 358; 182/Ms 398.
14. T.L. Stoate (ed.), *Devon Lay Subsidy Rolls 1524–7*, (Bristol, 1979), p.52; Stoate, *Devon Lay Subsidy Rolls 1543–5* (Bristol, 1986) p. 45.
15. Binney 40/Ms 183–4; 149/Ms 299–300; 193/Ms 32; 194/Ms 33.
16. Binney 64–5/Ms 210–11.
17. Binney 182/Ms 398.
18. Binney 178/Ms 393.
19. A.J. Howard and T.L. Stoate (eds.), *The Devon Muster Roll for 1569* (Bristol, 1977), pp.57–8.
20. Stoate, *Lay Subsidy Rolls 1524–7*, p.52; Binney 40/Ms 183–4.
21. There is no indication anywhere in the records where the manor court was held.
22. Below, chapter 3.
23. W.O. Ault, 'Manor Court and Parish Church in Fifteenth-Century England', *Speculum* 42 (1967), pp.53–67; Ault, 'The Village Church and the Village Community in Medieval England', *Speculum* 45 (1970), pp.197–215.
24. Bridget Cherry and Nikolaus Pevsner, *Devon* (Harmondsworth, 1989), pp.575–6: 'the saddle–backed roof obviously belonging to Butterfield's restoration'; Polwhele, *Devonshire*, p.377, and information from Jim and Mabel Vellacot of Bampton and Morebath.
25. For the Tudor building, I rely on the 18th-century description in Polwhele, *History of Devonshire*, pp.376–7, and details gleaned from the accounts themselves.

26. Derived perhaps from 'ambulatory'.

27. Binney 20–23 passim/Ms 341–6; 25/Ms 348.

28. Binney 92/Ms 103; 111/Ms 130; 142/Ms 231.

29. For discussion of which, see below pp. 77–81.

30. Binney 50/Ms 74; 159/Ms 370.

31. Binney 34/Ms 356.

32. For Devon church houses, G.W. Copeland, 'Devonshire Church Houses', *Reports and Transactions of the Devonshire Association* 92 (1960), pp.116–41; 93 (1961), pp.250–65; 94 (1962), pp.427–39; 95 (1963), pp.135–55; 96 (1964), pp.202–7; 98 (1966), pp.157–68; for Morebath church-house furnishings, Binney 124/Ms 150 and *passim*.

33. Binney 124/Ms 150.

34. Binney 69/Ms 218; 110/Ms 128.

35. Binney 49/Ms 72.

36. Binney 2/Ms 65.

37. The references are conveniently collected in J.W. Wasson (ed.), *Records of Early English Drama, Devon* (Toronto, 1990), pp.208–12: first reference to 'playing' 1565, to a harper 1578 and again 1579, 1582; for church ales more generally, Ronald Hutton, *The Rise and Fall of Merry England* (Oxford, 1994), pp.27–34, 59, 118, and the same author's *Stations of the Sun, a History of the Ritual Year in Britain* (Oxford, 1996), pp.245–57.

38. For the importance in late medieval England of feasting as a means of cementing unity and identity, Gervase Rosser, 'Going to the Fraternity Feast: Commenality and Social Relations in Late Medieval England', *Journal of British Studies*, vol. 33 (1994), pp.430–46.

39. Binney 82–86/Ms 92–95. For this dispute, see below p.61.

40. Binney 4, 26, 41, 42, 65, 82, 90; for the Bampton chantries, Nicholas Orme, 'The Dissolution of the Chantries in Devon, 1546–8', *Reports and Transactions of the Devonshire Association for the Advancement of Science*, vol. 111 (1979), pp.75–123 at p.93.

41. A corporas case is the container for the linen cloth on which the bread and wine were consecrated during the Mass.

42. Binney 25 (where her name is mistranscribed 'Grueway'), 47; the phrase quoted is from her will, PRO, Prob 11/27, fol 226v, (PCC 28 Dyngeley), 23 April 1539; see below, ch. 4, and colour illustration section pp. 8, 9.

43. Below, pp. 52, 115.

44. Binney 65, 90, 112, 250. The parishioner was William Hurley.

45. H.E. Salter (ed.), *The Triennial Chapters of the Augustinian Canons* (Oxford Historical Society 74, 1920), p.184; F.W. Weaver, 'Barlinch Priory', p.87.

46. Nicholas Orme, *Education and Society*, ch. 7, text of notes reproduced pp.117–21.

47. Exeter Cathedral Library D&C 4951, Court Roll 1508–9. I am grateful to Nicholas Orme for providing me with this reference.

48. Binney, *Accounts*, p.199; for Edward Sydenham's will (no bequest to Trychay or Morebath), see PRO 11/30 f18v (PCC 3 Pynnyng), and F.W. Weaver, *Somerset Medieval Wills, 3rd Series, 1531–58*, Somerset Record Society XXI (1905), pp.74–5; Binney 203/Ms 41 (great bell).

49. T.L. Stoate (ed.), *Devon Lay Subsidy Rolls 1524–7* (Bristol, 1979), p.52.

50. W.G. Hoskins, *Devon* (Tiverton, 1992), pp.125–6; W.B. Stephens, *Seventeenth-Century Exeter* (Exeter, 1958), pp.3–5.

51. A.E. Welsford, *John Greenway 1460–1529, Merchant of Tiverton and London, a Devon Worthy* (Tiverton, 1984).

52. W.J. Blake (ed.), 'Hooker's Synopsis Chorographical of Devonshire' in *Reports and Transactions of the Devonshire Association*, xlvii (Plymouth, 1915), p.346.

53. Binney 11/Ms 175; 13/Ms 177; 18/Ms 336; 32/Ms 354; 51/Ms 74.

54. Information from Mr Jim Vellacott, formerly of Wood.

55. This discussion of the building plan of Devon farmhouses follows Peter Beacham, 'Rural Building 1400–1800' in Cherry and Pevsner, *Devon*, pp.62–78. For Brockhole, see the illustration in the colour section, p. 4.

56. Described Binney 35–6/Ms 359.

57. Binney 97/Ms 108.

58. Binney 44–7/Ms 189–93; Katherine Robbyns's inventory may be compared with those of two other Devon widows in 1576, which it closely resembles, Ellin Dowdeny and Florence Pearsie: Peter Wyatt (ed.), *The Uffcolme Wills and Inventories*, Devon and Cornwall Record Society, New Series vol. 40 (1997), pp.1–3.

59. Binney 26/Ms 348; 58/Ms 200; 60/Ms 203; 132/Ms 160.

60. The technicalities of office-holding in Morebath are explained below, pp. 24–32.

61. Binney 184/Ms 289; 212/Ms 56; 234/Ms 255; 236/Ms 287; 249/Ms 17.

62. Binney 246/Ms 14: but there were special and tragic circumstances for this indulgence: see below, ch. 7, p. 184.

63. Binney 141/Ms 230.

64. Binney 109/Ms 128.

65. Binney 21/Ms 342; 55/Ms 196.

66. Binney 162/Ms 374.

67. Binney 244/Ms 11.

68. DRO: Morebath register, *sub* 22 March 1560, 22 November 1562, 9 August 1563, 21 October 1563, 19 October 1572.

69. W.G. Hoskins, *Old Devon* (Newton Abbot, 1966), 'Epidemics in Tudor Devon' pp.132–48; N.C. Oswald 'Epidemics in Devon 1538–1837', *Reports and Transactions of the Devon Association* 109 (1977), pp.73–116, esp. p.84; J.A.H. Wylie and I.J. Linn, 'Observations on the Distribution and Spread of the English Sweating Sickness in Devon in 1551', *Reports and Transactions of the Devon Association* 112 (1980), pp.101–15.

70. Examples culled from Binney 22–27/Ms 342–50: the story of 'the lad that was killed with the knife' can be reconstructed from Binney 195, 218, 203, 246.

71. DRO Register of Morebath, sub 31 May 1560, 13 and 22 October 1564, 10 February 1565, 4 and 20 October 1567, 22 October 1568, 3 July 1570.

72. Binney 64/Ms 210. John Timewell minimus was Young Men's Warden in 1532: Binney 38/Ms 182.

73. L. Stone, *The Family, Sex and Marriage. England 1500–1800* (Harmondsworth, 1979).

74. Binney 20/Ms 340.

75. Exeter Cathedral archives, D&C 5114; Stoate, *Devon Lay Subsidy, 1524–7*, pp.37–8.

76. Ordination lists, DRO. Chanter 13, Register of Bishop Oldham, 1504–19.

77. R.N. Swanson, 'Titles to Orders in Medieval English Episcopal Registers' in H.M.E. Mayr-Harting and R.I. Moore, *Studies in Medieval History presented to R.H.C. Davis* (London, 1985), pp.233–45; J.A.F. Thompson, *The Early Tudor Church and Society 1485–1529* (London, 1993), p.143.

78. R.J.E. Boggis, *A History of the Diocese of Exeter* (Exeter, 1922), pp.359–60: D.H. Pill, 'The Diocese of Exeter under Bishop Vesey', unpublished Exeter MA dissertation, 1963, pp.33–4; G. Oliver, *Monasticon Diocesis Exoniensis* (Exeter, 1846), pp.219–30; L.S. Snell, *The Suppression of the Religious Foundations of Devon and Cornwall* (Marazion, 1967), pp.47, 125.

79. Binney 21/Ms 342.

80. *Valor Ecclesiasticus Temp. Henry VIII* (1814), p.331.

81. Binney 20/Ms 340. Sir Christopher is of course quoting from the Latin Vulgate version of the bible, which follows a different numbering for the psalms from that of modern English bibles: Vulgate Psalm 117 verse 16 (118/16 in English bibles, where the sense is somewhat different).

CHAPTER TWO

1. J. Erskine Binney (ed.), *The Accounts of the Wardens of the Parish of Morebath, Devon. 1520–1573* (Exeter 1904 – Devon Notes and Queries, supplementary volume 1903–4); hereafter cited as Binney.

2. Unfortunately, the Devon Record Office does not appear to have preserved any information about the accession or binding of the manuscript beyond the summary in the text above, from a note written on the inside of the front cover.

3. Not 1526, as stated by Binney, p.1. The correct year can be established by comparing the names of the High Wardens (William at Pole and Geffery Smyth) with the list of wardens by year compiled by Sir Christopher, Binney 22/Ms 343).

4. Binney 32/Ms 354.

5. Binney 82/Ms 92; 205/Ms 45.

6. The first printed extracts from the manuscript, edited by Sackville H. Berkeley, appeared in the *Proceedings of the Somerset Archaeological and Natural History Society* in 1883 (vol. 29, pp. 69–83). Mr Berkeley commented that the manuscript 'had been rudely bound but is now in detached batches of folios, mixed together in no regular sequence' (loc. cit., p. 83).

7. Binney 11/Ms 175; 222/Ms 240.

8. For which, see below pp. 134–41.

9. The incomplete account of the store of St Anthony in 1529 is run into the account of the store of Our Lady for the same year: pp.180, 331–2 of the Ms, printed continuously as Binney 14–16.

10. Ms 267–8.

11. Ms 271–2.

12. Described in *Churchwardens Accounts of Croscombe, Pilton, Yatton, Tintinhull, Morebath and St Michael's Bath*, ed. E. Hobhouse (Somerset Record Society, 1890), p.208 (hereafter cited as *Somerset Accounts*).

13. Binney 171 Ms 384; 252/Ms 21

14. The fullest list so far available, county by county, is in Hutton, *Merry England*, pp.263–93.

15. Key works in this process: Ronald Hutton, 'The local impact of the Tudor Reformations' in C. Haigh (ed.), *The English Reformation Revised* (Cambridge, 1987); *The Rise and Fall of Merry England, the Ritual Year 1400–1700* (Oxford, 1994); Beat Kumin, *The Shaping of a Community: the Rise and Reformation of the English Parish c.1400–1560* (Aldershot, 1996); K.L. French, Gary G. Gibbs and Beat Kumin (eds.), *The Parish in English Life 1400–1600* (Manchester, 1997);

K.L. French, *The People of the Parish: Community Life in a Late Medieval English Diocese* (Philadelphia, 2001) unfortunately appeared too late for me to make more than glancing use of it.

16.　For example in R. Whiting, *The Blind Devotion of the People* (Cambridge, 1989); E. Duffy, *The Stripping of the Altars: Traditional Religion in England c.1400–1570* (New Haven and London, 1992); A.D. Brown, *Popular Piety in Late Medieval England* (Oxford, 1995); Hutton, 'The local impact'; Hutton, *Merry England*; Kumin, *Shaping of a Community*.

17.　See Clive Burgess (ed.), *The Pre-Reformation Records of All Saints Bristol*: Part I (Bristol Record Society, 1995), pp.xxxiv, xxxviii, xli; the argument is developed in the same author's 'Pre-Reformation Churchwardens' Accounts and Parish Government: lessons from London and Bristol', *English Historical Review*, forthcoming. I am grateful to Dr Burgess for an advance copy of this important and stimulating article. For a more upbeat assessment of the problem, see Kumin, *Shaping of a Community*, pp.87–9.

18.　*Somerset Accounts*, p.65.

19.　Robert Cornish (ed.), *Kilmington Church Wardens' Accounts* (Exeter, 1901), p.6.

20.　Powicke and Cheney (eds.), *Councils and Synods*, ii, p.1008.

21.　Alison Hanham (ed.), *Churchwardens' Accounts of Ashburton 1479–1580*, Devon and Cornwall Record Society N.S. 15 (1970).

22.　For example, Broadhempton, DRO 2659A/PW1, and Woodland PW1.

23.　DRO Tavistock PW1: 3210A/PW1: 1660A.

24.　DRO St Petroc PW1: DD 70868–70967.

25.　Katherine L. French, 'Local Identity and the Late Medieval Parish: the communities of Bath and Wells', unpublished University of Minnesota PhD dissertation, 1993, p.8 (quoting PRO C1 872/17, a Chancery case against two former wardens of the parish of Axbridge, 1536).

26.　I.S. Leadam, *Select Cases in the Court of Requests 1497–1569* (Selden Society, 1898), pp.18, 20.

27.　The accounts at Chagford were in Latin until 1543, those at Tavistock until 1535. The first English entries in the St Petroc accounts are in 1544, at St John's, another Exeter city parish, the expenses go into English in 1547 (though accounting reverts to Latin again in Mary's reign); the accounts at St Mary Steps in Exeter were still in Latin in 1547, but by 1551 the expenses

only were being reported in English. Katherine French provides a table of the move from Latin to English in Somerset parish accounts, *People of the Parish*, p.48.

28.　This seems to have been the practice at Dartington, DRO 009.4.c.F, vol. I *passim*, and at Chudleigh.

29.　French, 'Local Identity', p.32.

30.　*Somerset Accounts*, p.9.

31.　Binney 32/Ms 354; 61/Ms 205; 185/Ms 290. The editor of the Devon Volume of the Records of Early English Drama series considered that Morebath's George with his horse and dragon might be props for a play, procession or tableau vivant, but the fact that the George is gilded and located in a tabernacle that it is made by Thomas Glasse, the carver of other statues including a nativity of the Virgin for the church, and the context – all the references to the George occur in contexts concerned with the renewal or elaboration of devotional imagery – suggest that what is being referred to is a devotional carving with several figures, depicting the commonly represented legend of the rescue of the princess: J.W. Wasson (ed.), *Records of Early English Drama, Devon* (Toronto, 1990), p.448.

32.　Binney 22–3/Ms 344–5; below, ch. 4.

33.　F.W. Weaver (ed.), *Wells Wills* (London, 1890), pp.vii–viii.

34.　Binney 61/Ms 204; 71/Ms 221; 79/Ms 87. For St Sunday see Athene Reiss, *The Sunday Christ: Sabbatarianism in English Medieval Wall Painting* (Oxford, 2000).

35.　Binney 42/Ms 187; 62/Ms 206; 68/Ms 217.

36.　My thanks for this point to Nicholas Orme.

37.　K.L. French, 'To free them from binding: women in the late medieval parish', *Journal of Interdisciplinary History*, vol. 27 (1996–7), pp.387–412; 'Maiden's lights and Wives' stores', *Sixteenth Century Journal*, vol. 29 (1998), pp.399–421. Dr French, however, somewhat misleadingly equates 'stores' with guilds.

38.　Binney 6/Ms 70; 38/Ms 362; and esp. 72/223.

39.　Binney 103/Ms 117.

40.　Hutton, *Merry England*, pp.12–13, 17; Binney 164/Ms 376.

41.　Binney 241/Ms 6.

42.　Binney 56/Ms 198; 74/Ms 80; 75–7/Ms 82–4; 88–9/Ms 98.

43.　Binney 55/Ms 196.

44.　Binney 2/Ms 64–5.

45.　Binney 11/Ms 175; cf. the arrangements at Croscombe, where sheep were leased to parishioners who kept the wool in return for a rent paid to the church: Hobhouse, *Somerset Churchwardens Accounts*, pp.37, 40.

46. 'Sheep's lease': Binney 2/Ms 65; 53/Ms 77; 55/Ms 196; 56/Ms 198; 144/Ms 297; 145/Ms 298. Refusal: Binney 74/Ms 80 (William Norman); 108/Ms 125 (John Tymewell at Burston).

47. Binney 9/Ms 172–3; 36/359–60.

48. Binney 11/Ms 175.

49. When in the late 1540s church ales were banned by the Protestant authorities, the parish elected only a single warden annually; below, pp. 120, 124.

50. Binney 212–13/Ms 56 and see 51/Ms 74; 223/Ms 243; 229/Ms 287; for the late Elizabethan practice, Ms 303–4, 330. The parish reverted to the appointment of two wardens annually in the late 1590s.

51. Binney 220–21/Ms 402–3.

52. Binney 250/Ms 18.

53. D.H. Pill, 'The Diocese of Exeter under Bishop Vesey', unpublished Exeter MA dissertation, 1963, pp.45–6 (citing Exeter Consistory Court Act Book – CC.778 sub 12 January 1533, parish of Crediton).

54. Binney, 114/Ms 135.

55. Binney 73/Ms 224.

56. Binney 202/Ms 41; 250/Ms 18.

57. Binney 195–7/Ms 34–7; 243–4/Ms 9.

58. Binney 190/Ms 29.

59. Binney 146/Ms 275.

60. For which see below, pp. 107–10.

61. Binney 143/Ms 273.

62. Calculations based on the Morebath return in T.L. Stoate (ed.), *Devon Lay Subsidy Rolls 1524–7* (Bristol, 1979), p.52, and on the list of wardens provided by Sir Christopher, Binney 20–28/Ms 34–50 and Binney 199–202/Ms 277–8, 269–70.

63. Binney 74/Ms 79; 81–2/Ms 91; 119/Ms 143.

64. assessed at £14 in goods in 1524.

65. Binney 25/Ms 347; 47/Ms 194; 74/ Ms 80; 140/Ms 229; Stoate, *Devon Lay Subsidy Rolls 1524–7*, p.52.

66. Binney, 6/Ms 167; 21/Ms 341; 27/Ms 350; 61/Ms 204; 71/Ms 221; 86/Ms 96.

67. DRO 1429/PW3 (Chagford) fol. 161r.

68. DRO 009.4.C.F (Dartington CWA) vol. 1, fol. 51r.

69. Binney 6/Ms 167; 12–13/Ms 177; 33–4/Ms 356; 52/Ms 76; 79/Ms 87–8; 82–6/Ms 92–5, etc.

70. Binney 225/Ms 137.

71. Kumin, *Shaping of a Community*, p.155: Hanham, *CWA Ashburton*, pp.xii–xv and *passim*.

72. F.M. Osborne (ed.), *The Churchwardens' Accounts of St Michael's Church, Chagford 1480–1600* (Chagford, 1979), *passim*.

73. Binney 3–4/Ms 66–7.

74. Binney 9–10/Ms 173.

75. Binney 13/Ms 178.

76. Binney 19/Ms 336 (my emphasis).

77. Binney 91/101; 112/Ms 131; 120/Ms 143 (my emphasis).

78. Binney 98/Ms 110.

79. Binney 30/Ms 351(my emphasis).

80. Binney 5/Ms 69; 18/Ms 335; 137/Ms 225.

81. Binney 171/Ms 385; 252/Ms 21.

82. Binney 223–4/Ms 243.

83. Binney 116/Ms 138.

84. Binney 198/Ms 39; John Wood's fears were justified: 18d went missing, and he was pursued by the parish for it for years. See below, p.184.

85. Binney 206/Ms 46.

86. I give here just one reference per word: Binney 61/Ms 204; 5/Ms 69; 60/Ms 203; 16/Ms 332; 202/Ms 41; 248/Ms 16; 111/Ms 130; 60/Ms 204; 161/Ms 373; 44/Ms 189; 144/Ms 388.

87. Binney 114/Ms 135.

88. Binney 80/Ms 88 and *passim*.

89. Binney 86/Ms 96 and *passim*.

90. Binney 116/Ms 138.

91. Binney 120/Ms 143, cf Binney 23/Ms 344.

92. Binney17/Ms 333.

93. Binney 123/Ms 148; 118/ Ms 140 and *passim*.

94. Binney 9/Ms 172.

95. Binney 195/Ms 34.

96. Binney 70/Ms 220.

97. Binney 10/Ms 174.

98. Binney 16/Ms 332.

99. Binney 10/Ms 174.

100. Binney 16–7/Ms 332–3; 20/Ms 340.

101. Binney 4/Ms 67.

102. Binney 99/Ms 112.

103. Binney 112/Ms 132.

104. Binney 232/Ms 280.

105. Binney 182/Ms 398.

106. Binney 90/Ms 100.

107. Ibid.

108. Binney 95/Ms 105.

109. J.F. Williams (ed.), *The Early Churchwardens Accounts of Hampshire* (Winchester, 1913), p.159; DRO 1429A/PW2 (Chagford) fol. 155.

110. Binney 75/Ms 82; 135/Ms 165; 144/Ms 297.

111. Binney 75–6/Ms 82–3.

112. Binney 9/Ms 172; 86/Ms 96.

113. Binney 108/Ms 125–6; 72/Ms 80.
114. Binney 87–88/Ms 97–8.
115. Binney 135/Ms 165.
116. Binney 100/Ms 112–13.

CHAPTER THREE
1. Binney 150/Ms 296.
2. Binney 11/Ms 175; 30/Ms 351; 92/Ms 103; 114–5/Ms 135; 131/Ms 160.
3. For the bede-roll, E. Duffy, *The Stripping of the Altars, Traditional Religion in England c.1400–1580* (New Haven and London, 1992), pp.334–7.
4. Binney 106/Ms 123.
5. Binney 19–20/Ms 340.
6. Binney 22/Ms 343.
7. My emphasis.
8. Binney 22, 26/Ms 343, 349; Sir Christopher was a beneficiary, a witness and probably the scribe of Sir Edward's will: Weaver, *Wells Wills*, p.33.
9. Binney 21/Ms 341.
10. Binney 159/Ms 370.
11. Binney 34–5/Ms p.357.
12. Binney 38/Ms 181; my emphasis.
13. Binney 39–42/Ms 183–6.
14. Richard Polwhele, *The History of Devonshire* (London, 1797), p.375.
15. There is no doubt of the Ms reading, though nothing in the document explains how so long a period could have elapsed before a settlement.
16. It records a payment made on Trinity Sunday 1533 (8 June that year), and cannot have been made before then.
17. 23 Henry VIII c5, *Statutes of the Realm*, vol. 3 (reprint 1963), pp.368–72; S. and B. Webb, *The Story of the King's Highway* (London, 1913), ch. 6. I am greatly indebted to my Magdalene colleague Dr Neil Jones for help in teasing out the legal tangle behind these cryptic entries.
18. John Baker, *Order of Serjeants at Law* (Selden Society, 1984) pp. 168, 546, and private communication.
19. Binney 41–2/Ms 184–6.
20. Cornish (ed.), *Kilmington Church Wardens' Accounts*, pp.2–5.
21. Binney 42/Ms 186.
22. Binney 39–42/Ms 183–6, my emphasis.
23. Binney 35/Ms 358.
24. Kumin, *Shaping of a Community*, pp.41–2, 131; Peter Heath, *The English Parish Clergy on the Eve of the Reformation* (London, 1969), p.20; detail on Devon clerks in J.F. Chanter, 'The Parish clerks of Barnstaple 1500–1900', *Reports and Transactions of the Devonshire Association*, vol. 36 (1904), pp.390–414.
25. For contests, Peter Marshall, *The Catholic Priesthood and the English Reformation* (Oxford, 1994), pp.202–3.
26. Below, p. 190.
27. Binney 182/Ms 398. He was the son of Lewis Trychay, the priest's brother.
28. What follows is based on Binney 33–4/Ms 356–7.
29. My emphasis.
30. The discussion which follows is based on Binney 82–6/Ms 92–5.
31. Binney 116/Ms 138.
32. Binney 160/Ms 160; 200/Ms 278. See below, pp. 124–5, 165–6.
33. Thomas Norman, Richard Webber, William Norman and John Tymewell at Burston. Binney's edition gives no hint that these names were added as an afterthought, squeezed in above the line, and the priest evidently forgot one name – Ms 93.
34. Binney 34, 39/Ms 357, 183.
35. Binney 82/Ms 91.
36. In 1536 the Crown had ordered that the dedication days of parish churches should no longer be celebrated as holidays, but St George's day was specifically listed among the holidays which would continue to be observed; D. Wilkins (ed.), *Conciliae Magnae Britanniae* (London, 1737), vol. 3, p.824. Oddly, however, there appears to have been no Mass or office of St George celebrated in Morebath church that day.
37. For which see E. Duffy, *The Stripping of the Altars: Traditional Religion in England c.1400–1580* (New Haven and London, 1992), pp.136–8. Sir Christopher says the meeting was held on 'the Sonday a fore Rogation wyk': the Rogation processions began on a Monday, so this probably means Rogation Sunday itself, which in 1537 fell on 6 May, thirteen days after the quarrel on St George's day. Sir Christopher is unlikely to mean the preceding Sunday, since there would have been only six days between the disastrous betrothal and the proposed day of settlement, which does not allow much time for the involvement of the summoner and the Steward of the Manor which he goes on to describe, and in addition, it would in that case have been more natural for him to identify the date as 'the next Sunday'. These and all other calculations of dates derived from the calendars are in C.R. Cheney and Michael Jones, *A Handbook of Dates for students of British History* (Cambridge, 2000); however, it should be noted that although Cheney's table of Saints' Days and feasts, p.77, equates 'Little

Easter' with Pentecost, in the Morebath entry it quite certainly means the Sunday after Easter. 'Little Easter' was the day fixed by the Morebath parishioners for the temporary extension of the clerk's post 'at the busy time of Easter', and all the subsequent events occur in the space between Easter and Rogationtide, two weeks before Pentecost.

38.   Below, p. 90.

39.   Joyce Youings (ed.), *Devon Monastic Lands: Calendar of Particulars for Grants 1536–1558*, Devon and Cornwall Record Society, NS vol. 1 (1973), pp.3, 43, 44; Binney 91/Ms 101.

40.   Sydenham, *History of the Sydenham Family*, p.78.

41.   For the interweaving of parish business and the secular and ecclesiastical courts in general, see 'Parishioners in Court: Litigations and the Local Community' in S. Wabuda and C. Litzenberger (eds.), *Belief and Practice in Reformation England* (Aldershot, 1998) pp.20–39.

42 .   'Clerk ales', benefit ales the profits from which were used to supplement the clerk's wages, were a regular feature of West Country parish life in the late sixteenth and early seventeenth century; Chanter, 'Parish Clerks of Barnstaple', p.393.

43.   Binney 81/Ms 89; 94/Ms 104; 155/Ms 366; see below, pp. 80–1.

CHAPTER FOUR

1.   The 'pax' or 'pax-brede' was a carved or painted plaque kissed by the priest at the communion in the Mass, and then taken round the congregation by the clerk for them to kiss in turn, as a symbol of unity and peace. At Morebath the pax was of silver-gilt and depicted the crucifixion: the foot on which it stood on the altar until needed was kept by the wardens: the priest presumably was responsible for the custody of the pax itself, since it was considered a sacred object.

2.   Duffy, *Stripping of the Altars*, pp.11–12, 125–9; Binney 51/Ms 74; 100/ Ms 114.

3.   Binney 132/Ms 161.

4.   See above, p. 59.

5.   *Stripping of the Altars*, pp.29–37, 60–62.

6.   Hutton, *Merry England* pp.5–6.

7.   Binney 5/Ms 68.

8.   Binney 120/Ms 144; 125/ Ms 152.

9.   Binney 157/Ms 368.

10.   Wasson, *Records of Early English Drama, Devon*, p.448. Wasson also confuses the High Wardens' ale and the Young Men's ale.

11.   As indicated above (ch. 3, note 37), the Crown had abolished the local observance of the Dedication days of parish churches as hol-

idays, in the summer of 1536: St George's day, however, was one of the feasts specifically excluded from this prohibition.

12.   Below, pp. 93–103.

13.   Binney 100/Ms 114.

14.   Nicholas Orme, 'The Dissolution of the Chantries in Devon, 1546–8', *Reports and Transactions of the Devon Association*, vol. 111 (1979), pp.75–123 at p.93; L.S. Snell, *The Chantry Certificates for Devon and the City of Exeter* (Exeter, 1960), p.23. There were nominally three chantries, though only two Bampton chantry priests contributed to the Morebath chalice fund in 1534, 'Sir Thomas' (probably Sir Thomas Tristram, chaplain of Braddon's chantry) and 'Sir Hopper' – Binney 65/Ms 211.

15.   Binney 5/Ms 68.

16.   Binney 10/Ms 174.

17.   Binney 17/Ms 333 (vestments for deacon and subdeacon); 22/Ms 344 (high mass on feast days); 85/Ms 95 (diriges sung by note).

18.   Binney 23/Ms 345; 82/MS 92; *Wells Wills* pp.32–3: his will is witnessed by Sir Christopher and by John Scely, and he names John Nicoll as his father, a persuasive cluster of Morebath connections .

19.   Binney 46/Ms 192.

20.   see note 14 above.

21.   Binney 111/Ms 130.

22.   PRO Prob 11/54 fol. 257 (PCC 34 Holney), Will of John Norman at Poole , 6 May 1567; for the same formula concerning 'holie grave' see the will of Edward Sydenham, 21 May 1543, PRO Prob 11/30 fol. 18v (PCC 3 Pynnyng) and cf. Katherine Robbyns's bequest of her body '*sacre sepulture ubicumque Deus voluerit*': Binney 45/Ms 191.

23.   Binney 159/Ms 371; 162/374.

24.   Welsford, *John Greneway*, passim.

25.   Binney 25/Ms 347; 47/Ms 194.

26.   Ibid pp.12–14.

27.   Ibid p.15.

28.   Tristram Risdon, *A Chorographical Description or Survey of the County of Devon* (London, 1714) p.41.

29.   *Stripping of the Altars*, pp.212–13.

30.   For what follows, I rely on Nicholas Orme, 'Two Early Prayer-Books from North Devon', *Devon and Cornwall Notes and Queries*, vol. 36 (1991), pp.345–50.

31.   For such prayer charms, *Stripping of the Altars*, pp.266–98.

32.   West Country Studies Library, Exeter, Hennesy's Devon Incumbents, sub 'Morebath'. Morebath evidently encouraged

long incumbencies: Sir Richard came to Morebath in 1489/90, on the death of his predecessor Walter Atwell, who had been vicar for 15 years. Sir Christopher was to be vicar for fifty-four years, and his successor, Andrew Lake, would serve for thirty-two years (1574–1606).

33.   Cf Roger Martin's description of the figure of Jesus in Long Melford parish church, cited *Stripping of the Altars*, p.38; for the cult of Jesus, ibid., pp.113–16 and 284.

34.   Above, p.6.

35.   Athene Reiss, *The Sunday Christ: Sabbatarianism in English Medieval Wall Painting* (Oxford, 2000).

36.   D.H. Farmer, *The Oxford Dictionary of Saints* (3 edn, Oxford, 1992), pp.156–7.

37.   Ibid pp.25–6.

38.   Kathleen Ashley and Pamela Sheingorn (eds.), *Interpreting Cultural Symbols: Saint Anne in late medieval society* (Athens, Georgia and London, 1990).

39.   *Stripping of the Altars*, pp.38, 260–61, 332.

40.   Ibid., pp.260–61.

41.   For which see my 'The dynamics of pilgrimage in late medieval England' in Peter Roberts (ed.), *Pilgrimage: the English Experience* (Cambridge, forthcoming).

42.   Binney 22/Ms 343.

43.   Farmer, *Oxford Dictionary of Saints*, p.435; M. Swanton, *St Sidwell, an Exeter Legend* (Exeter, 1986); the best brief account, to which I am indebted, is Nicholas Orme (ed.), *Nicholas Roscarrock's Lives of the Saits of Cornwall and Devon* (Exeter, 1992), pp.170–72; Orme, *The Saints of Cornwall* (Oxford, 2000), pp.234–5.

44.   Binney 22/Ms 343.

45.   Binney 20/Ms 341.

46.   Binney 21/Ms 342.

47.   Bonney 22/Ms 344.

48.   Binney 23/Ms 344.

49.   Binney 47–8/Ms 194.

50.   Binney 11/Ms 175; 23/Ms 345.

51.   Binney 12–3/Ms 177.

52.   Binney 30/Ms 352.

53.   Binney 11/Ms 175.

54.   Binney 65/Ms 211 – Sidwell at Moore and Sidwell Morsse.

55.   Binney 10/Ms 174; 12/Ms 176; 24/Ms 345.

56.   Binney 10/Ms 174; 32/Ms 354; r7/Ms 360.

57.   Binney 16/Ms 332.

58.   Binney 18/Ms 334.

59.   Binney 52/Ms 76.

60.   Binney 70/219; 94/104.

61.   Binney 26/Ms 349.

62.   Binney12– 3/Ms 176–7; 18/Ms 335.

63.   Binney 60/Ms 203.

64.   These examples, a small sample, gleaned from the accounts 1527–37 *passim*.

65.   Binney 12/ Ms 176; 32/Ms 354; 81/Ms 90; 101/Ms 114; 111/Ms 130

66.   Binney 12/Ms 176; 13/Ms 177; 52/Ms 76; 59/Ms 202; 61/Ms 204; 72/Ms 222 etc.

67.   Binney 47/Ms 194; 115/Ms 137.

68.   Binney 101/Ms 115.

69.   Binney 32/Ms 354; see also Binney 12/Ms 176; 16/Ms 332; 18/Ms 335.

70.   SRO D/P/Banwell 4/1/1 sub 1521 (unpaginated).

71.   Binney 70/Ms 219.

72.   Binney 155/Ms 366.

73.   Alison Hanham (ed.), *Churchwardens' Accounts of Ashburton 1479–1580* (Torquay, 1970), pp.70, 85 and *passim*; Robert Whiting, *The Blind Devotion of the People: Popular Religion and the English Reformation* (Cambridge, 1989), pp.50–51.

74.   Binney 94/Ms 104.

75.   Binney 16/Ms 332.

76.   Binney 18/Ms 335.

77.   Binney 60/Ms 203.

78.   Binney 97/Ms 108.

79.   Binney 30/Ms 351; 53/Ms 77.

80.   Binney 153/Ms 364.

81.   Binney 16/Ms 331, cf 10/Ms 174 – '9d this ere habeo in mea custodia (tyll the wex be madyn)'.

82.   Binney 89/Ms 99.

83.   Binney 76/Ms 83, my emphasis.

84.   Binney 30/Ms 352; 113/132, my emphasis.

85.   Binney 94/104; 155/Ms 366.

86.   Binney 155/Ms 366.

87.   Binney 14/Ms 179.

88.   What follows is based on Binney 64–5/Ms 210–11.

89.   Binney 59/Ms 202.

CHAPTER FIVE

1.   26 Henry VIII Cap 1, *Statutes of the Realm*, vol. 3, p.492.

2.   R.A.W. Rex, 'The English campaign against Luther in the 1520s', *Transactions of the Royal Historical Society*, 5th Series 39 (1989), pp.85–106; R. Marius, *Thomas More* (London, 1993), pp.325–50; B. Bradshaw, 'The Controversial Thomas More', *Journal of Ecclesiastical History* 36 (1985), pp.535–69.

3.   E.W. Ives, *Anne Boleyn* (Oxford, 1986), chs. 13 and 14 ; M. Dowling 'Anne Boleyn and the Reform', *Journal of Ecclesiastical History* 35 (1984) pp.30–45; not everyone agrees with this account of Anne's influence: G.W.

Bernard, 'Anne Boleyn's Religion', *Historical Journal* 36 (1993), pp.1–20, and see Ives's reply in 'Anne Boleyn and the early Reformation in England', *Historical Journal* 37 (1994), pp.389–400.

4.   C. Haigh, *English Reformations: Religion, Politics and Society under the Tudors* (Oxford, 1993), pp.88–120.

5.   George Townsend and Stephen Cattley (eds.), *The Acts and Monuments of John Foxe* (London, 1838), vol. 5, pp.18–26.

6.   Ibid., p.26.

7.   Richard Rex, *Henry VIII and the English Reformation* (London, 1993), p.12; Andrew A. Chibi, *Henry VIII's Conservative Scholar: Bishop John Stokesley and the Divorce, Royal Supremacy and Doctrinal Reform* (Bern, 1997), pp.76–7.

8.   A.G. Dickens, *The English Reformation* (2nd edn., London, 1989), p.139.

9.   Diarmaid MacCulloch, *Thomas Cranmer, a Life* (New Haven and London, 1996), p.169.

10.   *Letters and Papers Foreign and Domestic, Henry VIII*, vol. 7, pp.107–8.

11.   Wallace T. MacCaffrey, *Exeter 1540–1640* (Cambridge, Mass., 1975), p.188.

12.   Nicholas Orme, *Exeter Cathedral as it was 1050–1550* (Exeter, 1986), p.94.

13.   P.L. Hughes and J.F. Larkin (eds.), *Tudor Royal Proclamations* vol. 1 (New Haven and London, 1964), p.231.

14.   Binney 34–5/Ms 357.

15.   This is the implication of the article on Cardinal Pole, see below, pp.128–41, esp. p.132.

16.   Dickens, *English Reformation*, p.144; Patrick Carter, 'Royal Taxation of the Parish Clergy 1535–58', unpublished Cambridge University PhD, 1995.

17.   Hooker's account, printed in Boggis, *Diocese of Exeter*, pp.356–7, and (slightly differently) in J. Youings (ed.), *The Dissolution of the Monasteries* (London, 1971), pp.164–5.

18.   Binney 91/Ms 101.

19.   Binney 93/Ms 103; 100/Ms 114; another Barlinch window went to the neighbouring Somerset parish of Huish Champflower: C.R. Elrington (ed.), *Victoria County History of Somerset*, vol. 6 (Oxford, 1985), p.88.

20.   A.G. Dickens (ed.), *Tudor Treatises*, p.125.

21.   *Stripping of the Altars*, pp.394–9.

22.   W.H. Frere and W.M. Kennedy, *Visitation Articles and Injunctions of the Period of the Reformation*, vol. 2 1536–1558 (London, 1910), pp.2–11.

23.   Below, pp. 174–6.

24.   The standard work is M.H. and R.

Dodds, *The Pilgrimage of Grace 1536–7 and the Exeter Conspiracy 1538* (Cambridge, 1915); the fullest modern treatment is Michael Bush, *The Pilgrimage of Grace: a study of the rebel armies of October 1536* (Manchester, 1996); M. Bush and D. Bownes, *The Defeat of the Pilgrimage of Grace* (Hull, 1999); for a brief survey see A. Fletcher and D. MacCulloch, *Tudor Rebellions* (4th edn., London, 1997), pp.22–49.

25.   Fletcher and MacCulloch, *Tudor Rebellions*, p.133.

26.   Ibid., p.136.

27.   C.E. Moreton, 'The Walsingham Conspiracy of 1537', *Historical Research* 63 (1990), pp.29–43.

28.   *Letters and Papers* XI, no. 405; XII, Part 1, nos 1000, 1001, 1126.

29.   G. Oliver, *Lives of the Bishops of Exeter and a History of the Cathedral* (Exeter, 1861), pp.477–83; there is a good account of Heynes in Orme, *Exeter Cathedral*, pp.95–8.

30.   *Letters and Papers* XII, Part 2, no. 557.

31.   Gilbert Burnet, *The History of the Reformation of the Church of England* (London, 1850), vol. 2, p.cxxxiv; for Heynes's authorship, *Letters and Papers* XII, Part 2, no. 409n.

32.   J.E. Cox (ed.), *Miscellaneous Writings and Letters of Thomas Cranmer* (Cambridge, 1846), p.351.

33.   *Stripping of the Altars*, pp.403–4.

34.   Nicholas Orme, 'Indulgences in the Diocese of Exeter 1100–1536', *Reports and Transactions of the Devonshire Association*, vol. 120 (1988), p.26.

35.   *Vistation Articles and Injunctions*, vol. 2, pp.61–4.

36.   *Stripping of the Altars*, p.401; Margaret Aston, *England's Iconoclasts*, vol. 1: *Laws against Images* (Oxford, 1988), pp.239–42.

37.   *Stripping of the Altars*, p.405.

38.   *Visitation Articles and Injunctions*, vol. 2, pp.34–43.

39.   Ibid., p.39.

40.   *Stripping of the Altars*, pp.413–14.

41.   Pill, 'Diocese of Exeter', pp.154–5; Orme, *Exeter Cathedral*, pp.95–7.

42.   Whiting, *Blind Devotion of the People*, pp.66–7, 75; C.S. Knighton, *New Dictionary of National Biography* article on Heynes: I am grateful to Dr Knighton for allowing me to see the typescript of this article; J. Youings, 'The Council of the West', *Transactions of the Royal Historical Society*, 5th Series, vol. 10 (1960), pp.41–59.

43.   *Visitation Articles and Injunctions*, vol. 2, p.34; MacCulloch, *Cranmer*, pp.226–7.

44.   For example see Binney 68/Ms 217.

45.   Binney 96/Ms 107.

46. Binney 98/Ms 110
47. Binney 97/Ms 108 and 46/Ms 192–3.
48. Binney 103/Ms 117.
49. Binney 99–101/Ms 112–15.
50. Binney 100/Ms 112–3
51. Binney 101 /Ms 115.
52. Binney 102/Ms 116.
53. Binney 102–4/Ms 117–19.
54. David Wilkins, *Concilia Magnae Brittaniae*, vol. 3 (London, 1737), p.846.
55. Whiting, *Blind Devotion of the People*, pp.190–91; *Ashburton CWA*, p.107; P.L. Hughes and J.F. Larkin (eds.), *Tudor Royal Proclamations*, vol. 1 (New Haven and London, 1964), pp.296–8.
56. Binney 105/Ms 121.
57. Binney 106/Ms 122.
58. Binney 105/Ms 120.
59. Binney 113/Ms 133.
60. Binney 106/Ms 123; he subsequently settled for the neutral 'Deus in adjutorium meum intende' [O god come to my aid] to start the account of the church sheep each year, reserving the invocation to St George for the High Wardens' accounts. .
61. Binney 110/Ms 129.
62. Binney 160/Ms 372.
63. Binney 124/Ms 150; 140/Ms 229.
64. Binney 112/Ms 132.
65. Binney 23/Ms 344.
66. *Ashburton CWA*, p.116; *Chagford CWA*, pp.174–6; DRO PW1 (Broadhempton) sub 1547; PW1 (Woodland) fol.13; E. Lega Weekes (ed.), 'The Churchwardens Accounts of South Tawton' (transcript of the subsidiary store wardens accounts), *Reports and Transactions of the Devonshire Association*, vol. 38 (1906), pp.522–3.
67. Binney 110/Ms 128.
68. Calculated from the accounts 1530–38, though the account for 1533 is missing.
69. Binney 113/Ms 133; 118/Ms 141.
70. My conjectural reading of what is going on in Binney 124/Ms 150 (High Wardens 1542); 132/Ms 160 (High Wardens 1543); 136/Ms 166 (High Wardens 1544).
71. Binney 137/Ms 166; 125/Ms 152.
72. Binney 12–13; 176–7; 32/Ms 353–4;92/Ms 102.
73. Binney 3–4/Ms 66–7.
74. Binney 114/Ms 135.
75. Binney 126/Ms 153; 133/Ms 161.
76. Christopher Haigh, *English Reformations: Religion, Politics and Society under the Tudors* (Oxford, 1993), pp.152–61; a slightly different reading of the balance between evangelical and catholic in the early 1540s is offered in MacCulloch, *Cranmer*, chs.

7 and 8. See also the very different case argued by G.W. Bernard, 'The making of religious policy, 1533–1456: Henry VIII and the search for the middle way', *Historical Journal* 41 (1998), pp.321–49 .
77. Binney 19–28/Ms 340–50.
78. Orme, *Exeter Cathedral*, pp.97–8; J.R. Dasent (ed.), *Acts of the Privy Council*, NS vol. 1 (1542–7), (London, 1890), pp.97–8, 117, 126, 150–51.
79. Orme, *Exeter Cathedral*, p.98.
80. 34 & 35 Henry VIII cap.1; S.E. Lehmberg, *The Later Parliaments of Henry VIII* (London, 1977), pp.186–8.
81. Susan Brigden, *London and the Reformation* (Oxford, 1989), p.348.
82. Nicholas Orme, 'Church and chapel in medieval England', *Transactions of the Royal Historical Society*, 5th Series, vol. 47 (1996), pp.75–102.
83. What follows based on Binney 126–9/Ms 153–8.
84. On the whole subject of communal feasting, Gervase Rosser, 'Going to the fraternity feast: commensality and social relations in late medieval England', *Journal of British Studies*, 33 (1994), pp.430–46.
85. Sir Christopher is expressing his appreciation in obsolete terms about money: an angel was a gold coin worth between 6/8d and 10/= and a noble was the sum of 6/8d.

CHAPTER SIX
1. Rex, *Henry VIII*, pp.157–8.
2. Binney 136/Ms 166; 141/Ms 229.
3. Binney 137/Ms 166.
4. Binney 147/Ms 301; 159/Ms 370–1.
5. M. Jurkowski, C.L. Smith, D. Crook (eds.), *Lay Taxes in England and Wales 1188–1688* (Public Record Office, 1998), pp.140–48; R. Hoyle 'War and Public Finance' in D. MacCulloch (ed.), *The Reign of Henry VIII* (London, 1995), pp.92–9 *passim*; F.G. Dietz, *English Government Finance 1485–1558* (Illinois, 1920), pp.159–67; Ian Arthurson, 'Fear and Loathing in West Cornwall: seven new letters on the 1548 Rising', *Journal of the Royal Institution of Cornwall*, New Series II, vol. 3, pp. 71–2; J.J. Scarisbrick, *Henry VIII* (New Haven and London, 1997), pp.424–57.
6. Scarisbrick, *Henry VIII*, p.440–41; Penry Williams, *The Tudor Regime* (Oxford, 1979), pp.115–20.
7. Binney 149/Ms 300.
8. Binney 140/Ms 229; 142–3/Ms 273.
9. Binney 143/Ms 273; 149/Ms 300 (retrospective settlement of previous collections).

10. 37 Henry VIII cap. 4, *Statutes of the Realm* vol. 3, pp.988–93.
11. Orme, 'The dissolution of the chantries in Devon 1546–8', pp.78–81, 93.
12. Below, pp. 172–3, and DRO 96M/86/13.
13. Binney 147/Ms 301.
14. Binney 149–50/Ms 295; 157/Ms 369.
15. Binney 147–51/Ms 295–6.
16. *Tudor Royal Proclamations*, vol. 1, no. 281, p.387.
17. John Strype, *Memorials of Thomas Cranmer*, p.209.
18. MacCulloch, *Cranmer*, pp.369–71.
19. *Salve, Alma Mater*.
20. Binney 152/Ms 254, 363 (the account has been separated in the middle and misbound).
21. Binney 153–5/Ms 364–6.
22. *Tudor Royal Proclamations*, vol. 1, pp.393–403; *Visitation Articles and Injunctions*, vol. 2, pp.114–30.
23. *Stripping of the Altars*, pp.450–53.
24. Ibid., pp.457–60.
25. 1 Edward VI cap. 14, *Statutes of the Realm*, vol. 4, pp.24ff.
26. *Visitation Articles and Injunctions*, vol. 2, pp.127–8.
27. Binney 156/Ms 367.
28. *Historical Manuscripts Commission: Calendar of the Manuscripts of the Dean and Chapter of Wells*, vol. 2 (London, 1914), pp.264–5.
29. David Underdown, *Revel, Riot and Rebellion: Popular Politics and Culture in England 1603–1660* (Oxford, 1985), pp.83–8; T.G. Barnes, 'County Politics and a Puritan cause célèbre: Somerset Church Ales 1633', *Transactions of the Royal Historical Society*, 5th Series (1959), pp.103–22.
30. Exodus 5/18.
31. The whole process is lucidly set out by Orme, 'Dissolution of the Chantries', *passim*.
32. Binney 158–9/Ms 370–71.
33. Binney 160/Ms 371.
34. Binney 159/Ms 371.
35. For which see *Stripping of the Altars*, pp.23–7.
36. Ashburton CWA, p.121; *Stripping of the Altars*, p.480.
37. Binney 164/Ms 376.
38. MacCulloch, *Cranmer*, pp.384–6.
39. *Stripping of the Altars*, pp.455–7.
40. Whiting, *Blind Devotion of the People*, pp.110–1.
41. Arthurson, 'Fear and Loathing', p.74.
42. *Tudor Royal Proclamations* vol. 2, no. 303, pp.421–3.

43. Binney 161/Ms 372; W.K. Jordan, *Edward VI, the Young King* (London, 1968), pp.269–70; M.L. Bush, *The Government Policy of Protector Somerset* (London, 1975), p.8, 22 and notes 112–16. I am indebted to Dr Charles Knighton for the identification of the 'oracion of the pece', and for a transcript of the copy in the Pepys Library at Magdalene (one of only two surviving printed versions, bound into Pepys's copy of the 1549 Prayer Book), PL 1976 (2); cf RSTC 16503, 'A prayer for victorie and peace': Ms version PRO SP 10/2, calendared by Knighton in CSPD Edward VI no.49.
44. Binney 160/Ms 372.
45. Binney 200/Ms 278
46. Binney 20–1/341–2; 115/Ms 135; 124–5/Ms 151; 199/Ms 277.
47. Binney 162/Ms 374.
48. Binney 162–3/Ms 374.
49. Binney 161/Ms 373; *Visitation Articles and Injunctions*, vol. 2, p.127 (Lucy's husband William Scely had dutifully left 6d to the poor man's box at his death, as the Injunctions required parish priests to encourage dying men to do – further evidence no doubt of Sir Christopher's conscientiousness).
50. Binney 173/Ms 387; 183/Ms 231; 184/Ms 289; 188/Ms 280; 196/Ms 36.
51. Binney 160/Ms 371.
52. Binney 172/Ms 385.
53. *Stripping of the Altars*, pp.487–9.
54. Binney 162/Ms 374.
55. 2 & 3 Edward VI cap. 1, *Statutes of the Realm* vol. 4, pp.37ff; Gerald Bray (ed.), *Documents of the English Reformation* (Cambridge, 1994); for Heynes's membership of the panel, see John Strype, *Ecclesiastical Memorials* (Oxford, 1828), vol. 2, Part 1, p.134, Part 2, p.52.
56. 2 & 3 Edward VI cap. 36, *Statutes of the Realm* vol. 4, pp.78–90; M.W. Beresford, 'The Poll Tax and Census of Sheep 1549', *Agricultural History Review* 1 (1953), pp.9–15, 2 (1954), pp.15–29.
57. Townsend and Cattley, *Acts and Monuments*, vol. 5, p.736.
58. Summary in J. Cornwall, *Revolt of the Peasantry 1549* (London, 1977), pp.8–40.
59. F. Rose-Troup, *The Western Rebellion of 1549* (London, 1913), p.134.
60. Brief overviews and up-to-date bibliography in A. Fletcher and D. MacCulloch, *Tudor Rebellions* (4th edn., London, 1997), pp.50–63 (Western Rebellion), 64–80 (Kett's Rebellion). The best modern treatment of the Western Rebellion is J. Youings, 'The South West Rebellion of 1549', *Southern History* vol.

1 (1979), pp.99–122; the best treatment of Kett's rebellion is MacCulloch, 'Kett's Rebellion in Context', *Past and Present* 84 (1979), pp.39–62. Documents for the Western Rebellion in N. Pocock (ed.), *Troubles Connected with the Prayer Book of 1549*, Camden Society NS vol. xxxvii (1884).

61. D. MacCulloch, *Tudor Church Militant* (Harmondsworth, 1999), p.122. See also MacCulloch, 'Kett's Rebellion' *art.cit.*, p.60, and, less guardedly, A. Fletcher and D. MacCulloch, *Tudor Rebellions* (4th edn., London, 1997), pp.79, 119.

62. Ethan Shagan, 'Protector Somerset and the 1549 Rebellions: new sources and new perspectives', *English Historical Review* 144 (1999), p.62.

63. Cornwall, *Revolt of the Peasantry*, p.137.

64. C.E. Moreton, *The Townsends and their World: Gentry, Law and Land in Norfolk c. 1451–1551* (Oxford, 1992), pp.37–8; F.W. Russell, *Kett's Rebellion in Norfolk* (London, 1859), 37–8.

65. Shagan, 'Protector Somerset', p.56.

66. Rose Troup, *Western Rebellion*, p.136.

67. W.J. Harte, J.W. Schapp, H. Tapley-Soper (eds.), *The Description of the Citie of Excester by John Vowell alias Hoker* (Exeter, 1919), Part II, p.57.

68. Ibid., pp.62–3; Rose-Troup, *Western Rebellion*, pp.145–7.

69. Ibid., p.145

70. Ibid., pp.212–13.

71. Long version of the rebels' demands, Rose-Troup, *Western Rebellion*, pp.220–22. Professor Youings considered this explanation of the demand for the recall of Pole 'far-fetched' – Youings, *art. cit.*, p.116.

72. Arthur Couratin, cited in MacCulloch, *Cranmer*, p.430; for the allegations about whoredom, Rose-Troup, *Western Rebellion*, p.430; Nicholas Orme suggests that the rebels were also disturbed by the presence of men and women together in the quire, previously closed to lay people except when husband and wife went there for the nuptial blessing at the wedding mass.

73. Pocock, *Troubles*, pp.12–13.

74. Ibid., pp.25–7, 30–33.

75. Ibid., pp.30–33, 40, 47.

76. Hooker, *Description*, p.95.

77. Ibid., p.94.

78. There were camps in other positions round the city: St David's Down was probably the nearest for Morebath men coming south down the Exe valley, but it may be relevant that Sir Christopher's friends the Sydenhams had a messuage and thirty acres of land in St David's Down parish: G.F. Sydenham, *History of the Sydenham Family*, pp.71ff.

79. Binney 163–4/Ms 375; for the detail about the collection at the church style, 169/Ms 381.

80. Hoskins, *Devon*, p.235.

81. Rose-Troup, *Western Rebellion*, pp.82–3.

82. Beatrix F. Cresswell, 'The Church Goods Commission in Devon 1549–1552', *Reports and Transactions of the Devon Association*, vol. 43 (1911), pp.243, 253–4.

83. Pocock, *Troubles*, pp.47, 63–4.

84. Eamon Duffy, 'Morebath 1520–1570: a rural parish in the Reformation' in J. Devlin and R. Fanning (eds.), *Religion and Rebellion* (Dublin, 1997), pp.17–39; I am indebted to Diarmaid MacCulloch for the scepticism of his response to this argument, which helped encourage me to press the material harder – MacCulloch, *Tudor Church Militant, Edward VI and the Protestant Reformation* (Harmondsworth, 1999), p.237.

85. C.S. Knighton (ed.), *Calendar of State Papers, Domestic Series of the reign of Mary I, 1553–1558, preserved in the Public Record Office* (rev. edn., London: Public Record Office, 1998), no.96.

86. Bush, *The Pilgrimage of Grace*, pp.117, 212.

87. Binney 140/Ms 229; 142–3/Ms 273; 145/Ms 298; 152/Ms 363; 197/Ms 37–8; 213/Ms 57; 218–19/Ms 400, etc.

88. P.F. Tytler (ed.), *England under the Reigns of Edward VI and Mary* (London, 1839), vol. 1, p.187.

89. Pocock, *Troubles*, pp.145, 148.

90. A.G. Legge (ed.), *Ancient Church-wardens' Accounts of the Parish of North Elmham 1539–1577* (Norwich, 1891), pp.55–60.

91. Pocock, *Troubles*, pp.23, 145–6.

92. Hooker, *Description*, p.75.

93. Rose-Troup, *Western Rebellion*, p.492; Susan Brigden, *New Worlds, Lost Worlds: the rule of the Tudors, 1485–1603* (Harmondsworth, 2000), pp.190–91; Fletcher and MacCulloch, *Tudor Rebellions*, p.60.

94. Youings, 'South Western Rebellion', p.104.

95. *Tudor Royal Proclamations*, vol. 1, pp.421–3 (no. 303).

96. MacCulloch, *Cranmer*, p.430.

97. Binney 167/Ms 380; 170/Ms 383.

98. Binney 164/Ms 376; 165/Ms 377; 166/Ms 378.

99. Binney 169/Ms 381.

100. Ashburton CWA, p.124

101. Binney 164/Ms 376; Whiting, *Blind*

Devotion of the People, p.39.

102. Binney 185/Ms 289.

103. Michael Sherbrook, 'The Fall of Religious Houses' in A.G. Dickens (ed.), Tudor Treatises, Yorkshire Archaeological Society, Record Series CXXV (1959), pp.138–9.

104. Butler's register was destroyed in a fire at Wynnstay Manor in 1859, but extracts made by an antiquarian clergyman were printed in the Cambrian Journal for 1861, and again in J.C. Cox, The Parish Registers of England (London, 1910), pp.25–35. I have worked from Cox's edition (quotation p.29), but Butler's remark about the Commissioners is included from the new edition of the Register beng prepared by Dr Will Coster of Simon de Montfort University. I am very grateful to Dr Coster for access to this work in progress; see also Dr Coster's essay 'Popular Religion and the Parish Register' in French, Gibbs and Kumin, The Parish in English Life, pp.94 –111.

105. Oliver, Lives of the Bishops of Exeter, pp.125–6.

106. Binney 166/Ms 378.

107. Binney 166–7/Ms 378–9, and cf. Binney 226/Ms 138.

108. The bells used at the Mass and rung before corpses as they were carried to burial, to call parishioners to prayer for the dead .

109. Binney 172/Ms. See below pp. 149–50.

110. Binney, 168, 175; Pill, 'Vesey', pp.313–4; Rose-Troup, Western Rebellion, pp.372–7; below pp. 157–8.

111. E. Green, 'Notes on the history of Dulverton', Proceedings of the Somerset Archaeological and Natural History Society, vol. 29 (1883), pp.68–82 at p.75.

112. Binney 165/Ms 377.

113. Sir Frederick Pollock and Frederick W. Maitland, The History of English Law, vol. 1 (Cambridge, 1968), pp.556–60.

114. Binney 175–8/Ms 390–93.

115. Binney 169/Ms 382.

116. Binney 167/Ms 380.

117. Binney 167, 169–70/Ms 379, 382–3.

118. Binney 167–8/Ms 380–81.

119. Binney 168/Ms 380.

120. Binney 168/Ms 380; 170/Ms 383, my emphasis.

121. Binney 169–70/Ms 382–3 passim.

122. Jonathan Vage, 'The Diocese of Exeter 1519–1641', unpublished Cambridge PhD thesis 1991, p.55.

123. Boggis, Diocese of Exeter, pp.343–9.

124. Vage, 'Diocese of Exeter', pp.41, 44, 80, 113.

125. Vage, 'Diocese of Exeter', pp.31–2; A.A. Mumford, Hugh Oldham 1452–1519 (London, 1936).

126. Pill, 'Diocese of Exeter under Bishop Veysey', pp.349–52; Binney 173/Ms 387.

127. Binney 173/Ms 386–7.

128. Binney 173/Ms 387: this form was still officially approved. The Proclamation of 1 October, announcing the regnal style of the Queen, called her 'defender of the faith, and of the Church of England and Ireland Supreme head' – Tudor Royal Proclamations, vol. 2, no.393, p.12.

129. Binney 171, 173; Ms 384, 387.

CHAPTER SEVEN

1. MacCaffrey, Exeter, p.189.

2. Whiting, Blind Devotion, pp.161–2.

3. Cattley and Townsend (eds.), Acts and Monuments, vol. 8, pp.497–503.

4. Fletcher and MacCulloch, Tudor Rebellions, pp.82–3; David Loades, Two Tudor Conspiracies (2nd edn., Bangor, 1992), pp.14–16, 18, 23, 34–46, 96.

5. MacCaffrey, Exeter, pp.191–2.

6. Vage, 'Diocese of Exeter', pp.92, 105, 113.

7. A.L. Rowse, Tudor Cornwall, Portrait of a Society (London, 1941), pp.304–5, based on PRO SP11/2 no. 2 Sir John Arundell of Trerice to the Earl of Arundel, 13 January 1554: I am grateful to Dr Charles Knighton for a copy of this document – see Knighton (ed.), Calendar of State Papers, Domestic series of the reign of Mary I, 1553–1558, preserved in the Public Record Office (revised edn., London: Public Record Office, 1998) no. 25, p.15.

8. MacCaffrey, Exeter, p.189.

9. P.W Hasler, The House of Commons 1558–1603 (London, 1981) vol. 3, pp.420–1; M. Bateson (ed.), Letters of the Bishops to the Privy Council in 1564, Camden Society NS 53, (1895), pp.67–70.

10. Binney 174/Ms 388–9.

11. Tudor Royal Proclamations, vol. 2, p.6 (no 390).

12. A.G. Dickens (ed.), 'Robert Parkyn's Narrative' in Reformation Studies (London, 1982), p.309.

13. Cox, Parish Registers, p.30.

14. Binney 175/Ms 389.

15. Binney 174/Ms 388.

16. Binney 175/Ms 389.

17. Binny 176–7/Ms 391–2.

18. Binney 178/Ms 393.

19. Binney 178–81/Ms 394–6.

20. Tudor Royal Proclamations, vol. 2, no. 407, pp.35–8.

21. Binney 181–4, 188/Ms 397–8, 231–2 (this is one of the places where the account has been broken up and bound in two widely separated parts of the manuscript book).

22. Binney 182–3/Ms 398.

23. Binney 183/Ms 231.

24. Binney 187/Ms 293.

25. Binney 187/Ms 294.

26. For the Marian restoration at parish level in general, *Stripping of the Altars*, pp.524–64; Haigh, *English Reformations*, pp.203–18; a somewhat different (and in my view mistakenly negative) assessment of the progress of the Marian restoration in the Exeter diocese, Whiting, *Blind Devotion*, pp.40–44.

27. All the above based on Binney 184–7/Ms 289–92.

28. Binney 185/Ms 290.

29. Binney 188/Ms 281; 191/Ms 29.

30. Binney 189/Ms 282; 201/Ms 269.

31. Binney 201/Ms 269.

32. Binney 188/Ms 281; 201/Ms 270.

33. Binney 197 Ms 36

34. *pace* Whiting, *Blind Devotion*, p.41; see R. Dymond (ed.), 'The History of the Parish of St Petroc Exeter, as shown by its church-wardens accounts', *Reports and Transactions of the Devonshire Association*, vol. 14 (1882), pp.402–92.

35. Cattley and Townsend (eds.), *Acts and Monuments*, vol. 6, p.500.

36. Binney 191/Ms 29.

37. Binney 17, 23/Ms 333, 345.

38. Binney 185/Ms 290; Nicholas Orme points out helpfully that St Clement's eve was 'one of the traditional disguising and begging times, when presumably people could be out and about at night in disguise, without exciting suspicion'.

39. What follows is based on Binney 199–202; Ms 277–8, 269–70 (this is one of the places where the document has been broken and misbound).

40. Binney 200/Ms 278, 269 (manuscript misbound).

41. Haigh, *English Reformations*, p.209; Duffy, *Stripping of the Altars*, p.501.

42. Reprinted in A.G. Dickens, *Reformation Studies* (London, 1982), pp.287–312; for Parkyn's career, see Dickens's essay 'The Last Medieval Englishman' in the same collection, pp.245–83.

43. Dickens, *Reformation Studies*, p.311.

44. Fletcher and MacCulloch, *Tudor Rebellions*, pp.131–41.

45. G.R. Elton, *Policy and Police: The Enforcement of the Reformation in the Age of Thomas Cromwell* (Cambridge, 1972).

46. Binney 189/Ms 282.

47. *A Profitable and necessary doctryne, with certeyne homelies adioyned thereunto set forth by the reverende father in God, Edmonde byshop of London*, London 1555 (RSTC 3238) preface (no pagination)

48. W. Haines (ed.), 'Stanford Churchwardens Accounts 1552–1602', *The Antiquary* XVII (1888), p.70.

49. Townsend and Cattley (eds.), *Acts and Monuments* 6, p.679; for an expanded version of this argument, see my 'The Conservative Voice in the English Reformation' in Simon Ditchfield ed., *Christianity and Community in the West: Essays for John Bossy* (forthcoming).

50. Binney 195/Ms 34.

51. Cox, *Parish Registers*, pp.32–5.

52. Injunctions and Articles in W.H. Frere (ed.), *Visitation Articles and Injunctions of the Period of the Reformation*, vol. 3 1559–1575 (London, 1910), pp.1–29. For this Elizabethan visitation in general, and its episcopal sequels, *Stripping of the Altars*, pp.566–77; Haigh, *English Reformation*, pp.235–50.

53. The return prepared by the wardens at Crediton in response to this requirement survives as DRO Crediton 1660/12 (*printed Devon and Cornwall Notes and Queries*, vol. 32 (1971), pp.15–17); a similar document for Morebath would be a treasure worth killing for, but Sir Christopher, sadly, did not keep a copy of it.

54. Binney 201–6/Ms 43–6.

55. H. Robinson (ed.), *The Zurich Letters*, vol. 2 (Cambridge, 1845), pp.44–5.

56. Binney 203/Ms 42.

57. Ashburton retained most of its vestments until 1568–9; Hanham, Ashburton CWA, pp.160–61.

58. Binney 208, 215/Ms 49, 59.

59. DRO Morebath Register, March 1559, 30 April 1570.

60. Binney 213/Ms 56; E. Lega Weekes, 'The Churchwardens Accounts of South Tawton', *Reports and Transactions of the Devonshire Association*, vol. 39 (1907), p.309; Whiting, *Blind Devotion of the People*, pp.183–4; Kilmington CWA, p.15; Ashburton CWA, p.152.

61. Binney 204/Ms 44.

62. Since Bishop Turberville stayed in office until the summer, and Bishop Alley did not arrive until 1560, it is unclear exactly what form this episcopal visitation can have taken: perhaps it was a routine visitation on behalf of the bishop by the vicar general.

63. Binney 247/Ms 14.

64. Binney 207/Ms 48.

65. Cf 'the settyng up of the 10 Commanndementts' the same year in Sir Christopher's other benefice at Molland: Sir John Phear, 'Molland Accounts', *Reports and Transactions of the Devonshire Association*, vol. 35 (1902), p.216.

66. DRO 96 M Box 86/13 (grant to William Portman of custody of third part of the rectory of Morebath and lands called Hawkridge Down, in the hands of the king by reason of the minority of Stephen Tristram). See also *Letters and Papers*, vol. 21, Part 1, p.472, no. 963, p.244 it. 104.

67. Binney 213/Ms 56; Ms 271 (account for 1571–2 not printed in Binney).

68. Joel Hurstfield, *The Queen's Wards, Wardship and Marriage under Elizabeth I* (London, 1958), pp.173–4.

69. Binney 214–5/Ms 58; 221/Ms 404; Ms 272 (memorandum of 'old debt' 1571–2, not printed in Binney).

70. Binney 208–9, 211/Ms 49–50, 53.

71. Boggis, *Diocese of Exeter*, p.385; Whiting, *Blind Devotion*, p.231.

72. J.L. Vivian, *The Visitation of the County of Devon* (Exeter, 1895), p.790; Francis B. Troup, 'A Forgotten Page of the Ecclesiastical History of Seaton', *Reports and Transactions of the Devon Association*, vol. 30 (1898), pp.331–49 at p.333; *Calendar of the Patent Rolls Preserved in the Public Record Office, Philip and Mary*, vol. 3 (1938), p.69; G. Oliver (ed.), *Westcote's View of Devonshire in 1630* (Exeter, 1845), p.280.

73. West Country Studies Library, Beatrix Cresswell, 'Notes on Devon Churches, p.125; Hennesey's Devon Incumbents sub 'Mugg', 'Knowstone', 'Newton St Cyres'; Mugg was deprived at Newton St Cyres in 1560, perhaps for rejection of the Elizabethan settlement.

74. Information from Hennesey index, West Country Studies Library. I am grateful to Nicholas Orme for alerting me to Hunt's career pattern.

75. West Country Studies Library, Exeter, Beatrix Cresswell, Notes on Devon Churches pp.117–24; records of Sir Christopher's institution have not survived: his presentation by Agnes has to be deduced from the fact that she presented his predecessor and his successor. For his institution by July 1561, see DRO Chanter 779 fol. 17v.

76. Public Record Office, E 334/7 Composition Book fol. 97r.

77. 'Molland accounts', pp.224, 235.

78. Corpus Christi College Cambridge, Parker Library, Ms 97 fol. 198.

79. Parishes with preachers listed, from DRO 009/9, Bishop Alley's report (a transcript of the Exeter diocesan material from Corpus Christi College Cambridge Ms 97) in Whiting, *Blind Devotion*, p.249.

80. M.S. Byford 'The Price of Protestantism: Assessing the Impact of Religious Change on Elizabethan Essex, the cases of Heydon and Colchester 1558–1594', unpublished Oxford DPhil thesis 1988, quotation at p.42.

81. Binney 234/Ms 255; 'Molland accounts', p.227.

82. *Stripping of the Altars*, pp.583–4.

83. Binney 239/Ms 3; 246/Ms 13

84. Binney 241/Ms 5; 252/Ms 20. For the campaign against chalices in Bath and Wells diocese, R. Dunning, *Christianity in Somerset* (Taunton, 1976), p.37. The Somerset parish of Langford Budville changed its chalice for a communion cup in 1573 – SRO DD/X/THR 9, c/3757 sub 1573, a representative date for the region generally: the campaign in the Exeter Diocese can be tracked through the Reports of the Committee on Church Plate, *Reports and Transactions of the Devonshire Association*, vol. 39 (1907), pp.110, 176; vol. 45 (1912), pp.96, 103, 111; vol. 49 (1917), p.116–7; vol. 50 (1918), pp.202, 206, 215; vol. 51 (1919), pp.93; the plate for the rural deanery of Tiverton, including Morebath, is in vol. 51 (1919), pp.98–113, but there is no surviving plate earlier than the last decade of Elizabeth's reign there. Morebath's exisiting communion cup cover is dated 1593, so nothing survives from Sir Christopher's time or its immediate aftermath.

85. Binney 246/Ms 13.

86. Binney 226, 228, 233/Ms 246, 265, 284.

87. Binney 221/Ms 403.

88. William Harrison, *The Description of England*, ed. G. Edelen (Washington, 1994), p.36.

89. Binney 228/Ms 264; W. Keatinge Clay (ed.), *Liturgies and Occasional Forms of Prayer set forth in the reign of Queen Elizabeth* (Cambridge, 1847), pp.524–39.

90. A revised edition of the second book of Homilies, including the Homily against rebellion, was issued in 1571, RSTC 13669, and it is probably this which Morebath bought that year.

91. Ms 271 (not printed in Binney): 'for the boke of the homiles and for the boke of the dissipline 3/6d'. The Morebath accounts description of the Articles as 'the boke of dis-

sipline' may suggest that Sir Christopher knew something of the controversy surrounding them in Convocation and Parliament W.P. Haugaard, *Elizabeth and the English Reformation* (Cambridge, 1968), pp.233–90; Binney 251/Ms 19–20.

92. Binney 228/Ms 264; 240/Ms 4. For these commissions, see C.J. Kitching, 'The quest for concealed lands in the reign of Elizabeth I', *Transactions of the Royal Historical Society*, 5th Series 24 (1974) pp.63–78; for a parish with something to hide, and managing to do it, Ken Farnhill, 'Religious policy and parish 'conformity': Cratfield's lands in the sixteenth century' in K.L. French, G.G. Gibbs and B.A. Kumin (eds.), *The Parish in English Life 1400–1600* (Manchester, 1997), pp.217–29.

93. Hasler, *The House of Commons*, vol. 3, pp.420–21, 567–8.

94. For its witholding, Binney 230/Ms 287.

95. A William Hurley married Dorothy Helior on 6 February 1565. It is possible, but highly unlikely, that this is the 'Young man' of 1549, more probable that either he was the son of John Hurley (Binney 202/Ms 39) or that William and Eylon Hurley followed the confusing Morebath custom of giving more than one male child the father's name.

96. Binney 241/Ms 6.

97. Binney 250/Ms 9.

98. Chagford CWA passim; Kilmington CWA

99. Kumin, *Shaping of a Community*, pp.241–55; J.S. Craig, 'Elizabethan Churchwardens and parish accounts', *Social History*, vol. 18 (1993), pp.357–80.

100. Binney 233–4/Ms 284, 256.

101. Binney 193/Ms 32.

102. Binney 212/Ms 55.

103. Binney 194/Ms 33.

104. Binney 197–8/Ms 37–8.

105. Binney 227, 229, 232, 237/Ms 264, 266, 283, 309.

106. Binney 233/Ms 283

107. Binney 240/Ms 4.

108. Binney 238/Ms 1.

109. Binney 213–4/Ms 57; 216/Ms 60.

110. Binney 209/Ms 401; 218/Ms 399; 228/Ms 265; 232/Ms 282; 251/Ms 20; similar military demands, including the maintenance of a fire–beacon, on another Devon parish, South Tawton, are usefully collected and set out in Ethel Lega Weekes, 'County armaments in Devon in the Sixteenth Century', *Reports and Transaction of the Devonshire Association*, vol. 61 (1909), pp.339–55, at pp.353–5.

111. Binney 246/Ms 14.

112. Binney 232–3/Ms 283–4.

113. 238/Ms 310.

114. Ms 272 (not printed in Binney); Binney 237–8/Ms 309–10; 241/Ms 6; Binney has confused this material by misplacing the incomplete accounts on page 237–8/Ms 309–10, identified by the names of the wardens as belonging to 1563–4, but printed by him as part of the accounts for 1570.

115. Binney 246/Ms 14.

116. Binney 250/Ms 18.

117. Binney 212–3, 215, 220/Ms 56, 59, 402.

118. Binney 234, 236, 249/Ms 255, 285, 17.

119. See the List of Wardens, appendix, below.

120. Binney 193/Ms 32 under 'not[e] Exbryge reparacion'.

121. Binney 237/Ms 309; 238/Ms 1.

122. D.E. Underdown, 'The Taming of the Scold: the Enforcement of Patriarchal Authority in Early Modern England' in A. Fletcher and J. Stephenson (eds.), *Order and Disorder in Early Modern England* (Cambridge, 1985), pp.16–36; for a corrective to some of Underdown's contentions, Marjorie McIntosh, *Controlling Misbehaviour in Early Modern England 1370–1600* (Cambridge, 1998), pp.58–63.

123. Binney 232/Ms 280.

124. Robert J. Alexander (ed.), *Records of Early English Drama: Somerset* (Toronto and London, 196), pp.212–19, 924.

125. For Morebath ale-going in other parishes, and the Wardens' involvement, Binney 42 (a rare pre–Reformation example) 207, 213, 217, 227, 231, 236.

126. Binney 230/Ms 287–8.

127. Binney 246–7/Ms 14.

128. Binney 249/17.

129. What follows based on Binney 233/Ms 283–4; 248–9/Ms 16–17.

130. West Country Studies Library, Murray Index of Wills, sub Trychay, Christopher.

131. Ms 13, 235 (not printed in Binney). Lewis Trychay was buried on 6 April 1575.

Index

Mercer
Chandler
Wright
Smith
Farmer
Sherman
Cooper
Carpenter
shoemaker
Thatcher
Pew
Miller
Warder
Tailer
Shepherd
Mason
Clark
Harper
Sawyer
Weaver

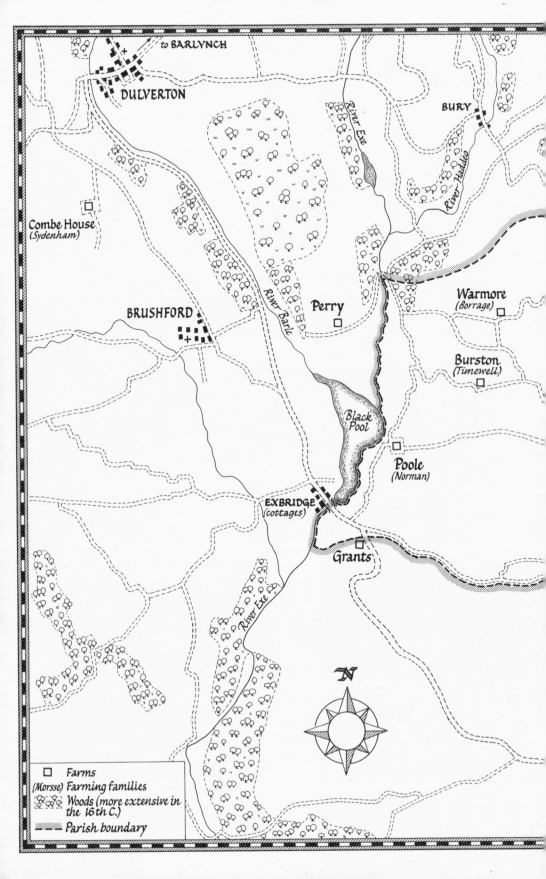

to BARLYNCH

DULVERTON

BURY

River Exe

River Haddeo

Combe House
(Sydenham)

Warmore
(Borrage)

BRUSHFORD

River Barle

Perry

Burston
(Timewell)

Black
Pool

Poole
(Norman)

EXBRIDGE
(cottages)

Grants

River Exe

N

☐ Farms
(Morsse) Farming families
🌳 Woods *(more extensive in
      the 16th C.)*
━━ Parish boundary